LEFTIES

ARE IN THEIR

RIGHT MINDS

LEFTIES ARE IN THEIR RIGHT MINDS
Part One

By
Beth K. Lamont
April 2009

And

A Re-Introduction to
Corliss Lamont's

You Might Like Socialism
First Published in 1939

HALF-MOON FOUNDATION, INC.

The Half-Moon Foundation was formed to promote enduring international peace, support for the United Nations, the conservation of our
country's natural environment, and to safeguard and extend civil
liberties as guaranteed under the Constitution and the Bill of Rights.

Preface

Actually, there's no need for you to read this book at all! The title sums up its whole thesis. When I say Lefties Are In Their Right Minds, I'm trying to give a whimsical approach to a very serious subject. The Righties of this world, who still believe that their might makes them right, have been wrong for too long. That's why I'm urging: Lefties, it's you who are right! Check-out a true Leftie-Life-Line: Pacifica Radio, especially its New York Station, @ FM 99.5 WBAI! We're gathering strength! We need to Unite!

And what perfect timing. Unbridled Capitalism is in disgrace; I picture rowdy, irresponsible teenagers behaving badly and Big Daddy having to bail them out of jail. Ethical control in behalf of the best interests of Society should be the first commandment of a Democracy if it is to flourish, let alone prevail. Might does not make right! Those of you who object to this vision, and actually identify instead with the Righties, might just as well close these pages immediately. Reading any of these words is a total and complete waste of your time!

Especially, if you believe that the Government of the United States of America, in its flaunting of military and economic power, deserves exceptional status, exempt from the laws of human decency, and deserves your own unquestioning obedience. Or worse, if you are convinced that this world is locked into some cataclysmic count-down in a battle between good and evil, then just don't bother reading any further. My contribution to these pages constitutes one long Granny-rant, an extension of my blog. Simply write me off as another Peacenik, a wimp, a bleeding heart, a tree-hugger, an impractical idealist, completely out-of-touch with the "real dangers" that you believe we face.

But if you believe as I do, that there's hope for humankind, and that, with courage, compassion and creativity, and most of all respect, I repeat, respect, working together, we might interrupt and dismantle all mercenary "empire-building." And that together, we will make the necessary changes that will produce a more humane and Humanistic Culture of Peace. People of the world are crying out for peace and justice!

If you can envision a world that will allow us each to follow our dreams, and what's even more important, to live our lives, unmolested,..... then please, Dear Reader, read on.   Beth K. Lamont, 2008

In my long lifetime there have been many moments of complete and ecstatic joy like the birth of my children. The election of Barack Obama, that brings tears of joy to my eyes, is right up there as an unforgettable event of my lifetime. Someone mentioned that this Man and his beautiful Family will occupy the White House that was built by slaves.

As a Humanist who celebrates the natural world and sees no need for any supernatural entity, I actually wish, at this time, that there really were a magical protector we could invoke in behalf of our President Elect. He will be surrounded with adversity, especially attempting to divert him from his stated wish to make changes. Always, those who benefit from the status quo will resist change. And those of us who are screaming for change, long overdue, will be impatient and see compromise as, instead, capitulation.

This Man has a "hard row to hoe!" He needs all the help and support that we can give him. His e-mail team is right on the ball, inviting our input, just as efficiently as it had invited our contributions. This is such a positive sign because accessibility is going to be essential. We have a cumulative history of being disrespected, discarded and rebuffed.

We are invited to go to: http://www.change.gov/. I hope that, besides providing information, this Web site will become an official two-way interactive site, and will be inundated with good suggestions from The People! I've already made a few suggestions on some of the multitude of problems that we face as a nation. Have you? Your perspective, gleaned from your own experience and your wisdom is needed.

This is actually a nation OF, FOR, and BY THE PEOPLE! We are a majority of ethical, hard-working and generous Americans. We will have a real democracy, and we must not allow our best interests to be thwarted, ever again!

~ ~ ~

My Son, Tim, just sent a message that astounded me. I see no mention of it in Corliss's works. He surely would have quoted it had he learned of it. In 1802, one hundred years before Corliss was born, Thomas Jefferson made this prophetic statement:

"I believe that the banking institutions are more dangerous to our liberties than standing armies. If the American people ever allow private banks to control the issue of their currency, first by inflation, then by deflation, the banks and corporations that will grow up around the banks will deprive the people of all property until their children wake-up homeless on the continent their fathers conquered."

In 1939 Corliss Lamont

wrote a book entitled,

You Might Like Socialism

~

Well, . . .sorry, Corliss;

they didn't like it then,

and

they don't like it now!

But, here are three provocative questions:

Who the hell are the "theys?"

How did we ever get Socialized Capitalism?
and
What are we going to do about it?

~ ~ ~

**This book is dedicated with love to the memory of
Corliss Lamont**

Lefties Are In Their Right Minds!

A Re-Introduction to Corliss Lamont's 1939 book:
YOU MIGHT LIKE SOCIALISM

**Introduction/update by Beth K. Lamont, wife, widow of
Philosopher, Corliss Lamont**

About Lefties:

We know that the left side of the human body is controlled by the right side of the brain. Therefore, I declare for all the world to recognize, that Lefties are in their Right Minds! And who, in their right mind, could dispute this anatomical, scientific fact?

But it is the symbolism that I appreciate. Lefties of the world are still scorned and maligned by the powerful for their Socialistic concepts, but they are the ones who champion the rights of the workers, the minorities, the indigenous, the persecuted, and the exploited. They dream of and demand true equality and a real Democratic society.

The analogy is even further symbolic in that the left is where the heart is. Hugo Chavez, President of Venezuela, speaking at the United Nations recently, reminded us of this fact, that on the left is the location of the heart. Even the valentine, a caricature of the human heart, is a symbol of love and caring, expressing compassion and nurturance. These expressions are the essence of family, the heartfelt concern for those we love. This heartfelt concern can extend also to the whole human family. Some humans are already thoroughly immersed and actively involved in this recognition of Universal Human Rights. If some of the family is in pain, we are all in pain.

In this present stage of human societal evolution, with its tantalizing potential for using universal peace-making mechanisms that might eventually render old fears and hatreds obsolete, and in this age of instant world-wide personal communications, the ultimate recognition that all Earthlings are of equal value and that all life itself is precious, is inevitable. That is, if we don't blow ourselves into oblivion first!

Corliss Lamont fervently believed that we could make changes

Corliss Lamont had been so inspired by the actual Ten Days That Shook The World, the actual Revolution by the People, the ideals of which appealed to the masses, that he made it a subject of his research. In 1939 he published what he hoped would be a reasonable and appealing explanation of a planned economy with full employment and other features of this new People's Movement that had the potential of sweeping the world. Thinking to offset the onslaught of propaganda that was pronouncing Socialism to be a frightening specter, and wishing instead to create a popular appeal, idealist and perennial optimist that he was, Corliss decided to entitled his book *You Might Like Socialism.*

I'm prompted to repeat that "they didn't like it then, and they don't like it now! But, the ideals of a Democratic Socialized Society are needed urgently now more than ever before. If you describe each feature, one by one, and how it will benefit the people, there will be applause! These benefits have their own appeal and might be consistent with the freedom and equality to which we Americans aspire; but once you label them with the dreaded S-word or the despised C-word, you scare the pie out of the brainwashed average person on the street. It's a toss-up; which have we been conditioned to fear more? Communists or terrorists?

Capitalism And Democracy Are Not Synonymous

One of our problems is the widespread confusion over the distinction between Capitalism and Democracy, one of which is clearly an economic system, and the other is distinctly a political system. Capitalism and Democracy are not synonymous, and have nothing whatever to do with each other, although adherents seem to use the words interchangeably, when they are actually describing our cherished American freedom, a totally different attribute! For my part, I maintain that Capitalism and Democracy are not even compatible; our democracy has been sold-out to the highest bidders, not meeting the needs of the people, but meeting instead, the will of those who are completely indifferent to the needs of the people, those who are callous, ruthless, and greedy. And as if that were not already confusion enough, just try further compounding the confusion by introducing the dreaded word **Socialism!**

We've Been Brain-Washed!

This system, Socialism, in both its economic and political sense, has been so maligned over the past century as to equate it in most people's minds as being inflammatorily anti-American, accusing it of advocating an alleged "violent overthrow" of our democracy, even identifying it with totalitarianism, dictatorship, and fascism, and certainly not to be tolerated even on our doorstep.

We've been convinced that we mustn't allow, no it's even worse than that, we are terrified to allow, Socialized Medicine, but look what we actually have: we have Socialized Militarism! And now, yeeegods, it's worse still! We now have government-backed Socialized Capitalism! What an insult to the American People!

Socialism: A Fearful Failure? What Of Capitalism's Failures?

Capitalism fails to honor its own workers, fails to nurture the new generation and the powerless, fails to protect and safe-guard our one and only human habitat, and creates without conscience, death-machines to sell to the fearful. Constant crisis and destabilization are the forces that have allowed the powerful to dominate us. The idea of a Free Market is free for whom? Certainly not the people. Capitalism's distorted values completely disregards our human need for stability in the workplace, our home lives, and our communities.

The ideal of valuing people over profits is a long-range wisdom that must re-invent itself as governments try desperately to deal with the societal problems emanating from an almighty profit motive. Only a political or economic system that meets these needs, especially for compassionate health care and equitable educational access, and most essential, an overall philosophy of respect for its citizens, is going to be acceptable in this more enlightened age. We have progressed light years beyond our heritage of helpless, grumbling toleration of tyrants!

Machiavelli Is Dead! Dead! Do You Hear Me? Dead!

Today's World is inspired by the Internet, the World Wide Web, by which the people of the world can communicate with each other, to compare notes, and most of all, to recognize bare-faced, blatant lies from the lips of those who would dominate us. This is a true counter-force that has become a powerful tool for the dissemination of information and inspiration like never before in history. A tool for resistance, a tool for ethical leadership, the ideal sharing marketplace of ideas.

I refer readers to *The Declaration of Independence of Cyberspace*, written by John Perry Barlow, a lyricist for the Grateful Dead, an originator of the Electronic Freedom Foundation. This eloquent and inspiring document proclaims against government, in behalf of the people that "You have no sovereignty where we gather.. . we are immune to your sovereignty. . . We will spread ourselves across the Planet so that no one can arrest our thoughts. We will create a civilization of the Mind in Cyberspace. May it be more humane and fair than the world your governments have made before." To be fully appreciated this Declaration must be read in its entirety. This little snippet does not do it justice.

Power And Profits And The Betrayal Of The People.

How it grieves me to recognize that we have been sharing our precious planet with some incredibly stupid, cloddish and unethical Earthlings who operate with such skewed, unexamined values that they might, metaphorically, slit a bird's throat to extract for sale its beautiful song. Several centuries of conscientious-less Capitalism have totally negated our need to live harmoniously in our neighborhoods, our own homes, our own hearts. The Capitalist power that permeates and fires-up ambitions for pure profit-making around the world has thwarted all of our tantalizing dreams

4

of Democratic societies. For a candidate running for President of the United States to boldly re-assert on national television that the US is promoting democracy around the world is truly laughable, except that this delusion being promoted, instead, makes me want to cry.

The Profit-Motive Is Totally Contemptuous Of Human Values.

Consider Maslow's hierarchy that places air and water and food as basic to our survival. Even these are ground-up in the money-making machinery. Harlow Shapley, the Astronomer, in reflecting upon the threats and fears that pit nation against nation, asserted that we Earthlings would get it together if Mars should ever declare war on us. One would think that the threat of global warming would be enough of an impending catastrophe that we Earthlings would begin to re-examine our values. A graphic illustration of this paradox is picturing a beautiful woodland that produces oxygen and a lovely setting in which to enjoy nature and restore our spirits, and then imaging its devastation, and the production of a giant load of lumber. Which is of more value? Right! Without a monetary value placed upon our shared worldly attributes, the trees must be killed and sliced-up to be considered of value. Disrespect for that which is precious and irreplaceable has us "Paving over Paradise to Build a Parking Lot."

The "Invisible Hand" Caught In The Cookie Jar!

And now, here we are in September 2008 with the Free Market in Free Fall! The mystical, thought-to-be market regulator, the "Invisible Hand" has been caught in the Cookie Jar! We might even call this event the Capitalist Casino Caper; no, it's more a Catastrophe! The gamblers can't cover their losses. As a result, the house can't pay the winners! Therefore, we ALL become losers for the gambler's losses in the unregulated out-of-control Capitalist Casino! The Free Market in Free Fall. What a shocking event for the Federal Government to be taking over and managing the giants Fannie Mae and Freddy Mac. This clearly indicates that the holy grail of Capitalism, the stock market system, is riddled with flaws, and can't be trusted, but on the other hand, "can't be allowed to fail." Taxpayers, workers, already in debt for a zillion-dollar-war that we didn't need and didn't want; with our jobs in jeopardy; with mortgages on our homes threatened or already foreclosed, we are the ones who are supposed to foot the bill for the gambler's follies? *No Way! No Way! No Way!*

Attention all patriotic Americans who don't recognize the country you pledged allegiance to as a child! Attention all patriotic Americans who still believe in the ideals of Democracy, but feel that somehow we've been screwed! (My apologies here; I tried other words, such as: cheated and thwarted. Nothing else fits!)

Members Of Congress, Your Seats May Be In Jeopardy

Congress, please have the courage to come to the rescue of, not the gamblers, but the hard-working American people. The suggested intervention of underwriting the market disaster with seven hundred billions of tax-payer's dollars is not to bail the people out of their plight, but instead, to support the threatened profit-of-the-investors, especially, foreign investors who are losing faith and bailing out! Help the people, instead! What about our foreclosed mortgages? How can we get re-financed? How can we override the tyranny of the too-powerful Credit Rating Companies who prevent our citizens from qualifying for **re-financing** once they have missed payments, ofttimes because of catastrophic health and employment trauma beyond their control, or even divorce.

Main Street Not Wall Street!

Protests are being staged as I am writing. A sign that I saw displayed was quite succinct, and right to the point of the protest: **Steel Bracelets; Not Golden Parachutes!** Putting things in perspective, please consider this question: is this truly a country of, and by, and for the people? Or,.............was this country established to promote free enterprise and profits, and to let the people be damned? If, indeed, we have a democracy in this country, the people should be in charge of the market, with a strong advocate in their behalf controlling the market, not the other way around. The market must not control and determine the economic well-being of the people. This is like the tail wagging the dog.

Congress, it up to you to have the courage to set things straight. There must be competent oversight and control. If you are working on a logical and long-range Bail Out Package, let it have provisions that will benefit the injured citizens of this country, not just Wall Street corporations and big investors.

Add These Considerations To The Bail Out Package

Here is some suggested wording for provisions to be added to the Bail Out Bill that is being considered by Congress and is due for a vote at this writing:

"Instruct the Treasury Department to immediately issue **Peace Bonds** (in small denominations to mature in five years, easily affordable on "Main Street,") that will be available to the Public immediately for the explicit purpose of providing an opportunity to invite active citizen involvement and participation in restoring the fiscal health of our economy, and a reaffirmation of trust in our Democracy. This will also constitute an expressed vote by the citizenry for **peace, itself**, to which Congress can refer in establishing a **Cabinet Level Department of Peace**

Also by way of the re-constructed Fannie Mae and Freddie Mac, "bridge loans" must be provided to prevent foreclosure of mortgages on homes that are now in jeopardy, and mandate lower monthly payment plans, as well as to provide some monetary compensation for families that have already lost their homes."

The Failure Is One Of Basic Philosophy!

This failure is such a threat to the Nation's economy in general and to the Capitalist system that, . . . guess what! The government must come to the rescue and bail out the capricious and undependable market! Whoa! Wait a minute! Isn't that what a **planned, controlled and stable economy** would have prevented and secured us against in the first place?

It seems that we have multiple failures operating here: first, the erroneous assumption that a **war economy** is profitable, is standing shamefully naked and exposed. There's lots more to tell about this travesty that has been perpetrated upon the American people. It constitutes outright fraud. We will go into more detail about Columbia University Engineering Professor Seymour Melman's study, showing how counter-productive war is to our economy, instead of generating profit! He established clearly defined methods of **Converting To A Peace Economy** that would actually enhance our productivity. We, as a nation, need a more peaceable world view and more truly honorable "employment."

Too Large To Fail? What An Insult!

Secondly, for entities to be considered "too large to be allowed to fail," is a direct insult to the rest of us. What are we chopped liver? Who cares that we've lost our jobs or pensions and gotten foreclosed; we workers, we citizens are too small to even bother with! Do we get bailed out? No! Any kind of a bail-out must support instead, home-owners, not just mortgage companies. How about a golden parachute to lessen the impact of our fall? Capitalism has proven conclusively that the people's plight is un-important to our leaders, it's no more than just "collateral damage."

Third, the ballyhooed belief in a free-market system is shown again to be pure hogwash! This really means that markets are **free to act unethically**. Basic ethical behavior will remind you that your freedom to swing your arm must stop short of my nose! For any Wall Street entity to have been allowed to be so free and to become so large and irresponsible that they are at risk of running amuck or running aground is not consistent with the needs for freedom of the people in a democracy.

The Only Remedy Is Ethical And Supervised Regulation

Government regulation and the oversight of the free market are shown to be absolutely essential. This need for strict control of the American economy is shown once and for all to be more powerful than the tantalizing lure of profit-making and the caprice of Capitalism. What the entire Capitalist system needs is a giant dose of **Socialist CONTROL!** The markets must work in behalf of the general public, not leave them hapless and helpless victims of its caprice!

In this land of the free, where corporate and monetary interests are allowed to dominate, and to ride roughshod over the rights of the people themselves, Socialist measures of control enacted into law is the only remedy, the only means of modifying this system in order to protect the people's own best interests, their own rights, their own safety, their own jobs, their own health, their own education, and their very own family values. Most Americans seem unable to make this connection; they have been so thoroughly brainwashed by the very interests that keep them enslaved!

What Does The General Public Actually Know About Socialism?

I tried a little experiment. Out of ten average persons that I questioned as to a definition or a description of Socialism, only one ventured the idea that it meant anything beneficial like our Social Security or workman's compensation or any useful regulation. The other nine were visibly disapproving, and believed that it meant complete government ownership and control of everything; the end of all freedoms! Little wonder that all of the potential benefits to the general public of a more Socialistic Democracy go unrealized and undeveloped, and that we allow and tolerate laws that are contrary to our own best interests, not to mention exploitive of the tax-payer's money, especially to pay for needless war expenses, instead of programs for health, education and our neglected infrastructure that will actually benefit workers and industry.

Don't Agonize! Organize!

The Lefties, those who advocate a Socialist Democracy, have steadfastly maintained that people are more important than profits, and that human needs, in the universal sense, are those that must be met. This is a cause that is ethical, just and humane. So,

I'm shouting from the rooftops! Lefties of the world unite! Even the Righties, whom I boldly declare have been wrong for too long, might be alarmed enough to recognize that we're heading in the wrong direction, and be ready to think of making changes!

We have the needed tools, the actual framework of our democracy to work with, but one of the major problems is that we, the people, have been totally betrayed. In a familiar religious reference: *Our precious Temple of Democracy has been foreclosed upon by the "money-changers." It's going to take heroic intervention to "throw them out!"*

There are things that we can do together about these screaming needs! Let's work together! Alert your Family! Alert your Friends! Alert your co-workers! Alert your neighbors! We can make changes! People are powerful! Be sure to vote! Urge others, who may disparage the value of their vote, to register! Please convince them their vote is essential. Prevail on Congress! What are the names and numbers of your Congress Persons? The time for determined and heroic action is now!

Democracy Has Not Failed!

We can't blame the democracy itself for these failings, but we certainly can properly blame the power-hungry Capitalist economic system. No matter how well-intended originally, if left unattended to run its own course, without the interjection of ethical considerations, a Democracy will no longer serve the best interests of the great masses of ordinary working people; their voices will have been effectively stifled. It will serve only the vested interests of the most powerful few. Power begets power! It chews up and spits out the powerless.

In effect, instead of a Democracy, our political system gradually becomes totalitarian, the very thing that we have been taught to fear; it serves to perpetuate only its own power, frightening and uniting the populace with threats, alleged and manufactured; even going to great extremes to blame and to deceive, and to guard its gathering power by thwarting dissent. Even further, to forcibly remove those whom it deems to be "enemies of the state" and to quickly undermine union power and political movements, and worst of all, to silence dangerous persons whose charisma will undoubtedly provide inspirational leadership to the angry, frustrated masses.

Threats To Our Civil Liberties: The Real Threat To Americans!

An especially frightening factor is that alleged "domestic terrorists" are attempting to have their voices heard, and to observe the National Political Conventions! Who would even have thought that these persons, cleverly disguised as peaceful protesters and journalists, were such a great threat to this nation? Let's hear it for freedom of speech, and of the press, and of the right of the people peaceably to assemble. When we petition for redress of grievances, how can we be heard? Perhaps we might have a day in court? As many of us as is possible need to be there in protest and support!

After the enactment of the so-called "Patriot Act," I stood in Times Square in Manhattan offering to passersby "souvenir copies of the Bill of Rights," calling out, "Get your copy now, before the final shredding!" Responses varied. Some who accepted the offered copy said they had never seen it before; some were wary and turned away, thinking I was trying to sell something; many gave a nod and a thumbs-up; a few were curious about the shredding, and believe me, I was most anxious to tell others about the real threats to our Democracy, about domestic spying, curtailment of free speech, and even torture.

Corliss Lamont was a passionate champion of The Bill of Rights. He'd be staging more powerful responses, alerting the public to these new dangers. His powerful voice would be heard!

Who Are The Terrorists?

Those of you who are old enough to recall a comic strip by Walt Kelly, will remember what his wise little Pogo told his Swamp friends: **"I have seen the enemy, and it is us!"** Walt, you were totally correct. So many patriotic Americans; who are honest, ethical and acutely aware of US leadership's blundering, flawed actions on the world stage, and the disastrous consequences of our domestic and foreign policies, wince at this shameful reputation. We Americans know that we are the good guys. Don't we come to the rescue when others are in trouble? We have been the light of the world, the beacon in the harbor, the place where the huddled massed are safe and welcomed. Well, not any more. The illusion has been completely shattered, once and for all.

Our Beacon In The Harbor Has Gone Out.

People are still huddled, they are not safe, and they are not welcomed. Our treatment of Native Americans and those persons we arrogantly "imported from Africa" and each new wave of immigrants, should have been a tip-off as to the reality of the inequities and the hypocracies of our hierarchically-layered society.

Presently, Immigration and Customs Enforcement agents are swooping down, wholesale, on workplaces with vengeance, confusing "illegals" with terrorists. The workers who have come here for a hoped-for livelihood being held or deported, and tearing families apart who have no resources at all. Children deprived of the parent who wasn't allowed to return home from work, or children held in detention centers: all violations of human rights. These atrocities would certainly make the workers wonder why on Earth they ever believed that there was an advantage and an economic opportunity in risking crossing the border. It would cause them to wonder, as well, whether they would ever wish to become a citizen of such a heartless country, if an avenue to citizenship were provided. Our damaged world reputation is a far cry from the illusions that we Americans hold about ourselves.

Acknowledging Our Real Danger

Those who recognize the fact that the whole human family is in mortal danger, and even our family home, Earth, the human birthplace itself, is threatened, are screaming just as ineffectively as Chicken Little was: "The sky is falling!" And what a normal human thing to do; we see danger and we're alarmed. Worse, is realizing that those with power to make needed changes seem totally unconcerned! Of greater danger is those who apparently have a "celestial escape-hatch" and actively promote an end-times scenario. We know our family is threatened; we must do all we can to protect it! We feel powerless, and too few are listening!

This is why I'm screaming: "Lefties of the World Unite! We need more power to protect our family!" Besides, it is the Righties, who still believe that their might makes them right, that have been wrong for too long! How on Earth can we alert them to our common danger and to the folly of their ways? The vision of Planet Earth from outer space showing a beautiful blue and green paradise in the whole bewildering universe and systems of galaxies should bring this folly home to our hearts. Nature have given us the most exquisitely fantastic gift. We are undeserving. We're not only unappreciative, even fighting to the death over what we have, we demand more. We are not satisfied with life itself. We want immortality.

From a sad, grandmotherly perspective, I'm heartsick and grieving over the selfishness and greed of Earth's children who haven't yet learned to share. Like, fighting-over and destroying a coveted toy, expecting that somehow they'll be provided another.

Nature's Rule: Adapt Or Die!

There is a law of biology that seems to apply to political entities as well as living entities, a simple matter of survival. An organism or an organization must do everything in its power to remain viable in order to fulfill its destiny. It must adapt or die! It must resist attack from without, and must survive betrayal from within, by protecting itself before all else. It cannot carry on its normal functions while under threat. The organism or organization that is under constant threat can become a distortion of its natural potential or its intended purpose. Nature provides armor, tooth and claw, and even camouflage to some of its creatures, but we humans are on our own, so to speak. We can hide, or flee, or fight, as dictated by our instincts. On the other hand, with our beautiful highly-developed brains, we can use our analytical reasoning skills, plus accumulated wisdom, and try to protect those values in which we believe, and to which we may be devoting our lives.

Sometimes it's not enough. Even when we may be doing all we can to influence decisions and provide leadership, trying to take responsibility for preventing our organization, whether it is Capitalist or Socialist oriented, from becoming a distortion of itself, it will instead lapse into a totalitarian, brutalizing regime that is hated and feared, no longer fulfilling its destiny, its leaders saying, that because it must protect itself, these extremes are justified and are absolutely essential to its survival. Does this sound like a would-be democracy with, testosterone poisoning?

Learning Ethical Behavior

Lawrence Kohlberg, a Professor of Psychology at Harvard, after a longitudinal study whereby he interviewed the same persons at different stages of their development, concluded that there are progressive levels of moral development, starting at the toddler's level, the simple fear of punishment and the anticipation of reward. Many religions still emphasize this simplistic approach. Good and evil. Heaven and hell. One of the next steps is the good citizen's unquestioning obedience to "the law," and then, on to some finely-tuned considerations of ethical principles when the law itself might be morally wrong. Welcome Earthlings all, who protest war!

In the schoolyard we learned some rudiments of ethical behavior: The parental admonition, "make nice and share your ball," really makes sense; it means we all get to play. Ethical observations, like not hurting others since we don't like to be hurt, seem fair and reasonable, even to a child. A sad and shocking vignette plays again and again in my mind's eye: I once observed a mother's response to her squabbling daughters, with a "smack-upside-the-head" to the eldest, and a loud and vehement announcement of, "I'll teach you to hit your little sister!" And so, of course, she did.

What About Killing Killers?

The newly-formed **International Criminal Court** pondered the dilemma of remaining ethical while punishing perpetrators of heinous crimes against humanity. If killing is unethical, then killing killers is also unethical. The Court has opted instead, for life-sentences, confiscation of property and restitution for survivors. This is a step in the right direction on the world stage. It envisions a day when, hopefully, age-old impunity to consequences is no longer granted to powerful perpetrators of unethical behavior, and will no longer be tolerated by Humans.

The perplexing perennial problem, however, of how to stop bullies, whether in the schoolyard or on the world stage, is no closer to a solution. Even though victims will always cheer when a bully gets his comeuppance, there's no denying that a bully's power itself, is awesome. A prevailing problem is that others may wish to associate themselves with it. It attracts those who want a piece of that power. Never mind that an action may be simply a show of force, an adolescent flexing of muscle, totally devoid of any mature ethical principles. Power takes on a life of its own. The phrase "Shock and Awe" comes to mind. This, alas, is the stuff that empires are made of. One would only hope that humans can and will evolve beyond this phase. Listen up, Rush Limbaugh!

The Muscle-Flexing Macho Stance

Unfortunately, the strong image of Man the Mighty Hunter prevails. This muscle-flexing Macho stance may look more like a cowboy these days, but the image is the same. Whether it's an inarticulate teenager punching-out someone who's "dissed" him, or an elegant Chief Executive Officer dealing a devastating corporate blow with his decision, it's the same wielding of power. It is man against adversity, whatever the threat may be. The myth of Man the Mighty Hunter, still prevails, and one can find evidence of it even in some anthropological theories that, if it were not for this powerful, action-oriented, manly mind-set, Humans would not have survived. Well, I beg to differ with the myth! Where the heck was Mrs. Mighty Hunter, meanwhile, while our hero was out doing battle? You know it! She was home taking care of the kids! She was the provider of the nurturance that really sustained the Human species. She was the keeper of the flame, the gatherer of the roots and berries, the tender of the young, the injured, sick and elderly. Without this nurturance, there would have been no ongoing existence, no home-base that needed protecting. Even with nomadic tribes there needed to be mobile mothering, or we surely would have become extinct long ago.

This was the Childhood Learning Stage of Humankind

And so, what's new? Today, Mrs. Mighty Hunter is still optimistically giving birth and nurturance to the children, who, if they are even lucky enough to stave off hunger long enough to grow up, may become either the victims or the perpetrators of violence. And this, because we still allow ourselves to be cowed or lured before the display of power. This primitive Macho culture of manly physical response to danger is a behavior that evolved in our Human baby stage. In the childhood of Humankind, we had no answers to our questions, no accumulated wisdom to address our dilemmas, so we did what children do: in the absence of knowledge and experience, we made things up! We had no science, no psychology, so we improvised, and we did the best we could. And for that phase of our evolution, it seemed to work pretty well; in some ways, remarkably well. For Humans to have survived at all is actually spectacular. Considering their risks: hunger, freezing, floods, predatory animals, plagues, earthquakes, drought, volcanic eruptions, and wars. Carl Sagan reminded us of our species' success, that we had survived against a lot of odds.

But, A Four-Million-Year Childhood?

We can be forgiven for our violent, confused, adolescent growing-up stages, even the need for the authority of vengeful, unseen gods to back us up. You know, the old ploy: "My father can beat up your father!" But what's our excuse now? Have we yet acquired the wisdom and the will to progress and evolve into the adult behavior that one would expect of an ethical Human species?

Let's get it straight. I dislike demeaning your gods, Allah, Yahweh, whoever, but if I were going to cite the authority of any supreme being, **I'd choose an ethical one!** Not one who is into vengeance, or who demands an eye for an eye, or sends curses upon humans, or welcomes to its throne, martyrs who have murdered for the cause. No way! If I worshipped any supernatural connection to the universe, it would be one that champions compassion, love, nurturance, respect, equality, equitable treatment, fairness, sharing, forgiveness, and one that would enable and encourage Humans to live rich lives of fulfillment and joy, developing all of their talents and potential, and living out their days unharmed.

Presidential God Bless Yous And pledges Of Killing

In the 2004 televised presidential debate, I watched in despair as two men, the leader, and the would-be leader, of the most wealthy, powerful, and previously-respected Nation on the face of this Earth, speaking in an age of modern miracles, fraught with amazing possibilities for the betterment of Humankind, men who might even have envisioned for us, a future of peaceful and productive existence, who stood before us and proclaimed to all the people of the world, their own belief in god. Apparently, they referred to the same god. What kind of god? A primitive god? They even issued "god-bless-yous." Incredulously, from the same assertedly civilized lips, they both spoke of killing!

Now, in a 2008 televised presidential debate I watched in horror as the candidates both made the very same mistakes of logic and ethics. They pledged to find and kill Osama bin Laden, as though he were a major symbol of our shame. Integrity and wisdom again have been sacrificed upon the altar of machismo.

We Need Ethical Leadership

So, how does the stated "integrity, integrity, integrity," and belief in god translate into ethical or unethical behavior? I might have been comforted somewhat, if instead of promising to kill, there had at least been reference to bringing terrorists to justice.

There are now 192 nations dealing with world problems, most of which are willing to sacrifice some measure of sovereignty, in order to create a system that can bring equitable justice to the long-suffering human beings on this Planet.

I grieve for all of the mothers and the fathers and the beautiful and precious lives, young and old, that are being wasted, wasted, wasted! Damn the unethical gods that condone this! Do you hear me? You believers in this god! Hear the cries of anguish! These precious lives are wasted! Wasted! And for nothing!

What it really boils down to is this: we Humans aspire to an ethical way of life. We have demonstrated this. The Human beings of this world gathered by the millions to say no to war. Our voices were not heard. We have not yet prevailed! Sadly, we are wiser than our lagging leaders.

This can only mean one thing! **We may have already evolved. Most Humans may be ethical! Now, what we need is ethical leadership!**

We Have Only Our Lives To Lose

So, I'm one of the many voices, along with other Raging Grannies, who have only our lives to lose, who are joining with all caring people, especially with our neglected, broken-hearted, broken-bodied veterans, and the grieving parents and loved ones of those veterans who have already been sacrificed, and of those serving this country who are still in danger, fighting an un-ending "war of terrorism" against an un-ending "terrorist enemy."

Bush and Cheney have been hell-bent on instigating a war on Iran; more insanity! Our warships are over there, inviting an attack (perhaps even a "false-flag" alleged attack, Gulf of Tonkin-style) for which we will be then be justified in retaliating by bombing Iran! Don't let them do this! Stop them now! This administration is guilty of War Crimes. Bush and Cheney must be impeached! The American People have spoken! Get out of Iraq! We have been "invited out" by its new government. We have no business there, except to dominate. Our mission there is not altruistic. We can best support our troops by bringing them home.

America, I hardly Recognize You!

Corliss Lamont would have been outraged at the recent shredding of our Bill of Rights, the erosion of our Civil Liberties; and at the Guantanamos where alleged "enemy combatants" are tortured. We hear about contracts to construct holding pens for dissenters. Or those who refuse the "vaccine" in the predicted Flu Pandemic. Plans for fascist-type domination of dissenters is alive and well. Sadly, we unsuccessful dissenters are the ones who have allowed it to overpower us all. This is not the country to which I once placed my hand over my heart, and pledged allegiance! America, I hardly recognize you! You, with the lofty dreams of freedom, and the promise of a bright future. You, the brash adolescent that might have matured so brilliantly in time; now turned into a snarling ugly bully, despised and feared, rather than serving as an inspiration to the rest of the world, and admired by other nations. How heartbreaking to all of us, who know that we are caring and generous, to be thought of as **The Ugly Americans.**

From The Halls Of Montezuma To The Shores Of Tripoli.

As long as ties to manufacturers of armaments prevail, and with former and current military leaders influencing the decisions being made as to the necessary responses to world situations, "in order to protect our interests and our investments," **we will have wars.** We are traditionally geared-up to make military responses. It's plain and simple. This is especially necessary to our economic expansionism, and now, the predatory and coercive doctrine of the so-called Free Trade Agreement. Always seeking cheaper labor, Capitalism is locked into an exploitive relationship with those developing nations it purports to help, damaging their resources and the health of their citizens, as well as thwarting their own democracies, by having the World Trade Organization's authority to override local protests, imposing fines against those who may regret having signed-on, and committed their country to such Un-Fair Trade practices. The ultimate plans to "protect our interests" is projected into Space, where it is asserted that we will "zap naughty nations," thereby protecting our interests AND our investments!

Information to this effect had been found on an actual dot.gov Web site, called Space Command, that has since been removed. What transparent, blatant and embarrassing war-mongering!

Can "Civilians" Assert Control Over A Militaristic Mind-set?

This is indeed the crucial question. The ability to sort-out our troubling confusion over the concept of moral strength and the entrenched reliance upon military and nuclear might, on the world stage, may be the real determinant to our ultimate survival. The decisions pertaining to whom and what constitute the real threat to our nation seems to be the exclusive domain of the Executive Branch, at least, after Congress handed-over to the White House its constitutionally-vested obligation to be the decision-makers on matters of war and peace. How can a candidate who purports to make changes toward more peaceful relationships with other nations, and who would strengthen diplomatic ties and encourage the establishment of a culture of Peace, make any headway in a presidential campaign that demands a show of saber-rattling? Just a flourish of saber-rattling is essential to convince the voters that the candidate is not a wimp and a pushover in a matter of needed response to an attack upon our nation by a terrorist. Oi! I think that the Yiddish expression of exasperation sums up the dilemma. Oi! How can the US ever get to where we need to be, **from here**? One simple plan might be by fostering truly respectful relationships and thereby surrounding ourselves with more friends than enemies?

The Necessary Taming Of Corporate Power.

The democracy to which we patriotic Americans aspire can only be achieved by the curbing and taming of corporate power, and demanding that human values and concern for Earth itself, replace the almighty, mercenary, monetary bottom-line.

Starting with adherence to the **Universal Declaration of Human Rights**; compliance with accepted **International Labor Standards**; total **protection for our fragile world ecology;** and absolute **respect for local democratic processes**, we must require corporations to comply with ethical standards, or they must cease to exist. State Governments allow them to be created and licensed. They can also judge them, expose them, and shut them down for non-compliance! Requiring, by new laws that can be enacted by Congress, the addition of these important phrases describing these new concepts and broadening a corporation's obligations, will give new legal recourse in cases of flagrant violations, and shatter the personhood immunity that corporations have enjoyed when being sued in courts of law.

The arrogant lawlessness, and complete disregard for truth and ethical behavior in the Executive branch of our government itself is even more frightening. Congress has been sucked into this morass, and has great difficulty making independent courageous stands on long-lasting, life-and-death issues regarding its rubber-stamp funding of military madness.

Drastic Changes Are Needed For Campaign Financing

Take the un-democratic US presidential nominating and electoral systems, for instance. What on Earth does raising millions of contribution dollars from Capitalist corporations, and well-off donors, have to do with selecting an ethical person to lead this nation? This nutty practice is totally counter-productive! Just simple logic dictates that any recipient of this largess is directly beholden to those corporate donors, rather than to the people! True Democracy cannot exist, much less thrive, in an untamed, I repeat, untamed, Capitalist economic system. Much more about taming the system will be next, in Corliss Lamont's own words, but first:

The "Airwaves" Belong To The People!

And one reason for raising millions of dollars is for the purpose of getting one's issues before the public via Corporate TV. All political discourse and campaigning could, and should be, free on C-SPAN-like channels and frequencies, eliminating much futile fund-raising simply for the purpose of having one's message heard. Free Public Access is the place for campaign issues to be discussed, without such staggering expense to candidates. Public financing of political campaigning will be more ethical as well as more equitable when this is established. It infuriates me to recognize that the "airwaves," such as they were at the time, were deemed to belong to the American People by the Communications Act of 1934, and that safeguards were actually installed to protect the people's interest. Too bad that the FCC, was entrusted with this task; and like the fox guarding the hen house, they have betrayed this trust, and sold-off the people's rights, yielding to powerful corporate interests. Free enterprise works in some respects, making some goods and services more available to more people, and, true, it does provide employment. But when it comes to buying-up and monopolizing the people's sources of information, free enterprise is actually prohibiting the ability of a democracy to sustain itself, much less to flourish, by limiting the **People's Right to Know**. What a paradox: free enterprise has also given birth to the Internet. This method for people to communicate with each other may ultimately become democracy's salvation.

So, Enough Of This Introduction.

I'll pick up this thought and many other ideas later on in the book, but now, here follows an introduction to Corliss Lamont, the Man, and a bit of information on how he came to write this serious study with the rather whimsical title, *You Might Like Socialism*, that he had hoped would actually make it more appealing:

The Chapters in his own words will be interrupted twice with my own commentaries on two separate topics. One of these is regarding specific plans for establishing Socialism in the US that are now less relevant than when written, with the need to rethink and establish new plans in light of newer technologies. Another break will delve into considerations of **means and ends**, and how any political entity, no matter whether Socialist or Capitalist, deals with dissenters. There will also be some reflections about the intervening years. Corliss lived to a very active age 93. He worked tirelessly in behalf of the Bill of Rights, and the virtues that he valued. He believed in this country and demanded that it live up to its promise without failing; he was a proud American Patriot!

Corliss Lamont, Was Indeed, An American Patriot!

Corliss Lamont, born a child of privilege in the beginning of the twentieth century, attentively absorbed in his formative years the serious issues of ethics and equality, right at the Family dining table, that would shape his life and his philosophy for nearly the rest of the century, the whole span of his life. And what an exciting and chaotic time in which to develop his principled, ethical, liberal point of view in listening to discussions of Wall Street and world affairs, and exploring the juxtapositions of labor and capital, of power and poverty, those of respect and contempt, of fairness and indifference. Corliss became a champion of the underdog, fighter for Civil Liberties, putting his reputation on the line, even going to jail in support of the rights of union strikers. Following the involvement of his own peace-supporting parents, he served as an enthusiastic guide to the League of Nations in Geneva, the summer of his graduation from Harvard in 1924, on his way to the Fall session at Oxford, where he then delved even deeper into philosophy. He was variously interested in the ministry and then the law, as a vehicle for his altruistic drive, but finally rejected pursuing either of these interests in favor of philosophy itself. He began to write and to explore the dynamics of the unfolding Socialist movement and to become enthralled with the potential for a more idealistic treatment of the working class and minorities, and a more equitable distribution of the world's assets.

Attempts To Assist The Bolshevik Revolution

Corliss recalled that at Christmastime of 1917, his Father, Thomas W. Lamont, cabled from Europe that he was coming home early. His return had urgencies other than spending the holiday at home. He proceeded down to Washington, with a long time friend, his classmate from Exeter and Harvard, William Boyce Thompson, who was then a Red Cross Executive, to attempt to persuade President Woodrow Wilson to support the Bolshevik Revolution that was already taking place in Russia. The thought in mind, already approved by England's Prime Minister Lloyd George, of helping the Russian Revolutionaries to sustain the war against

23

Germany, thereby keeping the Germans fighting on two fronts. It seemed a good plan for the Allies to join together against their common enemy, plus there'd be potential market ties with the newly emerging power that seemed to have the people's support. More about this later.

The Ideal Of Independence And Civil Liberties

I am, as Corliss Lamont was, a fiercely patriotic American! Neither he, nor I, have approved of the corruption of our core values, those of Democracy and of Civil Liberties. Corliss was a champion of Civil Liberties and the Bill of Rights. Think of where our ideas of Democracy came from! The Colonists rejected the imposition of taxation without representation, and with courage, acted-out this rejection, by staging the Boston Tea Party. We wanted to be in charge of our own destiny, and dammit, we did it! And at great cost, because many who had pledged their lives, their fortunes, and their sacred honor, died bereft of all three.

Never mind that this was a pact signed and executed by daring and principled white men land-owners only, some even slave-owners, actually pursuing their own vested interests, it was a beginning! It was a painful birth, and as a wise person observed: it had "birth-defects!" There would be centuries of struggle ahead. But, still, it left the dotted-line opening that inspired the landless, the poor, those of all religions, all colors, all ethnic groups, and yes, even women, even slaves, and streams of refugees from all nations, to risk and seek the benefits of this new-fangled dream of Democracy and to pursue the ideal of freedom! But, as the saying goes: "It ain't over yet!" The struggle continues. We are presently engaged in some hotly-debated questions: can diplomacy project a "proper" macho-stance? And can the demand for change protect enough beneficial vested interests? The 2008 Presidential Election will provide the answers. We may opt for change and diplomacy.

Where, Oh Where, Have We Gone Wrong?

The tantalizing ideal of freedom still beckons. This is the American Dream of the Democracy we would like to believe that we have! But freedom is fraught with pitfalls! I'm free to eat out of a garbage can if I'm hungry enough. I'm free to go without health care and education if these essentials are inaccessible. Believe me, freedom is not all that it's cracked up to be! You're free to swing your arm, but without some agreed upon protection, how can I safeguard my nose? Even worse, powerful entities and individuals who gain financial benefits from these very freedoms have been allowed to prevail and have been allowed to engaged in hideous and horrible deceptions, in undermining, in repression, in imprisonment, in aggression, in assassinations, in torture, and even in provoking wars to perpetuate these privileges. It is so hard to believe in this year of 2008, at the time of this writing, and after all these several hundred years, that our own Democracy could still be a work-in-progress. Where, oh where, have we gone wrong? And, what's more important: what will we do about it?

Corliss Was Thrilled With A Peoples' Revolution!

Corliss Lamont's passion as a champion of the ideals of Democracy, and being so painfully aware of its flaws and its inconsistencies under the Capitalist economic system, was thrilled with the Bolshevik Revolution, the emergence of a new ideal of a Peoples' Democracy, not as envisioned in the birth of this nation by slave holders throwing off the yoke of oppression from a King, and who were acknowledging only a portion of their own population, but by a whole new kind of all-inclusive Democracy as envisioned by the slaves themselves! This was the exciting thing that was happening! This was a genuine Peoples' Revolution from the ground up! Corliss Lamont was absolutely thrilled with the first-hand account of the Bolshevik Revolution written in the passionate, descriptive words of a fellow Harvard man and Journalist, whom he admired: John Reed, who participated in, and had written about, the *Ten Days That Shook The World.*

Corliss Lamont was intrigued with the concept of a planned economy guaranteeing full employment and equitable access to health care and education, and in the interest of human dignity wanted to see the "great experiment" succeed. He deplored the artificially induced anti-Communist hysteria and the over-arching fear of these Socialist concepts, and which still prevail today in the US, shaping our foreign policy and eroding our own democracy. This fear is what locked us into years of the futile "Cold War."

Who's Afraid Of The Big Bad Word?

When we decided to re-publish Corliss Lamont's book, *You Might Like Socialism,* originally published by Modern Age Books in 1939, a book that he thought at the time would be an easy read and an understandable explanation of the basic principles of Socialism, I remember quipping: "They didn't like it then! And they don't like it now!" Even as I'm saying aloud this rather trite phrase, the other half of my head is questioning: "Who the hell are the theys?" Who am I even talking about? And, even more, all of the "whys" that arise for me to question: why should this be so, why does this very idea of Socialism cause such fear, and what actually are these powerful people really afraid of? The quick answer is the successful Bolshevik Revolution in 1917, and the resultant fear that it would spread like wildfire across the industrial nations. It was a true and principled People's Revolt! This wasn't just Anarchy or the throwing off of all control, just the opposite. It would mean governmental "interference" and "regulation of corporate power," **in behalf of the people**. Government would assume greater control over public facilities, transportation and utilities, as well as a more equitable distribution of profits in behalf of the public and public works. Industry would need to share a greater percentage of profit with the unionized workers. These menacing threats of big-bad Socialism were enough to freak-out all of Wall Street from end to end, at the time. Nothing has changed!

Throwing Off The Power Of The Church As Well

Established religion also had a hand in the negative reaction because these Revolutionaries were throwing off the power of the Church, in addition, so we not only had "those damn Socialists to deal with, we had goddam Atheists as well." What a combination! A little funny aside here, that I must mention: a relative of Corliss Lamont who was an importer of goods, was offered the opportunity to have exclusive rights to the Caviar market during this time, but declined quite vehemently to have anything whatever to do with those goddam Commie Pinkos.

There was a futile attempt to muster some aid for the Revolutionaries, if only to keep them fighting against Germany and thereby occupying the German forces on two fronts. Woodrow Wilson's administration caved-in to pressure about the greater fears of Socialism. Many of you, and most Americans, will absolutely not believe what happened next!

I even did another little experiment inquiring of associates as to whether the US ever invaded the Soviet Union. Some were even shocked at my question, and answered most vehemently, "Of course not!" Not one person whom I asked knew the truth of it. The fact is not ballyhooed in our history classes, nor, to tell the truth, is the history of our invasions of other sovereign nations elsewhere, but you can actually read about our invasion of Soviet Russia, along with Great Britain and other allied nations, in a book called *Our Siberian Adventure*, by General William Graves, who led an American expeditionary force to the settlements of Vladivastok and Archangel in Siberia where so-called White Russians (Red was the Revolutionary color) had fled with their riches. Our forces were there to protect the elite Czar loyalists. According to Author Sheldon Drobney, "This pre-emptive invasion of a sovereign country was not well-publicized, and to this day most Americans are not aware of this shameful act by our country. An equivalent would be a European power having intervened in our own Civil War." US troops were actually there engaging in military intervention with resultant deaths on both sides. The asserted aim had been to *"strangle the menacing infant of Socialism in its cradle."* The infant didn't die. It grew strong enough to inspire others around the world with its Revolution.

Followers of Socialist Philosophy Must Be Punished

For most of the Twentieth Century this dichotomous dance

has prevailed: the haters and lovers of Marxian philosophy, the inspiration for the workers of the world to unite and to throw off the oppression and the exploitation of the Capitalists. While the fearful Capitalists, in cahoots with government forces, local and national, have taken it upon themselves to thwart and to punish its adherents. How ironic and infuriating in the face of our alleged democracy, that brags of the ideals of Freedom of choice and asserts that citizens can actually organize and associate freely with whomever they wish...just as long as it is **not** with Socialists or Communists or labor organizers or protesters against injustice. Even the ACLU, created to protect these rights, failed, in its fear of being considered a Communist-front organization, to protect its own members from being expelled from its very own Board of Directors. Then, through Freedom of Information releases, we've learned of long-time "infiltration," of people's organizations by government spies, such as was used in the Co-Intel-Program, purposely initiated by FBI Director, J. Edgar Hoover, for the purpose of destroying such "dangerous organizations" from within.

Corliss Lamont Was Denied A Passport.

On the accusation that he was a "dangerous person" and it was not in the best interest of the US for him to travel abroad he was denied a Passport, along with other "suspect persons" such as Rockwell Kent, who successfully sued the government to regain his right to travel. In the 50s there were 12,000 names on the list of persons to imprison in case of national emergency to "protect the country against treason, espionage and sabotage."

I'm tossing out a few names for you to Google, if you wish, like Palmer Raids, that swept up thousands of people suspected of being communists or radicals. Look for Haymarket, and Ludlow, even Paris Commune. We all know about the revered Peoples' heroes, Malcolm and Martin, and the falsely-accused Panthers, but look for hundreds of other heroes like Joe Hill, W.E.B.duBois, Elizabeth Gurley Flynn, Paul Robeson and Pete Seeger, just to name a few. If you are interested in this illustrative history, research will show that it is filled with thousands of, not only labor organizers and champions of the rights of the people, but countless unrecognized victims. *A People's History*, by Howard Zinn, would be a good place to start.

A Century Of Brainwashing!

More than a century of propaganda, indeed even Anti-Communist hysteria, exemplified by the McCarthy witch-hunt era, equating socialism and socialistic concepts with allegations of violent overthrow of the government, totalitarianism, repression and complete loss of freedom, has really done a number on our collective psyches. Hence, any such movement in behalf of the people is seen instead as a form of fascistic control, therefore we hear about "dictators" and "strong-men" that must be feared and reviled for leading their people into revolt, when all they may be guilty of is throwing off the domination of Capitalist exploitation, and even more threatening: claiming Capitalist assets in behalf of the people! Horrors! How shall the US respond? Pour money into promoting a coup? Assassinate? Invade? All of the above?

As recently as 2008, President Bush rejected Congress's attempt to give health coverage to more American children because he feared it introduced the horrors of socialized medicine!

In most political, and especially presidential campaigns, each candidate dare not associate too closely with the taint of socialized anything, for fear of creating an automatic revulsion in the potential voter. Statements of this type provide a heyday for rabid pundits who proceed to tell the public what to think! What to fear! And what to revile! Actually, it's a kiss-of-death. Even the accusatory L-word is a no-no! How I wished for Michael Dukakis, who was "accused of being a Liberal way back when," to have answered bravely, that yes, he was a Liberal, and mighty proud of it! This is such a strange and self-defeating paradox, for this unexamined fear of Socialism to prevail as a conditioned gut-reaction with the general public, when democracy's own social institutions and humankind itself will benefit in every way, when more humanistic, more liberal, more caring provisions are literally carved into this system of government to offset the indifference of the Capitalist economic system.

Human Values And Meeting The Needs Of The People Should Be A Primary Concern Of Religion!

Wall Street has its own fears, that of a socialist take-over of corporations in host countries, confiscating property and turning it over to "the state," or of even having to share more of their profits with would-be more-powerful unionized workers, but organized religion has had a part in this vilification, as well, because it feared loss of power over compliant and obedient people, as it always will be, when government and religion are in-cahoots and augment each other. The churches had been targets of angry overthrow in the Bolshevik Revolution. Iconoclasm was rampant with the tearing down of repressive elements of what was seen as the bloodsucking church. It had offered the poor only coercive and dutiful payments on some illusory "celestial real estate," but offered absolutely no remedy right here on this Earth against starvation.

But in this present day, religious leaders who are generally more enlightened and who possess a more worldly wisdom, will engage in what came to be known as "liberation theology" wherein Priests of the Americas sided with the plight of the people, against the rigidity of the Church and its collusion with power. And local churches offered sanctuary for refugees and political dissidents.

The Bushites Exploit And Abuse Their Religious Connections

Many religious persons in general, I'm observing, are feeling resentful at having been abused by the Bush administration as an ally in its war-mongering. Hooray for the good works of Faith Based Organizations in taking up the slack from the shameful neglect by governmental institutions, but, there should not be, nor should there have been, neglect of the needs of the American People by government in the first place! For any Faith Based organizations to obtain governmental appropriations for doing their volunteer work is doubly dangerous. It lets the government off the hook, allowing it to simply abandon its own obligations, and it is breaching the necessary constitutional state-church barrier. It is even unfairly aiding and abetting one religion over another.

What About Ethics Based, As Well As Faith Based?

At the United Nations, we Representatives of our Non Governmental Humanist Organization got so tired of hearing about faith-based this and faith-based that, that we formed The Council of Ethics Based Organizations, and were insistent upon reminding that faith is fine, if you have faith that we Humans can do better than we've done so far. And as long as you are faithfully working in behalf of the betterment of humankind right here on Earth! Never mind considerations of any supernatural. If they plan to go to heaven for their good works here and now, so be it. I won't quibble with their faith. It is those who are motivated by religion and expect to be "saved" somehow from earthly catastrophe, and believe that it is inevitable because "it is written" that terrify me.

Right at this moment, I am scared spitless at the very real possibility that a fanatical religious fundamentalist, who asks for god's intervention to secure a pipeline, might accidentally become the leader of the most powerful country on the face of this Earth, **and its military**! It is a fearsome possibility that "god's will" as interpreted by those who still believe in a primitive, simplistic good vs. evil model, might actually prevail, and set humankind, with its hard-won wisdom, reeling back to the stone age.

A Liberation Theology That Promotes Peace On Earth!

I know that rational minds will give this possibility serious thought! Tens of Millions of those who employ such logic were marching together in dozens of streets of the world way back in 2003, protesting the impending threat of misplaced "Shock and Awe" vengeance. Many in New York were even wearing religious robes; I know, because I marched alongside Nuns. **Besides the Catholics, there were Jews, Muslims, Quakers, Atheists and Humanists, as well as other Peaceniks,** all of us united in our

31

anti-war stance. I respect those of every religious faith for their work right here and now for the betterment of Earth and Earth people. If they plan to go to some other-worldly reward for their efforts, so be it. I cannot quibble with their motives; it is the believers in Armageddon that scare the hell out of me, also, those who would kill for their god. A cartoon; relating to a facet of this fanaticism, showed a message coming out of a cloud saying, "Forget it! There are no more virgins up here!"

Democracy and Capitalism Cannot Co-exist

If ever there were a case in point that Democracy and Capitalism cannot co-exist, it is the present dilemma of the American voters who sent the "other party" to tame the out-of-control radicals, only to watch them, with disbelief and disgust, instead, "make nice" with the warmongers. The ruthless, for-profit system, an economic system that is completely without conscience or ethics, will continue on its murderous binge, grinding up human beings in its bloody machinery, spewing out wretched victims, the world around, in its power-mad thirst for domination, its quest for empire, until the people rise up to take control and say, "Enough!"

But, when the dreaded fear of "socialized medicine" is cited as a reason for denying health care for children in this country, tromping callously over the people's own principled fears that children's lives are risked needlessly, this should have constituted a "last straw" event, hitting home the truth about this ruthless regime. But still, the people's resultant anger has not yet prompted impeachment. This is a sure sign that we are not yet ready for the ballot box "revolution!" But, let's acknowledge: it's long overdue!

Are You Now, Or Have You Ever Been...

Corliss Lamont did battle with Joe McCarthy in those intimidating witch-hunt years of anti-communist hysteria. "Are you now, or have you ever been, a member of the Communist Party?" The perceived, looming danger to church and state had caused such a tidal-wave of backlash that it has not even yet receded. Those godless communists! Smashing religious icons! Imagine! Workers forming unions, wanting better conditions, and demanding to share the wealth! Unheard of! Planning to overthrow the government? What? By non-violent Democratic means? Then we must guard the ballot box to prevent such a takeover! Throw those damn commies out, if they should ever get elected! This pervasive propaganda has in itself been quite un-American, illogical and completely reactionary. The US Government has been actively engaged in thwarting the development of Socialism in unethical and illegal ways, that even include outright aggression and assassination.

How Can The People Make Their Voices Heard?

Something that our Constitution failed to take into account, and to provide for, besides representation, (or non-representation, as the case might be) is the means by which the people can make their voices heard. The old Town Hall was a start, and back then, if you owned a printing press you were off and running. But today the voices of the people can only be heard if you own a Network! In 1934 it was established that the "airwaves" (such as they were at the time) belonged to the American people; the FCC was assigned to safeguard our interests. Guess who OWNS them now! Corporate interests are not synonymous with the best interests of the people; worse, even completely contrary to the people's best interest.

Who Decides? The Media Decides!

In order to regain some semblance of Democracy, all public discourse and all political campaigning rightfully belongs in the public domain! Not one penny should be spent on inequitable advertising and costly spots on the corporate media to promote one candidate over another. They should stand denuded of the backing of their vested-interest corporate sponsors, speaking before the American voters on public access channels only, articulating their principles; debating on an equitable footing; voters judging their merits, not influenced by the power of the machine behind them.

Dennis Kucinich responded brilliantly after he was insulted to his face for continuing to "stay in the debates" when he had no money behind him, as though raising money were a criteria for ethical leadership. He feigned surprise at the assertion that the media decides who runs for office or who gets elected, and pointed out that he thought this was "a matter for the voters to decide!"

Dennis Kucinich Is A Hero Of Giant Proportions!

This man had the courage, while others shrank from their duties, to read the 33 Articles of Impeachment against George W. Bush, standing almost alone on the floor of the US House of Representatives. He will see that the **US establishes a Cabinet level Department of Peace**. This is to be a UN initiative as well, urging all other nations to follow suit. When Dennis Kucinich was completely thwarted from incorporating even one of his liberal and humanistic planks into the Democratic Platform at the previous Convention, he tried to console his grieving followers, saying that we must go with the Democrats anyway, and hope to be of influence at a later date. We who had gone to Boston to promote these planks were subjected to some abuse for our signs advocating **Peace in Iraq, Repealing the Patriot Act, A US Department of Peace, National Health Care, equitable Civil Rights for all individuals, and getting out of NAFTA.** Some Bostonians gave us the thumbs-up and nods of approval, but others made snide comments, like: "What are you guys? A bunch of Commies? I thought I'd die laughing at a Gary Larson-like T-shirt that summed up the whole experience. This depicted two stand-up lady cows with hats and purses. One said, "I just learned how they make hamburger!" The other said, "Omygod! You must be a leftie-liberal-commie-pinko-conspiracy-theorist! Mable, get a grip!"

What We Have Is Electoral Insanity!

Complete campaign financing reform is essential in order to safeguard what's left of our cherished ideal of Democracy. It must include **establishing uniform nation-wide voting standards**, including same-day registration. The purging of voter rolls and the arbitrary disenfranchisement of those who would be eligible to vote must cease. A Voter-ID Card with a computer chip will help. Even the custom of voting only on Tuesday is total, counter-productive nonsense, left over from days long-gone. "All-week-end" open polls, even early voting; will help to accommodate this nation's workers and help to encourage participation. A new coalition-type multi-party system must be established rather than allowing the perpetuation of the entrenched power of the two-party system. It will be absolutely essential to eliminate the "winner-take-all" obsolete Electoral College. Also by demanding and installing uniform tamper-proof, electronic ballot box safeguards, that must produce a paper-trail, we will be taking further steps to assure that our votes are even worth a damn. Even then, we'll still worry that the courts may shred our paper trails. Much more about this later.

A War Economy Is Show To Be Counter-Productive.

Bombing, killing, terrorizing and torturing, as a policy of government, and even lying about it when exposed, is shameful, and immature. It is mistakenly believed that America's economic strength is linked to our military strength. Actually, even the belief is counter-productive. Our true strength is innovation; you toss us a lemon and what do we do? Forget plain old lemonade; We make lemon meringue pie! Americans are adaptable and inventive. We know how to get things done. We pitch-in and take the initiative. I'm remembering the poster of Rosie the Riveter rolling up her sleeve and flexing her muscle. Today, she could work in a factory that makes photo voltaic cells for solar collector technology. These newest technologies that the world needs for renewable energy can be American made. Let's get busy with new industries and apply this creative genius to good works that benefit humankind.

You may not know of the work of Seymour Melman, a Professor of Engineering at Columbia University, whose extensive studies proved conclusively that the war economy is counter-productive to the best interest of the American people by wasting its talents and resources. He promoted an extensive program called

Conversion to a Peace Economy that required every war-related contract to provide for a civilian peace-oriented use of its facility at the termination of a contract. Like, baby buggies instead of bombs!

Military Might Has Made Us Less Safe!

Using military might, muscle, rather than wisdom, has made us less safe now than we have ever been since the beginning of humankind. Cognizance of this fact and the influence of the arms trade on the International scene, prompted the suggestion by Lula DaSilva of Brazil and Jacques Chirac of France that the manufacture and trade of all war implements intended for the killing of humans be heavily taxed (better yet, outlawed and punished) and payable to the UN for humanitarian efforts, as an excellent way of interrupting this malicious and murderous money-making machinery, right on the way to the bank! Did the US sign on to such an effort? You can just bet your bippie it didn't!

US Efforts To Control Or Destroy The UN

The United Nations, though undercut, under-funded, and derided as "a useless debating society" by those who would prefer to dominate rather than engage in diplomatic leadership on the world stage, has the framework and the potential to really **"prevent the scourge of war."** John Bolton, who blatantly disrespected the UN, and described removing 10 floors of the building without affecting its operations, was assigned as US Ambassador to the UN on a search and destroy mission. The changes he demanded were not beneficial to the organization itself, but merely consolidated more lopsided power for the already too-powerful, veto-wielding, nuclear nations. The so-called Security Council is a relic from the 40s, now obsolete, needing to be phased out. It offers no security and it does not council; it dominates. Actions and decisions that affect all of our lives should be taken only in the more equitable General Assembly, which consists of the now 192 Nations.

Supporting The Goals Of The United Nations

Here are some ways we can help to make changes to bolster the efforts of the UN. First of all, we need the UNTV which sends out a 24/7 signal describing the historical achievements and current activities of the UN to be available to all TV outlets in the US. Most American are ill-informed about the UN, except for derogatory sound bites. This nation needs to be supporting the **Millennium Development Goals** to eliminate hunger and lessen poverty by the year 2015. We are not just failing to achieve these goals; we are slipping backward. **Human Rights** champions need to be actively advocating the newly developed UN policy assuming **Responsibility to Protect** those populations that can't protect themselves. This policy is contentious in that it seeks to override sacrosanct sovereignty. US policy will not relinquish one smidge of this country's sovereignty for any cause! We need to insist upon and to develop properly-funded and properly-mandated, stand-by **Regional Peacemaking-Peacekeeping Forces**. We also need to be supporting the newly formed independent **International Criminal Court** that has jurisdiction to prosecute such Crimes Against Humanity as the bombing of villages and the starving of children, and to put an end to the age-old shameful impunity of the powerful and to properly punish such crimes.

Human Rights and Humanism

In 1933, in a previous era of frightening military madness, concerned clergy and educators wrote a code of ethical concern that they named **The Humanist Manifesto**. Every single principle delineated in this document was incorporated into the subsequently created **Universal Declaration of Human Rights**, largely brought into being with the help and leadership of Eleanor Roosevelt. Humanism is consistent with the ethical stance of promoting respect and equality for all of Earth's beings. The United States of America has an obligation to provide ethical leadership. The people of this country have their own obligation to see that it does!

Corliss Lamont stated this idea of taking responsibility very well in his autobiography, *Yes To Life*. He is quoted here:

"My final word is that in the battles that confront us today for America's freedom and welfare, our chief aim as public-spirited citizens must be neither to avoid trouble, nor to stay out of jail, nor even to preserve our lives, but to *keep on fighting* for our fundamental principles and ideals."

Dear Readers, we will have the courage to make changes together. Let the peaceful "revolution" begin! Peace People of the World Unite! And unite we will with the help of our miracles of modern technology, under our multiple banners. We demand a peaceful ethical world! And you, government leaders, you will just have to put down the weapons, get in line behind us, and follow! Or it is inevitable: you will be rendered "absolutely obsolete."

Please help to spread the word to all the world. Join forces to demand ethical Leadership. The Lefties are in their Right Minds!

This heartfelt, but perhaps rambling, "Grannyrant" on so many different issues has been an attempt to update and review a bit, conditions and events that have been, and presently are, taking place in this country, even on the world stage, that are so relevant to the still-screaming need for us to tame Capitalism. If Capitalism indeed, has such indispensable attributes that the United States of America cannot survive without it, then there is only one recourse. Capitalism must be brought into line with the lofty ideals of true freedom for the citizens of this country.

A country that purports to be of, for, and by, its people cannot tolerate being controlled by its own economic system. We're familiar with analogy about the tail wagging the dog. It is the same preposterous illogic!

We can and will make changes. Yes, we can!

We can, and will, and must, create a Socialized Democracy that honors its own citizens, and that brings its economic system properly into compliance with the wishes and the needs of its own people; it must not be the other way around.

How I'd love to see a nightly news report focused on true human values and the celebration of progressive milestones: peace, diplomatic relationships among nations, participatory democracy, full employment, health services, educational facilities for all, the achievements of science in behalf of safeguards for humankind, endangered species and the survival of planet Earth etc. There could be a feature on the negative side: a Human Misery Index report, describing statistics of the as-yet-unfulfilled expectations, such as poverty, hunger, refugees, women, children, or whole populations living in intolerable conditions, who are still in jeopardy, indicating work that still needs to be done.

When I observe an account of the ups and downs of the stock market, delivered in all seriousness to investors, as though investors were the majority of Americans, I feel a revulsion at how pitiful and puny this information is in comparison to its impact on the greater majority of Americans of the working class, who may be impacted directly and negatively by a corporation's reported "profits," that were due to massive layoffs or outsourcing which benefited the corporation's bottom-line, meaning less payment of wages. How about an in-depth report on how corporations treat their own employees? Do they actively thwart the development of a union or collective bargaining? Or how do they truly respect the environment no matter what they claim? Or research whether they have exploited or terrorized others or used slave labor. I'm a 1929 model from the old depression. I can still remember having neither "a pot nor a window," as the old saying goes. Don't allow it again.

This the end of Beth Lamont's introduction.

~ ~ ~

39

And now, in the words of Corliss Lamont, his own introduction.

You Might Like Socialism
by Corliss Lamont
Preface

My purpose in writing this book is to give, in simple and understandable language, an inclusive survey of the main reasons that prompt contemporary Americans from every walk of life, including members of the upper and middle financial strata, to adopt Socialism as the way out for this country and the world. As the title indicates, I invite readers in the spirit of free and un-dogmatic discussion to consider the case for a Socialist society and to reach their own conclusions. It would of course be impossible, simply for reasons of space, to include the many different strands of study, discussion and personal experience which over a number of years have gradually led me to become a radical. Nor could I even recall all the impressions, some of them trivial in themselves alone, which have entered into my intellectual and emotional processes to stimulate and reinforce my Socialist position. A number of significant questions I have naturally not been able to treat very fully, and many matters of detail I have not been able to take up at all. Other volumes, classics in the field, perform these tasks.

My indebtedness is obvious and far-reaching to writers on Socialism such as Robert W. Dunn, L. E. Hubbard, Leo Huberman, George Soule, Sidney and Beatrice Webb, Albert Rhys Williams and, above all, John Strachey. But the opinions expressed in this book are my own, and I alone, bear the responsibility for them.

I wish to thank especially the following individuals for their valuable co-operation and counsel in the writing and publication of this book: Theodore Bayer, Alice W. Field, Henrietta Weigel, Josephine White, and my wife, Margaret Irish Lamont, whose sharing of common social aims and ideals with me is a steady source of strength and inspiration.

Since throughout this volume and particularly in the last chapter I have dealt to a considerable extent with contemporary affairs, it is quite possible that by the time this study is published, events, which move so swiftly these days, will have swept ahead of or contradicted me on one point or another. Hence it is necessary to say that this book went to press on August 8, 1939.

Corliss Lamont

This book is dedicated to
friends in the Harvard
Class of 1924

CONTENTS

Chapter I
Why Members of the Upper Financial Strata Go Left

1. *Why I Am a Radical*

"How does it happen, Mr. Lamont. that a person with your background is a radical?" I have been asked this question an infinite number of times during the past few years and by all manner of people, from incredulous workers coming up to speak with me after a lecture in some Midwestern city to perplexed plutocrats taking me aside for a confidential chat after a formal Manhattan dinner. Needless to say, I have never been able, in a brief conversation to give a very satisfactory reply. But I have always realized that it was a legitimate and important question. And in this book I want to try to answer it simply, honestly and thoroughly.

Yes, I am a radical. I am on the side of labor. I sympathize in general with the achievements of the Soviet Union. I am against Fascism. I want to see a life of abundance for all of the people. And I believe that Socialism can do the job both in America and the world at large.

At the same time there can be no doubt that in origin I come from America's so-called upper financial strata. I mean "upper" only in an economic sense, that top 1 per cent of American individuals and families whose incomes are $10,000 a year or more. (these were 1939 dollars at the time of writing, remember) From early childhood I have enjoyed certain undeniable advantages that wealth is able to assure. Two members of my immediate family are partners in the banking firm of J. P. Morgan and Company. And since coming of age, I myself have possessed considerably more than average economic security.

I betray no state secrets in citing these facts. And I mention them at the outset, not with any intention of embarking on a series of personal "confessions," but simply because they represent the truth and because they are objectively necessary for an understanding of what I have to say, I think we can take it as settled, therefore, that in the year 1902 I was born into what became soon afterward a prominent capitalist family. It was and is, I may add, a very congenial family. And in democratic, sometimes fiery, but always friendly discussion, with its various members, I have worked out much of the material which appears in this volume.

Why are persons from the capitalist class with backgrounds similar to mine today joining the ranks of the radicals? Though I can speak only for myself, I believe that I can throw light on this matter by telling the story of my own transition to a Socialist point of view. And perhaps I can clear up to some extent what, seems to be an endless source of amazement and alarm to so many of our fellow-citizens. They cannot understand how anyone who is normal, "Nordic" and economically privileged can become a sincere supporter of radicalism in economics and politics.

But even a cursory glance at the world at present ought to dispel any appearance of mystery in the fact that an increasing number of well-to-do Americans are following a leftward course. Here we are twenty-five years after the start of the Great War and ten years after the start of the Great Depression and we face once more, both nationally and internationally, an economic and political situation overwhelming in its extent and gravity. A vast and bloody conflict is raging in the East; the Second World War is an ever-present possibility; while behind the facade of so-called peace the brute force of Fascism is rampant and bludgeons its way to power in country after country.

And Capitalism in general has become so capricious, so utterly undependable, that even the wealthy cannot be too sure of their future and that of their children. The stock market reaches the heights one day and sinks to the depths the next; businesses both large and small, quickly go from boom to bankruptcy; great fortunes rise and fall; whole nations suddenly verge on economic collapse. Who is really secure? Businessmen and capitalist theoreticians more and more openly acknowledge that they do not know any way in which the ever recurring cycle of boom and crash can be halted. They piously hope that the next depression will not be so bad as the last, but beyond this they have nothing to offer a harassed and long-suffering humanity.

Now I definitely refuse to accept as the fate of mankind the defeatist attitude which condemns us to an unending repetition of the very processes that have brought about such overwhelming catastrophe and misery during the past quarter-century. I have only one life to live and I want to make it count for social aims that reach down to fundamentals. I do not want to waste my time by helping to bring about little improvements here and there and letting the big things go. I know of few greater personal tragedies than those of well-meaning, men and women who have devoted their lives to the achievement of some ideal only to find at the end that they were dealing with surface causes and cures. Such are the peace workers who think that war can be eliminated by governments formally agreeing to renounce aggression; such are the charity workers who think that poverty can be overcome by private contributions to the needy; such are all those who think that depressions can be avoided by tinkering with the capitalist system.

Reforms within the structure of Capitalism can result in genuine amelioration, but I do not believe that they can ever resolve our major dilemmas. One severe depression or one widespread international conflict can overnight do ten-fold more harm than all the good accomplished in the reformist gains of decades. I was once asked why I did not give over my entire energies to the establishment of unemployment insurance. My answer was that while I naturally was in favor of unemployment insurance, its enactment would not solve the problem of unemployment. The way to solve that problem is to establish Socialism and abolish unemployment. Socialism gets to the most of things. And I feel that it is more worth while to be the most insignificant worker on behalf of something that provides ultimate solutions than to be a big shot in a system which has terrible difficulty in providing even temporary ones.

These, then, are the main reasons in my opinion why men and women of intelligence and good will are everywhere today earnestly seeking to find a way out for society which will permanently put an end to the intertwined evils of war and poverty, of economic crisis and cultural retrogression. As one of the seekers I have tried to think through the deep-going problems of these turbulent times. And I have come to the firm conclusion that a Socialist order offers the most certain hope for the renewal of human progress. Specifically, to support Socialism means to work for, as the basis of a stable economy and a great culture, the goal of a planned and peaceful and democratic society, eventually on an international scale, in which the main instruments of production and distribution are publicly owned and operated.

2. *The Voice of Democracy and Reason*

I hold that the case for Socialism rests primarily on the belief in democracy and the appeal to reason. By democracy I mean the fair and equal opportunity of all individuals in all nations, regardless of race or religion, origin or occupation, to share in the good things, both material and cultural, of this life; and to participate genuinely in the economic and political decisions affecting their mode of existence. Only persons who subscribe to democracy in this inclusive interpretation of the word are capable, I believe, of possessing that passionate sense of outrage over the cruelties and injustices endured by humankind which has ever been an attribute of the world's great democrats. Only such persons are able to give their sincere and abiding loyalty to the happiness and progress of all humanity as the supreme ethical goal.

In general, it has been simply impossible for members of the upper financial strata to work sincerely for humanity as a whole, because they have always been filled with such profound sentiments of hatred and contempt for what they consider inferior classes, races and nations. They have accordingly felt that these groups were neither deserving of equal opportunity nor fit for it. Conversely, the upper classes have been so certain of their own inborn intellectual, moral and biological superiority that they have enjoyed with a good conscience the various economic and cultural privileges which have gone with their status in the community.

Upper-class ignorance of biology and social science often seems downright willful; but more often, I think, due to an unconscious bias which throws up a protective screen of rationalization and pure blindness to shut out unpleasant knowledge. And this is why in increasing measures today perfectly sane and sober capitalists refuse to acknowledge certain facts—commonly known facts—which they feel cast some sort of disrepute on their system.

These considerations explain why so many intelligent and formally well-educated persons uphold reactionary views that work hardship on the masses of the people. If your basic social assumptions are narrow and ungenerous, if you believe in a God-given right of an exclusive aristocracy to rule the world and enjoy its finest fruits, then reason may well lead you to support a social system that cares little for the rights and happiness of the majority. The exercise of reason alone, then, does not necessarily point in the direction of Socialism or any other particular form of society. It all depends upon what assumptions you start from in your reasoning, especially upon what general purpose you have in mind. Unfortunately, reason, as embodied for instance in scientific techniques, may operate on behalf of all sorts of anti-social ends such as aggressive war and unscrupulous profit making.

There are admittedly numerous exceptions among the ruling class to what I have been saying—men and women who are devoted to democracy in the broad sense. Yet surely most of these genuinely democratic capitalists, as even many members of the working class, do not believe in Socialism! True enough. And here is where the appeal to reason comes in. For I maintain that an objective intellectual analysis of the contemporary scene and of the lessons of history shows clearly that those who honestly desire the extension of democracy and the continued progress of humankind must sooner or later espouse the cause of Socialism. Only un-flinching reason and the democratic feeling working together lead to Socialist conclusions. And those believers in democracy and progress whose faulty thinking takes them in a non-Socialist direction are in the end bound to meet with defeat and disappoint-ment. Hence all liberals, for instance, or at least all liberals with guts, can hardly fail these days to become radicals.

Why Socialism should, I think, appeal to the reason of true democrats, to all those who are both tough-minded and tender-hearted, can be elucidated by reference to one or two of the most pressing problems of the day. We radicals hold, for example, that only Socialist planning within each country and between each country can eliminate the terrific economic pressures which, under Capitalism, and just now particularly in its Fascist manifestations, lead over and over again to the horror of international conflict. I shall later take up in detail the problem of peace and war. The point I want to make here is that the radical thesis on this grave question is a matter of intellectual analysis. It stands or falls on that basis.

What Socialism achieves in an international way is insepar-ably bound up with what it is able to do on a national scale and whether, as I allege, it can establish continuous prosperity and allay the economic discontent and distress of the various peoples. Here again 1 say that it is reason which must decide whether or not the Socialist analysis is correct, But in, this case it is not reason working merely with abstractions and projecting fine-sounding hypotheses. For the Socialist theory has for the first time been receiving a large-scale test, going through a prodigious pragmatic ordeal, in the Soviet Union. There a planned economy has actually been functioning for a number of years and, as I learned from my two trips to Soviet Russia, has achieved extraordinary success.

Turning to still broader perspectives, I want to bring out as a fact of the highest importance that Socialism is not concerned simply with economics and material things. The Socialist cultural synthesis does not have merely a theory of economics and politics; it has a theory of history and art and science; it has a theory of international and inter- racial relations; it has an attitude toward the universe. In other words it offers the individual an inclusive and rounded philosophy of life and one which provides him with a high and worth-while loyalty during his career on this earth. In Socialism, I and other non-proletarian radicals find an opportunity to fulfill ourselves. This ought to make it plain that, even apart from the hope of escaping death in some frightful Armageddon or economic ruin in some precipitous crash, we are not devoting our lives to Socialism simply as a beautiful, altruistic gesture. While I would not say that we are entirely selfish, we do believe that Socialism has at least as much to give us as we have to give the to ideals of Socialism.

We feel, too, that we are associating ourselves with the most vital thing in the world today, that we are becoming part of a great, ongoing and probably invincible tide in the affairs of humans, that we are casting our lot with the Future. All during the nineteenth century American Capitalism presented many challenging and exciting tasks. There was the opening up of the West, the building of a vast transportation system, the discovery and exploitation of our natural resources, the mechanization of industry and agriculture, the development of mass production and big corporate enterprise, the transformation of our country into a definite World Power. But now it appears evident that Capitalism has seen its palmiest days and that stirring opportunities within its framework are becoming increasingly scarce. The battle for Socialism—and for a long time yet in the United States it will be the uphill fight of a minority—seems to me much the most thrilling and at the same time intelligent movement in which one can participate today.

The general aims of Socialism which I have been reviewing, far from being alien to the spirit of America, are wholly in accord with our traditions. What indeed could be more American than the ideal of complete democracy, of social justice, of economic security, of cultural opportunity, of world peace and of the right of "all men to life, liberty and the pursuit of happiness" ? I am a radical precisely because such outstanding American ideals are daily stamped in the mire by Capital-Ism, whether in its Fascist or non-Fascist forms; and because they can be rescued and fulfilled only through the establishment of Socialism. These ideals, I may add, are sincerely shared by most Americans, including many honest conservatives and members of the upper financial strata.

Let me illustrate from personal experience the meaning of

this last statement. Two or three years ago a red-baiter by the name of Francis Ralston Welsh wrote an agitated piece about me and my parents called "Sowing the Wind and Reaping the Whirlwind," He pointed out that my mother, Mrs. Florence C. Lamont, was on the Board of such terrible "Communist" organizations as the Foreign Policy Association and the New School for Social Research, and that my father aided and abetted her subversive activities and was guilty of some rather liberal doings himself. "And so the wind was sown," the author said. Then came the inevitable "whirlwind," he concluded, and in no other form than my own humble self!

Now in spite of the absurdities of Mr. Welsh, he has a real point. For much of my radicalism is unquestionably due to my determination to see actualized certain of the ideals which were taught me in my home. I think especially of the goal of international peace and understanding, always a dominant concern of my parents and one which led my father to depart from his traditional Republicanism in 1920 and support Governor Cox, the Democratic candidate for President on the League of Nations issue.

Indeed, in my general family group there has long been a genuine tradition of independent and progressive thought. My uncle, Hammond Lamont, who died in middle age during the full tide of his brilliance, was managing editor of the liberal New York *Evening Post* for six years and editor of the militant *Nation* for three. Another uncle, John P. Gavit, was also managing editor of the *Post* for several years and later concentrated on the fight for a sane international order. My aunt, the former Mrs. Charles Corliss, is a popular novelist bearing the pen-name of Anne Parrish. A few years ago she wrote, under the title of *Golden Wedding,* one of the most effective contemporary satires on the wealthy American bourgeoisie. And one of my Father's first cousins, Robert Rives Lamonte, was for many years a prominent member of the Socialist Party and a prolific author on the subject of Socialism. All in all, then, I do not feel very much like a black sheep in the family circle.

Of course, if my position is sound on the ways and means

of achieving peace and other recognized human values, then all progressive minded and idealistic capitalists, including some of my close relatives, ought to seriously contemplate throwing their energies into the struggle for Socialism. I am convinced that many such members of the upper economic strata would be individually happier in a co-operative society where their social sensitivities would not be constantly outraged and where they would cease to lead lives which so often today are psychologically oppressed, spiritually frustrated, and weighed down by the very bulk of material possessions.

3. *Critique of Well-to-do Radicals*

The Marxists believe that the preponderant support for Socialism must come from the workers, because of their numerical strength and psychological cohesiveness, because of their basic and productive function in industrial life, and because their precarious economic situation more readily leads them to recognize a Socialist order as their chief hope. The radical movement has in addition always attracted an impressive number of the middle class, especially professionals and intellectuals, whose training is more prone to make them see the logical case for Socialism.

Members of the uppermost economic strata who espouse Socialism are relatively few and far between. The capitalists economic stake in the present order—or, rather, disorder—makes this understandable, but they have an important psychological stake as well. Not only do they possess on the whole, even in America, a very deep loyalty to their class as such; but also their careers and feelings of self-esteem are so bound up with the present system, that to admit that it is failing or that some other system is prefer- able would constitute, in their minds, an admission that their own lives had been a failure. That is why, in this era, members of the upper economic strata who come over to Socialism are almost always those of the second generation whose *amour pro pre* is not necessarily tied up with Capitalism.

When, despite all inhibiting economic and psychological influences, members of the upper class do come over to the Left, it is possible for them to be as dependable as anyone else. Like any other types in the radical movement, they may honestly change their convictions or lose their nerve, grow conservative with age or become tired of it all. But they can rarely be bought off, because they already possess a goodly measure of economic security. And they are not likely to be corrupted by the lure of social prestige because they had plenty of that commodity to begin with. There is little danger of their enacting the revolting spectacle of a Ramsay Mac Donald betraying British Socialism by gradually succumbing to the refined and aristocratic atmosphere of afternoon tea with the nobility.

We well-to-do radicals, however, have our own peculiar problems. There is the problem of what particular job will enable us to function most effectively in the movement, of how to handle the numerous and never-ending financial appeals, of making new and staunch friends on the Left who will give us understanding and moral support, and of adjusting our personal lives in a way that is appropriate to the beliefs we hold. The ordinary uppermost income conservative is quite prone to call us insincere because we do not at once reduce our standard of living to that of the most poverty-stricken group in the United States. I well remember an encounter some years ago with that picturesque blusterer, ex-Vice-President, ex-banker and ex-general Charles G. Dawes, who leapt up from an excellent Sunday dinner and paced around the table chewing angrily on his pipe and charging that I had no right to believe in Socialism until I gave away my last penny! I reminded him that it wasn't Lenin but Jesus who had advised giving away all one's goods to feed the poor. The Christian ex-general, himself a multi-millionaire at the time, did not respond to this observation.

The point is, that there are more significant things to do on behalf of Socialism than to make dramatic and half-baked gestures such as flinging away all one's money or moving to some city slum. It is well for at least a few friends of the radical movement to remain financially solvent. And it may be useful, too, for non-proletarian radicals to keep on working within the capitalist class where they were brought up and to try to win over more persons from it or at least to arouse them against Fascism. It is customary to jeer at what are sometimes known as "Parlor Pinks"; but as a matter of fact very good work can be done for Socialism in parlors both modest and magnificent. Some of the most flourishing seeds of the French and Russian Revolutions were planted in the salons of the high and mighty. And leftists like myself cannot help feeling that it is rather more important for us to be effective on behalf of Socialism than to try to satisfy the preconceived whims of upper-income folk as to how we should behave.

Finally, radicals like myself do not pretend to be either angels or martyrs; it is our unfriendly critics who concoct that myth and then accuse us of being hypocrites because we do not live up to it. Neither are we kill-joys who want to take all the fun out of life, gloomy fanatics who have no sense of humor, nor slaves to work who think that a cause can best be served by physical or nervous wrecks. The unexciting truth is that we are ordinary persons who like ordinary pleasures and recreations, who try to do a good day's work and who wish to provide our children with a decent environment in which to grow up. It would be folly for us, as for anyone else in this capitalist country, to attempt to act now in all respects as if full-fledged Socialism already existed in America.

Apologists for the present economic system, however, spare no efforts in their endeavor to discredit radicals of my type. Some- times they attempt simply to laugh us off; sometimes, like Sinclair Lewis in his recent novel *The Prodigal Parents*, they resort to absurd caricatures. But unquestionably their most frequent procedure is to try to explain us away by resorting to amateur psychoanalysis. Thus they claim that we are impelled toward Socialism by strange and obscure Freudian complexes. We have either a publicity complex, an Oedipus complex, an inferiority complex, a martyr complex or a romantic revolt-against-our-elders complex. We either were unhappy and neglected as children or became bored and took up radicalism as an engaging fad or had an ineffable, irrational yearning just to be "different."

Now a little psychoanalysis is a dangerous thing. And the first trouble with the psychoanalytic approach to non-proletarian radicals is that, even granting that some of us, like other people, are afflicted with Freudian complexes, personal neuroses and. social unpopularity, such psychological stimuli, while important to both thought and action, do not in themselves push a person toward any particular economic or political program. Even economic disaster does not necessarily lead a person leftward, since he may really think that his self-interest lies in some other quarter. These various types of pressure may, and no doubt usually do, move a person to some definite course of conduct in order to solve his personal dilemmas. He may then proceed to support Socialism and the labor movement; but instead he may join the Oxford Group, retire to an ivory tower of one sort or another, become a Fascist storm trooper or commit suicide. So again it seems to me that the deciding factor in bringing an individual around to the radical viewpoint must ordinarily be a deep but normal feeling for democracy and, reliance on the appeal of reason.

The second trouble with the psychoanalytic theory of radicalism is that radicals from the middle class or the so-called upper class do not appear to have been especially afflicted with psychological complexes. In the process of growing up we undoubtedly went through the average number of emotional difficulties, but nothing along these lines, I am sure, which would particularly distinguish us from the other 99 per cent of our social group who have faithfully stood by the existing economic order. Neither have we been in general unpopular among our fellows are denied social recognition, nor badly treated by our parents. Most of us graduated successfully from universities of long standing and high repute such as Harvard and Yale, Columbia and Chicago. And we are now engaged in congenial and productive occupations according to our abilities and training.

The third trouble with the psychoanalytic theory is, of course, that, conceding for the sake of argument that it is substantially true, it does not really undermine the case for radicalism. Even if personal mal-adjustments do drive people toward certain definite economic and political programs, this fact in itself, by no means discredits such programs, whether they be radical or conservative in nature. Intellectual propositions cannot be disproved by a parading of the various motives that have led persons to accept them, but only by other intellectual propositions which refute them.

Very pertinent to this discussion is what Karl Marx (1818-1883) and Friedrich Engels (1820-1895), the founders of modern Socialism., wrote in *The Communist Manifesto*. There they stated: "just as in former days part of the nobility went over to the bourgeoisie, so now part of the bourgeoisie goes over to the proletariat. Especially does this happen in the case of some of the bourgeois ideologists, who have achieved a theoretical understanding of the historical movement as a whole." The reference here to "theoretical understanding" is roughly equivalent to what I have been calling "the appeal to reason." True enough, Marx and Engels did not have Freud's very original and significant work to guide them. But if they had had, I greatly doubt whether they would have considered some sort of sexual neurosis or other psychological complex more important in bringing over members of the Bourgeoisie to Socialism than a certain modicum of good sound study and thinking.

As a matter of fact, as I have discovered after considerable experience, the primary object of the psychoanalytic attack on radicalism is to becloud the fundamental intellectual issues by what are in essence ad-homonym arguments. For years, starting during my term at Harvard, whenever I took some unorthodox stand which required a certain amount of open fighting, people would accuse me of personal publicity seeking. This developed in me a self-conscious fear of publicity about myself which was the nearest thing to a "complex" I ever had. Only later, when I came to under- stand the real purpose of such criticisms, was I able to deal with newspapers and reporters in a natural way.

There is one other ad-homonym argument used against

upper-class radicals that also warrants some attention. Since, as I have said, we usually belong to the second generation, the charge is made that most of us are either, too young in years, or too immature in mind, to know what is good for society. It is significant that as long as we agreed in general with conventional doctrines or did not go beyond a liberal position, such criticisms were never leveled against us. One is never too young to hold an opinion as long as it does not run fundamentally counter to prevailing views. But if one steps off the capitalist reservation, it is a very different matter; then one suddenly discovers that no one under fifty is entitled to an opinion about anything.

From time immemorial, the elder generation has used this deprecation of youthfulness in order to block progress and stop dissent. As far back as ancient Greece there was a proverb current, attributed to the Athenian Sage, Solon, to the effect that: "A young man who is not an anarchist is a knave; an old man who is not a conservative is a fool." The most familiar modern form of this saying runs: "A man who is not a Socialist before he is twenty-five has no heart; if he is a Socialist after twenty-five, he has no head." The delightful implication of this, of course, is that Marx, Engels, and Lenin have all been mere sophomores in their adherence to Socialism. They never became mature enough to think things through!

It is important to note at this point that Marx and Engels were themselves of bourgeois origin. Marx was the son of a lawyer and married the daughter of a high government official of aristocratic lineage. Engels was, in economic status, distinctly upper class, being the son of a wealthy German textile manufacturer whose firm owned factories in both Germany and England. He worked in the family business for more than twenty years, most of the time at Manchester. Out of the money he made as a functioning capitalist, and also out of an inheritance he received from his father, Engels supported Marx for more than three decades and enabled him thereby to pursue those research and writing activities which resulted in the production of *Capital*.

Two other able leaders with capitalist antecedents in the

German pre-War radical movement were Ferdinand Lasalle, who both co-operated and fought with Marx, and Wilhelm Liebknecht, one of the most active spirits in the founding of the Social Democratic Party. The latter's son, Karl Liebknecht, was one of the few German radicals who uncompromisingly opposed the Great War, spending two years in prison for his stand. Monarchist officers murdered him, together with his colleague and co-leader, Rosa Luxemburg, of middle-class Polish parentage, at the time of the Spartacus uprising in 1919. Today the German radical and anti-Fascist movement, necessarily either underground or emigre, probably contains more middle and upper-class elements than ever before. Perhaps best known in America are some of the outstanding anti-Fascist writers such as Thomas Mann and Lion Feuchtwanger, the late Ernst Toller and Karl Billinger, Prince Hubertus Zu Loewenstein and Ludwig Renn who inherited the title of Baron.

In Russia, Vladimir I. Lenin (1870-1924), the great leader of the Revolution and first head of the Soviet Government, was a middleclass intellectual; while his noted wife and co-worker, Nadeshda (aka Nadja) Konstantinovna Krupskaya, was the daughter of an impoverished nobleman. Upper-class authors like Prince Kropotkin and Count Tolstoi helped to pave the way for the overthrow of Tsarism. One of the heaviest financial contributors to the Bolshevik Party was a millionaire textile manufacturer named Alexander Morosov. Leonid Krassin, first Soviet Commissar for Foreign Trade and an executive of signal ability, was another wealthy businessman who had a hand in bringing about the Revolution. Felix Dzerzhinsky, a Polish nobleman, was for many years a member of the Bolshevik Central Committee, served as head of the secret police force to combat counter-revolution and became Chairman of the Supreme Economic Council. Of the fifteen original members of the Council of People's Commissars, the Soviet cabinet, eleven were middle-class intellectuals.

In France Jean Jaures, orator, parliamentarian and worker for peace, the leader of the Socialist Party for many years before his assassination in 1914, was of upper-class lineage. Leon Blum, who became first Socialist Premier of France in 1936, is the son of a rich manufacturer. Leading French intellectuals and writers like Romain Rolland, Andre Gide, Ramon Fernandez and Andre Malraux have been, among the most able and effective supporters of the Left. In Spain a large proportion of the bourgeois intellectuals supported the movement to overthrow the monarchy and get rid of King Alfonso XIII. While a few of them later deserted the Republic when the Fascist rebellion broke out in 1936, most of them rallied to the defense of the Loyalist Government. Manuel Azana, a Left Republican and lawyer by profession, remained as President of the People's Front Republic. And the Socialist Juan Negrin, Prime Minister in the cabinet which led such long and heroic resistance against the Fascists, comes from the professional class, having been a noted physician.

In England there has been a long tradition of middle and upper class radicalism, starting in the early nineteenth century with Robert Owen, wealthy and successful textile manufacturer, social idealist and experimenter with local Communist colonies. Later came William Morris, poet and author of the Socialist Classic, *News from Nowhere;* and after him the Fabian Socialists, including intellectuals like George Bernard Shaw, H. G. Wells and Beatrice and Sidney Webb (Lord Passfield). Among the present crop of radicals are members of the nobility such as Lord Marley and Lord Listowel, Lord Strabolgi and Sir Stafford Cripps; well-known authors such as John Langdon Davies, Harold J. Laski and John Strachey; the poets W. H. Auden, Stephen Spender and C. Day Lewis; and Major Clement C. Attlee, parliamentary leader of the Labor Party, and Oliver Baldwin, son of Earl Stanley Baldwin, former Conservative Prime Minister.

Throughout the world, in fact, and not just in Europe, members of the middle and upper classes are active in the radical movement. In China we find that Mao Tse-tung, son of a prosperous peasant, is head of the Chinese Soviets and the greatest Communist leader in the East, while Chu Teh, scion of a wealthy family of landlords, is Commander-in-Chief of the Red forces; in Japan the police are constantly arresting young Reds who prove to be the sons and daughters of bankers, generals or the nobility. In India, Pandit Jawaharlal Nehru, son of a rich Brahman, and Subhas Chandra Bose, of middle-class background, two leaders second only to Mahatma Gandhi in influence, are both militant left-wingers. In Brazil a middle-class lawyer, Luis Carlos Prestes, is the outstanding left and anti-Fascist leader.

In the United States a countless number of non-proletarians, most of them from the middle class, have served or are serving loyally and well in the labor and radical movements. It is possible to mention only a few of these Americans here. But they represent almost every field of endeavor, whether they be authors like Edward Bellamy, Jack London and Lincoln Steffens; Upton Sinclair, Harry Laidler and George Seldes; Theodore Dreiser, Ernest Hemingway and John Steinbeck; Anna Rochester, Anna Louise Strong and Dorothy Parker; journalists like John Reed, Heywood Broun and Louis Fischer; editors like Alfred Bingham, Jessica Smith and George Soule; artists like Thomas Benton and Rockwell Kent; civil libertarians like Roger N. Baldwin and Professor Harry F. Ward; political leaders like the Communist, Robert Minor, and the Socialist, Norman Thomas; clergymen like Reinhold Niebuhr and William P. Spofford; teachers like Robert Morss Lovett and Granville Hicks; labor organizers like Powers Hapgood and Lement Harris; or roving fighters for freedom like Ella Reeve Bloor, Gardner Jackson and James Waterman Wise.

History records that in times of great social and economic stress it is a common occurrence for a small minority of the ruling class, primarily for moral and intellectual reasons rather than from economic need, to sympathize with and take part in the movements of the under-privileged. Sufficient material is available to write a substantial volume on this phenomenon alone. Thus we upper-class radicals of the present day feel that we are carrying on a long and honorable tradition. While ancestor worship is not a very fruitful thing, a number of us can if necessary summon up the shades of our forebears to bestow a blessing on us; I myself had ancestors who sailed across the Atlantic in the good ship

Mayflower and who fought in the American Revolution. We are, then, by no means breaking entirely with the past; we are selecting out of that past what seems to us the highest course of conduct and are trying to follow it through.

On the Left with approval, on the Right with disapproval, we are sometimes called "traitors to our class." But I confess that I don't are for this negative formulation and find it very inadequate; I prefer to say that in trying to be loyal to humankind as a whole, we are compelled to oppose the economic interests of the capitalist class. At the same time we back the working class and accept its leadership because it possesses the potentiality of creating a new and better form of society, and because the labor movement everywhere is in the interests of the overwhelming majority.

Realistic radicals do not nourish the illusion, however, that we can get Socialism for nothing; we cannot take the greatest step forward in history without paying for it. Even where Socialism comes peacefully, as I trust it will in America, a lot of people especially among the capitalists, are not going to enjoy it one bit. And certain traditional values, closely bound up with the rise and rule of Capitalism, are bound to perish. I am sorry that these things have to be; but the universe decreed long ago that evolution, however healthy and desirable, must be a somewhat painful process. As long as mankind continues to grow, it must endure growing pains.

It is my thesis that if growth is to go on, it must be in the direction of a Socialist society. I cannot hope to argue people into that democratic feeling which is the emotional core of the radical movement; most Americans have that feeling anyway. What I aim to do, therefore, in the remainder of this book is to develop the intellectual case for Socialism, and in so doing, to reveal the path along which my own mind has traveled. I intend also to show in detail how Socialism's appeal to reason covers not only the realm of economics and politics but that of culture and philosophy as well. In short, Socialism, whether as a goal to be achieved or as an achievement to be experienced and enjoyed, represents a total way of life.

Chapter II
Capitalism Fails Humankind

1. *An Independent Analysis*

I am not an orthodox Socialist, an orthodox Communist or an orthodox anything else. I have never been an enrolled member of any political party either conservative or radical. So far as I can remember, in every election in which I have voted, I have cast my ballot for the candidates of at least three different parties. The most accurate label I can find for myself is simply that of independent radical and worker for Socialism. Being an independent has certain advantages and certain disadvantages, but anyway that is what I am. And in writing about Socialism I am giving my own interpretations and emphases, with both omissions and inclusions which any official account would no doubt consider unjustified.

At the outset I want to call attention to the fact that economics has traditionally been pictured as a terribly difficult and complex subject far beyond the grasp of the ordinary mind. This myth has been carefully fostered by the capitalist class in order to discourage people from asking embarrassing questions about the present system. And it is easy to see that if the capitalists can succeed in setting up themselves and their professorial henchmen as the sacred Priests of Economics, who alone know the inner workings of this abstruse discipline, then the person in the street will have no alternative except to bow down in awe before them. Indeed, if economics really were as difficult as is often claimed, only a few professional economists would have the intellectual right to hold opinions in this field and it would become all but impossible to develop a mass movement to change the existing order. Now of course there are details and ramifications of economic theory, whether Socialist or orthodox, which only specialists are equipped to follow. But I insist that the fundamental principles which explain the way in which Capitalism and Socialism function are comparatively simple. They can be understood readily by the average American citizen.

2. *The Profit System and Laissez-Faire*

Let us go back for a moment to 1776. That was a very important date in the history of America. I cite it, however, not in order to discuss the Declaration of Independence, but because in that same year, Adam Smith, Capitalism's most talented theoretician and probably the greatest of all the Smiths who have ever lived, published his famous book, *The Wealth of Nations*. This work became an international best-seller of the period and constituted, in a sense, world Capitalism's Declaration of Independence.

"It is not [wrote Smith] from the benevolence of the butcher, the brewer or the baker that we expect our dinner, but from their regard to their own interest. We address ourselves, not to their humanity but to their self-love, and never talk to them of our own necessities but of their advantages. . . . The consideration of his own private profit is the sole motive which determines the owner of any capital to employ it either in agriculture, in manufacture; or in some particular branch of the wholesale or retail trade. . . . Every individual is continually exerting himself to find out the most advantageous employment for whatever capital he can command. It is his own advantage, indeed, and not that of society, which he has in view. But the study of his own advantage naturally, or rather necessarily, leads him to prefer that employment which is most advantageous to the society."

Thus Adam Smith laid down the principle that if each capitalist tried to make the most profit for himself and was permitted unrestricted opportunity in this endeavor, everything would somehow work out in the end to the greatest possible benefit of the community as a whole. Complete liberty in the pursuit of profit implied an absolutely free market in which, Smith expected, free competition among the capitalists would result in the survival and success of the fittest and in the automatic adjustment of prices to the most efficient functioning of business and the maximum return for the consumer. A free market also assumed the right of free contract as between employer and employee, so that there could be unimpeded buying of labor-power by the capitalists and unimpeded selling of it by its possessors, the workers, Such a market, Smith thought, would create ever-extending spheres of economic activity and would stimulate that division of labor or specialization in production which was the surest way of increasing wealth.

He advocated the free market not just within countries but also between countries. For he was convinced that capitalist enterprise would reach the peak of prosperity only with the establishment of a market as wide as the world itself, and that international free trade would carry the division of labor to its logical conclusion by encouraging each nation to specialize in the production of those goods for which its particular economy was best suited. So Smith urged the abolition of all the cramping rules and regulations, monopolistic dealings and government restraints, burdensome taxes and duties—whether such practices affected primarily domestic or international trade—which had been the bane of business under the old system of Mercantilism. The new idea was well summed up in the French phrase *Laissez faire,* meaning Let us alone. Hands off.

Capitalists throughout the Western World hailed with acclaim the principles enunciated in **The Wealth of Nations**. And in varying degrees these principles became actualized in each of the chief capitalist countries. But the point I wish to stress here is that the capitalist does not run a business for fun, for charity, for love, for service, for the social good or any other such purpose; it is run, and must run, primarily for the sake of profit, for the return on the capital which he can earn in excess of all costs. And that holds as true today as in the eighteenth century when Smith wrote his book or in the sixteenth century when the capitalist era first began to come into its own.

Now there is no doubt that the profit system of *laissez faire* Capitalism, especially during the period initiated by the Industrial Revolution, and the new freedom of *laissez Faire*, succeeded in developing tremendously, the productive and technical powers of humankind. It subdued to a large extent the forces of nature and harnessed them to useful employment; it accumulated wealth on a scale far more vast than anyone had even dreamt of before; it extended the pattern of economic enterprise and progress to every part of the globe; it greatly broadened cultural facilities in the more advanced nations; and it brought into the realm of possibility, that Socialist form of society which it is the principal objective of this book to elucidate. I would not deny for a moment that Capitalism has advanced humanity an immeasurable distance beyond the previous system of Feudalism. Nonetheless, the costs of this advance in terms of human suffering and social waste have been frightful and enormous. And *laissez faire* itself proved unable to survive.

The results, of unbridled *laissez faire* have-everywhere and always been disastrous for the physique, the morale and general welfare of the working class. In England, for instance, during the first decades of the nineteenth century, scores of thousands of men, women and children (from the age of six upward) became broken in health and spirit, toiling in badly lighted, badly ventilated, crowded and unsanitary factories for twelve or even sixteen hours a day. No one has portrayed more truly the spirit of Capitalism in quest of profits than Karl Marx himself, on this very matter of the working day. He writes:

"In its blind, unbridled passion, its werewolf hunger for surplus labor, capital is not content to over-step the moral restrictions upon the length of the working day. It oversteps the purely physical limitations as well. It usurps the time needed for the growth, the development, and the healthy maintenance of the body. It steals the time essential for the consumption of fresh air and sunshine. It higgles over a meal time, incorporating this whenever possible with the process of production, so that the worker receives his food only as one of the means of production, just as coal is supplied to heat the boiler, and lubricating oil to facilitate the running of the machinery. The workers' hours of sleep, of what should be healthy sleep for the collection, renewal, and refreshment of the vital powers, become a spell of so many hours of torpor as are essential to the temporary revival of an utterly exhausted organism. Capital does not inquire how long the embodiment of labor power is likely to live. Its only interest is in ensuring that a maximum amount of labor power shall be expended in one working day. It attains this end by shortening the worker's life, just as a greedy farmer secures a greater immediate return from the soil by robbing the soil of its fertility."

Accordingly, the capitalists have always strenuously opposed limiting the hours of work to a decent length, fearing that such a step would reduce profits. And even when they have been forced by law or otherwise, to shorten the working day, they have in compensation to themselves, introduced into their factories the "speed-up," that is, an almost unbearable heightening in the tempo of the machines, and the "stretch-out," that is, a heavy increase in the number of machines to be tended by each worker. It is no wonder that the spurring on of production by such devices, putting the workers under a most fearful strain, eventually resulted in the well-known maxim of modern industry, "Men over 40 not wanted.

"It is not surprising, either, given the urgency of the capitalist desire to pile up profits, that businessmen have always contended they would be irretrievably ruined by the monetary loss involved in paying minimum wages, doing without child labor, or safeguarding the workers from the more obvious hazards connected with employment. When and where labor is cheap and plentiful, capitalists are only too likely to adopt the motto of "Safety Last"— for their employees. During the evolution of Capitalism literally hundreds of thousands of workers have met death, and millions have suffered permanent disability, through preventable occupational accidents due to neglect and stinginess on the part of management.

One of the worst results of the hard-boiled profit motive operating in its pristine state has been the constant creation of hordes of workers unable to find employment and, until recently, unable to obtain the aid of public, authorities in their plight. When business slackens and a capitalist cannot continue to make a profit on his regular program of manufacturing and selling goods, he curtails or stops altogether producing and distributing them. And he compels his employees, or a large proportion of them, to join the ranks of the jobless *because it is temporarily more profitable for him to leave them idle.*

In truth, though the capitalists have grown more and more exercised over the size of unemployment figures, they do not want to abolish unemployment entirely, for they need a substantial number of unemployed as a labor reserve to be available during the sudden expansions and sky-rocketing booms so typical of Capitalism; and, among other things, they are able to use such a reserve to hold down working standards and to break strikes. All the while, in spite of the appalling needs of the millions out of work, the average businessman has been extremely hostile to state aid on their behalf, both because this might mean an increase in taxation, and also might make the unemployed less amenable to wage exploitation.

Indeed, whether we study the history of unemployment insurance or workmen's compensation or some other reform, we see that there has hardly been one ameliorative measure of this sort in any country which has not at first been furiously contested by a large majority of the capitalist class. The movement, however, for eradicating the most glaring industrial evils has been so strong that in all the advanced nations of the West, numerous and far-reaching, though usually inadequate, statutes have been enacted, in the field of labor and social legislation, from the British Factory Acts of the early nineteenth century to the New Deal reforms of President Roosevelt. The government controls over business which were designed for the protection of the working class and which everywhere accompanied the evolution of industry constituted the first great breach in the system of constituted the first great breach in the system of *laissez faire.* And it is quite likely that even Adam Smith himself, had he lived to see the brutish way in which Capitalism developed, would have favored such measures.

Businessmen have from the start also fought tooth and nail

against trade unions, for fear that collective action on the part of labor would cut into profits by forcing employers to make expensive concessions to their workers. This is why in America during the past few years there has been such bitter and often violent capitalist resistance to the campaigns of John L. Lewis and the C.I.O. And it is likewise why one of the first important moves of a Fascist regime is to suppress the trade unions root and branch.

Toward the end of the nineteenth century in most capitalist countries labor had won, though only after long and arduous struggles, the legal right to organize. But many restrictions in law even then remained on such indispensable trade-union practices as collective bargaining, the strike, and peaceful picketing. Employer recognition of trade unions, which constitutes the very substance of labor's progress, has grown extremely slowly, with our own United States a laggard in this respect and nations like Great Britain and Sweden in the van. Here again, in the gradually successful efforts of the workers to organize and protect themselves against the intolerable effects of uncontrolled profit-making, there occurred, another significant lapse in *laissez faire.* For the whole idea behind trade unions has violated the *laissez faire* principle of an absolutely free contract between the individual employer and the individual workingman. (The word "free here was always a misnomer so far as the workers were concerned.) At the same time the more powerful the unions have become and the more able to win wage increases and resist wage cuts, the more they have interfered with that complete flexibility in the price of labor-power which, was such an essential attribute of the free market.

Meanwhile another change was taking place under Capitalism which was full of portent for *laissez faire* and directly due to factors inseparably connected with the profit system. I refer to the process of concentration and monopoly. In order to keep, making money, a capitalist business has to compete continually with formidable rivals in the same line. Even during fairly prosperous years an astonishing number of firms—more than 350,000, for instance, in the U. S. during 1937—discontinue operations because they cannot stand the pace. When we take bad times into account as well, it is conservatively estimated that at least one-fifth of all capitalist enterprises fall by the wayside. Up to a certain point, the bigger the business, the more cheaply it can sell its goods on the market and the more chance it has of coming out on top. For, other things being equal, large-scale organization and production, lowers the cost of manufacture by making possible comprehensive technological improvements, the standardization of output, the utilization of by-products, the general elimination of waste and the higher productivity of labor. Accordingly, there is a steady tendency for the bigger capitalist, through greater competitive strength and profit-making ability, to drive the smaller out of the field or absorb him by buying up his business and putting through a merger.

The fact of concentration and centralization in American business life is acknowledged in all quarters, though opinion differs as to its exact extent, and even more as to its exact significance. Adolph A. Berle, Jr., and Gardiner C. Means in their definitive study, *The Modern Corporation and Private Property*, show that out of approximately 300,000 non-banking corporations in the United States, some 200 control one-half of the total corporate wealth. We are all familiar with the names of some of these huge companies whose assets run into billions of dollars. Who has not heard, for instance, of United States Steel, General Motors, Pennsylvania Railroad, American Telephone and Telegraph, Standard Oil, General Electric, Anaconda Copper, United Cigar, Radio Corporation of America, Liggett Drug Stores, Metropolitan Life Insurance, the Great Atlantic and Pacific Tea Company?

The *Census of Manufactures,* compiled by the U.S. Department of Commerce, informs us that in 1929 out of 210,945 manufacturing plants in America, those with an output worth $1,000,000 or more, though constituting less than 6 per cent of the total number, and employed almost 60 per cent of the workers and accounted for almost 70 per cent of production. These figures do not reveal the full degree of concentration, however, since many of the plants concerned are simply units in huge industrial combinations or trusts. Even in retail trade, where the small shopkeeper is ordinarily thought to retain such strength, 25 per cent of the stores in 1929 enjoyed the lion's share— 75 per cent—of the business. The ever-growing chain stores alone accounted for 21 per cent of the total retail trade.

Concentration and centralization extend into the banking field where houses such as J. P. Morgan & Company, the Guaranty Trust Company, the Chase National Bank and the National City Bank, wield tremendous financial control Out of approximately 25,000 banks in the U. S. in 1930, 140, or 0.58 per cent of the total, held almost 50 per cent of the banking resources (excluding those of savings banks). Our whole economic life, whether in industry or agriculture, transportation or retail trade, is indissoluble bound up with the complicated system of credit which the banks administer.

Large-scale industry, with its huge expansion programs and capital requirements, has come more and more to depend on financiers to provide the necessary loans and to float the necessary stock or bond issues. Monopoly in industry and monopoly in finance have grown together; but the ultimate and greater power, exercised both nationally and internationally, now rests in the hands of finance. And this era well warrants being called that of Finance Capitalism.

I need not labor the point of capitalist concentration. While plenty of small business continues to function in America, big business has, without question, come to play the decisive role here. And in its rise to power and subsequent career it has ruined beyond recognition the original scheme of free competition in a free market advocated by Adam Smith and the other supporters of *laissez faire.* For not only does a business reach the monopoly stage by strangling competitors, but also, once it acquires something of a monopoly in its field, it is prone to boost prices inordinately and freeze them at a level which forces the consumer to take a severe drubbing. The net result is a market inflexibility that makes quick and. adequate adjustment: to changing economic conditions virtually impossible and that constitutes a major reason why depressions under monopoly capitalism have become deeper and more acute than ever before. True enough, the government may step in and try to remedy the situation by anti-trust laws and the like. Such measures, however, have had little more effect than King Canute's famous attempt to stop the incoming tide by decree; and of course *ipso facto* they have constituted yet another violation of *laissez faire's* principle of: *Hands off.*

Though unrestrained competition in profit-making leads inexorably to the stifling of competition, it is most necessary to add that the different monopolies themselves compete to the death with one another. Since, furthermore, it is the inmost essence of capita- list enterprise to expand or perish, when a business has exhausted the possibilities within a country it looks abroad for further spheres of conquest. Then the battle between monopolies proceeds to take place on an international scale; the giant trusts, which sometimes enter into international price and production agreements, to divide up the world among themselves; and the various capitalist governments, each one representing the profit-seeking urges and the monopolistic tendencies of a national capitalist class as a whole, struggle to obtain, through means fair and foul, peaceful and violent, trade advantages and territorial possessions from one end of the earth to the other.

One of the most common measures of economic warfare to which capitalist governments have resorted is that of the protective tariff. The reader will recall the strong emphasis which Adam Smith laid on the idea of international free trade. Great Britain, which had considerable head-start over every other nation in the new adjustments called for by the Industrial Revolution and which depended on foreign commerce as its very life-blood, naturally favored a free trade system. Thus, during the first sixty years of the nineteenth century British Capitalism, step by step, reduced and finally eliminated its protective tariffs on manufactured goods and foodstuffs.

But other countries wanted to stimulate their own industries and felt, that they must shield them from foreign competition, especially that of England. The United States, under the leadership of Alexander Hamilton, took this position from the beginning. France made only wavering gestures in the direction of free trade. And during the last part of the nineteenth century all of the European Powers except Britain, and most of the smaller nations as well, erected a system of high-tariff walls. This unhappy development continued in the twentieth century, reaching a culmination in the Great Depression of the nineteen-thirties when some of the tariffs grew into virtual embargoes. It was then that even England, the great and traditional free trade nation, finally succumbed to the pressure of economic self-defense, and enacted far-reaching tariff laws. Indeed, the protectionist idea has recently been stretched to such fantastic lengths that formidable trade barriers, with particular application to farm products, have been set up between different states in the U.S.A. "Today," reports Secretary of Agriculture Henry A. Wallace, "we cannot say that we have free trade between the states."

Though the tariff system has of course swelled immensely the profits of particular capitalists and corporations, its price to the peoples of the world has been incalculably high. It has proved a constant obstruction to the flow of commerce and the interchange of mutually desired goods; it has been a potent factor in causing ill feeling between nations and fanning the flames of international conflict; it has brought about an enormous loss of wealth by leading to wasteful duplication in production as between various countries; and has raised the cost of living by enabling capitalist business, protected from the competition of foreign imports, to push up beyond all reason the prices of goods on the domestic market; it has resulted in the establishment of high-pressure lobbies in all the chief capitals and has notably contributed to the corruption of public officials; and it has fatally disrupted the vast world market envisioned by *laissez faire.*

Since 1929 other changes have taken place in the capitalist system which have lent cardinal assistance to the tariff racket in ripping to pieces *laissez faire's* romantic picture of international free trade. Of primary importance is the fact that the monetary systems of the different capitalist nations have been experiencing extreme vicissitudes, with all the chief countries going off the gold standard and using their depreciated currencies as weapons to gain trade advantages over one another. The result has been that the value of money, at best never very stable under Capitalism, has come to fluctuate more and more on both a national and international scale, with dire consequences for the ideal of the freely functioning market.

Meanwhile the various capitalist governments, in their panic-stricken efforts to secure national self-sufficiency, or *autarchy* as it is called, have been striking out wildly in the most diverse directions. As the English writer John Strachey points out in his brilliant book. *The Coming Struggle for Power,*

> "A whole science, designed for maximizing the exports and minimizing the imports of each and all of the nations of the world simultaneously, has now been elaborated. Import 'Quotas,' import licenses, export bounties, subsidized railway rates to the frontier, penal railway rates from the frontier, subsidies to export industries of every kind, subsidized advertising of 'home' produced products, the systematic placing of all Government and municipal contracts 'at home,' regardless of comparative costs a whole labyrinth of measures for the restriction of international exchanges has been elaborated by the patient and devoted civil servants of every nation."

What tariffs, export bounties, and all the rest really amount to is intervention by the government, in behalf of certain favored business interests. And the capitalist class, in spite of .all its talk about rugged individualism and government coddling, has always enthusiastically backed those repudiations of *laissez faire* which have seemed to promise bigger and better profits. Professor W. Z. Ripley, formerly of Harvard, estimates that in the days of the great transcontinental railway expansion, federal, state and municipal contributions to construction costs came to no less than $700,000,000 and that the grants of public lands totaled 155,000,000 acres. Government authorities in America have in effect subsidized the automobile industry to the extent of billions-by constructing a vast network of concrete and macadamed roads running to every part of the country. And contemporary capitalists, however loud their outcries over public aid to the sick, the aged and the unemployed, have offered up hosannas of praise and gratitude for the timely loans which the Reconstruction Finance Corporation has granted to ailing banks and businesses.

The American capitalist class, too, has ever been most alacritous in attributing to governmental agencies terrible "wastefulness" and lack of foresight in public affairs. Yet it was this same class, which in its mad scramble for immediate monetary gain, recklessly gutted natural resources right and left throughout the country. That is why here in the United States we have witnessed the irredeemable waste of billions of dollars worth of oil and gas, coal and timber. And the tragic devastation of our forests has finally led, because of the interdependency of Nature, to chronic floods and the ruination of huge tracts of fertile land.

All the developments which I have discussed in this section—and I have by no means been able to include the whole story—are the direct outcome of the great find glorious profit motive in action. And they prove without a shadow of doubt that the pure and perfect profit system of *laissez faire* dreamt of by Adam Smith and the others is dead beyond all hope or resurrection and a future life. If you set up the aim of individual private profit as the central principle of economic enterprise, then you should not be surprised when the logical consequences of this principle actually come into being. But there is another consequence which has revealed itself with increasing sharpness during the more recent decades of Capitalism and which brings out most dramatically of all the fundamental weakness of the existing system. That is the well-known and ever more insistent paradox of unceasing want in a world of actual and potential abundance.

3. Poverty Amid Potential Plenty

Until the full unfolding of the Industrial Revolution, the many movements of social protest had little chance of achieving a high standard of living for the masses of the underprivileged, since there simply did not exist the productive equipment to, supply to everyone the necessary consumer goods. Hence those movements frequently ended up in a blind alley, though always keeping awake the spirit of revolt and the urge for a better life. Today the situation is very different. Today every schoolboy knows that in the industrially developed nations there is enough goods-producing machinery to insure a very fair level of existence to the entire populations of such communities. Today for the first time we have all the means to create that material well-being of humankind which the great Utopia-painters of the past have so vividly portrayed.

In the United States, above all other countries, we possess the natural resources, the mechanical equipment and the technical skill to provide all of our citizens with a thoroughly satisfactory standard of living. Yet President Roosevelt, in his second inaugural address, stated that even during the New Deal recovery one-third of the American people were "ill-housed, ill-clad, ill-nourished"; and the President was being conservative. This was proved in the autumn of 1938 when the National Resources Committee, a government appointed organization composed of Cabinet members, expert economists and private businessmen, made a report, after painstaking surveys and research, on income levels in the U.S. for the year 1935-36. The scientific findings of this committee were startling and demonstrated, on the most conservative interpretation; that at least one-half of this nation's population, or 65,000,000 people, fit the President's description.

The report showed that one-third of all American families and single individuals received during 1935-36, annual incomes of less than $780, with the average income of this group amounting to $471 or $9 a week. One-half of our families and individuals had incomes of less than $1,070 and two-thirds less than-$1,450. Even

76

this latter figure fell below the sum set by the U. S. Department of Labor as necessary for the average American family to live with a minimum of decency and comfort. Taking the figures for the 29,000,000 American families alone, we find that 14 per cent of them had incomes of less than $500, 42 per cent had less than $1,000, 65 per cent had less than $1,500 and 87 per cent had less than $2,500.

At the other end of the scale the National Resources Committee stated that a bare 3 per cent of American families received incomes of $5,000 or more and 1 per cent $10,000 or more. But this top 3 per cent got 21 per cent of the total national income and this top per cent 13 per cent of it, as compared with the 16 per cent share of the lowest 42 per cent of all families and the 10 per cent share of the lowest one-third of the families and individuals taken together. The Committee also established the fact that there is an unfortunate sectional concentration in wealth, with average family income in New England at the apex of the pyramid and that in the South at the bottom. Agricultural areas in general also have far less income than urban. The statistics of the National Resources Committee check fairly well, if allowance is made for the changed, economic situation, with those on the mal-distribution of American wealth worked out for the prosperity year of 1929 by the respectable Brookings Institution, a private research organization.

The full import of this discussion strikes home only when we contrast what might be with what is. The Brookings Institution published in 1934 an extremely significant volume entitled *America's Capacity to Produce.* This study reported that at the peak of 1929 prosperity in the United States our production of goods was about 20 per cent below the actual capacity of our economic plant. For the five-year period from 1925 through 1929 the loss of potential output was 22 per cent. Using these figures as a base, it can be shown that production in 1932, the worst year of the Great Depression, fell 45 per cent, or almost half-way short of its possibilities; in 1934, 40 per cent; and in 1935-36, 30 per cent. Reliable estimates show that full use of our economic resources from 1922 through 1934 would have increased the total income of the American people by 248 billion dollars, a sum more than half as large as the entire accumulated wealth of the U.S.A. and almost five times as great as the cost of America's participation in the First World War. Undeniably peace has its losses as well as war.

Another way of grasping the terrible waste that occurs under the capitalist system is to look at the unemployment figures. Even in 1927, a year of upswing and bustling business activity, there were around 4,000,000 unemployed in the United States. At the bottom of the depression the number rose to probably 15,000,000, not to mention the millions of others who were working only part-time. At the height of the first New Deal recovery, in the winter of 1936-37, there were still 8,000,000 without employment in the U. S. And with the recession that followed, this figure went up to at least 12,000,000.

What all this means is that year after year millions and millions of willing and able-bodied men and women are compelled to sit idly by instead of producing the billions upon billions of dollars worth of goods which could serve to enrich both themselves and others. It has been authoritatively reckoned, for example, by Mr. Franklin P. Wood of the Rural Electrification Administration, that ten million unemployed in the United States could, working forty hours a week with two weeks vacation, account for the following in one year: adequate food and clothing for 10,000,000 people, 5,000,000 five-room houses with proper furnishings, 100,000,000 radios, 10,000,000 refrigerators, 10,000,000 automobiles, 2,500 schools, 50,000 miles of rural power lines, 30,000 miles of highways, 10 Boulder Dams.

How much income could the average American family of four expect to earn if the tremendous wastes and inefficiencies of the present order were eliminated? Some years ago Howard Scott and his technocrats, in the first flush of their enthusiasm, said $20,000. That is obviously too high a figure. More modest and reliable was the estimate given by Harold Loeb and his associates in the *Chart of Plenty,* a solid and scholarly study issued by the National Survey of Potential Product Capacity. This report, proceeding from the basis of the plant and equipment available in

1929 and making allowance for two or three work-shifts wherever feasible, put the possible income for each family at $4,370. I do not wish to quibble over statistics. But after giving due attention to the various estimates made and to the more than 25 per cent rise in labor productivity over the, last ten years, I believe it is unquestionable that under a more rational system it would be possible to guarantee promptly an annual return to every American family of goods and services equivalent in value to at least $5,000, thus raising the present proportion of families attaining that level from 3 to 100 per cent.

Our economy of abundance, however, instead of being a blessing is turned into a curse. And we are told by the master minds of the capitalist system that this very abundance, in the form of a strange phenomenon known as "over-production," is the cause of all our troubles. In other words, the real reason for one-half the American people being ill-housed is that there is too much wood and steel and concrete; the real reason for these tens of millions being badly clothed is that there is too much cotton and wool and leather; the real reason for them being underfed is that there is too much meat and milk and wheat, I Instead of being thankful for the bounteousness of nature, we dread it as much as a drought. These and similar absurdities have been exposed many times, but they remain as completely repugnant to reason and common sense as before.

The truth of the matter is of course that, except perhaps in a few luxury trades, there is not and never has been an over-production of goods that the people need, but only of goods that they can afford to buy. It is far more accurate, then, to say that the root of the difficulty lies in *under-consumption* on the part of the masses of the population. And this under-consumption is forced upon them by the inexorable operation of the profit system itself.

For profit-making, to cite Mr. John Strachey again, is not only the motive of every capitalist; it is also the regulator of capitalist production.

"Under Capitalism it is not only the object, it is the very condition of production that a profit should result. Those things, that is to say, which will yield a profit can and will be produced, but those things alone. For anybody who produces things which do not, either directly or indirectly, yield a profit will sooner or later go bankrupt, lose his ownership of the means of production, and so cease to be an independent producer. Capitalism, in other words, uses profitability as the criterion or test, of whether any given thing should or should not he produced, and if so, how much of it should be produced."

This means that no matter how much the people may be in need of a commodity or how great may be the technical capacity for producing it, considerations of profit take precedence. For the capitalist system the general human welfare is merely a by-product which may or may not result from normal business activities.

If a business, especially one of the big monopolies I have described, decides that it can make more money by keeping its prices high and products scarce, then scarcity there must and shall be in that particular field, even if this entails the actual destruction of goods. Capitalist concerns, furthermore, in spite of the greater efficiency implicit in labor-saving machinery, are as likely as not to get the jitters over the prospect of fresh technological advance, because it may lead to the obsolescence and junking of present equipment and to an increase in that very abundance they so fear. In fact they suppress new inventions by the thousand. Though the Rust cotton-picking machine, for example, promises to bring about another progressive economic revolution in the South and to eliminate a huge sector of dreary and backbreaking toil, numerous businessmen all over America trembled at the thought of its widespread introduction. Indeed, throughout the capitalist world there has recently sprung up a whole philosophy of retreat from, modern technique, with its adherents crying out that the "machine is devouring humanity" and repeatedly urging "scientific holidays" and a "moratorium on invention."

The paradox grows even more fantastic during times of crisis when the population is more in need of consumers' goods than ever, but when the creation of artificial scarcity is carried on with redoubled energy. In his masterly book *Man and his Worldly Goods* Mr. Leo Huberman tellingly sums up what happened during the Great Depression:

"Confronted by the paradox of poverty in plenty, capitalist countries devised a plan for tackling the problem. The plan was to abolish the plenty. Who can possibly doubt that, whatever else is wrong with the capitalist system, it has come to represent stupidity incarnate and to be an intolerable affront to a sane man's intelligence?"

4. *The Central Contradiction of Capitalism*

Now obviously enough there would be no fear of plenty, nor would business ever slacken, if the capitalists could depend on a steady market for all the goods that they and their workers produce. Unfortunately, however, quite contrary is the actual case. The market is forever failing and fading away, so much so, in fact, that in the United States during the 150 years since 1790, we have gone through no less than fifteen major and twenty minor economic breakdowns, each of the major ones and several of the minor causing large-scale unemployment and untold hardships amongst the population. On the average during this long period there has been about one year of depression for every year and a half of prosperity. And much the same story of ever-recurring crisis has been true of the other capitalist nations. All of which constitutes an easily readable barometer of the "efficiency" of the profit system.

Now the basic reason for the continual failure of the capitalist market is simply that the masses of the people do not have sufficient purchasing power to absorb the plenty, to buy the vast abundance, of goods produced and producible. Hence the crucial question for Capitalism is: Why does that purchasing power remain insufficient? That question brings us straight up against the central and inescapable contradiction of the capitalist system; and the answer to it is in a nutshell this: On the one hand, you cannot raise wages high enough to give the people sufficient purchasing power to absorb all the available goods and services, without at the same time so reducing the total amount and rate of capitalist profit that economic crisis periodically results; on the other hand, you cannot hold down wages sufficiently to insure profits without keeping the purchasing power of the people so low that economic crisis periodically results. Whatever solution of this dilemma the capitalists attempt, supply and demand (the latter of which depends on purchasing power) are certain to become maladjusted every so often to a calamitous degree. And this brings disruption of the market and depression.

For the purposes of this analysis I include, under the heading of wages, 90 per cent of the fine-sounding category of salaries. Wages and salaries are of supreme importance in the picture because they constitute the mode of compensation for four-fifths of the American people and because, as Karl Marx showed so clearly in his *Capital*, the employers make their profit by underpaying their employees and thus exploiting their labor-power. In general, asserts Marx, it is the policy of the capitalists, unless under pressure by a trade union or some other extraneous factor, to pay their workers only the very minimum necessary to keep them alive and functioning and to insure the biological reproduction of more workers who will some time take their place.

But the workers in field and factory, in transport and store and office, turn out goods or services worth far more in value than their own pay, they are able to produce value equivalent to their wages in less than the total working day, say in five out of eight hours. The remaining three hours Marx calls *surplus labor-time* and the value produced in this period *surplus value.* The capitalist employer appropriates this surplus value, the amount of which will vary according to circumstances, and it enables him to make his profit. Thus all profit, which includes the categories of rent and interest, has its direct or indirect source in surplus value; and all surplus value is in substance "the materialization of unpaid labor-time."

I would consider it both unnecessary and unfruitful to take up in this book the widespread and unending controversy that has been waged over the Marxist theory of surplus value. I happen myself to believe that Marx is substantially correct. At the very least, however, all radicals must admit that this theory symbolizes most successfully the terrible exploitation to which the working class is subject under Capitalism; and that a very large proportion of capitalist profit, if not the whole amount, has .its origin in this exploitation. It also enables us readily to understand that constant strife I have already mentioned between capitalists and workers over the matter of hours and wages.

Even conservative capitalists and orthodox economists must admit that pay-rolls constitute both the largest and most flexible element in production costs, and that the favorite method used by business to economize, on behalf of profits, is to keep wages from going up or to force them to go down. To quote our old friend Adam Smith once more: "The workmen desire to get as much, the masters to give, as little as possible." I remember during the Great Depression talking with any number of businessmen who bewailed the efforts of both the Hoover and Roosevelt administrations to maintain wages at former levels. They insisted that recovery could come only through lowering wages so that the ball of profit could be started rolling again. I always surprised these capitalists by saying that this analysis was quite Marxian. For it was Marx's contention that a major part of the regular capitalist procedure of recovering, always temporarily of course, from economic crisis consisted of riding out on the backs of the workers by reducing wages; or by stopping wages entirely through dismissing workers from their jobs.

Though America has been able to boast of a rather high wage standard in comparison with other countries, the point about insufficient purchasing power applies here because that standard, in the light of our enormous wealth and economic resources, has never been relatively high enough to properly balance purchasing power and production. "If," as Professor Reinhold Niebuhr so forcefully puts it, "we produced ten times as much goods per capita as Europe and our millionaires were ten times richer than European plutocrats and our workers had a wage ten times higher than European proletarians, our economy would still be subject to violent dislocations if our markets could not absorb our productive capacity because of the faulty distribution of our wealth." The figures I have cited prove how dismally low our living standards are on the basis of even minimum needs. But it also remains true that, while most American businesses could well afford to pay considerably higher wages, and by all means should do so, they would cease to make a profit altogether if pay rolls went up beyond a certain point.

Another way of looking at what I have termed the central contradiction of Capitalism is from the point of view of prices. If prices go down on a widespread scale, then what economists call real wages (that is, wages fairly adjusted to fluctuations in the price structure or currency values) go up, since each dollar is able to buy more than before. An expanding consuming power results. This is the method of achieving economic stability advocated by a number of observers these days, prominent among them being Dr. Harold G. Moulton of the Brookings Institution. It is plain, however, that capitalist businesses cannot keep reducing prices indefinitely without also reducing profits to the zero point. And even if they could all be persuaded to lower prices to that minimum compatible with an attractive amount of profit, the masses of the people would not thereby sufficiently increase their purchasing power to solve Capitalism's problem.

As a matter of fact, aside from the ultimate implications of the price-reducing policy, it is extremely doubtful whether the capitalist world in the main, and particularly the monopolies, could be counted upon to put it into effect and establish it as a permanent program. Though individual firms may reap huge profits through continual price-cutting, nothing is more full of potential disaster for the average businessman. And regardless of the effect on the country's economy as a whole, he will boost prices whenever he thinks such a course will bring more profits. For example, the inveterate tendency of the capitalists, as soon as trade unions have won wage increases from them and have enlarged to that extent consumer buying power, is to cancel this gain by pushing up the prices of their goods on the market. This is exactly what has happened in America following the successes of the C. I. O. and the A. F. of L. during the past few years.

The fundamental dilemma of the capitalist system comes to light again when we investigate the question of private saving versus private spending. If we include, in addition to the earnings of those who work for average wages and salaries, the fancy emoluments of the upper-class executives and professionals, the incomes of all the capitalists and the profits of business in general, the total sum is sufficient to buy back the goods which the capitalist system produces. Then why docs not this fact counter-balance the lack of purchasing power on the part of the masses which I have already discussed?

The hitch occurs in that the small minority in whose hands the wealth of America is concentrated do not spend anywhere near all their incomes; they quite understandably save a large propor-tion. And they reinvest their savings or use them for speculation on the stock exchange or, in bad times, simply hoard them by letting them stagnate as deposits in the bank, which in turn is unable to find good investment opportunities for its assets. The more money you have, the more money you are likely to save. In 1929, for example, American families receiving over $20,000 annually saved more than half of their total incomes. And of the $15,000,000,000 of individual savings in that year, $12,000,000,000 came from persons with incomes of more than $5,000.

There are several good reasons for this phenomenon of saving on the part of the economically privileged. After all, the most opulent plutocrats possess only one stomach, a limited amount of energy and twenty-four hours per day. Try heroically as they may and gorge on luxuries as they will, our most consummate spendthrifts can only absorb a certain quantity of consumers' goods—food, drink, clothing, radios, automobiles, houses, yachts and so on—and no more. So even the most extravagant millionaires find it difficult to spend their entire annual incomes, though they sometimes resort to the most fantastic and wasteful extremes in attempting to get rid of their money. Besides, the profit motive, the fun of successful speculation, and ordinary convention spur on the rich to get richer: the lesser try to become millionaires, the millionaires to become multi-millionaires and all capitalists in the upper brackets to increase the family possessions as much as possible.

One of the chief ambitions of the average capitalist-minded individual is to amass enough property in stocks and. bonds and real estate so that he can support himself and his family indefinitely simply on dividends, interest and rent. This deep desire to maintain solvency through the magic of unearned increment is shared by the hospitals, universities and other institutions to which capitalists sometimes give a portion of their largess. Such institutions, in order to ensure permanent security, prefer to be always adding to their endowment and to spend only the annual return from it. Another significant item in the sphere of saving is the vast reserve funds, usually in liquid form (that is, in cash or easily convertible into cash), which businesses of every kind, feeling none too secure under their beloved Capitalism, build up for the inescapable rainy day.

Aside from all this, however, and more important than, anything else, is the fact that the very nature of capitalist business compels it to go on forever accumulating, to keep plowing back a big percentage of its profits into self-improvement and self-expansion or to seek outside financing for these ends. In Marx's words:

"The capitalist process of production is at the same time essentially a process of accumulation. The development of capitalist production necessitates a continuous increase or the capital

86

invested in an industrial undertaking; and Capitalism subjects every individual capitalist to the immanent laws of capitalist production as external coercive laws. Competition forces him continually to extend his capital for the sake of maintaining it, and he can only extend it by means of progressive accumulation."

The method of accumulation, of what might well be called dynamic saving, is to take profits and, instead of spending them on consumers goods, to use them to expand capital goods, that is, production goods, further and further. Capital goods consist of all the materials, machinery and other equipment produced by heavy industry and used by light industry for the direct manufacture of consumers' goods such as clothing, automobiles and .books. They include of course the various means necessary for the operation of heavy industry, and also most forms of construction and housing. It is generally agreed among economists of all schools that the mainspring of capitalist prosperity lies in continuous investment in a successfully functioning capital goods industry.

For a while, in a country like the United States, the new investment and expansion in capital goods heightens business activity and augments consumer purchasing power. But the fresh profits being garnered by the capitalists are, as always, based on the under-payment of the working masses; pretty soon the increasing supply of consumers' goods which the increasing quantity of production goods makes available starts to outrun demand, since the purchasing power of the population cannot keep pace with the new productive power of the capitalists. A glut of un-bought consumers goods, immediately reacting to create a glut of capital goods, quickly ensues. Light industry slumps and pulls down heavy industry after it; agriculture (in an unmitigated state of doldrums in the U. S. since 1920) sinks to still lower depths; and mounting unemployment and declining pay-rolls decrease ever more alarmingly the purchasing power that has already failed.

Thus over-investment, over-accumulation, over-saving on

the part of capitalist individuals, institutions and businesses bring on "overproduction." And economic crisis descends upon every section of the population. This tendency of savings to outstrip the possibilities for profitable investment used to be cyclical; the ominous thing now is that in recent times it seems to have become chronic. Year after year billions upon billions of capital has been lying idle in American banks. Such an enormous hoard of unemployed money inevitably leads to unemployed factories and unemployed workers. And it is a phenomenon which has received some well-deserved attention from Senator Mahoney's Monopoly Committee.

Of late, at all stages of the economic cycle, the capitalists have resorted to increasingly desperate expedients in order to evoke consumer demand. Everybody remembers the pathetic "Buy Now" campaigns of the early thirties. Everybody suffers from the high-pressure advertising that continually shrieks at one from magazine and newspaper, from billboard and radio. And everyone is led into the valley of temptation by our ultra-modern and streamlined methods of installment selling.

Previous to both the Great Depression and the 1937-38 recession millions of American citizens had over-extended themselves by installment buying of everything from perambulators to permanent waves, from refrigerators to radio sets. Of the vast number of automobiles sold in the U. S. A., 60 per cent are purchased on the installment plan. In 1937 total installment sales in all lines amounted to well over $5,000,000,000. In this way American consumers mortgage to an uncertain future, not just their houses and land; but their wages, salaries and entire means of livelihood. And when the inevitable crash comes, this mountain of indebtedness topples over to make the wreckage even worse. But the most important device of all in re-animating the dormant pocketbook of the consumer and one which gives another valuable insight into the great quandary of Capitalism has come to be government spending. What a government does in effect in a large scale spending program is to tap the surplus profits of the capitalists through taxes and especially through borrowing and to transform this money into fresh purchasing power by means of public loans and expenditures of a wide variety. But to distribute indefinitely sufficient purchasing power in this fashion for the masses of the people to buy back the output of business either would entail such burdensome taxation on profits (assuming that business was not able merely to pass on such taxes to the general public) that capitalist enterprise might not deem it worth while to go on; or would so strain the whole financial structure of the community through the huge, unbalanced budgets and the constant resort to borrowing by federal, state and municipal authorities that governmental bankruptcy would occur.

Such bankruptcy might well take the form of disastrous inflation, of the government setting its printing presses going full tilt and turning out paper money by the carload. If and when serious inflation comes to a country, the added purchasing power that a state spending program may have brought is quickly offset. For as more and more money is thrown into circulation, its value rapidly depreciates, prices rise sky-high in compensation, and the real wages of the people suffer a drastic decline. Public spending can go quite far, however, before bankruptcy or severe inflation begins to threaten. The federal debt of the United States, for instance, still remains, in terms of proportionate population figures, less than one-third the size of Great Britain's and could be enormously increased without bankruptcy or inflation necessarily drawing near. And income taxes in this country are much lower than in England.

Nonetheless, it is unquestionable that in this era of capitalist decline, the gigantic budgets for unemployment and social insurance, public works and armaments, are proving terrific burdens for the average capitalist government to carry. So it is quite natural for capitalist apologists like the Austrian economist Professor Hayek, to become fearfully worried over the expanding social services of the modern state. And the time may soon come when most capitalist economies can no longer afford to maintain even the present inadequate standards of unemployment and social insurance. Yet they cannot afford, either, to cut down on these expenditures very far. For to reduce government spending as drastically as Professor Hayek and the ordinary businessman so devoutly wish would not only cause millions of people—especially the unemployed—infinite hardship and stimulate dangerous unrest, but also would react most unfavorably on business by curtailing mass purchasing power.

Our American economic situation since 1933 provides convincing proof of much that I have been saying. In addition to the payment of the soldier's bonus, the indispensable and predominant factor in the partial recovery that culminated toward the end of Roosevelt's first term was the colossal "pump-priming" program which the President put across through such agencies as the FERA (Federal Emergency Relief Administration), the PWA (Public Works Administration) and the WPA (Works Progress Administration). But Mr. Roosevelt, under pressure to reduce expenditures by the very, capitalist interests which profited from his spending, decided that it was dangerous to continue this program. Accordingly, at the beginning of his second administration he started to reduce greatly the governmental outgo. And this was a decisive reason for the sharp recession that began late in 1937. Then in 1938 the Democrats again proceeded to prime the pump to the tune of billions, and an upturn again resulted.

If the "economy" conservatives and the budget-balancers sooner or later prevail once more at Washington, they probably will heavily slash public expenditures in hopes that business will be able to carry on by itself. We can be reasonably sure, however, that their hope will not come true, at least over more than a very brief period. And whether the Democrats or the Republicans happen to hold power, it will finally become plain that temporary primings are not enough for our ailing American Capitalism. For as soon as the new purchasing power due to government spending has become actualized in fresh consumer demand, a disproportionate share of it is promptly siphoned off into profits for the capitalists. This is exactly what happened during the first New Deal upswing when the rate of increase in real wages lagged far behind that of dividends, interest and other forms of profit; and also behind the increase in labor productivity. Hence the maldistribution of wealth continued much as before and the customary depression-making processes repeated their natural course.

So our analysis comes full circle once more. Neither extreme government economy, which in its lessening of purchasing power is comparable to extensive wage-reducing or price-raising, nor extreme government spending, which in its augmenting of purchasing power is comparable to extensive wage-raising or price-reducing (practices that the capitalists have never been guilty of over-stressing), nor any moderate program in between, promises any ultimate unraveling of Capitalism's Gordian Knot.

Finally, we discover that Capitalism's basic difficulty reappears, with some additional trimmings on the international scene. Not being able to sell enough goods in the home market to maintain prosperity, the capitalists, naturally try to get rid of them in foreign fields, sometimes going so far as to bolster up foreign purchasing power by lending huge sums abroad. But the desperate search for purchasing power in the world at large necessarily leads to all the characteristic ills of imperialism. And at best it affords but temporary relief. Today, even if a free international market existed or could be assured in the near future (suppositions wildly contrary to reality), so that each nation were at full liberty to find customers in every section of the globe, the same phenomenon of lack of purchasing power would eventually be repeated on a world scale. And a United States of capitalist Europe, for instance, would not necessarily solve any more economic problems in the long run than has the United States of capitalist America.

After studying, then, the central contradiction of Capitalism as it reveals itself in these various forms, I am ready to state definitely that Capitalism in the smallest and poorest country, Capitalism in the largest and richest country, Capitalism in all countries considered together, inevitably leads to an unbalanced and lopsided distribution of income, to lack of purchasing-power, to depression and crisis. To ask why purchasing power under Capitalism is always insufficient is really equivalent to damning the system, since there is no way of eliminating this insufficiency as long as we retain the present order. Therefore all those proposed remedies for the situation which leave the fundamentals of the profit system intact amount to little more than futile fumbling in the dark.

5. *Solutions Superficial and Retrogressive*

These observations about profits and purchasing power, wages and prices, private saving and public spending, show why I feel certain that no prescription short of planned Socialism can cure the creeping paralysis that has seized upon our contemporary world. The conjuring up of scapegoats such as Jews or Bolsheviks, politicians or trade unions, on whom to load the sins of the capitalist system is on a par with the ancient device of blaming everything that goes wrong on black magic and witchcraft. Coming to more substantial suggestions, I think it is patent that all the fancy currency schemes, with their almost inevitable tendency toward inflation, run afoul of Capitalism's inescapable and inmost contra- diction. The once much-vaunted "New Capitalism," with high wages as its chief ingredient, meets this same insuperable obstacle. And so does the panacea of a single tax on land and rent put forward by Henry George and his disciples.

There are those who argue that Capitalism has adequately solved the problem of production and that it falls down only in respect to the problem of distribution. While undoubtedly our present shortcomings become most obvious on the level of distribution, I hope that the analysis which I have been making shows how impossible it is to divorce the problem of distribution from that of production and the profit system in general. It is for this very reason that we must regard as superficial beyond measure the numerous "share-the wealth" schemes, from the dazzling proposals of the late Senator Huey Long to the old-age pension plans of the Townsendites and the recent $30-Every-Thursday idea popularized in California. These promised short cuts to Utopia are one and all variations on government spending as the way out. They at least

92

serve to dramatize the mal-distribution of wealth and the completely correct sense of the people that the American economy ought to be able to do far better by them; but they also shunt the minds and energies of millions into most wasteful channels.

To carve up, for instance, the cake of national wealth, and income into equal slices for everyone would not only be highly impracticable, but would be worse than useless if the underlying characteristics of the capitalist system were left untouched. Confiscating all at once and to such an extreme degree the profits of the more well-to-do sections of the community, would fatally cut the nerve of the money motive so essential to Capitalism. Thus the unplanned, competitive of the present order would remain, minus its chief driving force. And since the "share-the-wealthers" have worked out no alternative for such a situation, the certain consequence, as both radicals and conservatives agree, would be complete and fruitless breakdown.

What we radicals want to put through is not madcap projects to divide up the national income, but a program that will release to the utmost our productive potentialities. As a prominent New Dealer, Mr. Adolph A. Berle Jr., puts it: "The underlying and eternal problem is the problem of using our national plant and our resources in such a way that the income of the country may steadily and continuously rise. *The job is to level up, far more than, to level down.* Distribution is one problem, But if the ultimate goal is to be reached, there must be a great deal more to distribute." The millionaire Republican, the late Ogden Mills, Secretary of the Treasury under President Hoover said much the same thing when he asserted that the way to prosperity is not through "the sharing of poverty, but through the creation of new wealth. So Democrats, Republicans and radicals can all unite on this goal, however much they disagree about the requisite methods of arriving there."

What I have already said in passing should have made it evident that the methods of the New Deal are not in my opinion far-reaching enough to solve the economic problems facing the American people. Much of the legislation that has been enacted under the two Roosevelt administrations is all to the good. I give my wholehearted support to the National Labor Relations (Wagner) Act, the Social Security Act, the Securities Exchange Act, the Fair Labor Standards (Wages and Hours) Act and other federal or state measures of a progressive nature. Such laws ought to go a long way in bringing us abreast of advanced European countries like England in the sphere of reform.

I also much prefer government spending of the New Deal sort to government parsimony. For such spending genuinely, if only temporarily, relieves human misery; and an intelligent public works program, designed to fill basic community needs, can bring about lasting improvements and is akin to what a Socialist regime will itself undertake on an infinitely greater scale. Furthermore, the New Deal policy has been able to stave of economic disintegration during a period when, the American people still being unready to accept Socialism, such disintegration might have brought stark reaction or even Fascism into the saddle. At the same time President Roosevelt's measures have educated the people to realize that only government intervention can cope with present-day problems and that certain standards of welfare are to be considered the unquestioned right of the entire population.

It is, then, a hundred times preferable to have the Roosevelt Democrats holding political power than the Republicans. But extensive reform has not prevented economic depression and crisis in other countries; nor will it in the United States. And radicals as well as conservatives, Joseph Stalin as well as J. P. Morgan, know perfectly well that public spending within the limitations imposed by Capitalism can achieve, in an economic sense, little more substantial than the familiar "monkey gland" recoveries of recent years. On the other hand, the frenzied wail of the businessmen that all their troubles stem from government extravagance is about as far away from the truth as can be.

A secondary solution for Capitalism which seems to have been intermittently pursued by Mr. Roosevelt is that all would be well if we could replace certain, malevolent capitalists with certain noble-minded capitalists. This good-man, bad-man analysis of economics and politics will not hold water. It is an unrealistic approach because it does not get down to economic fundamentals. If the leading capitalists of the world were all able to qualify for the communion of saints, they would still find it impossible to make their system work satisfactorily: This is why appeals for a world-wide revival of religion or for the ethical regeneration of humankind, under the slogan of "moral rearmament" or anything else, cannot do much to eradicate the evils of Capitalism, unless they somehow stimulate people in the direction of a Socialist society.

It is a question of economics, not ethics. The capitalist cannot personally be held responsible for all the terrible things that happen under the profit system. That system is cruel, but the individual capitalists inextricably caught in its toils like everyone else, usually are not cruel. They act under the circumstances as psychologist and philosopher would expect the ordinary man to act, their behavior being conditioned by their environment and education. Thus, Karl Marx himself, in one of his prefaces to *Capital* said:

> "The persons of capitalists and landowners are not, in my book, depicted in rose-tinted colours; but if I speak of individuals, it is only in so far as they are personifications of economic categories, representatives of special class relations and class interests. Inasmuch as I conceive the development of the economic structure of society to be a natural process, I should be the last to hold the individual responsible for conditions whose creature he himself is, socially considered."

To my mind, more futile than any of the palliatives I have been discussing are those dreams of a return to some far-off Golden Age of Capitalism that supposedly existed sometime, somewhere in the shadowy past. Most of these nostalgic fantasies envision a revival of old-fashioned *laissez faire* or some variation of it. But if we could today somehow wipe the slate clean over the entire earth and begin anew with a *laissez faire* system, the inexorable workings of the profit motive would in all probability create a situation as far removed from *laissez faire* as the present one. The only possible way to have prevented the *anti-laissez faire* developments of *laissez faire* would have been to pass a drastic series of government acts in every nation which from the outset would have constituted a fundamental violation of *laissez faire*. In short, the history of the last 150 years has pretty well proved that Adam Smith, who undoubtedly had the best interests of humankind at heart, far from qualifying as the realist he has been reputed to be, was one of the most Utopian thinkers who ever lived. His blueprint for a capitalist paradise was doomed from the start.

Yet here is a well-known English liberal of the old school, the Marquess of Lothian, present British Ambassador to the United States, in an essay entitled **Liberalism in the Modern World,** naively calling for a re-establishment of the free market and calmly overlooking all those deep-lying capitalist tendencies which led businessmen themselves to whittle away that market with such devices as tariffs and huge monopolistic corporations. This noble lord proceeds to put the chief blame for the parlous state of the world on "international anarchy," especially as displayed in the First World War. Again, Lothian's mind never seems to have the faintest glimmering of the fact that the capitalist classes of the various nations ever ready to fight one another to the death in their imperialist ventures, were themselves responsible for the evolution of international anarchy and the disaster of the Great War. It is easy, but hardly profound, to push the cause-effect sequence back only as far as the cataclysm of 1914-18 and attribute all the current troubles of humankind to that one event.

A slight knowledge of history also plays havoc with Mr. Walter Lippmann's recent book **The Good Society** in which the author, like the Marquess of Lothian, advocates a return to the free market and true liberalism. Mr. Lippmann identifies the root of all evil in "authoritarian collectivism," which he sees as based on the principle that humans can be made happy through the coercive power of the state and centralized economic planning. It was after 1870, Mr. Lippmann claims, that the deplorable collectivist movement came into its ascendancy. Yet long before then, Capitalism was afflicted with its characteristic ills; and the free-market phase upon which Lippmann looks back with such longing was not, after all, a very happy one for the great majority of humankind. Like Lord Lothian, Mr. Lippmann almost totally ignores those inescapable aspects of the profit system which made it what it is today. And, fatal inconsistency, he finally outlines a series of social reforms much like those of the New Deal, one of the collectivisms he so despises, though these reforms would entail many of the same governmental controls that he denounces elsewhere in his book.

To put it briefly, Mr. Lippmann's facile remedy for the sickness of modern society is for Capitalism to return to the days of its radiant youth, but miraculously cleansed of all the original sin with which it was born, and rid of all the caprices and crudities of adolescence. The unfolding of nature, however, and the sequence of events in this hard, hard world are irreversible. It is not so simple to turn back the clock of history a hundred years. And I think it is true to say of Lippmann, what he himself says of Herbert Spencer: that he is defending positions which have in fact been abandoned by events.

Akin to Lord Lothian and Mr. Lippmann is that school of Utopian retrogressives—Distributists, Neo-Agrarians and others—who propose a return to a small-business economy as the solution of the world's present woes. Whereas in earlier days the crusade against big business came mainly from agrarian and petty bourgeois sources that feared the growing encroachments of large-scale enterprise and which focused upon the limited end of curbing this danger, now we have a pretentious little-business philosophy which brashly sets itself up as an economic cure-all.

The prime defect in this philosophy is the cavalier way in which it ignores how twentieth-century concentration grew naturally and inevitably out of the original capitalist competitive system, and the casual fashion in which it accordingly suggests an utterly impracticable about-face in the dynamics of history, a sudden and hazardous throwing into reverse of the speedily moving machine of modern industrialism. To actualize such a program, for instance, as Mr. Herbert Agar sets forth in his *Land of the Free* would mean scrapping the major portion of our technical improvements during the last 75 years. To overcome the immense economic and political obstacles involved would definitely require something in the nature of central planning and a government dictatorship, both of which loom as horrible specters in Mr. Agar's mind. And this dictatorship would need a huge bureaucracy to keep small business small and to enforce that 100 per cent system of competition so dear to the hearts of our backward-lookers.

Moreover, we must ask, even if the platform of the small-business enthusiasts were somehow achieved, where would we be then? Did the small-business era in America, prior to the eighteen-seventies, provide a solution for our economic problems? It did not. Beset always by the recurring failure of purchasing power, it brought that same cycle of boom and depression and unemployment that constitutes the worst economic feature of the capitalist system. More than that, the abolition of big business would, as Mr. Agar and his friends readily admit, result in a considerable decline in the American standard of living, a standard which even as it is rates abysmally low from the viewpoint of the masses of the population.

Inadequate or dangerous or both, as are the various proposals which I have been reviewing, I would prefer any one of them to the adoption of Fascism. For Fascism decrees the end of very nearly everything that I, and most other Americans as well, hold dear. Fascism means unceasing violence, in both domestic and foreign affairs; it means war and imperialism and the whir of bombers overhead; it means the erection of racial and national prejudice into a major principle of government; it means the death of democracy and labor's rights, of civil liberties and academic freedom; it means the burning of the books and the degradation of culture; it means a constant decline in living standards and a sharpening of all Capitalism's economic contradictions; including the central one revolving around purchasing power and profit.

Fascism represents the last desperate attempt, through resort to unprecedented force and savagery, of Capitalism and the capitalist class to survive in a world which has outgrown them. Fascist tyranny stands as the brutal and reactionary essence, undisguised and unashamed, of the capitalist system. Fascism is contemporary Capitalism in the nude, stripped of all garments that hide its ugliness. And neither Capitalist nor capitalists in any country can escape their share of responsibility for what Fascism, that is, Fascist Capitalism, does.

The capitalist supporters of the chief Fascist Governments, those of Italy and Spain, Germany and Japan, may have some mental reservations about the reckless dynamite-hurling of their dear dictators in the international sphere. But what promptly overrules such qualms is that the Fascist regimes put an end to the trade unions and other working-class organizations, shoot or throw into concentration camps all the liberals and radicals who do not succeed in fleeing the country, and check or drive into underground channels the movement toward Socialism. It is for these reasons that a good many upper-class Americans look upon Fascism with profound sympathy not only in its foreign aspects, but also as a possible program for the United States.

Though it is true that Fascism has been able to prolong Capitalism for a while in the totalitarian lands, the experience of capitalists in Germany, Italy and Japan ought not to make the businessmen of other countries any too enthusiastic over the prospects of Fascist dictatorship. For in the three main Fascist states there has been an ever-increasing encroachment by the government in the realm of private business, whether finance, industry or agriculture. When Capitalism becomes particularly hard-pressed, it extends its collective controls in order to make itself more efficient. This happened in the big capitalist powers during the First World War, and has been happening again since the Great Depression. The Fascist states being in the most precarious condition of all, capitalist collectivism has gone further within them than anywhere else. And we find in the Fascist economies a sprinkling of semi-Socialistic measures designed to head off real Socialism.; "a form of planning-to-avoid-planning," as Professor Max Lerner says in his discerning book *It Is Later Than You Think.*

More distressing than anything else to businessmen in the Fascist countries is that they are simply staggering under the load of taxation, mainly for armaments and other war purposes. In Italy Mussolini even went so far as to make a 10 per cent capital levy on all real estate and corporations in order to help pay for his Ethiopian venture. Able economists, both conservative and radical, increasingly agree that the eventual outcome in the Fascist states is likely to be national bankruptcy, either in a war or during the natural course of peace. So it is becoming more and more plausible to suggest that in Fascism, the capitalists have raised up a Frankenstein monster which in the end will get completely out of control and involve them in an unparalleled economic collapse accompanied by a holocaust of violence. When the Fascist dictatorships start to totter, we may be sure that the domestic scene will not be one of peace and politeness. And if Fascism really does lead ultimately to all this, the capitalists in democratic countries may well ask themselves whether a peaceful transition to a Socialist society, avoiding altogether the hideous Fascist episode, would not be a great deal better for themselves as well for everyone else.

Since none of the programs, Fascist or non-Fascist, conservative or liberal or sheer quack, which the capitalists and their varied assortment of theoreticians have proposed or put into effect, are anywhere near adequate to lead the world out of its economic morass, there can be no question that Capitalism stands today in a most critical state. Hardly anyone, even among conservative businessmen, can pretend that the future of either the Fascist, semi-Fascist or democratic Capitalism looks very bright. Whatever may be the defects of Socialism, it is impossible to discover any humane or workable alternative to it. And the proverbial observer from the planet Mars might well decide that it is not we radicals who are unrealistic and sentimental, throwing our lives away on behalf of a Utopian daydream, but rather the poor capitalists, those blind, pathetic idealists who will go down nobly with their lost cause singing one last hymn to Rugged Individualism.

Now conceivably, the reader will ask here whether Capitalism has not always surmounted its difficulties and gone on to better things. This was indeed true up to the Great War and, in the United States, up to the Great Depression. Since 1929 America, however, as well as Europe, has continually been in the midst-of or on the edge-of economic crisis; and the recovery periods between depressions are growing both shorter and less substantial. There is a mass of evidence on hand that henceforth whatever upward movements may take place, the course of Capitalism will be in general, downward in terms of living standards. In the chief capitalist nations and especially in the United States, no great new industries appear to be in the offing to spur-on that expansion of capital goods and productive equipment which formerly used to result in at least a temporary upsurge of mass purchasing power and business prosperity. Moreover, the mechanization of existing industries has already been carried out to a high degree; and in any case further mechanization, under our general conditions of decline, is nearly certain to swell mightily the ranks of the unemployed.

What bodes least well of all for Capitalism is the international situation. Never in the history of the present system has the export of surplus commodities and the profitable investment abroad of surplus capital been attended with such difficulties. It is not simply that the spheres of foreign exploitation have been fairly well exhausted or gobbled up and can be encroached upon only through new economic or military warfare; nor simply that one-sixth of the earth, Soviet Russia, lies outside the orbit of regular capitalist exploitation; nor that the colonial and semi-colonial areas are awakening and threatening to unloose the bonds of imperialist domination; nor that artificial barriers to international trade are more serious and extensive than ever before. On top of all this there looms a second world conflict, Which, if it comes, will probably be even more devastating than that of 1914.

This menace of war is everywhere having a ruinous effect. In Europe the big nations, and most of the little ones too, are spending far more on armaments than at any time except during the Great War itself. In the world at large the sums earmarked for military purposes have trebled during the past four years and during 1938 reached the staggering total of $18,000,000,000, a four-fold increase over 1913. If indirect military expenditures were added, the figure would probably go up at least 50 per cent. In most countries the huge armament budgets have been financed through government loans, a procedure which tends definitely in the direction of rising prices and perilous inflation. And it is undeniable, as the English review *The Round Table* reminds us, that in so far as rearmament heightens industrial activity, "it does so only at the cost of distorting the balance of the national economy, driving sound recovery into unsound boom and gathering labor into industries where its future employment depends on the continuance of world-wide political madness."

Even if the much-feared general war does not take place, economic catastrophe threatens. For in. most of the capitalist countries of Europe present economic activity is dependent in a decisive measure on the armaments race; and in America also heavy armament orders on the part of our own and other governments have contributed substantially to such prosperity as there has been in the past few years. The ghastly paradox is that when the armaments race stops or even measurably slows down, the effects on European and world economics may well be disastrous. Benito Mussolini himself, one of the chief offenders in the direction of armament and aggression, recognizes the economic dangers involved. To quote an interview from the Scripps-Howard newspapers in May, 1937: "So many people are now employed in the world-wide armament program, Il Duce holds, that if the wheels were suddenly stopped and the armament workers thrown out of jobs, the world might well be set back to where it was seven or eight years ago at the beginning of the depression." Unless, therefore, something drastic were done, "the consequences might easily be as terrible as war itself."

Even supposing, in spite of all these dire portents, that the capitalist system both in America and elsewhere does some day stage a complete recovery from its recent ills and achieves higher average living standards than before, such an outcome does not to my mind seriously affect the argument for Socialism. For I know that in any event Capitalism is doomed sooner or later to plunge downward again into another big depression; that mass unemployment, with millions and millions out of work, has become a permanent feature of the system; and that international wars, with their ever more scientific slaughterfests, will continue to afflict the peoples of the earth. Progress upward at the cost of so much misery and destruction is too frightful and senseless to contemplate. We have had more than enough of this unhappy muddling through; it is time to discover a better method. I am through with Capitalism because I want humankind once and for all to be through with the. wretched cycle of suffering and violence and cruelty that this system makes inevitable.

I recognize the historical function of Capitalism and the important part it has played in the evolution of mankind. But this system no longer has a useful role to fulfill; it is time for it to retire from the stage of history and permit a snore competent actor to take its place. In fact, in my opinion, the job which Capitalism alone was fitted to perform, the function in which it was unique and indispensable, was finished close to a century ago. Once Capitalism had broken through the cramping feudalist bonds and had developed to a substantial degree the factory system and the working class, the division of labor and the process of mechanical invention, it would have been desirable, 1 believe, regardless of how far politically possible, to establish a Socialist system in the "Western "World. And certainly this was the position of Marx and Engels, who as far back as 1848 were calling for the end of Capitalism in *The Communist Manifesto.*

If the chief nations of the West had been operating under Socialism these last hundred or seventy-five or fifty years, I am convinced that they would be far beyond where they are at present in terms or the wealth and welfare of their populations as a whole. And many of the most crushing costs, both material and spiritual, of capitalist evolution, such as the Great War and the Great Depression, would have been avoided. What I want to point out in addition is that equally heavy or even heavier costs face the world in the future unless it gets rid of Capitalism, and gets rid of it quick. Every year, every month, every day that we prolong the hopelessly infirm and decadent life of the present system, we prolong the agony of humanity and consign to limbo an infinity of splendid hopes and potentialities that could otherwise find fulfillment. This is the most poignant tragedy of our times and perhaps of all times that the finest and fairest new world that has ever been imagined lies within our grasp, but that we do not have quite the strength, quite the courage; quite the intellectual force to make it wholly and indisputably ours. The key that will open up that new world for us is Socialism and its planned economy.

Chapter III
Socialist Planning for Abundance

1. *Everyone Can Live Well*

Like anyone else I want to live well, and I want my wife and three children to live well. I believe in the wholehearted affirmation and enjoyment of life. There are surely few mortals who appreciate more than myself the simple material things that both sustain human existence and can bring to it such delight. I enjoy good food, comfortable living quarters and surroundings that are pleasant and healthful. I am very fond of sports, especially tennis, skating and swimming. I like to dance. And I enjoy, too, the pleasures of culture: the leisured reading of books and poetry, stimulating wit and conversation, evenings at the theater and concerts and motion pictures, the opportunity to write. Some of my conservative upper-income friends occasionally banter me on the exuberant way in which I relish the sweets of existence, as if such relish showed that I could not really believe in Socialism. But they miss the point. For it is precisely the destiny of Socialism to bring to the whole community those felicities of living that up to now only a small minority have had the chance to enjoy. I want everyone to live well. And I. am convinced that Socialist planning could quickly assure to every American family, not merely economic security, but also a fair degree of comfort. For this reason the idea of a Socialist society ought to attract profoundly not just the more poorly paid workers and farmers, but most of the middle income and many members of upper income as well. If we attain Socialism in the United States during my lifetime, I fully expect that I and other persons who are at present economically privileged will be able, if we work loyally under the new system, to maintain a very decent standard of living, though not one that is luxurious or extravagant. This Socialist promise, of general prosperity is one of the chief reasons why I consider so infinitely short-sighted and unintelligent those members of the upper class who oppose with such bitter-end stubbornness the passing of

Capitalism for they themselves can share to a substantial extent in the abundance which Socialism will make actual. And so long as they prevent this abundance from coming to fruition, they are playing the invidious role of dogs-in-the-manger.

They are saying in effect to the people: "It is true that we cannot ourselves unlock the untold possibilities of this modern economy, but just the same we don't intend to let *you* do it." Suppose the American people woke up some fine morning and read in the newspapers that every factory and farm in the country was operating at full blast, that all the millions of unemployed had been able to find jobs, that sweeping increases in wages would shortly go into effect and that for the first time in years federal, state and municipal governments saw the sure prospect of balancing their budgets. One can imagine the sense of relief, the happiness, the positive thrill that would be felt from one end of the country to the other; one can picture the rejoicing that would be called forth in every American home, in every place of business, in every public gathering. It would be like the end of the Great War; indeed, it *would* be the end of a Great War, the war on poverty, on unemployment, on depression and the thousand ills that accompany these major maladies of the capitalist system.

All this I have been depicting is no mere word-mirage. It is a close approximation of what would actually take place under full-fledged Socialism. For Socialist planning means that the American economic system would in fact be kept going at 100 per cent capacity, that its potential plenty would at long last be released, its productive resources and distributive techniques utilized and developed to the maximum for the people and by the people. The almost immediate outcome would be that $5,000 income for every American family that I mentioned earlier. And as time went on, this figure would steadily rise. These considerations spell out why *Socialism means wealth,* fabulous wealth, and eventually tenfold, yes a hundredfold, more wealth than Capitalism has ever been able to bring humankind.

2. *The Principles of Planning*

The fundamental principle that lies behind planning is fairly simple and one which we encounter in some form in many different realms of human behavior. It consists of coordinating our activities in the light of our capacities and of the objective external environment, especially its economic aspects. As individuals we all plan to some extent, whether it be for a day or a month, a year or a decade, always keeping a weather eye on the state of our finances. If we have a family, then planning becomes more complex and essential. The intelligent family looks into the future so far as is possible and plans, according to its resources, or the needs of its various members. If it is wise and has any sort of dependable income, it will make an annual budget, allocating definite sums to food, housing, clothing, recreation, baby carriages and the like. It will also probably try to set aside certain amounts as savings; and the most prudent heads of families will plan years and years ahead for the particular needs and vicissitudes of old age. Thoughtful people will take an even further step and, through the process of wills, lay careful plans for friends and family long after they are dead.

Coming to purely economic units, we find that every kind of business concern, no matter what its size and nature, must plan. The larger and more complex it is, the more attention it has to pay to planning. Any big corporation, for instance; with its many different departments, must have central planning in order to co-ordinate its various, activities and to function successfully as a business. This is true whether the U. S. Steel Corporation or General Motors is concerned, whether it is R. H, Macy and Company or American Telephone and Telegraph, whether Standard Oil of New York or the Pennsylvania Railroad. The planning necessary for the efficient management of huge businesses like these reaches out to all parts of America and in some degree abroad as well. And in certain fields where big business has come to be overwhelmingly predominant, the planning of a few large trusts or even of a single monopoly may extend over well-nigh a whole industry.

The purpose of planning in all capitalist enterprise is, of course, to make money. And this means that each business, in the process of continually establishing and re-establishing its own superiority, must plan against its rivals and win away from them more and more customers. Trusts in the same industry have to plan against each other and also, in order to capture a larger and larger share of the general consumer's income, against trusts in other industries. Thus, in enterprise both large and small, the plans of individual businesses and businessmen tend to cancel one another out to a considerable extent. The capitalist theory is that the most efficient and intelligently managed concerns come out on top. Undeniably this is frequently true; just as often, however, it is ruthlessness and lack of moral scruple that turns the trick, as has been amply illustrated in the lives of our "robber barons." But whether efficiency or ruthlessness or perhaps both together are operative in any particular case, the result for the community is in the end economic chaos.

In order to mitigate or prevent the disastrous results of anarchic Capitalism in some important field, capitalist governments sometimes put into effect a species of planning for an entire industry. In most European countries the telephone and telegraph are publicly owned and operated, and in several the railways as well. Then, too, there are public planning schemes in existence over particular localities. A good example of this is the Tennessee Valley Authority (TVA), which is exploiting the power resources of the Tennessee basin on behalf of the population of the vicinity, much to the chagrin of the private utility companies. These types of piecemeal planning, however, no matter how well they may work in the sectors allotted to them, cannot go far in solving the economic problems of a country as a whole.

It is characteristic that the most far-reaching schemes of public planning under Capitalism should be for profit, or for profit and war. The so-called planning of the New Deal during President Roosevelt's first term was directed, especially in agriculture, toward decreasing production in order to bring back profits by making, goods scarcer and prices higher. While the Great Depression was still ravaging the United States, the NRA (National Recovery Administration) and the AAA (Agricultural Adjustment Administration) nobly co-operated, through planned destruction, with the usual haphazard destruction-for-profit by individual capitalists. Those were the days when almost over-night a fourth of the cotton crop was ploughed under, the wheat acreage reduced by 20 per cent, and five million pigs destroyed. The AAA, doing its best under the circumstances to rescue the American farmer by boosting the price level, actually paid bonuses to all the producers who participated in this wholesale sacrifice to the capricious gods of capitalist economics.

During the Great War, America, and more than half the nations of the earth as well, carried out planned destruction on an even larger scale. Not only did this war planning entail the shooting away into nothingness of billions and billions of dollars worth of goods in the form of munitions; even the food, clothing and other supplies for the military and naval forces were for the purpose of enabling millions of men to engage in the entirely unproductive function of fighting to the death millions of other men. In order to wage war more efficiently, the American Government proceeded to co-ordinate in some measure the economic life of the United States by setting up the War Industries Board, the War Trade Board, the Shipping Board, the Fuel Administration, the Food Administration and the Railroad Administration. Since the railroads under private management could not stand the added strain of war conditions, the Government took them over entirely and administered them on a unified basis.

Unhappily, today again, the bulk of the planning that is going on in Capitalist countries is for belligerent purposes. This is especially true of the Fascist Powers—Germany, Italy and Japan— in each of which the whole economy has for a number of years been on a war basis. As these Fascist states push farther and farther their present aggressions and prepare for new ones, they are forcing the democratic Capitalisms to introduce ever more extensive planning for the object of armed self-defense. This brief review of the limited planning that takes place under Capitalism shows how far removed it is in aim and scope from Socialist planning. Planning under Socialism is for use not profit, for increasing production, not decreasing it, for peace not war. And it demands as an absolute prerequisite the socialization of production and distribution. For as long as private capitalists retain possession of a country's natural resources and transportation facilities of factories, farms, banks and all the rest, they have the power to throw out of gear the best-laid of plans. It is common knowledge that even with the minor public controls established under Roosevelt's NRA, the American capitalists, long before the law was declared unconstitutional, constantly sabotaged, dodged and defied the Act. But Socialist planning puts a finish to that unending tug of war, so characteristic of Capitalism, between the Government, supposedly representing the public in general, and various business interests jockeying for control of it and determined to carry out whatever profit-promising policies seem most advantageous. Under Socialism, politics and economics are thoroughly integrated.

The socialization of economic activity which I have in mind, however, does not necessarily entail either nationalization by the federal government or ownership by state or city governments. Many industries under Socialism the national government will certainly take over many other economic concerns, less far-reaching in their ramifications, state or city governments will own and operate. But besides all this, there will be a broad sector of enterprise which is socialized yet not governmental. It will be advisable to run some industries through the instrumentality of Public Corporations, which will be subject to control by the government planning authorities, but largely independent in their administrative work. In the non-governmental class will also be collective farms and fisheries, and indeed almost the whole of agriculture; co-operative societies for production and distribution; and much of journalism, art and culture in general. This means that there will be a sizable number, running into several millions, of independent individuals not on the pay-roll of any governmental concern. These will include a large proportion of the handicraftsmen, farmers, fishermen, inventors, teachers, authors, journalists, actors, artists and intellectuals. They will make their living by working in such organizations as I have just mentioned, or by selling their products or services to such organizations, to. public agencies or to other individuals. So, in the Socialist state there will be plenty of room for freelance workers of every type.

Socialist planning differs from any sort of capitalist planning, lastly, in that it is not confined to special localities, industries or periods of time, but is continuous and nation-wide. A genuinely planned economy demands not only that all individual businesses in one industry, whether it be concerned with hats, shoes, sugar, coal or anything else, be consciously coordinated, but that each industry as a whole, including the prices of its products and the wages and working hours of its employees, be coordinated with every other industry as a whole.

Think of the increase in efficiency and the decrease in waste that would result from planned, co-ordination among America's big energy-producing industries: coal, gas, oil and electric power. Such co-ordination, however, could reach its high point only when there was complete co-ordination also among the industries to be served. For only when we know how much energy is required throughout the whole country, and where and when, 'can we accurately gauge how much coal, how much gas, how much oil and how much electric power should, he made available in a given period and in a particular locality. Again, it is obvious that there is so much overlapping in the field of transportation— among railways, boats, busses, tracks and airplanes —that the situation cries out for unified planning. But it is not possible to separate transportation from the things to be transported. A plan for coordinated transportation implies a plan for coal and. steel, farm products and finished goods, just as a plan for all these things definitely implies a plan for transportation. And. of course all of agriculture must be carefully correlated with all of manufacture. The flow of foodstuffs to the cities must be coordinated with the flow of manufactured goods from them. The needs of the farmers must be estimated. Our steel plan, for example, must take into consideration the demand for tractors, combines and other agricultural machinery; and our agricultural plan the particular food requirements of the heavily laboring steel workers. Likewise there must be a well-worked-out plan for wholesale and retail trade, linking up these two main branches of distribution all along the line with industry, transportation and agriculture. The shops in town and city, the restaurants, the warehouses, the gasoline stations and other such distributive units all come into the planning picture here.

Since the planning that I envisage covers the entire socio-economic scene, it naturally extends into the fields of health and recreation, of education and. culture. Socialism is particularly concerned to bountifully provide all the different activities and services in these realms with the necessary equipment and other economic prerequisites. The educational plan of the country, moreover, must be always closely interrelated with the economic plan, so that there may never be a lack, of the needed technicians, scientists and other experts nor a deficiency of suitable employment opportunities for graduating students. Finally, the entire economic and cultural life of the country must be carefully correlated with finance under one vast, unitary budget that takes in all branches of industry and agriculture, or commerce and trade and extra-economic endeavor. This completes, in outline form, the picture of the great National Plan which Socialism sets in motion, a plan which brings into the economic and social affairs of any country that adopts it a closely knit unity, a smoothly functioning team-work, among all the myriad enterprises and individuals involved, making each one count for infinitely more, and lifting the collective achievement to new and unheard-of heights.

Because of its controls over production and distribution, currency and capital investment, prices and wages and hours, Socialist planning is able to overcome totally and permanently the central capitalist difficulty of lack of purchasing power. As more and more goods come out of the factories, wages go up throughout the land or prices decrease or the working day grows shorter. To take care of the increased turnover in commodities, currency may, depending on its velocity of circulation, be expanded. Since there are no capitalists to appropriate a large proportion of the value which the people produce, the full instead of only the partial value of their labor returns to them in one form or another. Thus, the unceasing abundance of goods is matched by an unceasing abundance of purchasing power. And this results in that depression-defeating, prosperity-ensuring balance between production and consumption, supply and demand, which every orthodox economist and capitalist has fondly dreamed of seeing Capitalism itself attain.

The United States and other capitalist nations are only as rich as the amount of goods that can be sold for a profit during any given period. But Socialist planning makes a country exactly as rich as its entire productive capacity during any period. This is why I say without hesitation that Socialism, in terms of sheer economic efficiency, is sure to far outstrip Capitalism. Since finance is the most important single element in Socialist planning and more crucial, if anything, than in a Capitalist economy—a fact which ought to give some slight consolation to Capitalist bankers—I want to discuss the subject in more detail. In a Socialist state the banking system, operates under and administers an all-embracing Financial Plan for the nation as a whole. This Financial Plan is the counterpart of the Material Plan and translates all the production and distribution schedules of the latter into dollar units. The dollar is the common denominator in which the various aspects of the National Plan can be accurately expressed and clearly related to one another.: The Financial Plan and the Material Plan are, in effect, two versions of the National Plan and each serves as a check on the other.

The Government Treasury Department, together with the State Bank and its numerous branches, acts as a great central pool for the national income. This it does not only through taxation of Socialist business concerns and of individuals, but also through receiving a substantial share of whatever surpluses the different businesses, including those involved in foreign trade, succeed in accumulating, A considerable portion of such surpluses, however, are retained locally by the factory or other unit earning them and are used collectively for expansion, improvements or social benefits connected with the same enterprise. The Government also raises a certain amount of capital through savings banks and through the flotation of public loans, which continue to be necessary during the first stages of Socialism. The surpluses or "profits" which economic enterprises build up under Socialism have a very different status and play a very different role from what we have been accustomed to expect under Capitalism. They are, in fact, mainly a book-keeping device. Socialist business is run, as I have said, not for the sake of making profits, but in order to provide goods and services to the community. The most convenient process of accounting and of distribution, however, demands the mechanism of buying and selling, of money and prices. Furthermore, identifiable "profits" are necessary so that our Socialist planners can set aside a certain proportion of the nation's income in order to meet depreciation and obsolescence and, above all, in order to expand the means of production. Soviet Russia, for instance, put into social savings for such purposes an annual average of one-third its total income during the first two Five-Year Plans, a feat which stands out all the more, owing to the fact that capitalist economists have always argued that a Socialist government would act like a reckless spendthrift and could not possibly exercise the foresight and intelligence to accumulate capital. Whereas under Capitalism, money and prices control the output of goods; under Socialism it is the output of goods that controls money and prices. Money is on a goods standard, not a gold standard. No real need exists for the latter unless to make the initial transition from Capitalism psychologically easier in the minds of the people. There can be no such thing as financial bankruptcy unless the supply of commodities proves inadequate; the value of the currency does not depend on any gold reserve, but on the quantity and quality of goods that nationwide planning has made available. Money ceases to be a commodity in itself, as under the capitalist system. It simply serves as the recognized unit of economic measurement and exchange, a function that some medium will have to perform in any future stage of society.

The most obvious advantage of a Socialist financial system is that it enables the public authorities to distribute and. redistribute the nation's capital resources according to the needs of the entire economy. The surpluses acquired in one sector of business can be transferred to other less developed and less lucrative branches of economic activity. This is analogous, on a national scale, to the various allocations within the huge budgets of some of the bigger capitalist corporations. Under Socialism a number of enterprises, particularly in the sphere of education and social services, will continue to show financial loss, perhaps permanently. And there will also be deficits in the industrial field, especially when some great new project; is getting under way.

Socialist financial planning requires that there be an ordered flow of capital investment all along the line in place of the slap-dash, haphazard methods prevalent in capitalist countries today. Instead of over-investment in some directions and under-investment in others, with crisis-causing disproportions as the certain result, Socialist planning ensures a balanced and even distribution of capital resources, that is, social savings, in the directions most useful and important. It would be inconceivable, for example, for vast quantities of capital to go into the building of palatial homes, yachts and other super-luxuries for a small class of the economically privileged, while millions of families lived in houses beneath even a minimum standard of decency. It would also be inconceivable for socialized capital to go into the production of things clearly harmful to health and well-being— such, as noxious drugs, patent medicines and deleterious foodstuffs—for which there might be unintelligent and perverse demand. It would be impossible, too, for capital to create manufacturing plants and services that would be continually duplicating one another, ruining one another through cut-throat competition, spending huge fortunes in misleading advertising, and inundating a locality or even the entire country with a bewildering flow of practically identical goods. The huge sums of money and the very large personnel involved in speculative activities in commodities, in land, and in stocks and bonds would also become a thing of the past. And, alas for the gamblers of high finance, that symbol of Capitalism at its worst, the stock market, would be no more. The perfect synchronization between savings and capital investment that Socialist planning makes possible is one of the weightiest arguments in its favor. Since the decision of how much and where and when to save and the decision of how much and where and when to invest rests in the hands of the Planning Commission and the Government, there is no danger that these important decisions will be at odds with each other as they so often are under Capitalism. The unplanned capitalist method means that two sets of different people, frequently with conflicting interests, save and invest as they see fit, with the result that the relations between saving and investment are always becoming maladjusted. Either savings cannot find an outlet in profitable investment or needed investment cannot find sufficient savings to put it across. In either case economic troubles are the outcome. Under the financial system. I have been outlining, every producing and distributing unit in the country has an account in the central State Bank or one of its branches. And it is the duty of each bank to check up on the use of the credits, long-term, short-term or emergency, which it issues at any time. It must make certain that the automobile factory, for instance, to which it has advanced a certain amount of credit, actually produces the motorcars called for by the Plan and supposedly made possible by the credit. The factory has the obligation of giving the bank definite reports on definite dates showing how it is fulfilling its program. If the bank discovers that the credit is being wasted or used inefficiently, it will at once stop further credits until the matter is cleared up, even instituting a special investigation if necessary.

Thus, under Socialist planning, the banks become the watchdogs of the whole economy by carrying on what amounts to a constant audit any gold reserve, but on the quantity and quality of goods that nationwide planning has made available. Money ceases to be a commodity in itself, as under the capitalist system. It simply serves as the recognized unit of economic measurement and ex-change, a function that some medium will have to perform in any future stage of society. The most obvious advantage of a Socialist financial system is that it enables the public authorities to distribute and re-distribute the nation's capital resources according to the needs of the entire economy. The surpluses acquired in one sector of business can be transferred to other less developed and less lucrative branches of economic activity. This is analogous, on a national scale, to the various allocations within the huge budgets of some of the bigger capitalist corporations. Under Socialism a number of enterprises, particularly in the sphere of education and social services, will continue to show financial loss, perhaps permanently. And there will also be deficits in the industrial field, especially when some great new project is getting under way, Socialist financial planning requires that there be an ordered flow of capital investment all along the line in place of the slap-dash, haphazard .methods prevalent in capitalist countries today, Instead of over-investment in some directions and under-investment in others, with crisis-causing disproportions as the certain result, Socialist planning ensures a balanced and even distribution of capital resources, that is, social savings, in the directions most useful and important. It would be inconceivable, for example, for vast quantities of capital to go into the building of palatial homes, yachts and other super-luxuries for a small class of the economically privileged while millions of families lived in houses beneath even a minimum standard of decency.

It would also be inconceivable for socialized capital to go into the production of things clearly harmful to health and well-being—such as noxious drugs, patent medicines and deleterious foodstuffs—for which there might be unintelligent and perverse demand. It would be impossible, too, for capital to create manufacturing plants and services that would be continually duplicating one another, ruining one another through cut-throat competition, spending huge fortunes in misleading advertising, and inundating a locality or even the entire country with a bewildering flow of practically identical goods. The huge sums or money and the very large personnel involved tin speculative activities in commodities, in land, and in stocks and bonds would also become a thing of the past. And, alas for the gamblers of high finance, that symbol of Capitalism at its worst, the stock market, would be no more.

The perfect synchronization between savings and capital investment that Socialist planning makes possible is one of the weightiest arguments in its favor. Since the decision of how much and where and when to save and the decision of how much and where and when to invest rests in the hands of the Planning Commission and the Government, there is no danger that these important decisions will be at odds with each other as they so often are under Capitalism. The unplanned capitalist method means that two sets of different people, frequently with conflicting interests, save and invest as they see fit, with the result that the relations between saving and investment are always becoming maladjusted. Either savings cannot find an outlet in profitable investment or needed investment cannot find sufficient savings to put it across. In either case economic troubles are the outcome. Under the financial system I have been outlining, every producing and distributing unit in the country has an account in the central State Bank or one of its branches. And it is the duty of each bank to check up on the use of the credits, long-term, short-term or emergency, which it issues at any time, It must make certain that the automobile factory, for instance, to which it has advanced a certain amount of credit, actually produces the motorcars called for by the Plan and supposedly made possible by the credit. The factory has the obligation of giving the bank definite reports on definite dates showing how it is fulfilling its program, If the bank discovers that the credit is being wasted or used inefficiently, it will at once stop further credits until the matter is cleared up, even instituting a special investigation if necessary.

Thus, under Socialist planning, the banks become the watchdogs of the whole economy by carrying on what amounts to a constant audit of all business enterprises. They act as the vital link between the various sets of plans drawn up on paper and the fulfillment of these plans in terms of concrete goods and services.

Their vigilance means that there can be no let-down on the part of either management or workers in a concern without the whole personnel being called to task. In this function the banks are aided by a system of accounting which penetrates into every nook and cranny of economic activity. Socialist accounting, organized on the strictest basis, aims to cut production costs and to attain the greatest possible results for the least possible expenditure. Book profits enter again into the picture here as a partial test of whether or not a plant is being operated efficiently. So the idea sometimes advanced that, under Socialism, extravagant executives will fling away heedlessly and without restraint the financial resources of the community is merely a caricature. Furthermore, besides the checks and. balances inherent in the technical set-up of Socialist planning, there is always the control exercised by the people themselves through regular democratic procedures. At established intervals they can approve or disapprove of the planning schemes in effect or proposed by electing representatives and officials committed to carrying out the popular will. And at all times they can bring pressure to bear by criticisms and suggestions through public meetings, the organs of opinion, individual or organized lobbying, and other such processes of democracy, Of paramount importance in this connection, will be the role of the trade unions, to which virtually all working persons will presumably belong. There is nothing, then, in the nature of Socialist planning which prevents it from being administered in a thoroughly democratic manner.

One can easily imagine some of the big public issues which are almost certain to emerge in the natural course of collective economic planning. Since the standard of living under Socialism goes steadily up, the question will arise as to how the people can most benefit from the increasing wealth. Shall our planners put the emphasis on raising wages continually or on providing more and better free services like libraries, parks and public concerts? How much of the national income shall be saved for the purpose of new capital construction? And in this connection will the time come when the population will prefer to stabilize the standard of living at a certain point and concentrate on enjoying the consumers' goods producible at that level rather than to continue with vast expansion programs? For under Socialist planning there is no categorical imperative, as under Capitalism, for an economy to keep on expanding indefinitely. This particular issue might well develop in relation to the matter of the average annual working time. In order that more leisure be secured, one political party might advocate reducing the work-day by a third or augmenting the number of holidays or cutting the age of retirement to fifty; another party might call for the maintenance of existing work-time schedules and for a mighty increase in production which would lift the standard of living to even greater heights. Or another burning issue might come to the fore, once the necessities of life had been provided for everyone, over whether to stress the provision of cultural amenities as distinct from material goods and services.

The exact planning techniques which I have been describing will certainly not be used in all stages of Socialism nor in all countries adopting the new system. For it is crystal clear that each nation will use somewhat different methods, adapting Socialism to its characteristic traditions, political institutions and degree or economic development. It would be foolish to imagine that if central planning were introduced in China at the same time as in the United States, it could be put into effect by precisely the same measures or at the same rate. Indeed, there will be plenty of differences even between two countries both as highly evolved industrially as America and Great Britain, one obvious reason being that the latter is in so many ways economically dependent on the outside world. But just as the general principles of the capitalist system were potentially applicable in every quarter of the globe, so the general principles of Socialist planning are applicable to the United States and all other nations.

~ ~ ~

This is the end of Chapter III Section 2 of You Might Like Socialism
An explanation of this break in the normal sequence follows

Note:

In Corliss Lamont's own Table of Contents and sequence of Chapters, the paragraphs that would normally follow here, his Chapter III Section 3, contain a very detailed expansion on how Socialist planning might possibly be organized in the United States. Remember, this was in 1939. We have new opportunities to make changes. At this re-issuing, in the editor's judgment, this chapter seems comparatively less relevant priority-wise to the present circumstances, and though Corliss Lamont's intent may have been to offer something concrete and tangible in the way of details, it might now be perceived as a little rigid in its specificity.

Therefore the major portion of Chapter III Section 3 has been respectfully relocated as an addendum, except for this inspiring closing paragraph in the words of Corliss Lamont:

"Socialist planning, carried out in America in the American way, will present to the citizens of this country the greatest challenge they have ever had. Limited as war planning was in the U.S. and destructive as was its objective, it did show that the theory and practice of nation-wide planning is not something entirely alien to the American genius. It is my firm opinion that under Socialism all the idealism and practical engineering technique for which America is so noted, freed at last from the shackles of the profit system, will have unprecedented opportunity for fulfillment in projects of almost unlimited scope, and grandeur. There will be no lack of tasks to appeal to the imagination and ambition of new generations. And the American people in their boundless energy will sweep forward to conquer new heights of economic and cultural achievement."

~ ~ ~

In proper sequence, Chapter III Section 4, of _You Might Like Socialism_ will follow after this brief commentary.

The thought that goes into this decision to tamper with Corliss Lamont's own judgment in his sequence priority is for a strategic reason: The intent for this re-issuing is to inspire new interest and hopefully **new action.** Especially, for those persons who might become newly interested, to inform them about how the ideals of Socialism have been completely denigrated in the eyes of the American public, in a way that they were never afforded the opportunity to explore these ideals openly and objectively before.

The whole intent of this re-issue is to invite new activists to collaborate with old activists and to raise their voices and their banners in mutual concern with human values. So many patriotic Americans are disgusted with the disgraceful performance and war-mongering of a duplicitous administration; of the dangers to our Democracy; of the complacency of Congress; of the venality and capriciousness of the stock market; of the dangers to our environment; of the complicity of the media. We must make changes! This is the time for assessing our options, working together, and making plans for creating a system more in keeping with the ideal that we believe in: a government of the people, by the people and for the people! Our problems are right now; this is immediate! It would be totally counter-productive to get bogged down in any nitty-gritty planning details from "yester-year" that might have been appropriate then.

Today, the necessary planning will be done by savvy young activists, with new tools, and will be meeting today's urgent need for drastic change in quite fantastic new, creative ways that were absolutely inconceivable in the "olden days" of 1939. Corliss Lamont himself would have been thrilled with the World Wide Web and its potential for the sharing of ideas and of inspiring and rousing whole segments of the population to work for change.

This is the whole point of this re-issuing after almost 70 years!

And now to resume with Corliss Lamont's next paragraphs.

4. Some Objections Answered

With this general view before us of Socialist planning and of how it would operate in the United States, I want to consider specifically some of the more common objections to this new way of handling the affairs of the world. What I have already said about democratic processes, administrative flexibility and local initiative in a planned economy ought to have made it plain that political dictatorship is by no means a necessary part of Socialist planning. Quite contrary to the truth, therefore, is this typical statement made by Mr. Walter Lippmann: "If the social order is to be planned, it has to be directed as it is in war time, and the liberty of private transactions has to give way to regimentation." This line of criticism has gained weight because in Soviet Russia, which is the only nation where Socialist planning functions today, a dictatorship still exists and aggression toward it from abroad unfortunately continues to be a grave menace. But with the steady democratization of the U. S, S. R., that dictatorship is gradually passing away. And the constant threat of war, while of course an important factor in Soviet policy, has in no sense been the guiding principle behind the planned economy of the country.

Mr. Lippmann, moreover, instead of acknowledging the obvious fact that the danger of war has enormously handicapped the Soviet Five-Year Plans, maintains the extraordinary thesis that the war danger is what has made any Soviet planning possible and that "when Russia no longer feels the need of mobilization, it will become necessary to liquidate the planning authority." Instead of recognizing the undeveloped state of industry in Tsarist Russia and its irrational, uneconomical concentration in a few regions, Lippmann argues that the laying of a heavy industrial base for the Socialist economy and the building of some of it in strategically invulnerable parts of the country demonstrates that the primary objective of Soviet planning has been military and not the improvement of the general standard of life. Crowning folly of all, in order to show that planning is incompatible with democracy, Mr. Lippmann tells us that "a plan subject to change from month to month or even from year to year is not a plan."

Since precisely such flexibility is a basic characteristic of planning, I submit that a comment of this sort could be made only by a person who has forgotten the commonplace planning procedures of daily life, who has ignored most of the extant literature on economic planning and who has been blind to events *in* Soviet Russia over the last fifteen years. And it is not surprising to learn that Walter Lippmann, the smooth and solemn refuter of Socialist economics, has never once bothered to visit the Soviet Union in the entire twenty-two years since the Communist Revolution, though it is his custom to make an annual pilgrimage to the other leading Powers of Europe.

While I propose to take up the whole matter of democracy at length in a later chapter, it is essential to state now that concepts like regimentation and liberty cannot be adequately considered apart from existing economic conditions. Who could be more regimented, for instance, than those wretched multitudes under Capitalism who are condemned through no fault of their own to unemployment? And if Socialist planning really does result in the elimination of depression and unemployment and in an enormous rise in the material and cultural standards of the whole population, then "regimentation" is hardly the correct word to apply to it. For such gains mean a very large increase in the liberty of the masses of the people. The end of unemployment not only creates a new life for the unemployed, but also puts a quietus on the fear of discharge that haunts the employed. The rise in the standard of living gives millions of workers and farmers and members of the professions a hundred freedoms which they never had before, infinitely enlarging the vistas of their lives and the opportunities of their children. As Mr. Lippmann himself writes in an unguarded moment, "The existence of plenty is a condition of liberty, and multiplies the individual choices. "The fact is that those capitalist apologists who are forever crying out that planning will exterminate freedom are thinking mainly of the unimpeded, godlike freedom of the present leisure class. They are afraid they may be curtailed by collectivism; and so it may. Indeed, "Share the freedom" might be rather effective as a slogan in the campaign for Socialism.

Closely akin to the charge that Socialism means some sort of dictatorship, is the claim that it will bring into power a vast army of government bureaucrats who will proceed to boss all of us about and tend to become a self-perpetuating body of slack, corrupt and privileged functionaries. While such an outcome may be theoretically possible, it is not inevitable nor even probable. For one thing, Socialist planning means the establishment of industrial democracy in business enterprise, where private capitalists have hitherto acted like little tsars, hiring and .firing, reducing wages and raising prices, restricting and expanding production all at their own sweet profit-motivated will. Then, too, since those elected to office will be dealing with the chief economic as well as political questions of the day, the people will presumably be a good deal more vigilant than at present in keeping abreast of public affairs and checking up on their representatives.

In the sense that any economic system must have the personnel to administer it, every economic system has a bureaucracy. And there is .no proof whatsoever that an administrative group working as public servants is any less efficient than such a group working at the direction of private business and constituting a private bureaucracy. Whether character or ability is in question, we should reflect that when the main economic enterprises of the nation are all parts of governmental or some other form of socialized service, the administrators of which are consistently well-paid, the highest talent available will enter that service.

Then there will .no longer exist the present situation in which a vast majority of the best men and women go into private business because of its greater rewards in terms of money, social prestige and sense of power. Today only too often those who have shown outstanding capacity as government servants are lured away by capitalist corporations which then use the experience and energy of such men to fight the Government. This has been particularly true in regard to the noble efforts of the capitalists to beat the income tax laws and to circumvent certain government restrictions and regulations imposed on, business in the public interest.

In spite, however, of the greater attraction that private business holds at present for average men and women of ambition and capacity, the public administrations in city, state and nation have on the whole done a pretty good job. Who would dream of suggesting, for instance, that we turn back into private hands the local fire departments, the postal service, the building of highways, or the water-supply systems of New York and other cities? And think of the splendid accomplishments of the TVA and the WPA of many city-owned utilities and power plants throughout the country; and of the Port of New York Authority, which has had charge of the construction and administration of the George Washington Bridge across the Hudson River and the Holland and Lincoln tunnels under it.

The fact that during the Great War the American railroads under Government ownership piled up large deficits is often cited as proof that public operation of a great industry is sure to be inefficient. These deficits were due mainly, however, to the Government's high-wage labor policy and to its holding down of railway rates, on behalf of the general war effort, in relation to the rising prices of coal and other materials. The fundamental purpose of the Wilson administration was, after all, to win the war arid not to make a success of the railroads ..in the usual business sense, This matter of the railroads also brings out the point that since governments usually take over weak or failing industries, public ownership and operation often start off with a heavy handicap and for this reason seldom receive a genuinely fair test.

Further objection is offered to public ownership and operation on the ground that government officials cannot be relied upon ethically. Now while it is true that the government of modern societies have been honey-combed with graft, it is probable that dishonesty and shady dealing in private business have been far

126

worse. At once there leap to mind the names of notorious capitalist crooks of the last decade such as Ivar Kreuger, the Swedish match-king and former extraordinary; Richard Whitney, Wall Street stockbroker and embezzler in the grand manner, and F. Donald Coster-Musica, versatile president of McKesson & Robbins, who juggled the accounts of the big drug company to the tune of $18,000,000.

Most essential of all to remember is that political life takes its color from the dominant economic institutions and practices of the time. Public officials are naturally affected by the prevailing motivations of the era. When making big money is held up as the big object of life, government functionaries as well as private capitalists are likely to nourish high pecuniary ambitions and not be too particular how they fulfill them. Corruption in politics is a function of the corrupt capitalist system. Almost always when a public official goes wrong, there is a private businessman on the other end of the transaction offering an outright bribe or some other form of speedy enrichment. The scandals of the Harding Administration, for example, were not due merely to weak and faithless officials; important oil interests represented by un-scrupulous businessmen, with their bribes and little black satchels and all the rest, played an indispensable role.

As Lincoln Steffens, the dean of American muckrakers, discovered over and over again, the badness of the bad men in municipal government, of the bosses and the lesser grafters, always in the end came down to "the system" rather than to the individual. And whenever he pushed his investigations toward the ultimate roots of the trouble, he ran into the sullen opposition of vested business interests frightened to death that they themselves would be exposed. Even reform administrations are able to accomplish little of a permanent nature. Steffens sums it up: "The same privileged interests which controlled the old rascals find ways to influence, moderate, and gradually to control the new reformers, and things go on as before." The peculiarly American institution of "rackets" also has a definite connection with our faulty economic order. As Thurman W. Arnold, Assistant United States Attorney

General, states: "The gangster with a racket is an answer to competitive conditions in which current ideals refuse to permit sensible organization."

Yet capitalist democracy, on those brief occasions when it becomes thoroughly aroused over government by thieves and thugs, can go quite far in cleaning house, as the accomplishments of Mayor LaGuardia and District Attorney Dewey in New York well show. Their work gives a hint of what an alert and determined Socialist administration would do. I do not claim that Socialism will completely put an end to graft; but by mercilessly prosecuting crooks of every variety, by eliminating permanently the private business elements that do so much of the grafting, by ensuring good pay to public officials, by steadily extending the civil service system and by changing the moral atmosphere of economic and political life, it will make corruption in government both more difficult to get away with and less tempting psychologically. In so far as Socialism discourages and rules out dishonesty, it. will of course increase the efficiency of government administration. One of the more important but less obvious reasons for this result is that today much of the red-tape in government services is due to the fact that they are organized on the basis of a lot of infuriating checks and balances designed primarily for the prevention of graft.

Another criticism of Socialist planning is that there is no man or group of men in a nation wise enough to carry it through. Says Dr. Benjamin M. Anderson, Jr., formerly of the Chase National Bank: "If a government of a collective system undertakes to regulate the business of the country as a whole, and to guide and control production, there is required a central brain of such vast power that no human being who has yet lived, or can be expected to live, can supply it." This is of course a naive caricature of the planned economy, since no one ever proposed that one man assume such an impossible burden. The fact is that the "central brain" for planning is the collective brain of the entire country. In other words, it's millions and millions of individual brains functioning through the multifarious planning commissions and attaining final co-ordination in the National Planning Commission and the Government.

Returning to Walter Lippmann, we find him arguing that planning cannot possibly operate in an economy of abundance as distinct from an economy of scarcity and that in America "the sheer complexity of the industrial system, would baffle any set of official planners who set out to direct it." What Lippmann really does in this statement, it seems to me, is to throw up his hands in despair before the mentally overpowering chaos he sees around him at present. And my comment on his capitulation is that precisely because the economic order has become so terribly complicated in the United States and other countries of a high technical development, that planning is now the most vital need of our times. The old capitalist methods become more and more disastrous as the economic repercussions of events in one area tend increasingly to spread throughout a country and the repercussions in one country throughout the world.

Mr. Lippmann buttresses his thesis by reference to Soviet Russia. Thus he writes that "what they may be able to do in a nation which has no capitalistic inheritance certainly provides no analogy for the United States, where the most highly developed Capitalism the world has ever seen, is a going concern. For Russia is still at a stage in the development of manufacturing industries where there is not enough of anything, where the demand outruns any visible supply; where, in short, no plan to increase production can be very wrong." Yet the indubitable fact is that the farther the Soviet Russians go in building up their economy, which is no longer exactly simple, the more smoothly and successfully does social-economic planning function. And as Lippmann himself would have to admit, there are very few, if any, high-grade industrial products even in America which have outrun the actual needs of the masses of the population.

The further assertion is made by Mr. Lippmann that "the more varied are the products of an industrial order the less possible it becomes to deal with it as a planned economy." Obviously such a statement conflicts with the very idea of Socialist planning, since the chief productive aim of this new system is that everyone should have an abundance of all sorts of personal possessions, including so-called luxuries. One of the most common misunderstandings about Socialism is the idea that it rules out the owning of personal property such as houses and automobiles, furniture and fountain pens. The point is that personally owned property must be for consumption, for use, for enjoyment. Only private property in the means of production and distribution is collectivized under Socialism; intimate personal things are not and never will be.

Mr. Lippmann's opinion to the contrary notwithstanding, the consumption goods which a planned economy turns out will be as different in quality and design as the consumer wishes. One of the main duties of a National Planning Commission and its country-wide agencies is to keep informed on the needs and desires of the consumers. And, as I have already pointed out, the Commission has a special Section on Consumers' Needs which will concentrate on this task. This Section will no doubt make special tests of consumers' habits and send out questionnaires on a large scale to the public, as many capitalist businesses and magazines do already. Occasionally, the Planning Commission would, I am sure, gravely over-estimate or under-estimate demand. In fact, almost all of its estimates would have to be approximate rather than exact. This means that undoubtedly a certain proportion of consumers' goods would be wasted. Some waste in the mechanics of distribution, however, is inevitable under any economic system; under Socialism it would be cut down to a minimum and would not be a very serious matter.

Furthermore, so far as quality and variety are concerned, with Socialist planning producing for use and beauty instead of profit, there is not the same pressure for utilizing cheap and non-durable materials and neglecting aesthetic considerations. Harold Loeb, one of America's most able economists, claims that the competition for cheapness which Capitalism makes inevitable "is particularly keen in clothing, utensils, household furnishing, and speculative building, and is characteristic of nearly all mass-production lines. A very small addition to the cost of the cloth, or of the plumbing, would result in an article likely to withstand a great deal more wear and tear. Unfortunately, under our present system the additional life that might be built into consumer goods, at so slight an additional cost, would in no way benefit the manufacturer. His pecuniary interest lies in selling a second article to replace the one that has been worn out." Planned obsolescence.

Another of our more progressive economists, George Soule, reminds us that "A certain amount of standardization is not incompatible with useful variety and freedom of choice. We should not suffer if we did not have to choose between hundreds of brands of canned fruits or vegetables whose relative merits we cannot know without laboratory experiments. The American public is not impoverished because its choice of automobiles is now limited to a few standard makes in each price range, nor is a rather strict planning and control in the manufacture of these cars incompatible with a satisfactory variety in style and color." In some fields, indeed, greater standardization, which will permit the economies of mass production, is a crying need. The whole sphere of housing, for example, is an outstanding case in point.

Naturally enough, errors will be made under Socialist planning, particularly at the start. And I hope 1 have not given the impression that I think a planned economy will result either immediately or in the long run in a final solution of all our problems. Humankind is always going to have plenty of stiff problems to keep it occupied. What Socialist planning does is to solve permanently some of our basic economic difficulties and to lift thereby all our other problems onto a higher level. Critics of Socialism, and sometimes its advocates, are prone to overlook the fact that a number of un-desirable things are bound to remain in some form or other under any economic system whatsoever. Thus in our planned society there will surely be a certain amount of favoritism; personal "pull" will continue to play a part in the obtaining of jobs. There will of course be leaders who achieve the more important positions and also-rans who hover around the bottom and bite their nails in jealousy. There will be some dishonesty and some red-tape. But a slight residue of such well-known human traits, could not be a very cogent reason for condemning Socialism.

Certainly our planners will have to be exceedingly stupid and perverse if they ever achieve mistakes as ruinous as the Great War and the Great Depression. And I cannot help thinking that critics like Messrs. Anderson and Lippmann are of the type who in the early days of the American Republic would have opposed the establishment of a United States Supreme Court on the ground that no group of men was wise enough to lay down the law for the entire country. Pursuing this thought further, I would say that the great issue facing America today is whether or not we are to have, as it were, a Supreme Court of Economics in the form of a democratically controlled National Planning Commission.

In the address from which I have already quoted, Dr. Anderson states that, "Our present system relies upon the unconscious, automatic functioning of the markets." Precisely! And we all know, both by reading history and experiencing the present, what calamitous results this "unconscious, automatic functioning" has brought upon the American people and the human race in general. We all know how tragically the countless splendid individual intelligences and abilities of humankind keep thwarting one another in the chaotic anarchy of unplanned Capitalism. Socialist planning with its collective coordination would release these now frustrated intelligences and abilities. It means just the opposite of what Dr. Anderson recommends in defense of Capitalism. In short, Socialist planning means the conscious, purposeful, non-automatic, un-ceasing functioning of the great community mind on behalf of the common good. It means embodying in human affairs what philosophers have called the life of reason. Thus Socialism not only appeals to reason, but also promises to give the method of reason far larger opportunities than ever before in history.

5. International Planning

Socialist planning can never be considered complete until, with the U. S. A. and. all other nations closely co-operating, it goes into effect on an international scale as the basic foundation of that great and peaceful world society which, long an ideal in the minds of statesmen, has become an acute necessity for our age.

Looking for a moment at the situation under Capitalism, we find that just as a species of planning can take place within nations under the present system, so also there can be certain forms of international planning within its framework. The most far-reaching example or capitalist international planning yet known was in the work of the Allied Maritime Transport Council, which during the last year of the Great War, carried out a program for coordinating the shipping of England, France, Italy and the United States. In peace times, too, there have been capitalist attempts at international planning. These have usually taken the form of "cartels" or other special agreements in which steel manufacturers, oil producers, rubber planters, sugar growers and other varieties of businessmen from different countries extend, internationally, the well-known capitalist device of fixing prices; curtailing production and restricting competition among themselves for the purpose of maintaining or restoring profit markets.

Socialism's goal of world planning has in view very different methods and very different ends. When the same general principles of national planning that I have proposed for America are in effect over a sufficient proportion of the earth, Socialism envisages a series of Twenty-Year World Plans that will immeasurably raise the living standards of all humanity and sweep unemployment, depression and war off the face of the globe. This would entail, besides the establishment of National Planning Commissions in each country, an International Planning Commission with headquarters at Geneva or some other appropriate city. There would also be Continental Planning Commissions for North America, South America, Europe, Asia, Africa and Australia, and, wherever necessary, sub-divisions of these covering several countries. It is quite possible that part of the mechanism of international planning could be worked out through a greatly revamped League of Nations, which, with its constituent members Socialist instead of capitalist-imperialist nations, would be a very different organization from what it is today.

All this, I admit, is looking rather far into the future, and I do not intend to be so presumptuous as to prophecy the details of the First Twenty-Year World Plan, A concrete illustration, however, of how international Socialist planning might function within the next five or ten years, is provided by imagining either Germany or Japan, or both, becoming Socialist commonwealths. In the latter eventuality they could immediately start to co-operate closely with the existing Soviet planning system. Germany and Japan, both of which lack foodstuffs and raw materials, would receive a proper proportion of these from the resources of the present U.S.S.R in exchange for their excellent finished goods. And these two new Socialist units would proceed to function in the production of abundance for a vastly enlarged planning area. The most vexing economic problems of Germany and Japan would quickly advance a long way toward solution. So, instead of attempting to solve their difficulties by foreign aggression, these two nations would obtain peacefully far more than they could gain through the most successful war.

In the Western Hemisphere, if the United States, with its immense prestige, power and economic potentialities, were to adopt Socialist planning, it would probably not be long before other countries in North and South America followed suit, Mexico in particular, where considerable strides in planning have already been made, and might speedily become desirous of co-operating with its northern neighbor in setting up a Socialist planning area of continental proportions.

But whatever may be the precise mode in which true international planning develops, the radical answer to the faint-hearted and timid-minded of these times is that modern human beings have the capacity to plan, and plan well, not only for a nation as a whole, but also ultimately for the world as a whole.

Socialism and Socialist planning will put a final end to the economics and politics of drift. They will bring to all peoples the abundant life promised by the potential of this good earth. They will make humankind at last the happy master of its high destiny.

Chapter IV
Socialism in Soviet Russia

1. The Russian Background

The only place in the world where country-wide Socialist planning exists is in the Union of Socialist Soviet Republics (U. S. S. R.). It is primarily for this reason that Soviet Russia has so much to teach the other nations of the earth, including our own American Republic. Yet, I must make the important qualification here that I by no means rest the entire case for Socialism on what has happened in Russia during the two decades and more since the great Revolution of 1917. For the fundamental logic behind Socialist planning would endure even if the Russian Revolution had never occurred; even if there had been no concrete example of Socialism so far in the world; or if the Socialist experiment in the Soviet Union had broken down. In other words, the principles of Socialism do not stand or fall because of what happens in a single nation; like experiments leading to new inventions, the initial efforts to establish a new form of society may fail in significant respects or even altogether. The basic principles of Socialism, international in their application, remain sound so long as the radical analysis of the socio-economic situation remains sound.

It was back in 1932 that, accompanied by my wife, Margaret Irish Lamont, I made my first visit to the Soviet Union. We spent six weeks in Russia at that time and traveled extensively throughout the western part of the country from Leningrad in the North as far as Tiflis and the Black Sea in the South. We stayed three weeks in Moscow, took a boat down the length of the winding Volga River from Gorki to Stalingrad, motored through the beautiful and awe-inspiring Caucasus Mountains, enjoyed ourselves in the warm and sunny resorts of the Crimea, and concluded our tour with the key cities of Kharkov and Kiev in the Ukraine. It was a splendid and rewarding trip. Then in the spring of 1938 we went to the U.S.S.R. again. This time we remained a month and concentrated on the larger cities and on collective farms. We did not get a chance to repeat our sail down the Volga or our tour of the Caucasus and the Crimea; but otherwise we covered about the same territory as before and were able specifically to compare conditions as between 1932 and 1938.

Before, however, taking up in detail the current situation in the U.S.S.R., it is essential to run the eye over a few simple facts about the physical characteristics and historical background of this remarkable land. The Soviet Union is the largest country in the world, covering a vast and sprawling territory representing between a sixth and a seventh of the entire land surface of the earth. It is greater in area than all of North America and two and a half times as big as the United States. When the American aviator, Howard Hughes, flew round the world, roughly one-half of his land flight was over Soviet territory. From the Arctic Ocean to Afghanistan more than 2,700 miles south, from Poland to the Sea of Japan more than 5,500 miles east, the Red flag flies; and over a total population of 170,000,000. In Bering Strait less than five miles of water separate islands belonging to the Soviet Union and islands belonging to the United States as part of the Territory of Alaska. And it is interesting to reflect that, if Secretary of State Seward had not put through the purchase of Alaska from Tsarist Russia in 1867, Soviet Socialism might today have a foothold on the North American continent reaching to within approximately five hundred miles of the United States proper.

These huge proportions of the Soviet Union entail immense advantages in the scope and variety of natural resources, making the country the most completely self-sufficient political unit in the world from an economic point of view. Within its extensive domains lie one-half of the earth's iron ore, one-third of the oil reserves, two-thirds of the manganese, and 95 per cent of the platinum. Its coal reserves are more than a thousand billion tons, the second largest in the world; while copper, lead, zinc, gold, bauxite, potash and apatite are plentiful. Its unending timber reserves cover two billion acres of forest-land; its harvests of grain, flax and sugar beets are larger than any other nation's; its cotton production stands third. And most of these figures are likely to need revision upward as further scientific surveys proceed throughout the Soviet Union and as its economy develops.

These almost infinite resources of the U.S.S.R. and its enormous territorial expense prove the truth of the old peasant proverb, "Russia is not a country, it is a world." Obviously the Soviet regime has been building Socialism in what amounts to a whole continent rather than in one nation in the ordinary sense of that term. These facts mean also that from a military standpoint the workers' and peasants' republic is all but impregnable. Yet at the same time these far-reaching boundaries and economic potentialities create a sheer problem of administration which is breath-taking in its extent and complexity, and which in itself alone explains many of the troubles that the Soviet Government has encountered in the first two decades of its existence.

This problem of administration is made even more difficult by the fact that within the U.S.S.R. and comprising nearly half of its population, there live, in addition to the Russians proper, 188 different minority peoples, speaking 150 different languages, and adhering to 40 different religions. Some of the better known of these peoples are the Ukrainians, the Tatars, the Armenians, the Jews, the Kazakhs and the Mongols. The Tsars cruelly oppressed all of the national and racial minorities, discriminating against them in many ways, forcing upon them a policy of strict Russification, and attempting to stamp out their native cultures. The Jews were, of course, especially subject to persecution, found themselves forced to live in ghettoes, and endured time and again the most violent reigns of terror. Co-operating closely with Government authorities in these atrocities was the corrupt and reactionary Greek Orthodox Church, the official State Church of old Russia with the Tsar himself as its head.

The semi-feudal Tsarist autocracy treated the masses or the workers and peasants with appalling brutality, condemning them to a wretched life of economic misery, political repression and cultural backwardness. Although pre-War Russia had a long revolutionary tradition and a most alert and able intelligentsia, the country had never experienced the progressive and invigorating

137

influences of a Renaissance and Reformation, an Enlightenment and Bourgeois Revolution. In 1917 capitalist industry was weakly and spasmodically developed, and largely dependent on foreign financing and technical management. About 85 per cent of the people were peasants (muzhiks) engaged in agricultural pursuits and using, for the most part, decidedly primitive methods. Up until 1861 these peasants had actually been serfs in the old medieval sense. Over 70 per cent of the entire population was illiterate; and enjoyment of the great Russian achievements in literature and drama and music was confined to a very thin layer of the economically and socially privileged.

Genuinely democratic institutions were practically unknown under the Romanov dynasty. The Duma or House of Representatives, conceded by Nicholas II as a result of the unsuccessful 1905 Revolution, soon became reduced to a parliamentary nonentity. At the same time the Tsarist Government was notorious throughout the world for its nepotism, its corruption and its impossible inefficiency—all of which contributed notably to the Russian breakdown during the Great War. Looking at Russia as a whole, we can say without exaggeration that in 1917 it lagged a century or more behind advanced nations like Great Britain and the United States in the development of industry and machine technique, of public administration and modern culture in general.

Such was the unpropitious setting in which the Russian followers of Karl Marx set out to construct the first Socialist commonwealth in history. Even had no other important factors entered into the situation, Lenin and his colleagues would have had a hard enough time, but other factors did arise which made their task at least twice as difficult. When in November of 1917 the Bolsheviks took over the state from the muddling liberals and middle-class republicans, Russia had already been through one revolution, that of March, which resulted in the abdication of the Tsar and the establishment of the Provisional Government. Meanwhile, in the intervening eight months, the condition of the country had gone from bad to worse, with the transportation system in collapse, the fields denuded of working hands and the bread lines in the cities growing longer and longer. The nation had endured more than three years of disastrous warfare and had undergone therein more than 9,000,000 casualties, with approximately 2,300,000 dead, 4,700,000 wounded and 25,000,000 taken prisoner.

Within a few months the Germans seized a large part of the rich, grain-producing Ukraine and forced the humiliating Treaty of Brest-Litovsk on the Soviet Government, But the troubles of the Communists were just beginning. For in spite of Lenin's sincere and continued efforts to establish peace, armed intervention on the part of the Allies began in the spring of 1918 and went on for several years, long after the defeat of the Central Powers had done away with the shadowy excuse of trying to re-establish the Eastern Front. During this period of intervention the armies of no less than ten foreign nations, including an expeditionary force from the United States,* invaded the Soviet Union, maintained a hostile blockade and gave lavish aid and comfort to the White counter-revolutionaries.

In fact, there can be little doubt that, had it not been for the support in men, munitions and money which the Allies contributed to the Whites, the civil war in Russia would have come to an end in rather short order. As it was, it lasted in extreme form three terrible years during which 2,000,000 people were killed, approximately $6,000,000,000 worth of property was destroyed and indirect losses were suffered amounting to some $20,000,000,000 more. Industrial production was reduced to less than 20 per cent of the pre-War level, while the Allied blockade almost completely eliminated foreign commerce When the Communists came into power in 1917, they admittedly did so with comparatively small loss in life and property; that later there took place a cataclysmic counter-revolution, stimulated and sustained by widespread foreign intervention, was certainly not of their choosing.

It. is illuminating to quote in this connection from the English writer Bruce Lockhart, who was a member of the British diplomatic corps in Russia during the exciting civil war period and who neither was nor is a Soviet sympathizer. In his book *British Agent* Mr. Lockhart writes, as of March 1918, that the Communists "had not yet embarked on their own campaign of suppression, I mention this comparative, tolerance of the Bolsheviks, because the cruelties which followed were the result of the intensification of the civil war. For the intensification of that bloody struggle, Allied intervention, with the false hopes it raised, was largely responsible. It sent thousands of Russians to their death. Indirectly it was responsible for the Terror."

The fact is that the "Red Terror," so played-up by foreign commentators, did not go into effect until the autumn of 1918 after the all but successful attempt on Lenin's life, and after Allied intervention had got well under way. Thus it becomes perfectly clear that the Communists, so often portrayed as bloodthirsty sadists, resorted to extreme measures only when internal and external violence forced them to do so in order to save the Soviet regime. But with their backs to the wall, they fought desperately and, like their opponents, with every weapon at their disposal. Both sides in this terrible civil conflict, fully bore out the old Russian saying, *"One life, one kopek,"* popularized by Mr. Walter Duranty, brilliant Moscow correspondent of *The New York Times*, as the title of his novel on the subject of these tragic years.

In the spring of 1920, when the Soviet Government had clearly gained the upper hand over the White armies, Marshal Pilsudski of Poland launched a totally unprovoked and temporarily successful attack on the Ukraine. The Red troops finally drove out the Poles and, indeed, carried their counter-offensive to the very gates of Warsaw, whence they were driven back. The added strain on the U.S.S.R. was very severe, Yet still another great emergency was to try the Soviets. In the autumn and winter of 1923-24 after the Government military forces had finally triumphed throughout the length and breadth of the land, a new enemy appeared on the scene. Its name was drought, failure of crops, famine. This crisis on field and farm, aggravated by the shattered state of transportation and the general war-weariness of the peasantry, brought another fearful toll of. death. Well over a million persons perished.

Besides the terrific inroads on life and property during this period of storm and stress, the Soviet Union suffered, either through military force or independence movements, the loss of all the western provinces: Finland, Estonia, Latvia, Lithuania, Poland and Bessarabia. In these regions had been many of the most highly developed industries of the Tsar's empire, including the Polish coal and textile centers and the Finnish pulp and paper mills. Though these districts comprised only one-thirtieth of the area of old Russia, they possessed one-fourth of its manufactures, one-fifth of its railway trackage, and nearly one-sixth of its population. They also embraced all of Russia's shipping outlets on the Baltic Sea. Hence the loss of these territories entailed such an extensive reorientation of Russia's economy as to constitute in itself a major task for the Soviet Government.

When one reflects, then, upon the Soviets' five-year ordeal of civil conflict, foreign invasion, territorial loss, economic breakdown and grueling famine, all following hard upon three calamitous years of the Great War and two far-reaching revolutions, it seems something like a miracle that they came through with their heads up and their colors flying. It was an epic triumph of unsurpassed energy and intellect on the part of an inspired people; and some day, I hope, will be described, as it deserves, in a literary document of Homeric quality and proportions.

When on this background which I have outlined, I view the picture of the Soviet Union's progress during the last fifteen years, I have no reservations in saying that the achievement of its people has been one of the greatest and most heroic in human history.

2. The Five-Year Plans

It required several years, as well as a number of concessions to the deeply engrained feudal-capitalist spirit and the traditional method of conducting business activities, before the Soviet Republic was able to recover from the destructive civil war period and work its way back to the economic level from which, had fate and history been kinder, it might have started forward in 1917. Then in the autumn of 1928, following three years of experimentation in comprehensive planning, the First Five-Year Plan went into effect. A year later such immense progress had been made that it was decided to attempt fulfillment of the Plan in four and a quarter years and thus bring it to a close December 31, 1932. While the revised and final schedules of the Plan were not all 100 per cent achieved by this date, the main objectives were carried out and the original 1928 estimates greatly surpassed.

In general the major goals of the First Five-Year Plan were to establish heavy industry on a sound and permanent basis, to mechanize and socialize agriculture, and to bring about the rapid technical training of the population. These achievements were designed both to provide a solid and lasting foundation for the building of complete Socialism and to make the Soviet Union, in case of need, independent of the capitalist world. The Plan admittedly cost a great deal in terms of human stress and strain, especially since the emphasis on heavy industry meant unprecedented savings for capital investment and therefore the temporary foregoing of consumers' goods. Accordingly, the Soviet people tightened their belts in order that the manufacture of producers' goods such as blast furnaces and steel foundries, tractors and agricultural combines, hydro-electric plants and all kinds of machinery, should go forward at top speed. Huge quantities of foodstuffs and raw materials, which could easily have been used at home, were exported in face of declining depression prices on the world market to pay for the import of machines and the hiring of foreign technicians.

The socialization of agriculture in Russia meant collectivisation, that is,- the merging of separate farms into large-scale collectives (kolkhosi) managed as a single co-operative unit by the individual peasant members and owners. The average size of the Soviet collective farm is about 1,300 acres. Usually each peasant family retains the ownership of its own dwelling, small kitchen garden, cows, pigs, poultry and perhaps beehives. In other words, the communal side of the collectives chiefly involves the major aspects of agricultural production in sowing, reaping, storing, making improvements and, above all, in applying machine technique and scientific methods in these various activities. Undeniably crucial in the collectivization program was the establishment throughout the countryside of the Government-run Machine-Tractor Stations, which rent to the collective farms tractors, reapers and other machinery as well as providing the necessary technical assistance or instruction for the operation of this mechanized equipment. Eventually more than 7,000 of these Stations were set up.

Besides the collectives the First Five-Year Plan saw instituted, thousands of huge State farms (sovkosi), owned outright by the Government and managed by a special Commissariat. These State farms are in actuality big agricultural factories with all their hands working for regular wages and organized in unions. One of their main functions has been to carry out large-scale agricultural experiments. In practice the State farms often proved, mainly because of the early Soviet tendency toward "gigantomania," somewhat unwieldy and inefficient. Hence they were later much reduced in area and in many cases broken up into collectives.

There can be no shadow of doubt that collectivization was an absolute necessity for the advance to Socialism in the U.S.S.R. The continued existence of some 25,000,000 scattered strips and separate peasant holdings throughout the nation meant, in the first place, production that was terribly inefficient and therefore insufficient for the needs of a growing population and an expanding Socialist economy. The obvious solution was to combine these innumerable small farms into two or three hundred thousand large enterprises (about 250,000 is the present number) in which the benefits of modern machinery and planned co-operative endeavor could be utilized. In the second place, the retention of the old individualistic agricultural system meant the persistence of the old individualistic psychology that went with it. And since the Soviet peasants constituted an overwhelming proportion of the population, it would very likely in the long-run have proved fatal for the new society had they gone on maintaining their anti-Socialist system and attitude. Hence collectivization had to come in the Soviet Union and did come—to stay.

Admittedly, however, certain organizers temporarily pushed the drive for collective farms too hard, as Joseph Stalin himself told them in his famous speech warning against "dizziness from success." This error in tempo markedly increased the amount of waste and inefficiency inevitable in the process of the peasants adapting themselves to the new system and did not give the factories time for the production of sufficient tractors and other agricultural machinery. In addition, there was widespread sabotage engineered by dissident Right and the Trotskyite-elements, the stubborn resistance of the kulak class naturally opposed to the whole idea of collectivization, and serious passive resistance stirred up by the Ukrainian nationalists who aimed at a separatist revolt. The combined result of these factors was a poor harvest in 1932 and a terrible slaughter of livestock by disgruntled peasants. An alarming food crisis developed. And during the winter of 1933 the entire Soviet Union felt the effects of food shortage, which in some areas undoubtedly was responsible for a heavy toll in malnutrition, disease and death.

But as so often happens in Soviet Russia, a bad situation quickly changed for the better. The Soviet Government made certain concessions to the individualistic tendencies among the peasants, established special political departments in the Machine-Tractor Stations, and dispatched 25,000-picked Bolshevik workers to some of the key agricultural districts to help in the 1933 campaign. At the same time the resistance of the kulaks was broken by severe measures which included deportation of the more recalcitrant ones to distant regions of the U.S.S.R. The result of these various moves became clear in the fall of 1933: the country had the biggest harvest in its annals. But even more important was the fact that collectivization, which means Socialism in agriculture, had won a great and lasting victory. This was one of the most significant agrarian revolutions in history; and without it, no matter what strides industry made, full Socialism in the Soviet Union would have been impossible and even partial Socialism endangered.

The accomplishment of the third great goal of the First Five-Year Plan, the mastering of modern technique, was likewise a costly process. A large proportion of the old skilled professional class left Russia at the time of the Revolution; many of those who remained continued to be hostile in their attitude and to sabotage whenever possible the economic program of the Socialist Republic. Hence, the Soviet Government had to train a whole new generation of Socialist technicians whose efficiency and loyalty could be counted on. This took time. It was also expensive in terms of production costs. Tens of thousands of unskilled workers and raw peasants from the fields started from scratch to learn how to operate complicated machinery. It is no wonder that they showed a great deal of awkwardness at first and that they ruined a great deal of machinery in the course of their education. In the end, despite these various obstacles, the objective was largely achieved. The Soviet workers demonstrated their proficiency in the arts of modern industry. The Soviet institutes of technical education turned out increasing numbers of engineers and other specialists fully capable of coping with the complex problems of the machine age. And the quality of all sorts of manufactured goods steadily and notably improved.

The Second Five-Year Plan, extending from January I, 1933, to December 31, 1937, continued in practically every respect the advances made under the First Plan. The chief differences were a greater stress on consumption goods—clothes, kitchen utensils, furniture, bicycles and the like—and a somewhat less arduous rate of expansion. As the Second Plan progressed, the Soviet people proceeded more and more to reap the benefits of their hard work and self-sacrifice under the First. Consumers' goods, the output of which had more than doubled by the end of 1937, poured out of the factories in vast quantities, causing an enormous retail turnover throughout the country, and quickly and noticeably raising the standard of living in urban and rural districts alike, Labor productivity in industry, stimulated especially by the Stakhanov movement to increase the workers' efficiency, went up 82 per cent and the average real wage more than 113 per cent.

The last year of the Second Five-Year Plan in the Soviet Union saw the gross volume of industrial output, with socialized property accounting for 99.8 per cent of it, rise no less than 800 per cent above 1913, and attain a place among the countries of the world second only to that of the United States. Taking 1929 levels as 100, Soviet industry had advanced 373 per cent at the end of 1937 compared with 103.5 per cent for industry in the capitalist countries as a whole. Today the U.S.S.R. is first in the aggregate production of tractors, agricultural combines, wheat and hemp; and second in respect to gold, coal, oil and the generation of electricity.

"Communism," Lenin wrote, "is Soviet power plus the electrification of the whole country." Lenin's dream has gone a long way toward fulfillment; for scores of huge, modern power stations now cover the Soviet land from one end to another and high-tension transmission lines carry energy to factories throughout the nation. The annual output of electric power in Russia today is more than twenty times that of the pre-revolutionary era. The biggest power plant in the U.S.S.R, and in fact the largest in all Europe is that of the Ukraine's Dneprogres, which American engin-eers helped to build. I was greatly impressed by my visit to this dynamic center in 1932 when it was under construction and again in 1938 when the magnificent dam and the nearby factory concen-tration, the Soviet "Pittsburgh," had been completed.

In agriculture, during the Second Five-Year Plan, the proportion of collectivized peasant households rose to 92 per cent of the total number and, together with some 4,000 State farms, covered 99 per cent of the cultivated land. Since 1933, with the exception of two years in which drought conditions were wide-spread, Russia's harvests have been progressively the greatest in its history. The biggest one of all in 1937 amounted to more than 110,000,000 metric tons of grain as compared with an annual average of 80,000,000 before the Great War. At the same time there have been enormous increases in industrial crops such as cotton, flax and sugar beets; while the livestock situation has rapidly improved since the tense days of the early collectivization period. Famine and the threat of famine, which for generation after generation in the old Russia constituted the major economic evil—there were nineteen famines in the last century alone—have become merely bad memories. And there has even been serious discussion recently about the free provision of bread to everyone on the same basis as water.

In the sphere of foreign trade the Soviet Union had, during the ten years from 1928 through 1937, a total business turnover of approximately $6,600,000,000 and imported $3,250,000,000 worth of goods without once defaulting on a single penny; and this in spate of the unusually severe credit terms imposed by capitalist business. Socialist planning has meant that behind every obligation, small or large, of the U.S.S.R., stand the resources of the entire nation. Soviet Russia for many years has been a very good customer of America and during the worst period of the Great Depression provided an invaluable outlet for certain of our machine-tool industries. Since 1935 the Soviet Government has made purchases in the United States averaging more than $40,000,000 annually, and since 1937 has done more buying in this country than in any other.

My own faith in the economic soundness and stability of the U.S.S.R. I put to a concrete test in 1932 when I bought a few Soviet Government 10 per cent gold bonds available then for foreign investors, I felt that this investment was about the best and safest that could be made at that time in the entire world market. A number of my American friends were exceedingly skeptical about my judgment, but future events decidedly bore me out. Interest payments, through the Chase National Bank in New York City, always came through fully and promptly, The exceptionally strong financial condition of the Soviet Government enabled it to call all of this issue of bonds for redemption late in 1936. During the slightly more than four years in which I held these 10 per cent bonds, their principal increased in dollar value, due to the United States going off gold, to the extent of 68.5 per cent. At the same time the average annual interest, in terms of the original investment, amounted to 16.5 per cent instead of merely 10.

When my wife and I made our second visit to the Soviet Union in 1938 we everywhere found evidences of the vast progress which the Second Five-Year Plan had brought. The contrast with 1932 was especially striking in the realm of consumers' goods, both foodstuffs and manufactured articles, which filled to overflowing the shops of Moscow and the other cities we visited and the villages through which we wandered in the Ukraine. The people in general were much better dressed than before, with both men and women, increasingly well-groomed and the latter paying much attention to manicure, coiffure and cosmetics. There was an abundance of bread, and pastry, milk and cheese, fresh eggs and vegetables, meat and fish, Spanish oranges and good ice cream, including delicious chocolate-covered eskimo pie. Wherever we went in the cities we found fleets of trim blue and white kiosks on wheels, selling nuts, fruits, soft drinks and cigarettes. At the many stations where we stopped on our three-thousand mile tour, women appeared with appetizing sandwiches, chocolate and other light edibles for sale. The meals on the dining cars were ample and well cooked. All this was very different from 1932. And there can be no doubt that for the first time in their age-long career the Russian people are getting plenty to eat.

Another of our chief impressions was occasioned by the immense amount of construction that was going on everywhere. The first thing we noticed coming into a city by train was that new buildings were rising wherever we looked. All of the chief cities have great five or ten-year plans of reconstruction and are in the throes of erecting factories, workers' apartments, offices, hotels, schools, theaters, stadiums and bridges. It is a sight that should make sick with envy those American economists who are always hoping to pull the United States out of the doldrums through big building booms. Despite all this Soviet construction, urban housing still lags behind the needs of the people, who have flocked to the cities by the million in the last decade and in some cases, like that of Moscow, have actually doubled the pre-revolutionary population. Another shortcoming in my opinion is the architectural quality of Soviet workers' apartments, which do not yet measure up to the splendid Vienna housing developments I saw in 1932 or the fine Stockholm co-operative apartments I visited in 1938.

I was struck, too, on this trip to the U.S.S.R. by the widespread mechanical development. Russian manufactured automobiles, buses and trucks now fill the newly macadamized streets of Soviet cities with quite heavy traffic and, I may add, with quite ear-splitting noise. The new Moscow subway, with its smooth-working escalators and beautiful, airy stations, runs with admirable efficiency and altogether constitutes a remarkable feat in the art of engineering. Soviet mechanical progress extends of course to military equipment, as we saw for ourselves on May Day when we stood for six hours on the Red Square and watched the tanks and artillery, the airplanes and other mechanized units, pass in review.

As for the Soviet people, they constantly impressed us with their spirit of gaiety and confidence. We saw them dancing and merrymaking in the public squares; we mingled with them in the streets and the parks, at workers' clubs and children's schools; we participated with them in festivities during holidays and other occasions; we enjoyed with them theater and movie, opera and ballet; we met them personally at their offices and homes, at lunch and dinner and during special outings. One of our more memorable days was a long boat trip down the new Moscow-Volga Canal with about thirty Russians—artists, authors, journalists, economists, professors and others—with whom we conversed freely and frankly, on topics both light and serious, for hours on end. And in all our contacts we found hardly a trace of that psychology of fear which certain observers have claimed was ruling the Soviet people on account of the recent liquidation of counter-revolutionary elements. Nor did we meet suspicion or hostility because of our status as foreigners.

The widespread idea that tourists in Russia are "shown" only what the authorities wish them to see and are strictly kept away from everything that might make a bad impression is simply fantastic. While my wife and I used an interpreter in talking with

Russians who did not know English, French or German, we wandered around alone a large part of the time and observed plenty of things that were far from ideal. As for our favorable impressions, it is rather difficult to believe that Stalin issued a secret decree ordering the Soviet people everywhere to smile and look happy on our behalf or that the bustling economic activity and large supplies of consumers' goods were in any sense faked.

It is no secret that in spite of the enormous increase in consumption goods, Soviet industry is not yet able to meet the ever-increasing commodity demands in either the urban or agricultural districts, demands to a large degree generated among the people by the economic and educational advances of the Socialist system itself. Prices remain relatively high in some lines, while in others new stock is quickly bought out. Distribution and retail trade are not yet as efficiently organized as production. And production of consumers' goods is itself handicapped by the degree of work-time which has to go to turning out military supplies for purposes of defense. Then there have been the widespread sabotage and wrecking activities of the past few years—activities which, in my judgment, probably set back the Soviet economy as a whole by 10 or 15 per cent.

But the human resources in the U.S.S.R, are just as great as the natural resources. New and younger elements, vigorous, able and well-trained, have come up from the ranks to fill the gaps left by unfaithful officials exposed in the purge. The Soviet economic machine is again hitting on all cylinders in its swift course forward, with industrial production for the first half of 1939 15 per cent above the corresponding period of 1938. The Army, too, has more than recovered from its personnel troubles and is unquestionably at its all-time high in strength and reliability. And the fast-growing Soviet Navy, its submarine fleet already the largest of any in the world, is a more powerful bulwark of defense than most foreign observers realize. Of the various non-Fascist peoples I observed in Europe in 1938, the Russians seemed much less nervous over the possible effects of a war than anyone else.

In a general sense, the most significant thing of all in the total Soviet picture is, I think, the fact that during the first two Five-Year Plans, the Russians have accomplished the unprecedented feat of eliminating the cycle of boom and decline by making controlled prosperity a continuous and permanent thing. Though various sores of growing pains will no doubt from time to time continue to cause trouble in particular industries or regions of the U.S.S.R., the general, countrywide breakdowns which character-ize capitalist crises seem to have become consigned to the past.

The fundamental reason is that wide-scale and long-range planning, which is the very heart of the Soviet or any other Socialist system, makes certain such a complete and harmonious adjustment between the purchasing power of the people as consumers and the productive power of the people as workers that the disastrous phenomenon of over-production cannot take place. There can be no piling up of un-bought commodities, as in capitalist lands, in profitless plenty in store and warehouse, so that a crisis for the owners as well as the would-be consumers inevitably results. If my opinion on this matter is correct, then surely Soviet Socialism has achieved a step forward in economic affairs at least equal in importance to the Industrial Revolution.

As regards the future, I think it can be said that the potential capacity of a people, even one with a relatively high standard of living, for absorbing consumers' goods approaches infinity. Yet it is conceivable that some day what we might call absolute over-production in one field —foodstuffs, for example— could threaten a Socialist economy like that of Russia. In such a case it will not be difficult to adjust the situation by reducing the hours of labor in agriculture or arranging for some of the farm workers to shift to other vocations. If, as I hope, Socialism comes about in the world at large, the possibilities of absolute overproduction in any field will become so remote as to constitute a purely speculative problem.

The Third Five-Year Plan started January 1, 1938, and will end December 31, 1942, The Soviet State Planning Commission expects that more will be achieved in this third period than during the First and Second Five-Year Plans together. Special stress will be laid on further increasing average labor productivity, which is admittedly still two or three times lower than that of American workers, and on improving the quality of goods. The Planning Commission is already looking ahead in a general way to the Seventh and Eighth Five-Year Plans which will be finished respectively in 1960 and 1965. It is expected that by the latter date the Soviet population will have increased from its present 70,000,000 to over 300,000,000. At the New York World's Fair which opened in the spring of 1939, Americans have been able to see, in the magnificent Soviet pavilions, representative exhibits showing past and projected progress under the Five-Year Plans.

3. *Soviet Cultural Progress*

I have been emphasizing so far the Herculean economic achievements of the Soviet Union, But we should not forget for a moment that cultural growth in the Socialist Republic has paralleled the material and has been just as striking. The ultimate goal of Socialism is to build., upon the foundations of lasting economic security and equilibrium, the greatest culture that the world has yet seen both in terms of its qualitative achievements and the number of people able to participate in it. I shall review a few outstanding examples of the Soviet advance toward this goal without in any sense trying to cover in total the country's many-sided cultural life.

It was Lenin himself who said: "Art belongs to the people. It ought to extend with deep roots into the very thick of the broad toiling masses. It ought to be intelligible to these masses and loved by them. And it ought to unify the feeling, thought; and will of these masses, and elevate them. It ought to arouse and develop artists among them."

These ideas of Lenin about art are daily becoming more and more of an actuality in the Soviet Union. Art there has become the possession of the entire people and has entered into the very fiber of their beings; it is no longer the private property of a small minority at the top. The whole population is sharing in the enjoyment and creation of literature and painting, the theater and the motion picture, music and dancing. Amateur art circles flourish by the tens of thousands. As so often among the Soviet Russians, a succinct slogan sums up the situation. In this case it is, "To live without work is robbery; to work without art is barbarism."

Socialist planning has made huge sums available in the Soviet Union for the encouragement of art. Already hundreds of new museums have been built, and Moscow alone has erected 125 since the Revolution. Millions and millions of people visit these Museums every year, absorbing the rich heritage of their nation's past and gaining a consciousness of the meaning of art. One of the busiest organizations in all Russia is the special Bureau for the Restoration of Historical Monuments, with its large staff of historians and technical workers. This Bureau has restored hundreds of ancient churches, mosques and other buildings, and has discovered countless rare art treasures, including many superb frescoes and ikons which had been hidden for centuries by whitewash and plaster applied to old walls by ignorant monks. In the realm of education the progress in the U.S.S.R. since Tsarist times has likewise been prodigious. Some of the statistics here are enlightening. During the First and Second Five-Year Plans illiteracy went down to 5 per cent of the population as compared with the 70 per cent pre-War figure of 1913; the number of children in primary and secondary schools increased from 8,000,000 to almost 30,000,000; and the total of students in a vastly augmented number of higher educational institutions grew five times over. There are 550,000 such students in the Soviet Union today as compared with a combined aggregate of 416,000 in the higher educational institutions of Britain, France, Germany, Italy and Japan, Ninety per cent of these Soviet students, moreover, are provided with free tuition, free living quarters and a monthly allowance for ordinary expenses. It is significant, too, that 33 per cent of them are women.

Lenin told the rising generation to do three things: to study, to study *and* to study. But everyone in Soviet Russia, of whatever age, has adopted this precept. In his absorbing volume *The Soviets* Albert Rhys Williams writes:

Schooling is in no wise a monopoly of the youth; nor is it confined to the regular system run by the State. Alongside of it rise up other systems conducted by and inside the Communist Party, Labor Unions, and the Red Army; some form of educational effort is an intrinsic part of the activities of every big enterprise. . . . There are Radio-schools broadcasting cycles of lectures, each one complete in itself, so the casual listener may profit thereby; home-study groups taking courses by mail; Workers' Faculties, Trade-schools, Night and Day "Universities."

Formal education will soon become compulsory between ages eight and fourteen. The eventual aim is to make it so for everyone throughout the land; and the Third Five-Year Plan will see this first step accomplished in the city districts.

At the same time the masses of the Soviet people have become voracious readers. In 1937, 2,000 magazines were being published in the U. S. S. R. with annual circulation of 391,000,000 copies; 7,000 newspapers, nine times the pre-War number, with a circulation sixteen times as great; and 53,000 titles in books and pamphlets with 1,300,000,000 copies, ten times the 1913 level. When Mr. Williams wanted to express what was going on in this field he did an article appropriately called **"Billions of Books."** "Today," he says, "bookstalls and bookstands are as numerous in the Soviet Union as are soda fountains in the United States. The problem is no longer that of awakening an interest in books, but rather of finding some way to satisfy the truly insatiable demand. In the last fifteen years seven billion copies of books have been published." Even in the rather abstract sphere of philosophy the Russians print editions ranging in number from 10,000 to 150,000, including translations of the chief classics from Plato and Aristotle to the twentieth century. Such publishing figures for philosophical works are unheard-of in any other country.

The spread of education in the Soviet Union has gone on; not just in the cities, but throughout the agricultural regions as well. The awakening of millions and millions of formerly ignorant and illiterate peasants to the new cultural life has been perhaps the most noteworthy thing of all. During my trips to Russia the young people with whom I talked in the villages and collective farms seemed just as intelligent and alert as the students I met in the urban centers. The educational program has also extended to all the national and racial minorities throughout the U.S.S.R. In many cases new alphabets have been created for the benefit of backward minority groups. And, exactly reversing the policy of the Tsars, the Soviet Government has not only permitted but has encouraged these minorities to develop their own languages, their own theaters, their own schools and their own institutions in general. The result has been a veritable renaissance of the various minority arts and cultures in Russia along the lines of the general principle, "national in form and Socialist in content."

Another group in the U.S.S.R. which has especially benefited from the cultural and social remodeling of the country are the women. They have experienced a far-reaching emancipation, and now are on a plane of equality with men, both legally and otherwise. It is revealing that as of 1938 there were in the All-Union Congress of Soviets 184 women, or 16 per cent, out of 1,143 deputies as compared with twelve women, or 2 per cent, in the British House of Commons and six women, or 1 per cent, in the Congress of the United States. In the extensive Mohammedan regions of Russia the women have gained through the abolition of the old custom of polygamy by act of the Soviet Government, so often portrayed as encouraging lax sex relations. In these districts, too, they have won freedom from wearing the veil and from the evils of child marriage and bride purchase. Again, it was Lenin who said that no nation can be free when half its population, the women, are household slaves and doomed to "daily sacrifice to a thousand unimportant trivialities," This saying has become a basic principle in the Soviet Union. Women in their function as mothers are provided for with particular care; babies and small children are allotted the best of everything that the land possesses. The Communists are not, in my opinion, breaking up the home; what they are breaking up is family drudgery and family egotism. They want people's ambitions and interests to extend beyond the domestic circle to the country at large.

Since the tumultuous years of revolution and civil war, the institution of the family in Soviet Russia has been growing more and more stable. Prostitution has been almost completely eradicated, Licentiousness is considered an offense against Communist ethics, not because it is a "sin" in the old religious sense, but because it is a self-indulgence which interferes with productive work and the welfare of the family. During the past few years the Soviet Government has enacted, primarily on the grounds of furthering physical well-being, decrees making abortions decidedly difficult to obtain. And it is encouraging modern contraceptive methods as the sanest and healthiest way of effecting birth control. No medical expert would for a moment dispute the wisdom of this policy.

In Soviet medicine we find established as axiomatic the idea which many eminent physicians and surgeons in America have recently been publicly supporting, that "the health of the people is the direct concern of the government," Since the Revolution the Soviet Government has increased the number of doctors from less than 20,000 to more than 100,000; it has increased the number of hospital beds from 175,000 to over 500,000; it has reduced infant mortality by more than 50 per cent and the general death rate by more than 62 per cent. Whereas in the United States only one out of every thirty dollars spent on medical care goes to the prevention of disease, in Soviet Russia the whole system of public health is built around the idea of prevention. And the guiding principle is the creation of the best possible conditions for work and living.

In the new Soviet Constitution there is a remarkable clause that reads: "Citizens of the U.S.S.R. have the right to rest and leisure. The right to rest is ensured by the reduction of the working day to seven hours for the overwhelming majority of the workers; the institution of annual vacations with pay for workers and other employees; and the provision of a wide network of sanatoria, rest homes and clubs serving the needs of the working people." In addition to these admirable provisions, the development of sports and all kinds of other recreational facilities has contributed greatly to the increasing health and well-being of the Soviet population. Stadiums, for example, have been built throughout the land; and the physical culture movement has millions of adherents.

An excellent measure of the difference between the old Russia and the new, is the situation in the sphere of science. Whatever political commentators may say about the Soviet Union, foreign scientists who have gone there and studied conditions in their specialty almost invariably bring back glowing reports. The number of professional scientists has increased from 3,000 under, the old regime to 40,000 now. In every field, from public health to archaeology, and in every locality, from the thickly populated industrial cities to tiny hamlets in distant Siberia, the truths and techniques of science are replacing the myths and methods of religious supernaturalism and are exerting a far-reaching and beneficent influence.

In their monumental and definitive book on the Soviet Union, the English authors, Sidney and Beatrice Webb, tell us:

"We find today in the U. S. S. R., what exists in no other country, an elaborately planned network of more than a thousand research laboratories, with their own extensive libraries and collections, scattered over the vast territory between the Arctic Ocean on the north, and the Black Sea or the Central Asian Mountains on the south, at each of which selected staffs of trained researchers, with salaries and expenses provided, are working in co-ordination on particular problems, allocated largely with special reference to local needs, opportunities, or resources."[*]

---

[*] Sidney and Beatrice Webb, *Soviet Communism: A New Civilization?* New York, 1938, p. 956. Quoted by special permission of the publishers, Charles Scribner's Sons.

While the Soviet Russians believe that in the long run all science should be made to serve practical purposes, they are thoroughly awake to the need of "pure" scientific research more or less remote from immediate utilitarian pressures.

The extraordinary scientific work which Soviet Socialism fosters has been dramatically symbolized in the stirring non-stop flights of Soviet aviators to the West Coast of the United States via the North Pole and to the East Coast of Canada via the Great Circle route. Of even weightier import have been the thrilling and successful efforts to explore and develop the Arctic regions. The Soviet regime has sent out expedition after expedition during the past fifteen years to these far-northern territories; has laid the ground-work for the exploitation of their fishing and other vast resources; set up seventy-five Arctic radio stations for the study of climatic and other conditions; established a regular Northern Sea Route from the West to the East of the Arctic Sea; and trained a special air fleet to aid and co-operate in these ventures. The high point of all this activity came in the spring of 1937 when Soviet airplanes flew a group of scientists to the North Pole itself to conduct scientific studies. Four of these men remained nine months on an ice floe, which finally drifted far from the Pole. In February of 1938, with their records and specimens intact, they were at last rescued off Greenland by Soviet icebreakers.

It is of course impossible to consider the present role of science in Soviet Russia apart from the new economic system. For that system of Socialist planning in effect turns the country into one huge laboratory in which, because of the central controls, scientific experiments of unparalleled scope can be carried on. Furthermore, in the economic realm, since there is no fear of overproduction, there is no fear of science. Thus the Science Section of the State Planning Commission encourages all kinds of new labor-saving inventions and experiments; every Government commissariat has a special experimental division; and each large industrial enterprise maintains laboratories for scientific work.

While the individual Soviet inventor is amply rewarded, the fruits of his work go to industry as a whole. There are no private interests in the U.S.S.R. to patent an invention and limit its use, for the sake of profit-making, to one particular business concern. If a worker or technician in a steel plant in the Ukraine invents an important instrument or process, every steel mill throughout the Soviet Union will as a matter of course soon be using it. Nor are there any private interests in the Socialist Republic which can buy up and put on the shelf new inventions lest they ruin existing investments. Under Socialism, science fulfills its proper end of serving humankind and does not, as under Capitalism, have a prior obligation to the cause of profit.

The evolution of experimental science in the U.S.S.R. is the best possible proof that the Marxism of the Soviet Russians will never succumb to the dead hand of a dead past and that it is not, as its opponents claim, a rigid orthodoxy laying down the law from a Bible interpreted by a Pope and a College of Cardinals. Lenin himself set the tone when he wrote: "We do not by any means look upon the theory of Marx as something final and inviolable; on the contrary, we are convinced that it only laid the cornerstones of the science which Socialists must advance in all directions, if they do not want to lag behind events." Applying this generalization to the individual, Lenin stated: "We do not want anything to be accepted with the eyes shut, to be an article of faith. Everyone should keep his head tight on his own shoulders, and think out and verify everything for himself."

Along with the educational and cultural developments in Soviet Russia there has occurred so profound an alteration in human motives that it is legitimate to call it a spiritual revolution. It may be asserted that the Communists have changed human nature, but it is more accurate to say that they have *channeled* it. That is, they have taken the raw materials of human impulse and set them going in certain specific directions both rewarding for the individual and beneficial to society as a whole. There is, for instance, more ambition in Russia than ever before; but this ambition, instead of finding an outlet in trying to make a million rubles, fulfills itself in doing a first-rate job for the community and climbing the ladder of achievement in socially useful ways. Not only is its fulfillment through the exploitation of others definitely ruled out; its expression in the form of personal vainglory or in ruthless careerism is an offense against Soviet ethics, as many an arrogant bureaucrat has discovered to his grief, The point is that in the U.S.S.R. ambition is fast becoming thoroughly socialized, which is to say that for the first time in human experience it is becoming truly civilized.

In their devotion to the great ends and inspiring philosophy of Socialism, the citizens of the Soviet Union have literally forgotten themselves. In their adherence to the new, invigorating loyalties they have been released from age-long economic fears, sexual repressions, and religious guilt-feelings. Their more personal problems and Freudian complexes have been driven into the background. Of course, the high purpose and enthusiasm of the Soviet Russians in their drive toward the goal of a free and class-less society has had its analogies in other countries. During the Great War some of the belligerent powers produced a somewhat similar mass spirit, thus bearing out the statement of Karl Marx that "The highest heroic effort of which old society is still capable is national war." But the Soviet Union is the first nation in history to harness the inspired imagination and devoted energies of an entire people to the constructive works of peace instead of the de-structive works of war. And this is a most important difference.

From all this it ought to be perfectly clear that, far from discouraging individuality, the Soviet Socialist order aims to give every member of the community the greatest possible opportunity for development. The Communists insist, however, that economic freedom is the basis of all others; and that only through planning can they free humankind from the chaotic control of the market and its blind, unconscious forces. The much-publicized issue of individuality versus collectivism or Socialism is a totally false one. The truth is that in the industrialized and mechanized world of the twentieth century some sort of collectivism is necessary in order

160

that individuality may flourish. Socialism only rules out individualism in the narrow, selfish sense of people exploiting, harming, ruining others for the sake of their own personal advantage. Marx himself wrote in *Capital,* of Socialism as a "higher type of society whose fundamental principle is the full and free development of every individual." And the motto he chose for himself was "Follow your own bent, no matter what people say."

4. *Democracy and Peace*

The deep concern of Soviet Socialism for the individual is clearly discernible in its aim of developing a democracy in the fullest sense. The very term Soviet, has a democratic connotation, since it is the Russian-word for council. In Marxist theory the dictatorship of the proletariat has always been considered a temporary phase for a transitional period, an adamantine instrument in the creation of the Socialist society and for defense against its class enemies. This dictatorship, however, disappears as the need for it disappears. Here we have one of the most important differences between a Communist and Fascist dictatorship. People are habitually lumping the two together as if they were in essence the same, but with Fascism the dictatorship has a very different purpose and is supposed to go on forever; there is no thought of, or provision for, the ultimate transition to democracy. Hitler talks of the Nazi form of government lasting a thousand years, while Mussolini revels in calling democracy "a putrid corpse." Stalin, on the other hand, only recently made the following characteristic statement: "Leaders come and leaders go, but the people remain, Only the people are immortal. Everything else is transient."

Undoubtedly, the Communist Party still remains the most important and powerful organization in the U.S.S.R. Composed now of about 1,600,000 members, subject to strict discipline and expected to set an example in both public affairs and personal behavior, this body has been since the Revolution the greatest cohesive and initiating force in the growth of Soviet Socialism, giving an indispensable and decisive impetus to everything from economic planning to the formulation of the new Constitution. It has provided, as the Webbs put it, an organizing group for "the vocation of leadership." This does not mean that the many non-Party sympathizers and the masses of workers and peasants do not themselves demonstrate the qualities of initiative and leadership; but the best of them, as they reveal their ability, tend to gravitate toward the Communist Party and become members of it. The same tendency exists in the two large youth groups closely associated with the Communist Party: the Young Communists or Comsomols, numbering 8,000,000 between the ages of fourteen and twenty-three, and the Pioneers, numbering 11,000,000 between the ages of ten and sixteen.

It is true that at present no other political party besides the Communist exists in Soviet Russia, As time goes on, however, and democracy develops more and more, it is my guess that important disagreements over Socialist policy will result in groupings which, whatever their formal position or designation, will act in some sense as parties.

In America itself, it is appropriate to recall, the theory of the Founding Fathers did not make a place for parties; two distinct and functioning political parties did not come into existence for a good fifteen years after the Revolution; and George Washington was unopposed in the first two elections for President. Whatever the particular evolution of democracy in the Soviet Union, and whether it eventuates in a multi-party system or adopts more effic-ient forms, that evolution must be judged chiefly in terms of the particular conditions which come to prevail in the country. For we can neither expect nor wish Socialist democracy in the U.S.S.R. to follow the pattern of the democracies or rather pseudo-demo-cracies, with which the world is already acquainted.

The most convincing sign that the Soviet Union is putting democracy into effect was the enactment of the new Constitution in the latter part of 1936. Since the Soviet idea has been from the start that true democracy demands certain economic and cultural foundations, this Constitution reflects the tremendous progress that has been made. Its epoch-making new "rights of man," the right to employment, the right to leisure, the right to free education, the right to material security in old age or in the event of physical disability, the right of sex equality, the right of racial equality, show that, in Stalin's words, "the complete victory of the Socialist system in all spheres of the national economy is now a fact." Soviet Russia is surely the only nation in the world that would dare make unemployment unconstitutional.

The socialization of agriculture and the remarkable growth of education in the rural areas have written themselves into the Constitution in the important provision establishing electoral equality between the workers and peasants. Formerly, the workers had a relative advantage in voting power of about two to one. The Constitution gives the franchise to all persons of both sexes eighteen years of age or over, which automatically means restoring the ballot to certain groups which, like the kulaks, the clergy and former Tsarist officials, were for many years disfranchised for political reasons. This step signifies to what a large degree the old class lines have been obliterated and to what a large extent there has been actualized the policy announced by a leading Soviet official several years ago that "All those who work for the Socialist State are comrades, including those who have joined the working class in that work as well as those born in it." The Constitution also guarantees by law freedom of religious worship, freedom of speech, freedom of the press, freedom of assembly and meetings, and freedom of. street processions and demonstrations. The creation of a second legislative chamber, the Soviet of Nationalities, ensures that the particular interests of the various minorities shall be protected.

There can be no doubt that prejudice as between the many different nations and races making up the U.S.S.R. has all but disappeared, both because the security and well-being guaranteed by Socialism has removed the roots of economic jealousy and because all of the minorities feel a new sense of unity in their common endeavor to carry out the overall objectives set up by the present regime. In view of the growing persecution of Jews in many countries, it is of profound significance that in the Soviet

Union the expression of anti-Jewish prejudice, like that of any other racial animosity, is treated as a crime under the law, and that Joseph Stalin, himself a native of once oppressed Georgia, now one of the eleven constituent Republics of Soviet Russia, should specifically denounce anti-Semitism "as a relic of cannibalism" and "a lightning conductor" which enables the exploiting capitalists to evade basic economic issues.

It is easy to say that this new Soviet Constitution is only a "paper" one, however, it is obvious in the nature of the case that all written constitutions are paper constitutions. The extent to which constitutional provisions become actualized is always dependent on the good faith of the government and people involved. Now I do not contend that the new Soviet Constitution will be observed 100 per cent, especially during the first years of its existence; yet I venture to say that its fundamental principles will become the law of the land sooner than in most other instances. The United States Constitution has been in effect for one hundred and fifty years, but we know how frequently it is violated even today, particularly its guarantees regarding civil liberties and minority rights. And those who laud the British parliamentary system as the last word in perfection should remember that it has been in process of development upwards of six hundred years.

An element of primary importance in the functioning of Soviet democracy is the trade union. Out of a working population of 28,000,000 eligible for membership, almost 24,000,000 belong to one of the 166 different unions, a far larger proportion than in other countries. Since in a Socialist society the economic well-being of every individual is a universally acknowledged right and since the exploiting capitalists, together with the class struggle, have disappeared from the scene, the Soviet trade unions have little trouble in negotiating favorable contracts as to wages, hours and working conditions. Hence they are able to put much of their energy into educational and administrative work, and have full charge of administering the extensive social insurance benefits which so substantially supplement wage income in the Soviet Union.

What about the recent purges in the U.S.S.R., and do they indicate a trend away from democracy? I do not think so. The purges are now definitely over, it seems. In any case they were transitory phenomena which do not represent the fundamentally democratic direction in which the country is moving. I do not like violence, I do approve of executions, I do not like any sort of bloodshed. But I can hardly blame the Soviet Government for dealing sternly with the plotters and wreckers who aimed to pull down the structure of the first Socialist society. Whether these enemies were out-and-out Fascist agents from abroad; followers of Leon Trotsky or Nicolai Bukharin aiming to overthrow by force the present Soviet regime; generals with Napoleonic ambitions; or White Russians seeping over the far-eastern border from their big emigre settlements in Manchuria, it seems to me that they may have deserved the utmost severity.

I, like so many others, was deeply shocked and troubled by the series of treason trials at Moscow. But after reading the long and detailed verbatim testimony of the three big trials—a check-up which few critics of Soviet justice have bothered to make—and after careful consideration of the main factors involved, I felt no doubt of the defendants' guilt and of the genuineness of their sweeping and frequently surprising confessions. For years Trotsky, burning with resentment because the Soviet people refused to follow his hair-brained policies, and driven to the most fearful extremes by his megalomaniac itch for political power, has been openly agitating on behalf of a violent counter-revolution against the Soviet Government. Both he and his followers have made it clear that they consider any means toward this end justified, And they actually succeeded in 1934 in assassinating Sergei Kirov, one of the top Soviet leaders. Since Trotsky and his fellow-conspirators could count on no mass support in Russia, it is easy to see why the natural result was terrorist plotting and, as a last desperate measure, even co-operation with foreign governments interested in bringing about the downfall of the Soviet regime.

History clearly shows, not only that the defenders of the *status quo* always fight a new social order to the last gasp, but also that bitter dissension usually develops among the makers of far-reaching revolutions. And because the Revolution in Russia is the most far-reaching that has ever occurred, because it abolishes and not just re-arranges private property in production and distribution, the struggles revolving around it are bound to be more ferocious than in other cases. The Webbs give us the correct historical perspective when they say:

> Even England and Scotland, in the small population of the seventeenth and eighteenth centuries, with a much less fundamental revolution, produced generation after generation of conspirators, to whom treason and killing, with lies and deceit, were only part of what they felt to be a righteous effort. . . .
>
> The French Revolution of 1789-95 ushered in a similar period of conspiracy and struggle, leading to a whole succession of counter-revolutions, not reaching the stability of a democratic republic, with its large measure of personal security and social equality, for nearly a century. . . . In Russia (which was in 1900, in the matter of morals and civilization, very much where Britain and France stood in 1700) the pattern of behavior of the revolutionary conspirators culminated in a bitterness and mutual antagonism more acute and all-pervading than in any other example.[*]

The Soviet Republic, I may add, is not going to permit the unhappy French experience of successful counter-revolution; nor the unhappy American experience of dreadful civil war long after the founding Revolution; nor the unhappy Spanish experience of

---

[*] Sidney and Beatrice Webb, *op. cit.*, pp. 1158-59.

bloody, Fascist militarist rebellion throttling the emancipation and progress of the people. These things are simply not going to happen in the Soviet Union. And I for one am glad that at least in one land violent revolution is once and for all over and done with.

Unfortunately, however, many liberals and radicals in foreign countries have become quite confused over the internal troubles which the U.S.S.R. has experienced. A number of them have joined either the international brigade of Soviet-haters or the association of fair-weather friends. Intellectuals such as my former teacher and colleague, Professor John Dewey of Columbia University, have aligned themselves with the professional enemies of the Soviet people and have allowed themselves to become regular publicity agents on behalf of the Trotskyites. Most of Trotsky's defenders in America, are, like Dr. Dewey himself, New York intellectuals. Trotsky as an individual seems to have a fatal fascination for such people. They view him as a brilliant, dashing, heroic, misunderstood intellectual, quite similar to themselves, whose dra-matic role as Lucifer of the world revolutionary movement arouses all their sentimental impulses. To these incurable romantics Stalin appears prosaic and unexciting in comparison, despite the fact that in a quiet and unspectacular way he has played the outstanding part in the consolidation of Soviet Socialism.

I am convinced that today the chief factor holding back the full flowering of Soviet democracy and especially of the proper psychological atmosphere for it, is the constant threat of military aggression on the part of foreign powers, together with their constant attempts within the borders of the U.S.S.R. to sabotage and carry on espionage work and enlist for their own hostile purposes whatever dissident individuals they may still discover. With spies of the German War Ministry developing into a regular plague in the United States and all over South America, we can be sure that the Nazis are stopping at nothing in nearby Russia, which they regard as their foremost enemy. Hitler's recent annexation of Czechoslovakia and Memel, makes the peril to the Soviet Union greater and nearer.

It is to be remembered that at present, international war, open in Asia and underground in Europe, is actually going on, with the Fascist states of Germany, Italy and Japan everywhere the aggressors. The ultimate aim of the Fascists and their allies in every nation is to crush the Soviet Republic, to put an end to the ever more successful Socialist commonwealth whose stirring example fills the masses of the people in capitalist countries with what the Japanese so charmingly call "dangerous thoughts." As long as the foreign situation remains as menacing as it is today, one can hardly expect the Russians to act as if they were surrounded by nothing but sweetness and light. Toward the enemy within the gates and the enemy outside they must necessarily maintain an attitude of stern vigilance.

For some strange reason persons who admit that the Soviet Union was justified in using armed force in its early stages to defeat the interventionists argue today that this country is hypo-critical in building up a large army while its representatives unceasingly talk .about the establishment of international peace. But the Soviet people remember only too well the extensive efforts of the capitalist powers to overthrow their republic during the civil war years. In this turbulent period of world history, there can be no doubt that the U.S.S.R. is fully justified, nay, morally obligated, to maintain its own defenses. And radicals must necessarily view an attack on the Soviet Union as an extension of the class struggle into the sphere of international war, with foreign capitalists, Fascists or otherwise, launching violent counter-revolution in the form of unprovoked aggression upon the first Socialist state.

That the U.S.S.R. does not itself harbor aggressive military designs is proved by its whole conduct since the founding of the Republic. **It was on the day following the October Revolution that Lenin proposed to all the belligerent powers that they start negotiations at once for "a just and democratic peace." But the answer of both Germany and the Allies was invasion**. It is hardly too much to say that the idea of peace was treated as a sinister Bolshevik plot! Even after the period of civil war and intervention came to a close, the Soviet Union found great difficulty in establishing normal relations with the capitalist countries, One would have thought that Soviet Russia had been invading *them* rather than the other way round. Nonetheless, as time went on, most of the capitalist nations, both big and small, entered into Commercial and diplomatic relations with the Soviet Union. Of the larger powers the United States was most stubborn, holding off recognition for sixteen years until the late date of 1933.

Shortly after it came into power, the Soviet Government proceeded to publish the secret imperialist treaties connected with the Great War, a step which the capitalist nations have never forgiven, and to renounce the imperialist aims of the former Russian Governments. Instead of continuing to cherish the romantic Tsarist vision of annexing Constantinople and the Dardanelles, the Soviets initiated cordial relations with Turkey and even ceded that country certain territory near Armenia. In China the U.S.S.R. gave up all its extra-territorial privileges. In Manchuria, it sold its rights in the Chinese Eastern Railway to Japan in order to lessen the chances of friction in the Far East.

The Soviet Union's policy of international amity registered particular progress during the period from 1930 to 1939 when Maxim Litvinov, who carried through the difficult negotiations for American recognition, was the Soviet Commissar for Foreign Affairs. Under Litvinov's leadership, Soviet Russia signed the Kellogg Peace Pact and later entered the League of Nations. Mr. Litvinov negotiated non-aggression pacts, marking a new stage in strictness and clarity of definition, with all twelve of the states bordering the U.S.S.R. except Japan, which steadfastly refused to enter into any such treaty. In conference after conference at Geneva the Soviet delegation demonstrated its sincere desire for disarm-ament and consistently made proposals toward that end far more concrete and drastic than those of any other nation.

At the same time the Soviet Union has been thoroughly realistic and, since the open Fascist offensive against world peace, has supported more stoutly than ever the principle of collective security. **This principle is based on the belief that aggressors can be stopped dead in their tracks if those nations truly**

desiring peace will band themselves together and unequivocally declare their intent to invoke economic and, in case of final necessity, military sanctions against war-makers. The Soviet Government stood willing and ready to participate in sanctions when Fascist force was used against Ethiopia, Spain, China, Austria and Czechoslovakia. And not only was it foremost in exposing and opposing these acts of aggression; it also sent substantial aid to the invaded Spanish and Chinese peoples, to the latter in fulfillment of its pledges as a member of the League of Nations.

I have often heard it said that the main reason for the peace policy of the Soviet Union is that it has plenty of territory for its present purposes. Now while it is certainly true that the U.S.S.R. is not land-hungry, it should be recalled that the Tsarist Empire, one of the most imperialist, war-mongering regimes in history, possessed much more territory than the new Russia, which lost so heavily in the West after the Revolution of 1917; and that Nicholas II aimed to enlarge his domains greatly following the expected victory in the World War. The point is, that Tsarist imperialism, no matter how much land it acquired, was always hungering for more.

But Soviet Russia, with its Socialist economy, has neither the need nor desire to expand, It has eradicated within its borders all those economic factors that make for war. Because the Soviet people as a whole own the productive property of their country and because they have abolished private profit-making, the possibilities of war-profiteering are nil. Because Socialist planning has put an end to capitalist crisis and has brought under its control the country's foreign trade as well as its domestic, the Soviet Union has been able to pass sentence of death upon the chief practices of war-provoking economic imperialism. Surely the most prejudiced Soviet-hater can see that from the point of view of sheer self-interest, the U.S.S.R. most ardently wants peace. For the most important and pressing item on the agenda of Soviet Russia is the unimpeded building of Socialism throughout its vast homeland.

In addition, there are the moral considerations involved in Socialist Russia's attitude toward world affairs. There is the fact that the Soviet Republic, from the very start, has stood for full equality between the various races and nations of the earth. On account of the many different minorities living in happiness and harmony within its borders, it is in itself a functioning and splendid example of international cooperation and understanding. As the first existing Socialist state, Soviet Russia believes in internationalism as a basic principle and refuses to admit that geographic boundaries or differences in physiognomy should be allowed to limit the expression of the human spirit and the interchange of human values. There can be no doubt in my mind that collaboration with the Russian peace efforts is one of the categorical imperatives for both nations and individuals that are sincerely working for the abolition of war.

5. *Some Criteria of Judgment*

In formulating a final judgment on the economic and cultural achievements of the Soviet Union since the Revolution of 1917 and during the first two Five-Year Plans, it is highly necessary to keep in mind certain general considerations concerning the particular characteristics of the U.S.S.R. I have already mentioned the very special historical background of the country. Now given that background, it is obviously absurd to expect that Russia could completely catch up in twenty years in all respects with nations such as England, Germany and the United States. As a standard of reference in regard to things like modern technology and administrative efficiency, these countries must always be held in view. But one cannot be fair to Soviet Russia without constantly taking into account the question: How much have conditions improved since the time of the Tsars? In other words, we cannot afford to neglect the important principle of historical relativism.

Consider the matter of shoes. It can easily be demonstrated that the Soviet masses are still in need of more and better shoes and that it will be some time before they overtake the people of the U.S.A. in this important sphere of equipment. The most significant point to remember, however, is that the Soviet Union is turning out nine times as many shoes as in pre-War days, that is, 180,000,000 pairs per year in comparison with 20,000,000. Moreover, before the Revolution, the shoes were distributed mainly in the cities and among the upper classes. The great majority of the peasants went barefoot in the summer and fashioned themselves straw footwear in the winter. When the average peasant wanted to get married he had to hire a pair of decent boots for the occasion from one of the well-to-do farmers in the community. Today, on the other hand, the shoes which are manufactured are distributed to all sections of the population and not just to a privileged group.

This same principle of making comparisons between Soviet Russia and other countries on a relative rather than an absolute basis holds in other fields. I think especially of the modern conveniences and mechanical gadgets so dear to the heart of Americans. Anyone familiar with traveling in Russia before the Great War knows that conditions were unclean, uncomfortable, and generally unsatisfactory. The last edition of Karl Baedeker's Russian guidebook, published in 1914, makes this very plain. It is hardly to be expected that the Soviet Russians, who have had world-shaking and world-making problems on their hands, could have turned the U.S.S.R. into a tourists' paradise over-night. Yet tourists continually come back from Russia disgruntled and disgusted with the whole country because it was so difficult to find taxicabs in Moscow, because meals in the hotels were not always served with the accustomed American dispatch, and because they could buy only drugs in the drugstores and not milk-shakes and fountain pens.

Now everyone knows that Europe in general lags far behind the United States in its provisions for creature comfort. From personal experience I have learned, for example, that plumbing in France and Italy, especially in the provinces, is in drastic need of improvement—where it exists at all. Yet American tourists are willing to overlook or even to romanticize the discomforts which they meet in traveling through European countries other than Russia, For some strange reason, though, they will return from the U.S.S.R. and construct whole books or lecture tours around the profound subject of their troubles with trains and hotels, food and insects. As time goes on, such lopsided travelogues should occur less and less frequently, since, as I discovered myself in 1938, the Soviet Russians are becoming increasingly efficient in the small things that often loom so large in the consciousness of travelers from abroad.

Another misunderstanding on the part of foreign observers is in reference to the various compromises and shifts in policy that occur in the Soviet Union from time to time. Now, no intelligent Marxist ever dreamed that it would be possible for Socialism in any country to leap up full-fledged all at once from the chaos of the old order. How much less so, then, in a land which was as far behind as the Russia of 1917. There one could see that the building of Socialism would quite obviously entail a long, difficult struggle even had there not been an immediate background of international and civil war. In such a struggle there are bound to be bad years as well as good, failures as well as triumphs, detours as well as marches straight ahead. And it is essential to distinguish temporary setbacks from permanent defeats.

Since the Soviet Union was the first nation in history to attempt the construction of a Socialist society and had no precedents on which to draw, serious and unforeseen problems have inevitably arisen and unfortunate mistakes have on occasion been made. Far from attempting to cover up their blunders, the Soviet officials and workers have set them forth in self-castigating detail in the press throughout the land. Their frank self-criticism has become a veritable institution, and has been an exceedingly effective weapon in combating bureaucracy and inefficiency. At the same time, thanks to it, foreign detractors have obtained some of their most potent ammunition, A naive reader of the average Soviet newspaper can easily get the impression that the whole country is daily going to the dogs.

Lenin's formula of "one step backward, if necessary, in order to take two steps forward" has seemed to be just plain common sense in the Soviet Union. What temporary compromises or changes in policy indicate is not failure, as hostile critics are always claiming, but a willingness on the part of the supposedly dogmatic Communists, controlling a radical Government actually in power, to face the facts and to exercise an intelligent flexibility in carrying out their program. Certainly no other compromise compares in extent with the N. E. P. (New Economic Policy) which was introduced by Lenin himself in 1921 in place of the stringent "War Communism." Yet this far-reaching but transitory move in the direction of capitalist principles did not result, as the outer world predicted, in the abandonment of Socialism in Soviet Russia. Indeed, not many years later the First Five-Year Plan was dis-placing the N. E. P. In other words, the Soviets always eventually take those two steps forward.

An excellent example of Soviet procedure and foreign reaction to it is to he found in the handling of the 1932-33 food crisis which I have already described. In November of 1932, when the agricultural outlook was rather gloomy, the New York *Herald Tribune* published an editorial entitled *"The Retreat from Marx,"* in which it said that the Soviet agrarian problem could be solved "only by such a swift retreat from Marxian first principles as will leave no doubt in any Russian or foreign mind of the collapse of the Communist experiment under the relentless pressure of faulty but unalterable human nature." In point of fact, "a swift retreat" did take place, a wise and statesmanlike one that abandoned certain extremist policies which were provoking opposition among the peasants; but it was not a retreat that sacrificed any fundamental Marxist principle. By November of 1933 things had improved in such a startling measure that, as I stated earlier, a harvest breaking all records was the result. Hence, the only thing that collapsed was the prophecy of the *Herald Tribune*, originally made, I suspect, "under the relentless pressure of faulty but unalterable" editorial policy.

Not only internals but also serious external difficulties arise to confront the U.S.S.R. and to make its general forward march follow something of a zigzag pattern. Ever since the Japanese militarists invaded Manchuria in 1931, the Soviet Union has been faced with the acute possibility of aggression in the Far East. Then in 1935 the rise of the Fascists to power in Germany brought a serious threat from the West, with Adolf Hitler stating that the dearest aim of his life was to make large portions of the Soviet Union part of an all-conquering Nazi Empire. These dangers have forced the Soviet Government to make extensive alterations in the Five-Year Plans and to allocate to the manufacture of munitions and other military equipment men and materials that could ill be spared from normal productive operations.

There remains to be mentioned one compromise which the Soviet Union supposedly makes, but which is not really a compromise at all because it has never been part of the Socialist program. Some critics assert that the new regime has failed in Russia because it has not established equality in wages. Wage equality under Socialism, however, was at no time an item on the Soviet agenda. In a speech at a recent Congress of the Communist Party, Stalin took especial pains to make the present Soviet policy clear, "Equalization of needs and personal living conditions," he said, "is a reactionary, petty-bourgeois absurdity, worthy of a primitive sect of ascetics, and not of a Socialist society organized on Marxist lines, because we cannot demand that everyone have similar needs and tastes, that everybody in personal life live according to one model."

Indeed, *absolute* equality in wages is not even an aim under that far-off Communism toward which Soviet Socialism is beginning gradually to evolve under the Third Five-Year Plan. According to Marx, the eventual Communist stage of society will see actualized as its chief distinguishing characteristic the ideal formula: "From everyone according to his capacities, to everyone according to his needs!" But .though this means an approximate equality in compensation, if allows for a certain amount of variation due to the fact that everyone's needs are not the same. Thus a man with a weak heart or some other physical disability will require more to support himself comfortably than a perfectly normal person. A scientist is likely to need more than a retail clerk. In any kind of society men, who like Scientists, are performing certain highly complicated functions must have more extensive

175

material facilities than others, for carrying on their work. It makes little difference whether the community provides for such requirements by a special grant from the budget or by paying the individual a higher salary. But the need must be met.

Because so many people seem to think that Soviet Russia and the Fascist states are basically the same, I want to sum up briefly here, at the risk of some repetition, the twelve most fundamental respects in which the Soviet Union differs from Hitler's Germany and Mussolini's Italy: The U.S.S.R. has been and is a bulwark against world war, and envisions a peaceful Socialist internationalism as the final goal; it has practically eliminated racial and national prejudices within its borders; it has instituted the public ownership and operation of all industry; it has socialized agriculture through the process of collectivization; it has established nation-wide Socialist planning; it has built the trade unions into the very fabric of its society; it has emancipated woman and the family; it has brought about a most far-reaching cultural and educational advance among its people; it believes in the philosophy of anti-supernatural Dialectical Materialism; it follows the method of experimental science in social and economic affairs; it has abolished the old social structure of classes based on the exploitation of man by man; it considers political dictatorship as a transitional measure and has shown a steady growth toward democracy.

Any proper evaluation of a country, besides taking into account its past and present, also demands some estimate of its probable future. The Soviet Union is certainly no millennium as yet; and simple-minded folk with an essentially religious psychology, like Eugene Lyons, author of *Assignment In Utopia* who have gone to Russia expecting to find paradise were bound to become disillusioned and bitter. It can hardly be doubted, however, that from both a material and cultural standpoint the direction in the U.S.S.R. is steadily, sometimes spectacularly, but in any event on the whole, upward. The problems are very definitely those of growth and not decay. Undeniably the Soviet people have made great sacrifices since the Revolution, But these sacrifices have been, I think, worthwhile and constructive, and made with a high purpose held consciously and continually in mind. In the rest of the world, too, millions and millions of people have been making sacrifices; but these sacrifices for the most part have been purposeless, muddling and to a large extent useless. There has been no plan behind them. They have not led anywhere, unless to a new world war and fresh economic crises.

What compensating gains, for example, resulted from the sufferings of the fifty million unemployed in the capitalist nations during the four years of the Great Depression? And does it not seem likely that the sufferings of these millions and their families—and of other millions and their families—will continue indefinitely under Capitalism? In the final perspective of history this distinction between constructive and fruitless sacrifice is bound, I believe, to be of the utmost importance. History judges no great event or social change simply by tallying up the number of lives lost and the amount of suffering that went on. It always asks what was the total situation: what kind of a past were the people trying to escape from and what kind of future were they trying to build? And I am confident that the ultimate judgment of history on these first twenty-two years of the Soviet Republic will be a most favorable one.

It might be well for us in the U.S.A. to remember that during the first two decades after the American Revolution our own Republic went through a rather trying period. In 1798, twenty-two years after the Declaration of Independence, the youthful United States was still experiencing grave troubles. The Constitution had been in effect comparatively few years; the country was in a turbulent state, chaotic, disunited and poor; European observers were predicting failure; foreign powers loomed menacingly on the horizon. And, paradoxically enough, the most reactionary of the old world nations, Tsarist Russia, refused to recognize the American Government for thirty three years after the break with England. No one could have foreseen in 1798 the immense and startling developments which would come to the United States in the next century of its existence. Yet I venture to say that relatively speaking, equally unforeseen and remarkable things will take place in the U.S.S.R. during the next hundred years.

Today, as the U.S.S.R. swings into the full rhythm of the Third Five-Year plan, it looks very much as if the Soviet people had finished the most difficult and grueling stage of Socialist construction. The Third and Fourth Five-Year Plans, in comparison with the First and Second, are going to be comparatively easy. This does not mean that there will not be plenty of good hard work to be done. But the tempo will be slower and the nervous pressure less. Meanwhile the standard of living will continue to rise rapidly; and it would seem that the future in Russia has more than just hope, indeed that it has promise of a steady and almost limitless advance in every field of human endeavor. Of course if the U.S.S.R. is forced into war, another period of storm and stress will sweep the Russian land and the people will again have to live twenty-four hours per day in the heroic mood.

It is my own feeling that the Soviet people are well-nigh invincible in an economic, moral and military sense. From without, Soviet Socialism can undoubtedly be set back, but hardly destroyed; from within, there is about as much chance of its being brought to an end as of the United States voting to become again a colony of Great Britain. The idea to which the Trotskyites still cling, that there can be a successful revolution against the present Soviet regime, is fantastic, since the class divisions and economic discontent which are the Marxist prerequisites for revolution simply do not exist in the U.S.S.R. I do not consider it over-optimistic to state that, happen almost what may, Socialism has come to stay in the world. This is the portentous fact that all the dire prophecies about the impending "collapse of civilization" so blindly ignore. For civilization has undeniably taken a new and lasting lease on life in the Soviet Union.

Though my enthusiasm for the U.S.S.R. is profound, I do not want to claim too much on its behalf. Yet this, finally, can be added with no danger of exaggeration: The very fact that, over a territory far larger than the United States and non-Russian Europe combined, Socialist economic planning has for many years been operating on a fairly efficient basis proves that it can be done. It proves that though the opponents of Socialism may continue to talk themselves blue in the face, Socialist collectivism is a system which can maintain itself and make both substantial and rapid strides ahead. It proves that, while in no country can the capitalists possibly get along without the working class, in the Soviet Union the working class has got along swimmingly without the capitalists. And if Socialism works in the Soviet Union, a country so indescribably backward in 1917, then how would it work in this mechanical wonderland of America? My own opinion is, though any guess may soon be out of date because the Soviet Union is catching up so fast, that Socialist planning would at present work at least twice as well in the U.S.A. as in the U.S.S.R.

End of Chapter IV of You Might Like Socialism

~ ~ ~

Here follows Beth's Commentary on some philosophical and historical considerations regarding "Means and Ends," loyalty, and justification of violence as regards Socialism:

Note: It seems appropriate at this point to add some commentary about the preceding chapters. Corliss Lamont was exploring, in 1938, the thorny questions regarding resistance to Socialist collectivism, treatment of dissidents, and philosophical and political challenges to Stalin's leadership. These following selected paragraphs, also found elsewhere in his book, describe the thoughtful considerations in the writings of Corliss Lamont regarding whether a "noble end" justifies a "violent means." He was dealing with the ideas of dictatorship, repression, revolution and violence, all of which, regardless of the cause, many will still find repulsive today. At that time the world was hearing about executions!

179

How was he responding to those who were asking these serious questions? One three-paragraph response by Corliss Lamont is as follows:

"What about the recent purges in the U.S.S.R., and do they indicate a trend away from democracy? I do not think so. The purges are now definitely over, it seems. In any case they were transitory phenomena which do not represent the fundamentally democratic direction in which the country is moving. I do not like violence, I do not approve of executions, I do not like any sort of bloodshed. But I can hardly blame the Soviet Government for dealing sternly with the plotters and wreckers who aimed to pull down the structure of the first Socialist society.

Whether these enemies were out-and-out Fascist agents from abroad; followers of Leon Trotsky or Nicolai Bukharin, aiming to overthrow by force the present Soviet regime; generals with Napoleonic ambitions; or White Russians seeping over the far-eastern border from their big emigre settlements in Manchuria; it seems to me that they may have deserved the utmost severity."

"I, like so many others, was deeply shocked and troubled by the series of treason trials at Moscow. But after reading the long and detailed verbatim testimony of the three big trials—a check-up which few critics of Soviet justice have bothered to make—and after careful consideration of the main factors involved, I felt no doubt of the defendants' guilt and of the genuineness of their sweeping and frequently surprising confessions. For years Trotsky, burning with resentment because the Soviet people refused to follow his hair-brained policies, and driven to the most fearful extremes by his megalomaniac itch for political power, has been openly agitating on behalf of a violent counter-revolution against the Soviet Government. Both he and his followers have made it clear that they consider any means toward this end justified, And they actually succeeded in 1934 in assassinating Sergei Kirov, one of the top Soviet leaders. Since Trotsky and his fellow-conspirators could count on no mass support in Russia, it is easy to see why the natural result was terrorist plotting and, as a last desperate measure, even co-operation with foreign governments interested in bringing about the downfall of the Soviet regime."

Another relevant quote, from Corliss Lamont's writings is as follows:

"However, let no one think for a moment that I like dictatorship of any variety as a form of government. In fact I sharply dissent from these radicals who sometimes portray a Left dictatorship as a lovely and beautiful thing in itself. But when it is obvious that dictatorship is essential for progress, I cannot do otherwise than to grit my teeth and support it, bearing as best I can the many cruel and violent things that it implies. I do not expect a dictatorship, even when managed by the most idealistic radicals, to avoid becoming involved in very un-idealistic actions. And that is why I have never been greatly surprised at the violence which has taken place in the Soviet Union, much of which I am convinced is an integral part of dictatorship as such, whether proletarian or otherwise.

As I have shown elsewhere in this book, the trend toward democracy has been very marked in Soviet Russia. There, in the world's one Socialist country, the people already enjoy economic, cultural, sex and racial democracy; they are well on their way toward full political democracy, and they stand unwaveringly for international democracy. This outcome of events in the U.S.S.R. is by no means the first example in history of democracy being advanced through revolution. It is, indeed, only the latest instance of this phenomenon. For it should not be forgotten that the democratic privileges and the civil rights to which we have grown accustomed in the West were the result of centuries of bitter and violent struggle against monarchical and religious absolutisms upheld by intransigent ruling classes.

I was once cut off the radio when I came to a passage in an address in which I made a mild and qualified comparison between the Russian and the American Revolutions. But I think that I can safely state here that the American nation actually did win its characteristic institutions of democracy through a revolutionary war of five years duration. And for many years following the end of that war in 1781, the American Government did not treat at all gently the Tories who had sided with King George III or who still wished to see the newly founded Republic return to his rule. Americans, therefore, cannot with consistency deny the present right of oppressed peoples to throw off the yoke of twentieth-century autocracies, even if revolutions are essential to do the job; nor criticize too harshly drastic measures on the part of recently liberated nations to secure their gains against domestic and foreign enemies."

Another of Corliss Lamont's observations:

"History clearly shows, not only that the defenders of the *status quo* always fight a new social order to the last gasp, but also that bitter dissension usually develops among the makers of far-reaching revolutions. And because the Revolution in Russia is the most far-reaching that has ever occurred, because it abolishes and not just re-arranges private property in production and distribution, the struggles revolving around it are bound to be more ferocious than in other cases."

Another quote follows:

Corliss Lamont then goes on to say that a counter-revolution against the established Socialist government in U.S.S.R. is not likely to be successful, because of "the progress of the people. These things are simply not going to happen in the Soviet Union. And I for one am glad that at least in one land violent revolution is once and for all over and done with."

What a shame that this turned out not to be true. But, at the time, this is what he truly believed. Further, he points out his disappointment, especially in the US, with those whom he expected to be idealistically open to a more long-range view of the situation, in these next three paragraphs:

Disappointed in Intellectuals

"Unfortunately, however, many liberals and radicals in

foreign countries have become quite confused over the internal troubles which the U.S.S.R. has experienced. A number of them have joined either the international brigade of Soviet-haters or the association of fair-weather friends. Intellectuals such as my former teacher and colleague, Professor John Dewey of Columbia University, have aligned themselves with the professional enemies of the Soviet people and have allowed themselves to become regular publicity agents on behalf of the Trotskyites. Most of Trotsky's defenders in America, are, like Dr. Dewey himself, New York intellectuals. Trotsky as an individual seems to have a fatal fascination for such people. They view him as a brilliant, dashing, heroic, misunderstood intellectual, quite similar to themselves, whose dra-matic role as Lucifer of the world revolutionary movement arouses all their sentimental impulses. To these incurable romantics Stalin appears prosaic and unexciting in comparison, despite the fact that in a quiet and unspectacular way he has played the outstanding part in the consolidation of Soviet Socialism.

I am convinced that today the chief factor holding back the full flowering of Soviet democracy and especially of the proper psychological atmosphere for it, is the constant threat of military aggression on the part of foreign powers, together with their constant attempts within the borders of the U.S.S.R. to sabotage and carry on espionage work and enlist for their own hostile purposes whatever dissident individuals they may still discover. With spies of the German War Ministry developing into a regular plague in the United States and all over South America, we can be sure that the Nazis are stopping at nothing in nearby Russia, which they regard as their foremost enemy.

The ultimate aim of the Fascists and their allies in every nation is to crush the Soviet Republic, to put an end to the ever more successful Socialist commonwealth whose stirring example fills the masses of the people in capitalist countries with what the Japanese so charmingly call "dangerous thoughts." As long as the foreign situation remains as menacing as it is today, one can hardly expect the Russians to act as if they were surrounded by nothing but sweetness and light. Toward the enemy within the gates and the enemy outside they must necessarily maintain an attitude of stern vigilance."

Another observation by Corliss Lamont , in commenting on his 1938 trip to the Soviet Union is as follows:

"And in all our contacts we found hardly a trace of that psychology of fear which certain observers have claimed was ruling the Soviet people on account of the recent liquidation of counter-revolutionary elements. Nor did we meet suspicion or hostility because of our status as foreigners."

Commentary, from Beth's Human Values Blog:
For Corliss Lamont to have made, even at the above date, such an accepting and even blasé comment about "liquidation of counter-revolutionary elements," sounds to me quite shocking, even looking backward, even understanding his passion and fervor for the cause. Today, we might shrug and say that, obviously, "he had drunk the Kool-Aide." This poses an interesting paradox: the man who continued to champion our own Civil Liberties and later, the Universal Declaration of Human Rights for all of Humankind, to be beguiled into believing that executions were essential in order to protect the newly-developing system that he passionately believed would in-time promote human progress and equality. There is something definitely discordant in this disconnect between "means" and "end."

Strangely, in 2008, we've not progressed in the matter of ethics as a nation. This is still a popular and patriotic stance: kill those whom you deem to be enemies. I heard the words, "find and kill Osama bin Laden" from the lips of one whom I expected, instead, might use the words, "bring to justice," in a more statesmanly pronouncement. Unfortunately, one must not be seen as a wimp when running for office in the country whose leaders have been hell-bent on military domination of selected sovereign nations, and whose citizens have mostly been beguiled into believing the "irrationale" (new word?) for doing so.

No Google in those days!

We must remember that Corliss Lamont did not have the luxury of instant information resources that today we have at our fingertips. There were official observers and writers about these trials-for-treason who vouched for their authenticity and the "confessions" of those who were accused. He must have had much difficulty in determining and searching-out what he believed to be the truth and weeding-out what he surely believed to be pure anti-Socialist propaganda. So very much has transpired since Corliss Lamont wrote this book in 1939. First of all, he himself, during his lifetime began to re-appraise some of the events that had taken place in the Soviet Union. For instance, his previous comments about Leon Trotsky and Nicolai Bukharin as surely being guilty, when in later years he acknowledged that the "show-trials" as they came to be known, were unjust and violations of the civil liberties of those who were accused during that specific time, and alas, even subsequently.

Strangling the "infant:"

I can understand his mind-set and the rationale, and his recognition that the Soviet Union had been militarily attacked for the purpose of "strangling" the menacing infant of Socialism in its cradle, with tragic loss of lives. The threat was not imagined; it was real, since, in 1918 the United States and its allies had actually sent troops into Russia to fight against the Bolsheviks, who had since established themselves as the legitimate government of Russia. The Allies, including U.S. President Woodrow Wilson personally, were fearful that the Russian Revolution might have a dramatic negative effect on the workers of capitalist countries.

Corliss Lamont, only 20 years later, was dealing still with these realties. On the one hand he saw the ideal of Socialism as a shining beacon in the darkness toward which to aspire, with it necessarily needing to struggle and to protect itself against all obstacles that it was encountering on the way. On the other hand he placed undeserved trust in Joseph Stalin, who had risen ruthlessly to the top leadership position. Hindsight allows us to call it naiveté; when immersed in the movement, we call it steadfast and unwavering belief in the cause. Some in the Russia of today still champion Stalin, believing that his heroic efforts in the "great patriotic war" saved the nation. Would dissidents in Siberia agree?

Struggle for power! Who betrayed the Revolution?

Other students of U.S.S.R. history, as the extensive writings of Nicolai Bucharin eventually began to come to light, and he was somewhat rehabilitated posthumously by official recognition, know that he is fully vindicated and was faithful to Socialist ideals, but differed in leadership decisions. Had Lenin lived, or Bucharin been able to prevail, the ultimate damage and the mistrust that was generated by Stalin's fears and over-reaction to all threats perceived and real, and that moved the country into totalitarian control, might have been averted. We can never know.

Nicolai Bucharin was perceived to be a threat. He became an "enemy of the state; therefore he must be eliminated." Leon Trotsky must be tried, even in absentia, to show that he was an "enemy of the state." Both of these men were intelligent, charismatic leaders with strong ideas and who constituted a real challenge to Joseph Stalin. I truly believe that Stalin was responsible for Lenin's death as well, seeing Lenin as being the ultimate obstacle to his own leadership. Lenin, himself, had even warned that Stalin was untrustworthy. But, none of this information was available at the time that Corliss Lamont was appraising the situation.

Continuing threat to Russia:

Observing world situations in this year of 2008, ninety years later, it occurs to me that even after the Soviet Union has been dissolved, that Russia is still under assault from hostile forces that surround it. NATO is designed to protect whom from what? I would feel terribly threatened. The installation of radar in the Czech Republic; creating missile bases in Poland; the meddling by the US in Georgia to secure a pipeline that bypasses Russia? All of these instances are of a provocative nature. How should Russia respond?

That old ploy: "he did it first!"

Try as I might, I simply cannot advocate or condone the use of violence as justified when threatened or even assaulted. To defend oneself against an aggressor is one thing, but then, at what point does the defender become the aggressor? My criticism of the aggressive, outrageous murderous, tactics employed by the Zionist leadership of Israel against Palestinian citizens is based on the same principle. In a justified fear of genocide they over-react to terrorist attacks and become perpetrators of genocide. My kids learned that they couldn't use that old ploy: "But, he did it first!" The ethical answer is still the same: if you judged it to be wrong, then it's twice as bad to repeat it! The one-upmanship tactic is rendered obsolete in the same way. Ask the International Criminal Court how crimes against humanity shall be dealt with!

Negotiating with power?

Being a staunch supporter of the potential for peace that is embodied in The United Nations, I keep saying: negotiate! Negotiate! Negotiate! But then, whoa, wait a minute! A picture of the murderous Siege of Stalingrad pops into my mind! How do you negotiate with the onslaught of an advancing army? Or in the face of overwhelming, devastating power, as in Rwanda? How do you negotiate your way out of the Gulags? Treblinka? Auschwitz? Guantanamo? We need the interception of a Real Peacemaking and Peacekeeping Force to intervene in behalf of the People and to protect those who cannot protect themselves! Now, at the United Nations this principle is called *The Responsibility To Protect*. It needs to be implemented with law, power and consistency.

Would I have killed Hitler?

When I even speak of negotiations, I'm accused of being a "wimp." My accuser challenged me with this question: "If you had a crystal ball and could have seen into the future in 1933, would you have killed Hitler before he could commit his heinous crimes?" Well, besides being a metaphysical nightmare, in which the necessary hindsight after a "future" fact was not available, nor could there have been clairvoyance in which the crimes might have been anticipated, no crime would yet have happened. I had no definitive answer. To base an execution on your belief that someone will commit a crime is in itself, a crime. Isn't this what happened to Nicolai Bukharin?

Unethical to willfully kill!

My son, at age seven, was questioning capital punishment, saying, "If killing is bad, then the guys who kill the killers are bad, too!" Seemed like perfect logic to both of us. I was privileged to be in Rome to attend the founding of the now newly operational International Criminal Court which opts for no death penalty, even as punishment for Crimes Against Humanity, but imprisonment and restitution, instead. I listened intently to all the arguments preceding this decision that was finally taken after great debate. The worries were that the Court would be a "toothless tiger" without a death penalty. The majority of nations represented there opted for a more ethical approach of not killing convicted killers but sentencing them to life imprisonment instead. The US position favored capital punishment. US Ambassador Scheffer did not sign the founding document, citing another concern: that American military personnel might be accused of War Crimes, as the US meets its military obligations around the world!

One of the last things that Bill Clinton did before leaving the Presidency was to sign the International Criminal Court Protocol. One of the first things that George Bush did after the Supreme Court put him in the White house was to UN-sign it! Never before in the history of the United Nations had a document been UN-signed. It is not enough to cause 'collateral damage" by accidentally bombing villages or inadvertently starving children, **apparently the US actually intends to commit crimes against humanity, for which it does not wish to be charged! Why else would our Leadership take this stand, refusing membership?**

My own personal Code of Ethics reminds that there are things that I would die for, but there is nothing that I would kill for, regardless of what the perceived benefits might be.

Corliss Lamont said he "stayed loyal over-long."

Corliss Lamont was subject to much criticism when he tended to justify the "show-trials" of dissidents, under Stalin, as they have come to be called. I can certainly understand his "believing over-long," as he put it," that the show-trials were legitimate. With the luxury of looking backward and reviewing more information that has come to light, we can confirm that the bedazzlement and continuing faith in the ideals of the Bolshevik Revolution, envisioned as a means of promoting the democratic rights of the people, the "soldiers, the sailors and the peasants" to live in peace and prosperity, actually became its own litmus test of one's ability to remain steadfast in an atmosphere of hate and fear.

Sidney Hook's Erroneous Statement in his book "Out Of Step"

Appropriate here is a little vignette from personal conversation with Corliss Lamont. One of his cohorts and critics was fellow philosopher, Sidney Hook, whom he actually admired, although Hook ultimately and vehemently renounced his own original approval of Socialism, even Party membership, almost to becoming a right-winger. When Hook's book *Out Of Step* was published, Corliss laughed aloud at reading Hook's description of himself. Hook had boldly stated that he had recruited Corliss and his wife, Margaret Irish, into the Communist Party. Corliss thought that this was immensely funny and was shaking his head, saying that this was utterly preposterous! When we urged him to publish some kind of response, since he was already in his nineties, and it seemed very important for him to do so during his lifetime, he literally boomed out his reply: "Why should I bother refuting such an allegation? It is total nonsense, but it doesn't make much difference now, does it? Besides, anyone who knows me, knows that it isn't true. I was, and still am, an Independent! Even Party Officials criticized me for not being supportive enough!"

The following paragraph is commentary written by Beth Lamont regarding Corliss Lamont's stand on these issues taken from the Preface to his Eighth Edition of the Philosophy of Humanism, re-printed in 1996, a year after the death of Corliss Lamont.

"In these recent years some earth-shaking events have taken place. One of them was the end of the Cold War between the U. S. and the Soviet Union, strangely leaving those persons who had long promoted friendship between the two countries still un-forgiven for their "un-American activities" —among them, Corliss Lamont. He deplored the artificially induced anti-Communist hysteria which still prevails in the U. S., shaping our foreign policy and eroding our own democracy. Corliss Lamont was intrigued with the concept of a planned economy guaranteeing full employment and equitable access to health care and education, and in the interest of human dignity wanted to see the "great experiment" succeed. But if Socialism has failed, what of Capitalism? Capitalism fails to honor its own workers, fails to nurture the new generation and the powerless, fails to protect and safeguard our one and only human habitat, and creates without conscience, death-machines to sell to the fearful. The ideal of valuing people over profits is a long-range wisdom which will re-invent itself as governments try to deal with the societal problems emanating from the almighty profit motive."

Father and Son at the same podium in support of the Soviets!

Corliss Lamont's participation in support of Socialist ideals over the years never wavered, even though he suffered accusations from Joseph McCarthy and insults from his philosopher peers. In 1941 at Madison Square Garden in New York City both Corliss Lamont and his Father, Thomas W. Lamont, a J.P. Morgan partner, spoke on the same podium in behalf of American Soviet Friendship. This was doubly supportive, in that an "Ambassador" from Wall Street was acknowledging the need for help of the Soviet Union while publicly endorsing his own Son's pro-Socialist stance.

Corliss Lamont, throughout his full lifetime, continued supporting Leftist ideals, especially his Leftist friends, and Leftist publications and their courageous and heroic informational efforts. Still on Corliss's agenda were many Socialist activities and even Communist Party appeals, for instance, but, in his role as a fiercely "Independent Thinker," he often voiced disapproval of some of their "bungling and inappropriate" organizational efforts, plus some ineffective, even counter-productive rather rigid and strictly top-down leadership and planning.

Socialism in the Sate of New York:

He identified more with the American Labor Party, even running as a Candidate for United States Senator from New York State in 1952 on the ALP ticket. Always, he continued to be extremely sympathetic and supportive to all who were being maligned and accused, even coerced and intimidated, during the height of the fearful, reactionary anti-Communist hysteria in the United States.

Most Americans know nothing of the fact that in 1920 five members of the Socialist Party were elected to the New York State Assembly, but were expelled on the grounds that as members of the Socialist Party, they were, as the report of the Judiciary Committee put it, part of "a disloyal organization composed exclusively of perpetual traitors." These members were Louis Waldman, who had also run on the Socialist ticket for Governor, Samuel Orr, Charles Solomon, August Claessens and Sam Dewitt. This case was brought before the Supreme Court, and the five members were ultimately permitted back into the Assembly. One accusation stated that they were "little Lenins, little Trotskys in our midst." A quite conservative Republican, Charles Evans Hughes, was derided as a possible "parlor pink" himself, for voting against their expulsion.

Again, in the words of Corliss Lamont:

We should not forget, either, that the defenders of the *status quo* always tend to minimize the amount of violence which is implicit in the functioning of the ordinary capitalist state. Without repeating my story of extra-legal violence on the part of government officials and of international war on the part of whole governments, I want to call attention to the fact that coercion or the threat of it, on behalf of certain socially recognized purposes, has been a necessary element in every state that has ever existed. The majesty of the law is only a shadow unless there stands behind it the physical power of enforcement. And the Marxist theory is that the coercive power of the state has on the whole been used, and often very harshly, on behalf of the ruling class in the community.

Since radicals are in general idealists and, in the ultimate sense, pacifists, they have often played into the hands of the reactionaries, who are almost always hardheaded, realistic men who do not hesitate to use force whenever convenient. What Marx and Lenin and Stalin have taught the radical movement is that in order to succeed, or even survive, it must on occasion fight fire with fire and employ some of the traditional capitalist methods to defeat the capitalists. This does not imply the principle that the end justifies the means; what it implies is that *some* ends justify *some* means. Those liberals and radicals who have become disillusioned with the Communist dictatorship in the Soviet Union have in my opinion overlooked the fact that until we have a perfect society, we cannot expect to arrive at new social and economic forms through perfect methods; that until we have a perfect democracy, we cannot expect to bring about fundamental changes through perfectly democratic means. Communists and Socialists, who are in accord on most of the chief *ends* of Socialism, have disagreed primarily on the *methods* of attaining it."

Trying to insulate from a Barrage of "anti" propaganda:

When immersed in a movement, it is difficult to evaluate all criticisms from the "outside" for any grains of truth. One is apt to ignore such criticisms completely, as merely constituting anti-movement propaganda, thus it would seem essential for fervent adherents to simply disregard all unfavorable observations, even to steel oneself against such maligning, and to shrug off all caustic commentaries that will come to be seen only as blatant attempts by the "enemy" to undermine the effectiveness of the movement.

De-humanizing "the other"

Justification of use of brutal tactics or extreme measures seem always to abound; it doesn't matter which side of any struggle is using them. Witness the Gulag 1953! Witness Guantanamo 2008! The great cause, whatever it is, demands dominance! Enemies are almost essential to the cause! Demeaning, racial, religious or ethnic slurs help to dehumanize the other, and to focus attention on their "inferiority" or their "dangerous beliefs." Kill them before they kill you! State-sponsored violence can fan ethnic animosities, even hatreds, and can turn genocidal. Some brutality that is instigated, even covertly, against an alleged, illusory enemy by government or military, soon becomes officially entrenched and subsequently becomes a matter of policy.

Kill them before they kill you!

Some actions of the individual might seem a little more spontaneous in the heat of battle. When the passions are aroused and the adrenaline is pumping and you feel that your life or your cause is on-the-line; powerful issues are at stake; you do not hesitate; courage sustains you and enables you to do what is expected of you. Just think how this principle plays out in millions of situations. This is not the time to stop and think things over, is it? No way! What are you? A shirker? A coward? You don't desert your comrades or your cause! Your basic beliefs are threatened!

"Trained" to cancel our human connection

It is happening at this very moment in hundreds of places around the world. The efforts of our US troops in Iraq and Afghanistan, the retaliation of "insurgents" or "terrorists;" all these responses are determined by the circumstances in which one is immersed, and what one believes. How can we know the Freedom Fighters from the "terrorists?" Would I "take out" a suspected sniper who might, or might not, be firing on my unit? Would I shoot an intruder who might threaten my own children? Would I fire on a car that defied my authority and raced through my checkpoint, believing they were terrorists, learning too late it's just a family rushing to the hospital, or would I neglect "my duty" to kill, and let them pass? I grieve for all the victims of such a situation.

How to be a hero?

For my own part, personally speaking, there are many things that I would die for, but there is nothing on Earth that I would kill for. The very idea of strapping explosives onto one's own body for the purpose of killing others in a desperate valiant effort, believing fervently that it will "further the cause," is to my thinking, an act of total insanity. Giving one's own life to actually save others would be more understandable, and is an act that we could, under any circumstances, consider truly heroic. But to be so immersed in such belief that killing for the cause gives one heroic stature in the eyes of one's fellows, or in the approval of a deity that is believed to have the power to confer immortality or special privileges, is incomprehensible to me and most other Peaceniks.

The struggle to Humanize our Democracy

Someone always seems to suggest that you can't make an omelette without breaking some eggs. For creating breakfast, this is necessary advice. For creating a just and peaceful world the advice is a bit counter-productive, not to mention hypocritical. And, in the US for more than a century now, despite heroic efforts by hundreds of thousands of political and labor organizers and workers in behalf of justice, equality, freedom of speech, civil and human rights, many of whom have been beaten, jailed and killed, remaining defiant in the face of sometimes armed and violent over-reaction in opposition to their efforts, the struggle still continues. So much for democracy! Some say that especially in light of our "exporting of democracy" often at gunpoint to other countries, that the word should be pronounced, instead: hy-poc-racy. And with apologies to Emma Goldman, I say, if I can't vote for Socialist ideals in this country, you can keep your democracy!

Even today in 2008, as we are witnessing a presidential campaign in the US, trying to promote the ideals of peace-lovers in the face of war, and struggling to establish any true semblance of democratic process for providing continuity of leadership is tenuous. Both candidates promote the use of military might rather than the wisdom of statesmanship and differ only in where the troops should be sent. My sincere hope is that wisdom will prevail.

Making War for fun and profit!

The incongruity of using military might to further the progress of humankind, I fear, is absurd! You simply cannot foster Peace by making war! It's rather like sponsoring a sex-orgy as a fund-raiser to support a program that promotes chastity. You might have heard this paradox described more bluntly in street language. Some other crazy ironic juxtapositions pop into my mind. Never mind such creative advice as "Making Backyard Gardens for Fun and Profit." The corporate powers-that-be are more intent on "Making War for Fun and Profit." Invest in the military industrial complex corporations and make a killing! Be all that you can be! Join the Military; kill people with whom you have no quarrel and get your college education! Such absurdities as putting these two words together: "war" and "games," no doubt was originated to teach strategy in the various war colleges, but has permeated the general culture. Children, practice your eye-hand coordination skills now; learn to kill "the other" (whatever it might be) quickly, before it kills you; you needn't bother discriminating between friend and enemy, or right and wrong, just eliminate all threats immediately, the moment they appear, and be a winner!

Watch dogs? Lap dogs?

The nightly news on all channels promotes "The War" as sensation, glitzy excitement in a cheer-leading manner, all reporting from "embedded journalists" Even tolerating government bans on photo coverage of the coffins of our own war heroes returning home; never acknowledging deaths of innocent civilians, only "insurgents" or "the enemy-du-jour." At all costs to the public's Right-to-Know, truthful information is not consistent with the illusion that must be perpetuated in the patriotic American mind-set, especially to insist that Congress keep funding the war.

195

The message is always: "We ARE the good guys; and you'd better believe it! Fear terrorists, Muslims and immigrants!"

Who are the Good Guys?

In 1945 I was already attuned to a Universal Ethics, but still expressed in religious terms, as I hadn't yet learned that I am a Humanist. When upon hearing of the bombing of Hiroshima, I knelt to "ask god's forgiveness." I had already suspected that our reputation as the good guys might be flawed or had been sacrificed upon the altar of vengeance. I learned of our bombing, not just munitions plants, but the fire-bombing of civilian populations in non-industrial cities like Dresden.

So, where are we, as a nation, positioned on the stage of world leadership? You, Dear Reader, may have a completely different perspective on this matter. I have been participant and observer of activities at the United Nations enough to know that our position, as well as our reputation, tilts toward profit-making rather than protecting the vulnerable people of the world. This is not the stance of a promoter of Peace! The good people of this nation are unaware of the Peace possibilities that are squandered with our coercive participation in the forum of the United Nation's so-called "Security Council." This position is actually more the stance of a ruthless, conscienceless, chauvinistic, arrogant flexer of just mere muscle, rather than an exerciser of long-range wisdom, a plotter of strategy, a power-monger, a war-monger, un-heedful of all consequences to the rest of the world, unintended or otherwise. How shameful that Colin Powell was sent to purposefully deceive.

"Civil" Society versus Un-Civil sovereignty

The real need is real reform of the United Nations, in which the Security Council is disbanded and the General Assembly of the whole 192 nations will make decisions that are in keeping with the best interests of the majority of Earth's inhabitants, rather than the few. The now seldom-used Trusteeship Council Chamber needs to become the People's House, wherein Civil Society will discuss the issues that transcend sovereign borders and recommend solutions wiser than the dangerous power-posturing of the nuclear nations. The US must be reminded: it is a member of the family of nations.

Here follows suggested Criteria for United States Leadership

1. The simplistic concept of good and evil is not a proper focus for ethical world leadership; it establishes an absolutist, arrogant and reckless mindset for determining courses of action that have proven to be counter-productive to the well-being and protection of Americans and the citizens of other nations.

2. The pursuit of empire by vested interests, commercial and military, with visions of dominating Earth and Space, is not in the best interest of Americans or other nations, or even Earth itself, and will necessitate violence to enforce.

3. The United Nations' concept of "eliminating the scourge of war" by peaceful means, respecting the Universal Declaration of Human Rights, and upholding the International Criminal Court, all need strong United States' support.

4. The United States is responsible for unleashing the threat of nuclear annihilation; it must demonstrate by its own leadership to take the initiative to curb its own proliferation of nuclear weapons, helping to reverse an escalating "doomsday" one-upmanship.

5. The production of so-called "conventional arms" and other lethal instruments of war, benefits only the arms manufacturers, and must be brought under control, with the ultimate aim of phasing out such primitive means of pursuing objectives or settling disputes. Violence is not in the best interest of any of the Peoples of Earth.

6. The argument of "necessity" is invalid; basic logic dictates that one does not counter a wrong with a greater wrong, thinking to overcome it. If it is deemed to be wrong in the first place, by having judged it so, then it is an even greater wrong in the second place, to willfully proceed to do the same thing, or worse!

7. The American People are patriotic and proud of what they have believed to be their tradition of being "defenders of freedom." More and more, upon examining previously-secret historical documents, we learn US leaders have often been provocateurs and instigators of unscrupulous domestic and foreign actions. This is no way to uphold a democracy; this is more indicative of the very totalitarianism that we have been conditioned to denounce. There must be transparency. No secrecy in domestic and foreign policy.

8. The American People have allowed this patriotic passivity to cloud their collective judgment, and even when periodically aroused in massive anti-war demonstrations, they are rendered impotent in the face of the war machinery mindset. Worse, they are considered anti-American, non-supportive of "the troops," and even subject to arrest. This is intolerable and needs Federal Law.

9. The vested interest of corporations, including the corporate media, are complicit in this thwarting of democracy. The voices of the people, as well as potential candidates for public office must be promoted on non-commercial TV and Radio. The "airwaves" belong to the American People according to The Communications Act of 1934. UNTV must be carried on every cable station.

10. The anti-communist hysteria that has dominated US foreign policy for a hundred years, causing irrevocable damage to humankind, has run its course, and has become exposed as a frightened pose. The People will have their rightful share of the wealth. With education of the populace, religions of the world will no longer be able to wield such power over their adherents with extreme coercive and skewed notions of morality and immorality.

11. The American People demand ethical leadership on the world stage, and drastic change in the leadership at home. We need uniformly non-tamperable elections; the abolishment of the antiquated electoral college; 2-term limits in Congress to prevent entrenched power; the full restoration of our Bill of Rights; and the establishment of absolutely transparent and accountable domestic

and foreign "surveillance" systems that may collect appropriate data, but will have absolutely no power to execute actions.

12. The American People demand that care and relief be given to their own needs. The tyrannical banking, mortgage, and credit-rating systems must be curtailed. Universal Health Care and equitable access to all educational levels must be mandatory nationwide. Innovative new energy sources must be subsidized, and our infrastructure must be restored. The repression of alternative political parties and of collective bargaining and union representation must cease.

~ ~ ~

HUMANISM AND DEMOCRACY
by Corliss Lamont

Humanist principles demand the widest possible extension of democracy to all relevant aspects of human living. The Humanist conception of democracy naturally incorporates earlier contributions to the democratic ideal such as the guarantees embodied in the American Bill of Rights, and the stirring battle cry of the French Revolution, "Liberty, Equality, Fraternity." Also Humanists the world over subscribe to the internationally valid tenets of the Universal Declaration of Human Rights adopted by the United Nations General Assembly in 1948.

Democracy is of course a method as well as a goal. It is the most intelligent method of conducting political life, of carrying through social changes, and of settling disagreements in the realm of public affairs. The life of reason—the appeal to the supreme court of the mind for which philosophy stands—implies in its very essence peaceful persuasion through the free exchange and competition of ideas in the wide arena of social discussion. The philosophic ideal is the transformation of our bitter social and economic disputes.

As a minority position at present, Humanism must defend democracy on the grounds of both the social good and sheer self-interest. Only if the channels of opinion are kept open, can the Humanist viewpoint hope to win the respect of a majority of thinkers in the nation and the world.

A true democracy welcomes differences and disagreements and cherishes, as a creative force in society, minority criticisms of existing customs and prevailing patterns of thought. The democratic spirit is not dogmatic, for it recognizes the value of constant challenges to basic assumptions.

The crackpot may turn out to be the trailblazer; the genius usually starts off as a dissident minority of one; and many outstanding leaders of the human race spent much of their earlier life in a jail or prison camp.

Humanism, then, urges complete democracy as both an end and a means; and insists that the idea of democracy has great Platonic dialogues carried on in legislative bodies and the organs of public opinion—dialogues, however, that in due course have a definite outcome and therefore do not end as inconclusively as most of those in which Socrates took part.

Humanism's support of the democratic way is a matter of both idealism and realism. To quote Professor Reinhold Niebuhr's epigram, "Man's capacity for justice makes democracy possible; but man's inclination to injustice makes democracy necessary." Democracy is a comparatively new thing in the world; and a very radical thing. Violence, bloodshed, coercion, and war—both civil and international—are the old, traditional methods of resolving deep-going conflicts of opinion and interest. Such methods have been wasteful, in terms of human life and economic dislocation, beyond all computation. Often they have succeeded in curing one evil only by substituting another.

Since Humanism as a functioning credo is so closely bound up with the methods of reason and science, plainly free speech and democracy are of its very lifeblood. Reason and scientific method can flourish only in an atmosphere of civil liberties. Humanism envisions a republican society where Humanists and everyone else can express unorthodox ideas on any subject without risking persecution, prosecution, execution, exile, or loss of employment.

Here follows a relevant brochure published by Beth Lamont

Humanist Healing for the Woes of the World

Planet Earth, the home of all living things and life as we know it, is in mortal danger. Fundamentalist religious fanaticism, greed, and exploits of empire, have brought us to this brink.

The Humanist Philosophy respects and embraces the efforts of all caring persons, of all faiths, of all ethnicities, of all traditions, of all nations, who take responsibility, for trying to make changes to improve the perilous conditions of Humankind, working together to foster understanding among the diverse Peoples of Earth, working toward the development of a respectful, lawful, equitable, compassionate and care-taking Culture of Peace that most of Earth's Peoples long for.

Strangely, some beliefs hold to ancient notions of vengeful deities that champion one segment of humanity over another, giving rise to fears and hatreds, militarism, fascism, violence, vengeance, exploitation, inequities, and injustices that still abound, endangering our survival as a species, jeopardizing the lives of our children, grandchildren and all future generations.

I am concerned about this danger and, as an individual, I have the power to raise my own voice in protest. I value Life; I love my own Family and the larger family of Humankind. I revere the Human Species, and believe in the right to peaceful pursuit of individual and societal happiness. I pledge to support the ideals of a Culture of Peace, and will encourage others to do likewise. I, therefore, pledge to take responsibility to promote the following Human Survival Principles:

I, personally, and as a representative of my own ethical perspective, life-stance or faith, pledge to act with courage, in all ways short of violence, to renounce and thwart the various adverse forces that have gained the power to dominate Earth and its inhabitants. I renounce all systems of repression, whether by governmental or economic control. I support only systems that are in the best shared-interest of all of Earth's Peoples and of Earth itself.

I, personally, renounce violence and vengeance as an option to redress grievances for wrongs done to me, my people, or my ancestors. I pledge to seek justice and compensation, never before feasible, through pursuit of new lawful means, consistent with the recognized principles of the United Nations and the newly established International Criminal Court.

These new tools must be fostered and ultimately established, for all times, promoting the pursuit of justice in every village and in every community. No longer will there be impunity for perpetrators of Crimes against Humanity. There will now be justice in the Courts! I pledge to support this goal.

I agree that technology, medicine, science and biology must be harnessed to serve only the best interests of all Humankind, whether it be our means of communicating freely with each other in the pursuit of truth and democracy, and the sharing of information regarding our common interests, or for the creation of power sources that do not damage Earth's ecosystem or harm living things.

Biotechnology must not modify or claim ownership of Earth's bounty, and the benefits to Humankind in all of these areas must not be tied to a corrupt and capricious profit motive, enslaving the many and ignoring the most needy.

I pledge to work in behalf of the survival and best interests of Humankind right here and now, because I believe in the basic goodness of other human beings. I will willingly join with them in order to help to create a Culture of Peace, regardless of any known traditional beliefs that aspire to other worlds or any belief in end-times scenarios.

I will not allow my name or my belief to be used to endorse actions that are contrary to my own personal beliefs. I will not allow my faith to be conscripted or construed in order to justify support for actions that are harmful to others, such as seeking retaliation and vengeance, or to justify terrorist acts, or the making of war against alleged and illusory enemies, with whom I have no quarrel.

If my tradition aspires to a Heaven elsewhere, I will surely have earned my place in it as a Peacemaker. Meanwhile, I will do my best to help make Peace on Earth, and to keep my pledge in behalf of the Human Survival Principles. In doing so, I reach out my hand in respect for others of good will, showing that I hold no weapon or animosity, and expect that others will do likewise, in recognition that we humans are more alike than we are different.

These Human Survival Principles are logical and important to me and I will do my best to promote them.

~ ~ ~

The following essay is a blog post on our Human Values Web site, entitled:.... How Tolerant shall we be of other's Intolerance?

An abiding dilemma for Humanists who are in the "ecumenical" position of working closely with people of all faiths, is how patient and understanding we need to be in our relationships with the rest of the world. There is the especially perplexing dilemma of how tolerant to be of other's intolerance. An old and reliable admonition that flashes in my head like neon, simply states: Do not alienate those whom you might persuade!

Those of us who are working toward a goal with other dedicated activists, are often in the position of censoring our own comments so as not to blow away our colleagues. We understand so very well that the only way that this old world is ever going to improve at all, is through cooperation and respect among those of all beliefs, cultures, and traditions, so simply out of respect for these differences, we may find ourselves limiting our own exercise of free speech. I say to myself: Try not to criticize! Be constructive! You know, the old..."don't throw the baby out with the bathwater" routine. Do the Mommy-thing: encourage others to become aware and involved in the project or activity at hand. This is all well and good for the shared goal...up to a point!

But what can we say or do about those practices and beliefs that are completely beyond comprehension? How long to ignore or look away, or bite your tongue, and wish that you didn't have to know or feel this shame or anger. How can we contain our anger at those who refuse to acknowledge and respond to whatever "emergency" we may be dealing with. I picture some of us bailing frantically in our sinking ship, while some of our fellow passengers are outright denying that the water's even rising, and treat our concern with contempt, while still others feel there's no need for them to worry because god will save them. Yet we can't simply write-off those whose beliefs clearly endanger us; we share our sinking lifeboat with them! Not only will they not bail, some are even shooting more holes in the boat!

No wonder we get frantic and impatient! They've got to

come to their senses! How can we get them to come around to a more "logical" way of thinking? How can we get them to recognize the real danger that we're in, instead of their mistaken constructs of how-to, by ignoring or worse, exacerbating, deal with world problems? How can we persuade the powerful to relinquish a portion of their power? How can we intervene to stop the inhumane militarized mentality that prevails on this Earth? How to stop the bullying, hatred, murder, torture, ignorance, greed? Then, how to stop fear and hunger and homelessness?

Our expectations that those in power will recognize their errors and set about correcting the horrible mistakes that they've set in motion are continually dashed in disappointment. What a shock it can be to learn that those whose opinions you might once have valued, no longer meet your standards or your expectations. You can shrug off the stupidity of a stranger, but what an extra shock when a member of the clan or the club fails you. That really angers you; how could they be so stupid? Perhaps it's human nature for us to expect those closest to us to think and behave "normally" as we do; they, of all people in the whole world, should know better!

The principles delineated in the Humanist Manifesto say it all! What more is there to ask than respect for all human beings and life on Earth? So then, we're back to the issue of needing to respect our differences: a principle which is essential to our own integrity and our own code of ethics. What a paradox!

We feel the urgency for making changes, but this heavy responsibility is, indeed, fraught with complex dilemmas. When shall we be courageous and uncompromising? When shall we be patient and conciliatory? Speak-up! Shut-up! The ideals of freedom of speech and democratic participation are precious and need to be fostered and protected, but unless they get a lot of exercise, they're going to get flabby. We will no longer be able to protect these freedoms.

We who recognize this syndrome of self-censorship may remember that in our first declarations of independent thinking we drew negative responses, even shock or derision from our more traditional relatives or co-workers. We gathered courage over a period of time to begin to articulate the logic of our point of view more persuasively, and perhaps we learned that some even agreed with us in our Humanistic values. And what a joy it is to connect with like-minded truth-seekers! How delightful to find others who reject the so-called "authority" that has been thrust upon us, and who acknowledge that the universe is indifferent to us, and that moral responsibility is completely up to us humans.

From whatever source we draw our strength and wisdom, we know that it will take human interaction only, right here and now, for us to create our own purpose and our own Peace on Earth!

In the arrogance of my youth, I had pasted onto my old manual typewriter these urgent and altruistic marching orders: **Words that might help to persuade and promote Peace on Earth are trapped inside this machine! Get them out!**

There will be more discussion about these important issues and many other dilemmas in the next book that will follow this one: *Lefties Are In Their Right Minds - Part Two.*

~ ~ ~

Note: And now to resume with Corliss Lamont's own words :

Chapter V
The Road to Peace

1. *The Awful Malady of War*

To write about peace at all in these days might well be interpreted as optimism of the most unrealistic variety. As I start this chapter (March, 1939) Adolf Hitler and his Nazi legions are on the move in Eastern Europe. Within the short space of two weeks they have annexed Memel and the greater part of what was once the free, proud state of Czechoslovakia. No man can tell what another day will bring forth. Though the civil war in Spain, in essence an international conflict, has simmered down, Mussolini keeps the Mediterranean pot boiling and can be counted on to cause plenty of trouble in the near future. On the other side of the world, in the Far East, Japan and China are still locked in deadly combat. The war is likely to be long drawn-out. As it proceeds, the Far Eastern interests of France and Great Britain, the United States and Soviet Russia, are certain to become increasingly jeopardized. All Europe, all Asia, are in turmoil, And the fear of war and its horrors hangs like a black shroud over the peoples of the earth. Meanwhile the whole world feverishly arms and during 1938, as I stated earlier, spent at least four times as much on armaments as in the year prior to the outbreak of the Great War. The three aggressor states—Germany, Italy and Japan-—naturally lead the way, each of them devoting well over half of its national budget to military expenditures. The non-Fascist powers are straining to the utmost to meet the threat. Britain alone, in its enormous rearmament pro-gram, will have expended nearly $8,000,000,000 during the five, years from 1935 through 1939. Since it cannot make up this terrific sum out of its regular budgets, it is saddling its already heavily taxed citizens with huge armament loans. France and Soviet Russia are financing comparable programs. Even little Switzerland has been trebling its armaments for fear of aggression from the direction of Fascist Italy and Nazi Germany.

Nor does the United States lag in military outlays. For the

fiscal year beginning July, 1939, the American Government appropriated more than $1,600,000,000 for the Army and Navy, the biggest peacetime budget since the immediate post-War years. It constituted approximately 37 per cent of the total budget; but when we include pensions, the bonus, and interest and retirement on our past war debt, our annual tribute to the greedy appetite of wars is approximately 31 per cent of the annual budget.

It is clear that today's colossal armament programs are, in terms of economic waste, equal to or greater than full-blown wars in previous centuries. And if the armaments race continues on its present scale much longer, the capitalist powers of Europe and Asia will, even without a world conflict, find themselves in a condition of bankruptcy or close to it. Their unmistakable drift in this direction is meanwhile hastened by their suicidal efforts, again motivated by the war danger, to become economically self-sufficient. At the same time the threat of foreign conflict retards all sorts of reforms long overdue at home, not simply because there is not sufficient money left over from the armaments budgets, but also because the minds of whole peoples are anxiously intent on the international scene and because they fear that the readjustments involved in drastic social and economic change would weaken resistance to a potential enemy. So everything must wait until the war menace ends, which it shows no sign of doing.

I am not trying to prove the self-evident proposition that war is bad. But it may be well to refresh our memories on what the Great War actually cost mankind. While absolutely exact estimates are not possible, reliable and conservative figures inform us that from 1914 to 1918, 13,000,000 combatants lost their lives, almost three times as many men as were killed in all the major wars from 1790 to 1913, including the American Civil War. Due to causes directly connected with the Great War, 13,000,000 civilians perished, thus making a grand total of 26,000,000 dead. Among other results of this enormous death toll were 9,000,000 war orphans and 5,000,000 war widows. There were 22,000,000 fighters wounded, 7,000,000 of them being crippled, blinded or otherwise permanently disabled.

One powerful reason for the madness of post-War Europe, culminating at the present time, has been that so many of the potential leaders, the best minds and wills, of the belligerent states were killed off in mutual slaughter or returned from the trenches too physically or nervously scattered to take their rightful places of responsibility.

The direct financial costs of carrying .on the struggle on both sides amounted to slightly more than $186,000,000,000; but if we add the indirect costs such as property losses on land and sea, the decrease in production, and the capitalized value of the lives lost (at about $2,500 per person), the final total comes to $337,000,000,000. Statistics alone, however, cannot possibly .give an adequate conception of the unending series of ills that have flowed from the Great War, especially when we consider the long-range as well as the immediate effects.

Whoever is the victor and whatever the terms of settlement, the economic and political problems to which international conflict gives rise make no treaty of peace; when the soldiers and the diplomats go home, these problems everywhere go marching on. The far-reaching consequences of the holocaust of 1914-18 for both victors and vanquished—the huge burdens of debt piled up by the participating nations, the disastrous dislocations of complex economies, the bitterness and misery of the exhausted peoples, the unholy encouragement to the methods and morals of violence— will still be felt, directly or indirectly, for generations yet to come.

Fascist force was used against Ethiopia, Spain, China, Austria and Czechoslovakia. And not only was it foremost in exposing and opposing these acts of aggression; it also sent sub-stantial aid to the invaded Spanish and Chinese peoples, to the latter in fulfillment of its pledges as a member of the League of Nations.

I have often heard it said that the main reason for the peace policy of the Soviet Union is that it has plenty of territory for its present purposes. Now while it is certainly true that the U.S.S.R. is not land hungry, we should recall that the Tsarist Empire, one of the most imperialist, war-mongering regimes in history, possessed much more territory than the new Russia, which lost so heavily in the West after the Revolution of 1917; and that Nicholas II aimed to enlarge his domains greatly following the expected victory in the World War.

The point is that Tsarist imperialism, no matter how much land it acquired, was always hungering for more. But Soviet Russia, with its Socialist economy, has neither the need nor desire to expand, It has eradicated within its borders all those economic factors that make for war. Because the Soviet people as a whole own the productive property of their country and because they have abolished private profit-making, the possibilities of war-profiteering are nil. Because Socialist planning has put an end to capitalist crisis and has brought under its control the country's foreign trade as well as its domestic, the Soviet Union has been able to pass sentence of death upon the chief practices of war-provoking economic imperialism. Surely the most prejudiced Soviet-hater can see that from the point of view of sheer self-interest the U.S.S.R. most ardently wants peace. For the most important and pressing item on the agenda of Soviet Russia is the unimpeded building of Socialism throughout its vast homeland.

Surely, of all the evils that beset our tortured civilization, war is the most hideous and devastating. Its ever more awful actualities, paralyzing the minds even of those who view from afar, dramatically sum up and symbolize as nothing else can do the degradation and dilemmas of this age. But however fearful the horror, this is no time to throw up our hands in despair and abandon the struggle for peace, On .the contrary, it is a time to renew as never before our energies and our efforts; to seek out the reasons for past failures; to discover the proper cure for war by unraveling its true causes. The task is pressing; for unless we humans can put an end to war, war will most certainly put an end to us.

2. *False Theories of War*

Homer tells us that centuries before the flowering of Athenian culture and the imperial sway of Alexander the Great, the

Greeks and Trojans waged a terrible conflict over the wrongs done to a very beautiful and alluring woman by the name of Helen. But 1 have an idea that back of that famous Grecian campaign against Troy, back of the immortal exploits of Achilles and Hector and Ulysses and the others, there lay much more fundamental causes. And I also suspect that the Greek ruling class of that time, in order to arouse the ardor and fighting spirit of its warriors, tried to conceal the real reasons for the war by trotting out Helen, just as in our own day and age the ruling class has tried to camouflage its actual war aims by claiming that the fight is over that beautiful woman variously used to symbolize justice or Democracy or Liberty.

It is a commonplace knowledge that during the Great War the different capitalist governments invented romantic symbols of precisely this nature. And they likewise broadcast all sorts of other myths and propaganda tidbits for popular consumption, Both the Allies and the Central Powers alleged that they were fighting a purely defensive war to preserve the fatherland; that they were struggling to save culture from barbarians who would destroy it. Both sides concocted hideous and fantastic atrocity stories about the other; both played tip inherent national or racial superiorities in order to make it appear that God, or at least Nature, regarded their cause as just and their victory as necessary. The Germans carried this strategy farthest with their elaborately constructed theories of the Teutonic supermen. The British and French were not at all enthusiastic about such theories when directed against themselves; yet for a century and more they, too, had been using biological apologies of a like variety, which propounded the natural superiority of the white race and particularly themselves, in order to justify their imperialist exploitation of the colored and colonial peoples. The manifest lesson of the past is that if we are to be realistic, we must not confuse what the capitalist class persuades the people to believe about its policies, either in times of war or of peace, with the true causes and aims of such policies. Nor can we afford to accept at their face value the resounding rationalizations with which capitalists persuade themselves that they are the true saviors and redeemers of mankind. Individual men go out to fight for their country for a variety of reasons, ranging from the most intense sentiments of patriotism to the simple fact of being conscripted. But the reasons why capitalist controlled governments become involved in war are very different.

Among the other myths there is the one, disseminated by hardboiled militarists utilizing half-baked psychology, which attributes wars to something called "the instinct of pugnacity." Since this instinct is inherent in man, the argument goes, war must always remain inevitable. Furthermore, nature's great law of the survival of the fittest operates through this instinct. Now aside from the fact that in modern warfare the fittest from each side are likely to kill each other off, there is the fact that there are other and more intelligent criteria of men's ability than their prowess in fighting, and the fact that on the human level, at least, it is mutual co-operation that has the greatest survival value—aside from all this, scientific psychology does not recognize a separate and identifiable instinct of pugnacity. Men are moved on occasion by a variety of competitive and combative impulses, but the mode of expression that such impulses assume depends on the conditioning circumstances, including both environment and upbringing, They may find their outlet in the constant battle that Man wages against Nature in the wide realm of sports or in definitely anti-social activities such as commercialized gambling and violent crime. The point is that the many different sorts of impulse for which "the instinct of pugnacity" stands as a rough summary term have no single natural outlet. There is no more reason why these impulses should be expressed in warfare between nations, which is civil war in the great world community, than in civil warfare between rival groups within a nation or in warfare between city gangs or racketeers. And there is no more reason why they should be expressed in any kind of warfare than for men's impulses of self-preservation to be expressed in sun worship, human sacrifice and other superstitious practices to appease the forces of Nature.

Another common illusion as to the causation of wars is that which assumes they are brought on by what is known as "over-population." But as any competent economist will agree, the extent to which a country is either over-populated or under-populated is primarily a function of the economic situation, At the height of the Great Depression when there were 7.5,000,000 unemployed in the United States, this country, assuming an average of only two dependents for each of the unemployed, was over-populated to the extent of 45,000,000. In 1939 on the same basis, with 10,000,000 unemployed, we are over-populated by 30,000,000. Yet no one dreams of proposing that the U. S. A. should acquire more land to accommodate these surplus millions, since even the simplest mind understands that the real trouble is mismanagement of our economic resources and technical equipment, China, the largest country in the world next to Soviet Russia and with a population density one-half of that of "underpopulated" France, is nonetheless very much over-populated with, its 450 millions.

There is hardly a nation on earth which, if it had a rational economic system together with rational relations in the international sphere, could not adequately cope with present population figures. This is not to assert, however, that every country has that size of population best suited to its inherent resources. Of course governments which believe that their people are over-crowded could easily institute effective educational campaigns on the subject of birth control. But the truth of the matter is that the "talk about over-population is usually little more than a pretext for imperialist expansion. While one day Mussolini makes a speech about how the Italian people are being suffocated from lack of space, the next day he makes another speech urging all mothers to have more children and signs a decree imposing extra heavy taxation on bachelors. In Germany and Japan the same sort of thing goes on. As a matter of fact, even when these so-called over-populated nations have acquired extra territories, their teeming millions have not emigrated to them in any substantial degree. Back in 1895 Japan vanquished China in a short war and annexed the large and fertile island of Formosa. Yet the Japanese population there today is still only about 5 per cent of the total. In 1910 Japan annexed Korea, but today its nationals number hardly more than 2 per cent of the population, The same story has been repeated in Manchuria. The same story is also true of the African colonies which Germany and Italy acquired before the Great War. And this makes patently hypocritical the Nazi outcry for "living space" and for the return of the former German colonies to absorb an overflowing population.

Closely associated with the over-population fable is the claim on the part of Germany, Italy and Japan that they are poor and oppressed "Have-not" nations striving to obtain economic justice in a world controlled by the "Haves" This apology for the Fascist drive toward war, though it has the merit of bringing certain economic problems into the open, is nonetheless almost altogether specious.

As the Raw Materials Committee of the League of Nations reported in September of 1937, these countries, far from requiring colonies for basic industrial products, could buy all the raw materials they need were it not for their feverish construction of armaments. Not only do they put into guns, tanks and military planes,, wantonly excessive proportion of commodities which are the lifeblood of trade and industry; but they use up most of their foreign credits purchasing more and more raw materials for war purposes, General Goering tells the suffering German people that they must forego, butter in order that more guns may be manufactured; and then a little while later Adolf Hitler gives a fiery address demanding colonies for Germany in order that its people may have sufficient food!

But suppose that the "Have" powers,—Britain, France, Soviet Russia, and the United States—agreed to hand over peaceably to Germany, Italy, and Japan substantial colonial areas in various parts of the earth. Would this do away with, the threat of war? It would not, The colonies which the Nazis have been demanding as part of the price of peace, the imperialist Germany of Kaiser Wilhelm II possessed before the Great War; but their possession did not prevent Germany from marching to Armageddon in 1914. Has Italy become less warlike since seizing Ethiopia, and Japan since seizing Manchuria?

Just open your morning newspaper and see. Capitalist imperialism is never content; it has an infinite itch to expand. Were Britain, France, and Russia satisfied with their huge empires before 1914? They were not, When the war was over Britain and France were only too happy to add to their domains at the expense of the defeated imperialisms. And had Russia been able to see things through under the Tsar, it would have followed suit.

Even if what the so-called Have-not nations consider a more equitable division of colonies could be made today, it is not likely that general satisfaction would result or that many years would elapse before revisions were called for. Such a settlement could be made only on the basis of numerous compromises. And as time went on and the different capitalisms involved developed in their different ways, new pressures for expansion would come to the fore and a new inter-relationship of forces take place. What Lenin said in 1910 in his brilliant little book, *Imperialism,* holds as true as ever: "There cannot be, under Capitalism, an equal development of different undertakings, of trusts, and branches of industry or countries. Half a century ago, Germany was an insignificant country, as far as capitalist strength is concerned, by comparison with Britain. Japan was similarly insignificant as compared with Russia. Is it thinkable that in ten or twenty years' time, there will have been no changes in the relative strengths of the capitalist powers? Absolutely unthinkable."

While today the threat of the Fascist nation's, overshadows everything else in international politics, tomorrow it may be the aggression of a non-Fascist power or group of powers that takes the limelight. Thus, the theory of the Have-nots vs. the Haves is also misleading in that it pictures the Haves as being altogether peace-loving and Christian. Quite possibly, too, some of the colonies of England or France, awakened to national consciousness and stimulated to action by the revolutionizing influence of Capitalism itself, v/ill attempt, like the America of 1776, to cast oft the imperialist chains. In which case Britain and France, so long as they are controlled by the capitalist class, will respond, we can be sure, with all the force at their disposal.

The smug, self-righteous imperialists, repeating their unctuous platitudes about "the White Man's burden" would not have us too cognizant of their Unceasing exploitation of the colonial and semi-colonial territories in Asia, Africa, and Latin America. World Capitalism wrings its profits not only from the toil of the under-paid laboring classes within the various industrial countries, but also from the misery of economically subject peoples throughout the earth. At least half the population of the world, a billion people, live in the exploited colonial and semi-colonial areas. All of us who are citizens of the rich lands of the West, including radicals and the working class, participate to some degree, at least indirectly, in this crime of imperialist parasitism. And in all the chief capitalist nations the ruling classes, have long distributed part of the booty of imperialism to quiet and confuse the upper layers of the proletariat.

In the colonies as at home the foremost object of the capitalist is to make money. The welfare of the subject peoples, most of them belonging to colored races which he regards as "inferior," is almost his last consideration. Whatever wealth the capitalist is able to find or develop in the colonial areas goes primarily to enrich himself and not to benefit the land and the people whence he has extracted it.

The history of modern colonial expansion is one long tale of blood and terror, enslavement and impoverishment of native populations, from the time of the Spanish rape of Mexico and Peru in the sixteenth century to the latest sanguinary exploits of Germany, Italy and Japan. No capitalist nation, small or large, that has or ever has had possessions abroad can boast of clean hands.

Among the most iniquitous and injurious forms of present-day imperialist exploitation is the international traffic in opium throughout the East. One of the first steps of the Japanese Government in Manchuria and the conquered provinces of North China was to set up a monopoly to promote the trade in opium and its derivatives in these districts. The Japanese Government, however, prohibits opium smoking among its own nationals. It is to be observed in general that government opium monopolies in the Far Eastern territories under control of Great Britain, France, Holland, and Portugal sell prepared opium to the native orientals, but are sufficiently solicitous of the welfare of Europeans to forbid the sale of this commodity to them. Yet despite the long and scandalous story of imperialist stimulation of the opium traffic, westerners will still tell you that the oriental peoples are inferior because of their weak-minded addiction to the drug habit. The opium traffic has, to tell the truth, become one of the great vested interests of international Capitalism.

The liberation of the colonial countries from such an evil and from their long nightmare of oppression in general is something that lies entirely outside the purview of the Have-not vs. Have theory. For that theory, as the English writer R. Palme Dutt so clearly explains, "is built on the vicious imperialist assumption of the necessity and permanence of the subjection and exploitation of the colonial peoples, and finds the 'injustice' and source of conflict only in the non-possession of colonies by certain Powers, not in the colonial system itself."

A lasting peace, however, demands a just and democratic settlement among the nations of the earth. And that means the finish of the colonial system; it means a world order in which the principle of international democracy holds sway, with all countries, whatever their present status, living on terms of equality, freedom and friendship and not interfering with the legitimate and peaceful aspirations of one another. Nothing short of this can destroy the existing germs of war and insure the healthy sort of international environment in which no new ones can be bred.

3. *The Economic Causes of War*

It is the radical thesis that war and the menace of war will not end until their 'primarily economic causes, which are part and parcel of the capitalist system, are obliterated never to return. I believe that the history of war up till 1914, the Great War itself, and the course of international politics since the downfall of the Central Powers in 1918 all substantially support this conclusion.

Naturally, economic factors are not the *whole* story behind war; there are a number of *contributing* causes such as dynastic ambitions on the part of royal families, the influence of professional military and naval castes, the existence of huge and provocative armaments, the clash of opposing ideologies. But factors of this sort are not sufficient either separately or together to bring about war: in my opinion at least 80 per cent of the story remains economic, meaning in this connection largely the attempt to make up for domestic deficiencies in the way or gold, raw materials and, above all, purchasing power as embodied in markets.

To quote one of our most conservative and respectable economists, the late Professor E. R. A. Seligman of Columbia University: "if I read history aright, the forces that are chiefly responsible for the conflicts of political groups are the economic conditions affecting the group growth." And he goes on to say: "The great wars of the seventeenth and eighteenth centuries, fought in order to control the sea and to expand the colonial empire, all had in view the development of nascent industry on capitalist lines," In other words; all those wars between the growing imperialist powers, between the English and the Spanish and the French and the Dutch and the rest—conflicts which the accepted history books not so long ago pictured mainly as quarrels between rival dynasties—all those wars were economic in their roots. If we go back to ancient times and consider the wars between Egypt and Assyria, between Greece and Persia, between Rome and Carthage, We see that the same thing is true. And I feel certain, also, that the even earlier struggle between the Greeks and Trojans had its basis in hard, unromantic economic fact.

Turning to the origins of the First World War, we find general agreement on the fact that the assassination of the Archduke Ferdinand of Austria-Hungary at Sarajevo was only the *immediate* cause, the accidental spark that lit the very ready and omni-extending dynamite fuse. Everyone might agree, too, that the fundamental cause was, in a general way, "uncontrolled nationalism." But this does not get us very far until we determine exactly what "nationalism" is. And what a careful analysis reveals is that modem nationalism is nothing more nor less than an expression of the economic status and political power, the habitual attitudes and prevailing ambitions, of the ruling class in any country, however qualified by internal opposition and however camouflaged by high-sounding doctrine. For the capitalist classes of the various countries war has ever been one of the mightiest instruments of national policy. British "navalism," for instance, no less than German militarism, was from the start the most sure and potent means available to the domestic capitalists for economic expansion and for directing an ever-increasing flow of the world's wealth into the home coffers. We have a special word to describe the capitalist nationalism that reached its zenith early in the twentieth century, when the partition of the earth into colonies or spheres of influence had been almost completed and monopolies and finance capital had risen to domination on a world scale. That word is imperialism.

When German patriots before the Great War waxed warm over the subject of the Fatherland obtaining its rightful "place in the sun," they were either consciously or unconsciously expressing in grandiloquent fashion the wish of German capitalists for more territories to exploit in the accustomed imperialist manner. Not until the last third of the nineteenth century did Germany obtain unification as a nation and become a powerful capitalist state in the modern sense. By that time most of the choice and weakly defended regions of the world had been appropriated by Great Britain, France, Russia and Austria-Hungary; or were the properly of empires in their dotage like those of Portugal and Holland. In 1870 Germany robbed France of Alsace-Lorraine, with its rich coal and iron deposits, picked up some fairly worth-while territories in Africa, and got a foothold in China.

Its empire, however, seemed to its proud and ambitious ruling class "cabbin'd, cribb'd, connn'd" in comparison with the country's fast developing economic and military power. Of this undoubted power the capitalists of Great Britain, France, and Russia were only too well aware. Britain, especially, seeing the speed with which Germany had built up a powerful navy, a great merchant marine and widespread foreign markets, feared its economic competition in the international sphere. Russia feared the German program of economic penetration in the Balkans and on. through the Near East, centering around the idea of the "Berlin to Bagdad" railway and the slogan of "Drang nach Osten" (the Drive toward the East). The Tsarist Empire itself had long cherished the thought of expanding in this direction and held as its fondest wish the acquisition of Constantinople from the Turks. In the middle of the nineteenth century England and France had trounced Russia in the Crimean War to prevent this very dream from coming true.

In 1914 Russia and Germany's chief ally, Austria-Hungary, were also jockeying against each other for a superior imperialist position in the Balkans. Italy, too, though nominally an ally of the Central Powers, was jealous of Austria-Hungary's influence in the Adriatic Sea and longed to detach certain territories in that vicinity from the Empire of Franz-Joseph, Capitalist France not only nourished deep lying feelings of revenge toward Germany for the humiliation of 1870, but also, like England, greatly feared it as an economic rival.

The French, to be sure, wanted Alsace-Lorraine back on the grounds of sentiment; but more basically they wanted it back because of its rich mineral deposits and because its possession would bring them certain definite industrial advantages over Germany. The most conclusive proof that the Allied governments were the faithful servitors of collective capitalist greed on a national scale lies in the secret treaties which they concluded at various times during the war. In 1915 and 1916 the Allied Powers agreed that Russia was to annex all of German and Austrian Poland, Constantinople and the Straits, a large part of Turkish Armenia, and most of the land immediately south of the Black Sea; that France was to have Alsace-Lorraine and huge sections of the Turkish Empire; and that Britain was to appropriate the greater proportion of the German colonies and gain control of lower Mesopotamia. In similar treaties the Allies promised important territorial gains and spheres of influence to Italy, Rumania, Japan and Greece, Because, however, of the collapse of Tsarist Russia, the recalcitrance of the new Turkish Republic, and the restraining influence of the United States, the final peace settlements did not follow out a number of these earlier understandings for dividing up the plunder.

Versailles and the other treaties did put into effect a substantial proportion of the secret agreements and also added significant provisions of an imperialist nature. Germany was forced not only to yield valuable territory to Poland and Czechoslovakia, but to surrender its merchant fleet to the Allies and the United States, to permit French exploitation of the rich Saar basin for fifteen years, and to agree to pay reparations tribute in the staggering total of $31,500,000,000, According to Allied estimates Germany never paid more than $5,500,000,000 of this amount. But the crushing terms imposed upon her were clearly designed permanently to end the threat of successful economic competition with the capitalisms represented by the Allied Powers, It is indisputable that wiser and more generous statesmanship on the part of the Allies, a more equitable and far-reaching Treaty of Versailles, could have done much to establish a more stable post-War world. But we might as well recognize that it is not in the nature of things, and especially not in the nature of international Capitalism, for countries seeking economic gain and winning a long and devastating war to deal, over-gently with those whom they have conquered.

Had Germany and Austria-Hungary been triumphant in 1918, they would in all probability have imposed an even more humiliating and hate-provoking settlement on the Allies than the Allies did on them. In the Draconic treaties which they crammed down the throats of defeated Russia and Rumania everyone saw how overweening were the imperialist ambitions of the Central Powers. One does not have to be any kind of radical or Socialist or Communist to hold that the underlying reasons for the First World War Were economic. Plenty of liberal historians and economists take this same view. In a well-known speech in 1919 one eminent person in public life made the following statement: The real reason that the war we have just finished took place was that Germany was afraid her commercial rivals were going to get the better of her, and the reason why some nations went into the war against Germany was that they thought Germany would get the commercial advantage of them. This war, in its inception, was a commercial and industrial war. It was not a political war.

Was this Lenin speaking, perhaps, or Eugene Debs or some other radical leader? It was not. It was President Woodrow Wilson of the United States. Though Mr. Wilson was referring to the European origins of the conflict, this statement nonetheless looks passing strange when compared with his idealistic message to Congress in 1917 calling for the entrance of the United States into the war in order to save civilization and make the world "safe for democracy," with scarcely a word about America's economic stakes. As everyone knows, President Wilson had a passionate fondness for rhetoric and was one of the most effective slogan-makers who ever entered American public life. Moreover, he was the head of a Government which had to arouse sufficient enthusiasm in its people to win the greatest war of all time. But regardless of these considerations, is it reasonable to conclude, in view of the fact that the Allied Powers were fighting for primarily economic reasons, as asserted by Mr. Wilson himself, that the United States went to war in 1917 entirely apart from motives connected with trade and commerce? I do not think so.

In the very first stages of the Great War it became apparent, since Britain and its associates controlled the seas, that if America, apart from all sentimental considerations, was to do business with any of the belligerents, it would have to be with the Allies. And a very big business indeed it did do with them, for almost three years prior to its own participation in the struggle. During all this time America was the chief market of supply for the Allied Governments, which spent billions of dollars here purchasing munitions, food and other commodities necessary for the conduct of the war. As part of the financing of these vast purchases the British and French Governments floated loans in the U.S.A., through J. P. Morgan &Co., which totaled $1,550,000,000 up until America's entry into the war in April, 1917. These two governments pledged American stocks and bonds mobilized from their own citizens as security against approximately two-thirds of the loan total. The bulk of the loans were undoubtedly distributed far and wide throughout the regular American investment community and were not held to an unusual degree by banks and bankers. Moreover, the purchases which the Allies were able to make through the proceeds of these loans—as, indeed, their huge purchases in general—were of immense economic advantage to business of all types throughout the United States.

As my father, Thomas W. Lamont, a Morgan partner during the war years, writes in his biography of Henry P, Davison, another partner: "During this two-year period, roughly from the spring of 1915 to the spring of 1917, almost every department of American industry .and commerce was stimulated by the business proffered by the Allied Governments." Mr. Lamont goes on to say: "It was almost a romantic story,—that of the Allied purchases in America: how from small beginnings they grew in an orderly way to the great totals that manifestly spelled such high degree of prosperity for American agriculture and industry, and that brought increased wages to the workingman; how the favorable effect of these purchases of all sorts of farm products and of manufactures spread and reached even the remote corners of the country."

In another place in his book Mr. Lamont, speaking of the Anglo-French loans, states: "It was manifestly to the distinct advantage of the American community to extend credit on such a scale to the Allied Governments as would enable the latter to continue their enormous purchases of American grain, cotton, copper, steel, leather, and other products." Undoubtedly so. And if this was true in 1915 and in 1916, it was also true in 1917 when the Allies were becoming so hard-pressed that probably America's support as an out-and-out belligerent could alone save them and guarantee continuance of their purchases. Mr. Walter H. Page, our Ambassador to England, undoubtedly expressed a thought quite widespread in highest circles, when he cabled President Wilson a month before the American declaration of war: "The pressure of this approaching crisis, I am certain, has gone beyond the ability of the Morgan financial agency for the British and French Governments. It is not improbable that the only way to maintain our present pre-eminent trade position and avert a panic is by declaring war on Germany."

The point which I am driving at is that by the spring of 1917 it was not just an inside group of international bankers or a small coterie of big munitions manufacturers, but the entire business enterprise of America, agriculture as well as industry and finance, which had a tremendous stake in the solvency and the victor of the Allies. Here, in the country-wide capitalist involvement in the lucrative war trade, is where I see the fundamental, economic motivation for America's finally taking up the sword. Bankers, munitions makers, industrialists, farmers, ambassadors, politicians, journalists, writers and even so-called liberals all did their share in bringing about this result. And whatever other factors contributed to America's joining in the Great War, I am certain that we would never have done so if it had run counter to our basic economic interests at the time.

The official reason for America's resort to arms, the immediate reason, and what many Americans still consider the main reason, was the ruthless and unrestricted submarine warfare of the German Government. Yet while the natural human indignation of the American people over the suffering and loss of life brought about by the U-boat campaigns was deep and genuine, the respective policies adopted by the German and American Governments *vis-a-vis* those campaigns had economic roots. Germany was not interested in torpedoing ships, whether Allied or neutral, unless they carried supplies directly or indirectly useful to the enemy's war effort. And that is exactly what they did carry, including the S. S. Lusitania. In other words, it was the close economic relationship between the Allies and the United States that drove the Germans to the desperate recourse of unrestricted submarine attack. This attack on Allied and neutral shipping constituted a direct and serious threat to America's great war, trade. It was an open violation of "the freedom of the seas"; but what that freedom concretely meant under the circumstances was the freedom of the United States to trade with belligerent nations and the freedom of its citizens to travel across the Atlantic for business purposes. So again we come back to economics.

The most important factors of a non-economic variety contributing to America's participation in the war were the three years of pro-Ally propaganda, the numerous, heavy-footed German diplomatic blunders and our natural feeling of kinship toward the Allied countries: toward England because of ties of blood and origin; toward France because of a traditional friendship starting with La Fayette and the American Revolution; toward England, France, Italy, and—for eight months in 1917—Russia, because they were in form, like the United States itself, political democracies. Germany, Austria-Hungary and Turkey, on the other hand, the American people looked upon as despotic autocracies. But such feelings in themselves alone could never have drawn the United States into the world conflagration.

Like the planned propaganda that so exploited them, they performed a martial function only in conjunction with the more fundamental economic forces. Logically enough, I think that the economic interpretation also applies to the foreign wars fought by the United States during the nineteenth century, not to mention the Revolution and the Civil War.

The War of 1812 with England, the Mexican War of 1846, the many Indian Wars in the West, and the Spanish-American War of 1898 (in which humanitarian idealism was admittedly an important factor) were all waged for good economic and imperialistic reasons. And in the course of these conflicts America acquired one of the world's richest empires, stretching from the Atlantic to the Pacific, from the Great Lakes to the Rio Grande, and including colonial possessions and spheres of influence throughout the region of the Caribbean Sea and even thousands of miles away in the Pacific Ocean. In the same category, as parts of the imperialist game, were the numerous expeditions led by the navy and the marines to protect and extend American business interests in places like Haiti, Honduras and Nicaragua.

Particularly brusque and cold-blooded was the manner in which President Theodore Roosevelt managed to obtain sovereignty over the Panama Canal Zone for the United States. Everyone agrees that the world as a whole loses through modern imperialist war. Yet undoubtedly in the past certain national capitalisms have profited economically and politically through war; and no sure proof exists that they cannot continue so to profit in the future. There is no question that Prussia gained immensely in the War of 1870 with France, that Japan gained in the War or 1905 with Russia, that Britain gained—in fact, won the world's greatest

empire—in the many and bloody wars that it fought before 1914. Whether a war is profitable in this modern era all depends on the kind of war. A quick and relatively inexpensive victory, such as that of the Germans over the French in 1870 is of course what every nation hopes for when taking up arms. Though the Great War resulted in a long and unbreakable deadlock that impoverished all of the chief European participants, this experience by no means conclusively shows, as many commentators seem to think, that future struggles or another World War will follow the same pattern. Even if it could be demonstrated that wars are no longer worth while even for the victors, it still remains true that they can be most profitable for individuals or groups within a belligerent state. While America by its participation in the Great War ran up a debt of some $32,000,000,000, capitalist business here profited hugely from our martial adventure; and the war boom temporarily increased prosperity even among the rank and file of the population. In England, where the national debt due to the war rose to $12,000,000,000 more than in the United States, private war profits in excess of taxes and losses amounted, according to the late Viscount Snowden, former Chancellor of the Exchequer, to approximately $15,000,000,000. Of the $186,000,000,000 total of direct expenditures for the waging of the Great War, an enormous proportion went to swell the profits of businesses furnishing to the different governments all the varied materials required by armies, navies and air-fleets.

All this is not to deny that there are forces within Capitalism which, in their limited way, have made for international peace. During the nineteenth century and the first decade of the twentieth, capitalist economic internationalism took considerable strides. International economic agreements in the form of trusts and cartels sprang up here and there; finance capital extended its influence and. operations over the whole earth; international trade and transport reached new highs and drew the various countries more closely together. Imperialism itself is quasi-international in spirit and can impose temporarily the peace of conquest. But the war-making factors in Capitalism, the intense economic rivalries of the more powerful nationalisms and of the nationalisms become imperialisms, far outweighed the peacemaking factors and dealt the latter their death-blow in the Great War.

Today international antagonisms are far deeper and more widespread than in 1914. Despite this fact, certain capitalist theoreticians have recently broached the fond notion that beyond our present trials and tribulations lies a period of "ultra-imperialism" in which a political federation of great powers and an economic structure of international trusts will bring an end to war, John Strachey effectively punctures this babble of an idea when he states that if Capitalism "leads to the peace of world monopoly at all, it does so by a series of the most gigantic and devastating wars between the great monopolist groups, and the nations which they own. It leads only to a desert peace, established by some victor empire after the last supreme war of the world."

The economic interpretation of war that I have been trying to elucidate does not include the naive thesis that the capitalist class in most countries today goes about secretly plotting inter-national conflict. The majority of capitalists throughout the world feel that large-scale modern war has become such a frightful Juggernaut of ruin and revolution that it no longer constitutes one of the better business risks. And they are well aware that their own children and relatives may get killed and wounded in the fighting and that they themselves may meet death in some terrific air raid.

Yet the fact is that war is almost as ranch as integral part of the capitalist system as the cycle of boom and depression. Now the capitalists do not want economic depressions. What happens is that they drift into them, since they cannot prevent the occurrence of phenomena which are inherent in our present economic order. In somewhat the same haphazard manner most capitalists and the nations they control drift into Armageddon. Let me be frank. So deep-going are the roots of war in Capitalism and so far-reaching are the contradictions of the system, that even radicals in capitalist countries find great difficulty in following, in every aspect of their existence, a course which consistently makes for peace and discourages war.

Though it is true that certain munitions manufacturers have been and are consciously active in fostering war and provocative armaments, I would not say that most armament-makers are actually against peace and in favor of war. What they are in favor of is selling their wares; and since in the present state of the world someone is sure to make money from munitions, they figure that they might just as well cash in on the job themselves. When a government puts in an armaments order they are naturally glad, because armaments is their business. Thus the producers of munitions are primarily concerned with the fact that they are engaged in a legitimate means of livelihood; and if the armament business happens to help pave the road to war, they feel that that is hardly their fault.

This matter of armaments indicates the tragic dilemma of the entire capitalist class: all capitalists, no matter how worthy their motives, must in their characteristic economic activities do things which, though somewhat more indirectly than in the case of the munitions-makers, definitely sow the seeds of war. Consider the question of tariffs. Many capitalists, sincerely opposed to war and intelligent enough to know that the high tariff system is an all but impenetrable obstacle in the way of international peace, are nevertheless constrained in their capacity as private businessmen to acquiesce in this fundamental cause of war. They will even sit on the Board of Directors of corporations the profits of which depend in some measure on the tariff system and which carry on propaganda for the maintenance or raising of current duties. And never, never will their minds come down to real bed-rock and recognize that the competitive economic nationalism which tariffs represent is simply the expression on a national scale of the competitive economic individualism which is the motive-power of the capitalist order, I have granted that many individual capitalists honestly desire international peace. This should not lead any reader, however, to overlook the fact that there is a considerable section of the capitalist class which frankly and consciously supports war and the threat of war as a means of attaining certain economic and imperialist ends. In the world of today this group is made up chiefly of those Fascist-minded gentlemen who either give their direct allegiance to the aggressor governments of Fascism or collaborate with them in their efforts to make the rule of blood and iron supreme in all parts of the earth.

4. *The Fascist Menace*

In all the tumult and the shouting over the Fascist onslaught on peace and civilization, we are likely to forget that economic causes lie behind the present international crisis just as behind that of 1914-18, It is assuredly no mere coincidence that today's three big war-making states, Germany, Italy and Japan, set out on the path of military conquest in the years subsequent to the Great Depression of 1929. The world-wide economic and political troubles of the past decade have aggravated all the existing forces making for international war. Internal and foreign tensions have multiplied on every hand; whole classes and nations have grown desperate; and in their desperation they have resorted to the most extreme measures, finally falling back on brute force as the way to solve their problems.

The Fascist governments particularly, confronted with increasingly unstable economic conditions at home, have been anxious to divert the attention of their restive peoples from domestic woes to exciting and glamorous foreign adventure. When a regime can no longer provide its population with sufficient bread or circuses, then a great military crusade may temporarily stave off disaster; such a crusade can itself be considered as the necessary circus. And it is plain enough that if the governing castes of any capitalist nation feel that their control is on the point of crumbling from within, they will not refrain from precipitating even a general war as a final madcap throwing of the dice to keep themselves in power.

The militaristic ruling class of Japan started the imperialist parade of the thirties with its assault on Manchuria in 1931, continued later with the seizure of several provinces in North China, and enacted a grand finale in 1937 with outright war on the whole of China, What the Japanese capitalists mainly want in Manchuria and China proper is a sure and handy source of food and raw materials, a market all their own for the disposal of surplus goods, and an exclusive outlet for the profitable investment of capital. They also hope to set up undisputed Japanese dominion over the Far East by incorporating large blocks of rich Chinese territory within the Empire, by erecting a solid barrier against the spread of Soviet economic and political influence, and by squeezing out the commercial interests of the three great Western democracies.

In 1935 and 1936 came Fascist Italy's invasion and annexation of the Ethiopian Empire, when Mussolini's legions, opposing a primitive and ill-armed people with the latest and most efficient machine guns, tanks, bombing planes and poison gases swept through to easy victory. The complete pacification of the country, however, has been proving a most formidable task. The primary aim of the Duce and his capitalist henchmen was to obtain for exploitation the valuable raw materials of Ethiopia, especially the large oil deposits it was reputed to have. Secondly, they desired this colony as a base from which to threaten the Suez-Red Sea lifeline of Britain to India and the Far Ease. And, thirdly, they were anxious to bolster up the dwindling prestige of the Fascist state.

The behavior of Nazi Germany in Central Europe likewise can be understood only when seen in relation to the economic background. One of the cardinal factors in Hitler's rise to power in 1933 was the misery and unrest of the German population during the Great Depression. And economic considerations have played by far the largest role in the policies followed by the Nazi Government since; it first took over the state. Since, as every student knows, the economic stresses and strains within the Third Reich have grown by leaps and bounds, it is quite natural that the dominant Nazi-capitalist elements should try to ease the pressures through outward expansion. Hitler himself in a speech early in 1939 cried out that his country must "export or die."

The Nazis annexed Austria, to be sure, partly because they wished to unite its German-speaking population with the Reich. But they also had a heartfelt yearning for its timber and its gold reserve, its manpower and the beauties of its strategic geographical position—all of which could be used for further imperialist ends. By the spring of 1939 conditions had so deteriorated within hard-pressed Germany that Hitler, in spite of the riches he had plundered from the Jews, needed some more quick booty. This he obtained in large quantities when he seized Czechoslovakia according to his regular routine of bluff, blackmail and brigandage. And in addition he got control of the great Skoda munitions works and of very considerable material resources of a permanent nature.

To think that calling the Nazi Chancellor a "madman" gets to the bottom of the problem is equivalent to the superstitious practice of ascribing human ills to the malevolent activity of a Devil. Hitler is no madman, but on the contrary, the very able representative of a particularly reactionary and brutal plutocracy, led by the armament capitalists, which is hell-bent on gambling for the economic hegemony of Europe and the world, even at the cost of drenching the whole earth in blood and even with the definite possibility that it will be digging its own grave beneath the crashing pillars of the temple. After all, the motto of the capitalist class in every nation is "Rule or ruin." And if Hitler is crazy, he is crazy only in the same degree and manner as the German capitalist system that produced him. We can never afford to forget that Fascism is a form of Capitalism.

What those two faithful friends, the dictators of Germany and Italy did together in Spain was in some respects most enlightening of all, as to the mind and morals of Fascism. In the summer of 1936 a group of Spanish army officers and reactionary capitalists, advised and aided from the outset by Messrs. Hitler and Mussolini (both of whom later openly boasted about it) started a rebellion against the legitimate, democratically elected and moderately reformist People's Front Government of Spain. There is no question that the Loyalist Government could have quelled the revolt in short order had it not been for the assistance that General Franco, the Fascist leader, received from Germany and Italy. Throughout the nearly three years of civil war the two major Fascist Powers provided him lavishly with munitions, airplanes and technicians; transported to Spain a combined army of more than 100,000 men for his support; and co-operated in the blockade of the Loyalists by sending to Spanish waters warships and submarines, the latter of which sank neutral vessels at will until nine of the nations affected instituted an anti-piracy patrol.

Moreover, all this help from Mussolini and Hitler, which eventually carried the day for Franco, was in complete and cynical violation of the Non-intervention Pact into which the Great Powers of Europe entered during the early days of the revolt. Only when the extent of German and Italian intervention had become a world scandal did Soviet Russia and France put into effect substantial counter-measures and only then did the anti-Fascist volunteers' start flocking to Loyalist Spain from the ends of the earth to form the famous International Brigades. Unfortunately the United States, by invoking its very un-neutral Neutrality Act and imposing an embargo on military supplies to both sides in Spain, collaborated with the other democratic nations in strangling the Spanish Republic, which was fatally handicapped in the purchase and delivery of munitions from abroad, though Franco and his Fascists got everything they needed from their foreign allies, Time and again the representatives of Loyalist Spain at the League of Nations rose to protest the outright invasion of their country by the Fascist Powers, but they received scant support except from the delegates of. Soviet Russia and Mexico.

Indeed, the attitude of foreign capitalists in the so-called democracies toward the Spanish imbroglio was one of the most disgraceful things in the entire situation. For years the upper classes of America, England and France had asserted that they were for democracy and opposed to violence and revolution; yet when a Fascist revolt broke out against a democracy which they feared had some radical intentions, they suddenly found themselves in favor of revolution of the bloodiest variety. For years they had made loud protestations of their desire for peace; yet when the Italian Fascists and the German Nazis dispatched all the engines and materials of war for the subjugation of Republican Spain, these noble-minded capitalists readily excused any and all acts on the part of the aggressor governments. Their hypocrisy, however, was fully matched by their folly; for unquestionably the Spanish triumph of international Fascism gave a far-reaching stimulus to aggrandizement against the democracies and much strengthened the Rome-Berlin axis by creating for it a new partner, committed like its big brothers to the principles of war and violence.

Similarly shortsighted has been the covert encouragement that an number of influential foreign capitalists have exerted on behalf of a Japanese victory over China, Some of these businessmen, particularly in the United States, are motivated by their economic ties with Japan; others feel a real kinship with the Japanese aristocracy. Some think that Japan, cramped for space on its little islands, has the right to expand like Britain of yore; all profess to see a red star or pink rainbow in the ascendant over China and fear that the defeat of Nippon would mean the downfall of Capitalism and the rise of Sovietism in the Far East.

No one should be surprised that a sizable proportion of those same capitalist elements who have previously been friendly toward Fascism in Europe should feel favorably inclined toward the Tokyo extension of the Berlin-Rome axis, no matter what this implies in condoning aggression and barbarity. The Fascist governments all claim that their military actions are on behalf of the great and holy cause of halting the spread of Communism.

Thus the Japanese have constantly attempted to excuse their robberies on the mainland of Asia by conjuring up the Communist bogey. Yet up until recently the present Chinese Government was engaged in fighting the Chinese Communists with all the resources at its command. It was precisely the continued aggression of the Japanese Government that finally resulted in a truce and a united anti-Japanese front between the Chinese Reds and the Chinese bourgeoisie represented by Chiang Kai-Shek's regime. As a matter of fact, nothing could be better calculated to help bring about Communism in China and Japan than the disastrous economic repercussions that the present war is having in both countries.

So far as the Spanish situation is concerned, every impartial observer realizes that Hitler and Mussolini wished primarily to extend their spheres of influence, to obtain concessions in respect to the valuable mineral resources of Spain and to win a military ally and geographic bases—in the Pyrenees region, the Balearic Islands and near Gibraltar —with which to threaten France's rear and British communications in the Mediterranean. In one of his more indiscreet moments, Hitler, referring to the Third Reich's need for iron, imports, publicly stated:

"That is why we want a Nationalist government in Spain, so as to enable us to buy Spanish ore. And for the Italian Fascists to claim that they, sent armies into Spain solely for the high and altruistic purpose of fighting the Reds, is only slightly less absurd than if they had said that they invaded Ethiopia and Albania to save those countries from the influence of Moscow.

Let me momentarily grant, for the sake of. argument, that the Fascist triplice has been waging aggression for the sole purpose of putting an end to the alleged menace of Bolshevism. Can any sincere believer in peace take for a minute the position that governments are justified in making war on other governments whose forms they happen to dislike? If so, then the Fascist states will be justified in next hurling. themselves against the democratic nations, whose political systems they wholeheartedly hate and consider as only a step removed from Communism itself. In fact, the Fascists constantly talk about wiping out Communist "and similar regimes. To uphold war and armed intervention on such principles is equivalent to eliminating permanently the chances of international peace. Those who really wish for a warless world must make up their minds once and for all that individual nations have the right to determine their own destinies, whether in the direction of Communism, Fascism, capitalist democracy or anything else. I do not mean to imply that the Fascist nations would not go to war to suppress Communism. They would; and in fact they already have well-laid plans afoot for attacking Soviet Russia. Up to date, however, they have been using their anti-Communist slogans to cover up their felonies against non-Communist countries and to confuse world public opinion. Under the guise of a pact to oppose the machinations of the Communist International (the Comintern), the Fascist International (the Fascintern) has been extending its rule to nation after nation as part of a grandiose plan for world domination. Though not one single country has yet followed the example of Russia in successfully setting up a Socialist or Communist regime, the Fascist pattern spreads like a cancer to every section of the earth. And only the mentally blind can deny that the great and immediate threat to national integrity comes from the Axis Powers and their satellites.

That war which the Fascist governments, and perhaps other governments as well, may some day undertake against Socialism in its Soviet form will not be merely or even mainly a conflict motivated by ideology. It will be another call to arms the causes of which are basically economic. For it will be grounded in the capitalists' dread, lest the Soviet system so incontestably prove its superiority over Capitalism that the people of other lands will throw off the shackles of the present order; and in the capitalists' desire to bring back once more the rich expanses of Russia into the orbit of imperialist exploitation, either through the setting up of spheres of influence or through out-and-out annexation. The Soviet Union, on the other hand, will defend to the utmost its material resources, its economic interests and its Socialist system in general.

The Japanese imperialists have made no secret of their profound longing to take over the Far Eastern provinces of the U.S.S.R. Nor have the Nazis attempted to conceal their ultimate intentions toward the Soviet Union. In his definitive book, *Mein Kampf,* Adolf Hitler asserts: "We stem the eternal Germanic migra tion to the south and west of Europe and direct our eyes toward the lands in the East. If we speak today in Europe of new land and soil, we can primarily think only of Russia and its subject border states. Providence herself seems to point the way."

The new German War Lord enlarged upon this thought in a famous speech during the summer of 1936 when he shouted to a large assembly of his followers: "If I had the Ural Mountains with their incalculable store of treasures in raw materials, Siberia with its vast forests and the Ukraine with its tremendous wheat fields,. Germany and the National Socialist leadership would swim in plenty," Never in the history of modern times has the head of a state expressed with such brutal frankness his hopes of annexing extensive territories in a nearby and peaceful country.

It is not surprising that a number of capitalists outside of Germany should have felt that it would be wonderfully convenient if it were possible to appease Hitler and his Nazis by letting them carry through their project of expanding eastwards and incorporating choice slices of the Soviet Union. This sentiment is the key to much of the shilly-shallying in international politics during the past few years.

However annoyed American, British and French capitalists may have grown over the ungentlemanly behavior of the Fascist states, they have ever regarded Socialism as the arch-enemy. And the perfect solution for the capitalist classes of the Western Powers would be for Germany, Italy and Japan to concentrate their bellicose attentions on the U.S.S.R., deliver Soviet Socialism a perhaps mortal blow, and in the process exhaust their own fighting energies for a long time to come.

The non-Fascist capitalists have all along been terribly apprehensive over the possible collapse of Fascist Capitalism, fearing it would be supplanted by a Socialist system which would confiscate their investments within the Fascist nations and set a very bad example to the people of the remaining capitalist states. So, up until the Nazis seized Czechoslovakia, the Cliveden sets throughout the capitalist democracies were principally worried, not that their own countries would be defeated in war, but that the Fascist countries would be. As a corollary of this attitude they were extremely averse to having their Governments co-operate in any way with Russia on behalf of international peace. There have always been plenty of die-hards who hate Socialism and the Soviet Union more than they do war!

The brilliant idea of unloosing the wolves of Fascism against the U.S.S.R. played a large part in the settlement which Prime Ministers Daladier and Chamberlain made with Hitler and Mussolini at Munich in September of 1938. It did not work out well for two main reasons. First, the Nazis became so impressed by the very great economic and military strength of the Soviet Union that they decided they should seek easier prey in Central and Western Europe. Second, bourgeois public opinion in France and England finally awoke to the fact that the Fascist dictators really meant what they had been declaiming for so long about partitioning the French and British Empires.

It became obvious that whatever gains Hitler made in Eastern Europe would be only the prelude to his marching straight on toward Turkey, Iraq and India or to his turning directly, with vastly augmented resources, toward the West with the purpose of overwhelming the capitalist democracies. And it likewise became evident that Europe must take seriously even Mussolini's fantastic talk about re-creating the ancient Roman Empire and turning the Mediterranean into an Italian lake. When one of the Duce's leading newspapers justified the sack of Albania because it had been part of a Roman province in 250 BC, Frenchmen and Englishmen, who remembered some of the other territories Rome had held, at last began to sit up and take notice.

Finally, the ruling classes of Britain and France decided, though, with the utmost reluctance, to institute apparently genuine measures for resisting Fascist aggression, including the long negotiations for a joint alliance and peace front with Soviet Russia, These steps they took, not because of any ardent desire to defend peace or democracy or the rights of small nations, but because they realized that the British and French peoples would no longer tolerate the old appeasement policy and because they saw that their own economic interests were becoming gravely and directly jeopardized. Had the Chamberlains and Daladiers taken the trouble merely to thumb through the book, *Mein Kampf,* they could easily have learned what was in store without first surrendering Czechoslovakia and Spain to the enemy.

In spite of Herr Hitler's Napoleonic complex and his fanatical determination that Germany should dominate the world, we find that after all he has a big heart. For, though first making it clear in his book that in the "eternal struggle" between nations "all considerations of humaneness or aesthetics crumble into nothing," he tells us later that "the ideas of pacifism and humanity may be quite good after the supreme race has conquered the world in such a way as makes him its exclusive master. . . . Therefore, first fight, and then perhaps—pacifism." Hence, "Anyone who really and sincerely would desire the victor of the pacific idea, should back by every means the conquest of the world by Germans." This indeed shows that the Fuehrer has thought long and deeply and has even studied history; for what he evidently intends is a Pax Germanica along the lines of the old Pax Romana.

It is to be noted that Hitler makes no room in his unique world Utopia for forms of national Fascism other than German. This omission gives a clue to what would happen if the present Fascist bloc were victorious in an international war. Its members, like thieves in general, would eventually fall out among themselves and fly at one another's throats. Since intense nationalism and imperialist aggressiveness are integral parts of both the Fascist creed and need, a world under the thumb of Capitalism in its Fascist uniform would be more than ever a prey to internecine struggle. And it is not unlikely that the first inter-Fascist war would occur when Germany and Italy started to quarrel over the spoils of conquest and their respective roles in the Danube Basin and the Balkans. Benito Mussolini, like his co-dictator, from time to time has also expressed with admirable clarity the true Fascist attitude toward war, "Three cheers," he wrote in 1914, "for war in general. War, a physical and spiritual fact combined, cannot: fail to exist in a world which has always seen it and always will." In speeches more than twenty years later the Duce repeatedly affirmed this position as a basic tenet of Fascism. "War," he asserts, "is to man what maternity is to woman. From the philosophical and doctrinal viewpoint I do not believe in perpetual peace. Only a sanguinary effort can reveal the great qualities of peoples and the qualities of the human soul," Again: "We reject the absurdity of eternal peace, which is foreign to our creed and our temperament," It was only natural that Benito Mussolini's eldest son, Vittorio, in telling about the Ethiopian campaign, should call, war "the quintessence of beauty." In his book, *Flights on the Ethiopian Plateau,* Vittorio Mussolini recounts with glee how much he enjoyed bombarding the defenseless Ethiopian villages, "I had never seen a fire in my life," he writes. "Every time I used to run after a firemen's car to see one, I was chased away. Thus, perhaps because someone had learned of this unsatisfied desire of mine, one day an order was issued to bombard the territory of Adi-Abo with incendiary bombs only. I do not think there existed any more important reason for this order. We received the order to repeat the bombardment, It was a pleasure." Like his father, young Vittorio has worked out a general philosophy of war. "War," he says, "certainly educates, I recommend it to everybody. I believe that every man must at least make one war. War for us has been a sport, the most beautiful and complete of all sports."

Naturally the Japanese militarists have not lagged behind their Western brothers in butchery and have tried hard to break the morale of the Chinese people through the method of unmitigated ferocity. Not even the Fascist aerial bombardments in Ethiopia and Spain have been able to match in horror those that the Japanese have let loose upon the civilian populations of Chinese cities. And recently the Japanese military even issued an order forbidding the

International Red Cross to send medical supplies to the wounded or food to the survivors in the bombed areas. The Japanese Government also has an extraordinary sense of humor. Shortly after its planes, raining high explosives and incendiary bombs on the city of Chunking, had killed some 5,000 Chinese in the most terrible air-raid in history, its representatives at the New York World's Fair released into the open sky 150 doves of peace to show the Japanese love for their fellow-men.

Undeniably the armies of the Fascist states have manifested a savagery till now unknown in modern warfare and have solidly established themselves as the world's most wanton Killers. But not forever will the peoples of the earth put up with these new barbarians and their philosophy of frightfulness. The heroic defenders of undefeated China and defeated Spain have given an example of what intrepid resistance can do. The Fascists can be stopped.

5. *The Cure for War*

I strongly believe that the only feasible way of meeting the current crisis in international affairs is through the application of the principle of collective security. This means that the peace-loving nations of the world stand together to take co-operative and affirmative action against aggression. The first step is an open pact of mutual assistance, either inside or outside the framework of the League of Nations, that puts every government on notice that any aggressive military move on its part against, any other government whatsoever in any section of the globe will immediately make it subject to certain definite and drastic penalties and bring into operation collective aid on behalf of the victim nation. The second step, in case of an act of aggression, is the imposition of economic sanctions on whatever country or group of countries are violating the peace. The third step, to be taken only when all other measures have failed, is to" put into effect military sanctions against the aggressor state or states.

The theory, behind the principle of collective security is that the threat of economic and military sanctions by an overwhelming majority of existing states would probably be sufficient to prevent war by making a potential aggressor afraid to go ahead. If nonetheless such an aggressor did go ahead, the aggregate strength of armed power against him would be so formidable that he could be crushed in short order. Moreover, the combined might of the peaceful countries would be so great that vast increases in armaments on their part would not be necessary.

A good example of how collective security would work is to consider what would have happened if the United States and other countries had put economic sanctions into effect against Japan when it proceeded to the invasion of China in 1937. Sanctions in this case would have entailed a complete financial embargo against the Japanese so that they could not obtain loans or credits abroad and a. complete embargo on the shipment to them of all war materials such as munitions, oil and scrap iron. Since the United States has recently been exporting about $200,000,000 worth of goods per year to Japan, primarily for war uses, and in 193S provided 57 per cent of her imports of essential war materials, our nation alone, through the proper economic measures, could probably fatally cripple the continuance of the Japanese military effort. When Mussolini invaded Ethiopia in 1935-36, the League of Nations voted to put into effect economic sanctions against Fascist Italy. Nazi Germany of course opposed this policy; the United States refused to co-operate; and France and Great Britain supported it with faint-heartedness, Soviet Russia was the only Great Power willing to go through with the sanctions campaign as originally planned. Hence the League sanctions soon faded away and only served to goad the Italians to anger and rally them around the Duce's imperialist venture.

Yet had a majority of the members of the League been faithful to their principles in this instance, the economic strain on Italy in the end would have been overpowering. There is grave doubt whether any capitalist government would ever apply sanctions on an effective basis, for fear that a temporary letdown or dislocation of business would ensue. For this reason the peace-loving peoples of the different countries must either bring enough pressure on their governments to make them take sanctions seriously, or carry out anti-aggressor measures on their own initiative.

One such measure is a consumers' boycott against imports from an aggressor nation, cutting down the trade balance of the aggressor abroad so that it is handicapped in getting foreign exchange to buy further supplies. The impressive results, particularly in America, of the consumers' boycott against German and Japanese goods show what can be accomplished along the lines of peaceful, non-governmental action.

The Roosevelt administration's imposition of a prohibitive 25 per cent duty on German imports following the forceful Nazi annexation of Czechoslovakia was the sort of "short-of-war" economic move that may help to bring an aggressor nation to its senses. In the same category was the American Government's denunciation, in the summer of 1939, of the 1911 trade treaty with Japan, which had enjoyed definite commercial advantages under the pact. Whatever private boycott movements are able to achieve, it is obvious that official action by a government, including within its possible scope all business transactions with an aggressor state, can be very much more effective.

I would be the first one to admit, however, that there is no assurance that the threat or application of economic sanctions against a warlike state will prevent its committing or continuing an act of aggression. If economic measures are unsuccessful in their aim, there is no guarantee, either, that even the prospect of military sanctions will serve to calm down a potential or actual aggressor who is perversely insistent on playing with fire come what may. Yet collective military sanctions against an aggressor are in the last analysis the only immediately practicable alternative to permitting gangster governments to ride roughshod over the whole earth, killing, conquering and annexing at will. And there is an excellent chance that the imposition of such sanctions on the part of a large group of states will at least doom the aggressor or aggressors to rapid defeat.

Though the ideal would be an agreement by all nations to

undertake economic or military sanctions in case of need, the sanctions method can be extremely effective if only a few of the big countries and a few of the little ones participate. It is most significant that when Prime Minister Chamberlain finally set about creating a stop-Hitler bloc, he had to fall back on the old League idea of collective security, though in a decidedly limited form. Again, while the ideal is for collective, security at once to include in it's scope the entire world, it may be necessary to apply it to one crisis at a time; to attempt to extinguish the blaze lit by the Fascists in the West before turning to the conflagration raging in the East. Of course Japan, as a member of the Fascist triplice, might well forestall this strategy by entering promptly into any general war precipitated by its German and Italian partners in crime.

The utilization of sanctions is not something that can be done lightheartedly. But when all is said and done about the dangers involved in sanctions, the fundamental question remains, How much are we willing to pay to stop war? For the prevention of war is bound to cost something, though its non-prevention is bound to cost a hundred times more. While conceivably individual nations, like individual persons, may rise on occasion above material self-interest, it is clear that modern states, whether Socialist or capitalist, will not enter into programs for collective security unless they are convinced that they will benefit economically thereby. It is the blindness of the capitalist democracies in discerning what is their true self-interest that has largely been responsible for their lukewarm or hostile attitude toward the principle of collective security. For an armament-saddled, war-ridden world will in the long run do far more harm to the capitalist system than any immediate losses from boycotts or sanctions if a sufficient number of nations do finally come to rely on economic and military sanctions and use them successfully against aggression. Such measures must nonetheless be regarded primarily as emergency stop-gaps in a world where the main economic compulsions toward war continue to exist. The whole international capitalist system still is ultimately responsible for the curse of war and the threat of it. Even so, with the development of international law and consultative techniques, it is possible today as never before to identify the aggressors.

And sanctions are assuredly worth while as a means of arresting the current Fascist onslaught, a goal which is unquestionably the most pressing item on the agenda of those working for peace. What course in international affairs should America follow in these perilous times? Most of our people are, I think, thoroughly disillusioned over what our country's participation in the Great War accomplished. There can be no doubt, either, that the geographical position of the United States, as distinct from some of its possessions, insulates it to a certain degree against the danger of aggression. This insulation, however, is relative and not, as some isolationists and pacifists argue, absolute. When one reflects that it is already possible to fly from the United States to Europe in sixteen hours, it is not difficult to see that the science of the not so distant future may well make deadly aerial attacks from the other side of the Atlantic or Pacific a comparatively simple thing. In the words of President Roosevelt, "Beyond question, within a scant few years our fleets will cross the ocean as easily as today they cross the closed European seas."

Then, too, there is the possibility of a warlike Fascist bloc, under the influence of Germany and Italy, coming into power in Latin America and challenging the position of the U\ S. A. in the Western Hemisphere, The victory of General Franco in Spain has given a strong stimulus to Fascism on the South American continent. And the Nazis are angling for military and aeronautical bases ail the way from Patagonia at the southern extremity of Argentina to Iceland in the North Atlantic. If, furthermore, the Fascist triplice should decisively crush the European democracies; the United States might well face the unenviable assignment of simultaneously repelling the Japanese fleet in the Pacific and the Italo-German fleet in the Atlantic.

Whatever the implications of geography, .that policy of international political isolation which many sincere workers for peace have been urging for the United States is to my mind utterly impracticable unless we also have international economic isolation. Our trade involvements abroad are so great that we could not attain economic isolation without throwing into reverse and indeed ruining vast sectors of our business life. Sooner or later a major war in any part of the world is bound seriously to affect America. Though an isolationist policy may keep us out of war temporarily, it will not do so permanently. And by yielding to the blackmail tactics of aggressor nations, the day of reckoning is merely postponed and made more catastrophic. "Keep America: out of war by keeping war out of the world' is one of the soundest slogans ever invented.

As President Roosevelt stated in his notable Chicago speech of 1937 against the aggressions and inhumanities of the German, Italian and Japanese Governments: "If those things come to pass in other parts of the world, let no one imagine that America will escape, that it may expect mercy, that this Western Hemisphere will not be attacked and that it will continue tranquilly and peacefully to carry on the ethics and the arts of civilization. There is a solidarity and interdependence about the modern world, both technically and morally, which makes it impossible for any nation completely to isolate itself from economic and political upheavals in the rest of the world, especially when such upheavals appear to be spreading and not declining,

"International anarchy destroys every foundation for peace. It jeopardizes either the immediate or the future security of every nation, large or small.." Mr. Roosevelt went on to say: "The peace-loving nations must make a concerted effort in opposition to those violations of treaties and those ignorings of humane instincts which today arc creating a state of international anarchy and instability from which there is no escape through mere isolation or neutrality. . . . It seems to be unfortunately true that the epidemic of world lawlessness is spreading. . . . When an epidemic or physical disease starts to spread, the community approves and joins in a quarantine of the patients in order to protect the health of the community against the spread of the disease."

I agree with the implication of the President's address that America has the obligation, both from considerations of self-interest and international morality, to participate in collective agreements and actions with other nations, not "to save democracy," but with the definite and limited aim of preserving world peace. Fulfillment of this obligation demands the immediate repeal of the present Neutrality Act which makes no distinction between attacked and aggressor nations. The obligation is binding even if it leads America eventually to take up arms. I do not think that "peace at any price" is a very noble sentiment; and I hold that our country can be faithful to its highest destiny only by contributing its full part to the peaceful advancement of mankind.'

There are those who argue that participation by the democracies in any sort of war, even one to curb Fascist aggression, is certain under present circumstances to result in Fascism at home. I confess that this argument sounds farfetched to me. While a war would undoubtedly mean a great increase in state controls and capitalist collectivism, such steps do not necessarily have to take the form of Fascism or continue after military activities cease.

Long before the more or less international crisis of today, I was in favor of the principle of collective security. In fact, the first thing I did after my graduation from Harvard, was to spend a summer at Geneva studying the workings of the League of Nations under the tutelage of my old law teacher, Professor Manley O. Hudson, who later became a Judge of the Permanent Court of International Justice at the Hague. In connection with the League, I had the opportunity of meeting many of the prominent international figures of the day. Of all those with whom I came in contact, the English Statesman, Lord Cecil of Chelwood, still stands out in my mind as the one with the most understanding and integrity. Year in and year out, Lord Cecil, though a conservative and a leading member of the .British aristocracy, has supported unyieldingly the principle of collective security and has opposed the fatuous maneuvers of his class to save Fascism and to isolate Soviet Russia at the expense of world peace.

For several years I gave considerable time and effort to the .America's entrance into the League of Nations and the World

Court. In so far as the League has stood for international peace and cooperation, for disarmament and collective security, it has always represented a sound idea; but in so far as it has stood, the enforcement of the Versailles Treaty and has reflected the imperialist ambitions of the various powers, it has actually been a factor in preserving the war system. Unfortunately, the basic contradiction between these two different sets of tendencies within the League weakened it and in the end well nigh ruined it. In addition, it was crippled all along by the absence of The United States, and during the greater part of its career, by the absence of Germany and Soviet Russia, as well.

Now most radicals condemned the League of Nations from the start as worse than useless. This was a bad mistake, I think, since the organization always had real possibilities for good. And when Soviet Russia became a member of it in 1934, a number of these same radicals felt rather embarrassed. There can be no doubt that the constant presence at Geneva since that time of a Soviet delegation, pledged to uphold without compromise collective security and the principle that :Peace is indivisible" and unafraid to name names and call bluffs, has had a wholesome effect on the deplorable international situation. The Soviet leaders thought that they might be able to reduce the chances of immediate conflict by working through the machinery of the League and using its meetings at Geneva as a means of educating world opinion, But they never had any illusions that the League, as it stood, it was an adequate instrument to abolish war in a mainly non-Socialist world. For the only certain path to peace is to make Socialism and the Socialist principles of international conduct predominant.

World Capitalism is quite clearly caught in the twists and turns of a descending spiral. Its national economic difficulties lead to international economic difficulties; these latter complications result in war or near war; war and the threat of war bring about an ever more critical economic situation; this stimulates further war; and so it goes indefinitely.

Capitalism cannot escape from its own nature, But there is a way by which humanity can escape from Capitalism, can break free from the fatal spiral. That is the way of Socialism. Socialism will eliminate the economic causes of war by eliminating the capitalist evils of depression and unemployment, cut-throat competition in international trade and private profits from armaments and Armageddon. Public ownership of the instrumentalities of production and distribution means that no individuals or groups can make money from manufacturing munitions or selling any other goods or services .needed in armed hostilities. Socialist planning, by establishing a just and rational economic system at home, makes it unnecessary for governments to attempt to extricate themselves from domestic troubles by adventures abroad. Because their own people will always have the purchasing power to buy what is produced, Socialist nations will feel no irresistible economic pressure driving them on to get rid of surplus goods in the foreign market or to compete with other countries in vicious hunting expeditions for colonies, protectorates and spheres of influence. Likewise, since the Socialist economies will put into effect a planned investment of capital and since there will always be plenty of opportunities for it on the domestic scene, there will be no great, compelling need to send capital abroad for investment. Moreover, since planning will take place between the different Socialist states, no national unit need longer fear that it may be cut off from essential sources of raw materials or lose out in some disastrous currency war. Socialist international planning, in conjunction with the disappearance of special business interests lobbying for protection in the various countries, will also lead to the abolition of tariffs, except perhaps for the minor purpose of raising revenue.

Thus there will be removed one of the chief impediments to world trade and commerce and a factor that is acknowledged on all sides as a primary cause of international friction. The natural exchange of goods will accordingly increase on a vast scale and all the advantages for which free traders have been agitating ever since the time of Adam Smith will come into being, Paradoxically enough, only Socialism, which liberals fear and oppose, can ever fulfill the old free-trade ideal of liberalism.

Socialism, then, as it unfolds internationally, puts a finish once and for all to the fierce struggle, with the whole world as the arena, among the capitalist imperialisms, minor and major, to survive and expand at the expense of one another and of exploited peoples. And it forever sets free the colonial countries from the heavy bonds of imperialist overlordship and control. The point of departure for international Socialism is the fact that Capitalism has laid the material foundations, at least, for a truly world society, even though it is incapable of erecting upon them the firm edifice of a peaceful and co-operative international order. The unceasing development of long-distance transportation facilities has been bringing the different countries of the earth nearer and nearer to one another in a physical sense. Today New York is closer to London than Boston was to Philadelphia at the time the thirteen American states, each in reality an independent nation, adopted a federal Constitution. Also, the speedily evolving transoceanic air services will knit the world together ever more tightly. And an international federation, a United Socialist States of the World, somewhat along the lines of the American union, is by no means beyond the bounds of possibility for this twentieth century.

There are reasons other than strictly economic ones why the influence of Socialism is so fundamentally on the side of peace. Socialism works everywhere for the liberation of the masses of the people—workers, farmers, and middle-class employees—from the ills inherent in the capitalist system. Now it is just these masses who arc always hardest hit in war. They constitute the bulk of the fighting forces; they are the ones who meet suffering and hunger, mutilation and death, by the millions; they are the ones who bear the brunt of the economic aftermaths of international conflict. All this is especially true in modern warfare, in which the demoralization of whole peoples is a primary objective. In the First World War we became used to the blockading and starving out of belligerent countries; today, in addition, the scope of hostilities includes the ruthless bombardment of civilian populations in the biggest and most crowded cities.

The extreme disdain with which the Fascists and their

supporters look down upon the masses of the people everywhere is an important factor in their readiness to resort to violence and war. Their aristocratic political morality, or rather immorality has no place in it for the worth and dignity of human life outside of a small ruling clique at the top. And the pseudo-biological principles which they invent to rationalize their international policies make scorn and abuse of other races and nations an integral part of their philosophy. It is not just the Jews who are held in contempt. At the 1936 Olympic Games in Germany, the Nazis accused the U. S. team of bad sportsmanship for entering "fleet-footed animals," that is, Negroes, in the races. Likewise it is an essential element in the official Fascist creed to look down upon the English and the Americans, the French and the Czechoslovaks, the Poles and the Russians and the Chinese, as degenerate peoples.

Nothing could present a more complete contrast to all this than Socialism's unyielding opposition to every form of racial and national chauvinism. Socialism does not believe that there is any "chosen" race or nation; and it takes this position on the grounds of scientific fact as well as ethical principle. Neither modern biology nor anthropology recognizes the existence o£ races which are inherently superior or inherently inferior. Indeed, these two sciences can find no such thing as a pure race. Peoples such as the Anglo-Saxons, the Teutons and the Slavs, to all of whom there has been ascribed at one time or another a god-given superiority entitling them to rule the world, are themselves the result of biological mixtures so complex as to defy analysis. Hitler's notion that either in Germany or elsewhere there exists a pure-blooded" Aryan" race is as fantastic as the superstition still accepted in some quarters that the earth is flat.

No genuine radical ever analyzes the international or other troubles of the world in terms of "the German menace," "the Jewish menace, "the British menace," "the Japanese menace" of "the Yellow menace." The enemy from the Socialist point of view is never a race or nation as a whole, but always a ruling class forcing some race or nation into an un-resolvable predicament. Socialism's analysis cuts across all national frontiers to find the explanation of things in the class alignments which are much the same the world over. It holds that only action by the entire international working class and its allies can bring a victory over the international capitalist class and that the outcome must be Socialist reconstruction on an international scale. All this is, indeed, so central in Socialist doctrine that the official song of the radical movement is entitled "The International."

Precisely because of this generous and open devotion to internationalism, Socialism's enemies are constantly denouncing it. But Socialism openly accepts the challenge of the reactionary cult of hate, war and world anarchy. Yet at the same time the adherents of the coming society remain nationalists in the best sense of the word. They take pride in and encourage the peaceful flowering, of Rational cultures; they see, however, no more reason why an integrated international commonwealth should prevent the expression of the spirit and genius native to the various nationalities than why a closely knit nationalism should do away with the characteristic contributions of city, state or region. Clearly Socialism stands as the greatest hope for those ideals of international peace and understanding which have been both an inspiration and a goal for countless men and women of good will in all ages.

The ideal of human brotherhood throughout the earth, regardless of race, nationality or religion, is one of the oldest in the history of thought. In every ethical philosophy worthy of the name from the ancient Greeks to the twentieth century, this ideal has had in some form or other a rightfully important place. The Stoics expressed it in the term cosmopolitanism; the Christians in the precept, Love thy neighbor as thyself, the slogan-makers of the French Revolution in the word "fraternity." This conception of human brotherhood has often been scorned as sentimental, but today the most hardheaded realist must agree that our civilization can hardly be saved without it.

As we look forward into the future in this year 1939 the prospects for international peace are not auspicious. It may well be already too late to stave off the Second World War. I do not grant that such a conflict will mean the end of civilization. There is little danger that any of the countries on the two American continents will become major scenes of battle and carnage; Soviet Socialism is too powerful utterly to collapse; and in any case I imagine that the belligerent nations, when the holocaust is over, will start building again from the ruins.

Yet unless Socialism grows sufficiently strong, unless enough of the more important countries go Socialist so that they, supported by the radical movement in other lands, possess the power and the will to make peace prevail, mankind will again build only to stumble almost surely once more into the awful abyss of new wars. The best and the living proof of what Socialism means for world peace is the splendid record of the Soviet Republic in international affairs since it came into existence in 1917. That record, which I outlined earlier, and the argument of this chapter show that Socialism proceeds to the permanent outlawry of war, not through drawing up nobly phrased documents and instituting pompous organizations, nor merely through education on the horror and stupidity of modern war, but through drastically altering the most fundamental and pervasive relationships—the economic ones—of society. It is the supreme opportunity of peace-loving men and women from every nation and every class to grasp the Socialist vision of a planned and democratic international order and to help actualize it in the affairs of mankind.

~ ~ ~

Chapter VI
Toward Greater Democracy

1. *What Democracy Is and Is Not*

I have found that most Americans tend to think of democracy mainly in terms of free political activity and traditional civil liberties. Democracy does include, of course, as most essential elements, complete political democracy and complete civil liberties. .But it means in addition economic democracy, in which no class can exploit another class, in which everyone possesses material security and in which all adults have a voice in the conduct of economic affairs: cultural democracy, in which everyone has an equal opportunity to share the fruits of culture; sexual democracy in which legally and in all other relevant ways women stand on an equal plane with men; racial democracy, in which all racial .groups, whether they be minorities within a state or nations in themselves, are on a par with other racial groups and not subject to any sort of discrimination; and, finally, international democracy, as defined in the preceding chapter.

The emotional drive behind the ideal of full democracy is distinctly not a sentimental or condescending sympathy for the underdog as such; when it comes to Soviet Russia, I, along with most radicals, support and sympathize with the top-dogs, the workers and their leaders who have built a Socialist society in the face of tremendous odds, Nor is this feeling for democracy quite what Christianity means by brotherly love, though it is akin to it. Rather, the democratic attitude that I have in mind is best expressed as a general one of well-wishing and friendliness toward all humanity and of faith in the ultimate common sense of the common man to make reasonable decisions in the adventure of self-government.

As far back as I can remember, my natural feeling toward people, whether as individuals or en masse has been one of warmth. That was always the way I felt toward everybody: toward members of my own economic strata, toward the workers, toward foreigners, toward unjustly treated racial groups such as the Negroes and the Jews. From the start I followed the principle that every man was my friend until he proved himself my enemy, and that is still my philosophy today, When I went away to the Phillips Exeter Academy, probably the most democratic private school in the country, my equalitarian feeling was strongly reinforced. But even at Exeter there were snobs; and 1 constantly felt offended by their haughty, anti-democratic attitude and by that of the upper-class boys I later met at Harvard College. The parents were usually even crasser in their Bourbonism.

Equally repulsive to me was my discovery of the inveterate propensity of the American capitalist class for social-climbing within its own ranks. This phenomenon it was easy for me to observe during my college days when so many of my fellow students, egged on by expectant relatives, nourished as their dearest ambition election to membership in Harvard's exclusive clubs and an entree into Boston high society. Since then I have witnessed time and again the fatuous competition for social prestige among different individuals and groups in the "upper class." The topmost stratum of American capitalist society itself does plenty of climbing in the direction of the much longer established European, and especially British, aristocracy, which social climbs in its turn, toward King and God. Not a few of our society leaders, both male and female, look wistfully across the water at the highly stratified English social system, ever feeling homesick for that deferential subservience to name and money which so disgusts democratic-minded Americans traveling in the British isles. And many an American magnate, in the full flush of wealth and success, has sighed sadly to himself, "Oh that this were England where they would make me Earl." The marital scramble after titles is the most brazen example of American social-climbing under foreign inspiration, with the racket of being presented at the Court of St. James running a close second. The inferiority complex of the American bourgeoisie also takes more subtle forms such as the continual kowtowing to old-world culture and the acceptance of old world leadership in the intricacies of international diplomacy. For example, it would be impossible to exaggerate the effects that the slightest whispered hint from an English Lord or Lady has upon members of the American ruling class and its representatives in the diplomatic service. I first began to recognize the extent to which the spirit of democracy is violated in America when A. Lawrence Lowell, Boston blueblood and former President of Harvard, ruled that a Negro boy I knew could not room in the Freshman Dormitories with the other members of his class. This act of discrimination was later reversed by the University authorities; but in the public uproar over the incident and the many arguments back and forth, I learned a lot about racial prejudice in the United States. Soon after graduating from college I spent several weeks in the South studying the "Negro question" at firsthand from Washington to Atlanta. And I later served on the Board of Directors of the National Urban League, an organization devoted to the social betterment of the Negroes.

The position of the Negro in this country and particularly in the South, excellently illustrates how the different types of democracy, or rather un-democracy, are linked together. The Negro minority, originally introduced into America on account of the lust for profits of planters and slave traders, has remained a subject class economically from the beginning; and has therefore naturally been unable to establish for itself political, cultural or racial democracy. Though the Negro race supposedly won political freedom almost seventy years ago through the ratification .of the Fifteenth Amendment, it has in actuality largely been disfranchised in the southern states right up to the present day.

As for sharing equal rights under the law and the advantages of ordinary civil liberties, everyone knows that the Negroes below the Mason and Dixon Line have had less than a beggar's chance. Thus we have a group of native-born American citizens in the South numbering no less than nine million, to whom the ruling class openly refuses to grant the political guarantees of the Constitution. Turning to the sphere of culture, we find that the allocation of funds in the South as between public educational facilities for Whites and for Negroes is nothing short of scandalous. Throughout the fourteen southern states the expenditures for each white child range from three or four times to ten times as much as for each Negro child. In a recent study the National. Education Association reports: "In South Carolina the annual expenditure for education is $4.48 per child for Negro children and $45.45 per child for white children. In Georgia, where the Negro population is 36.8 per cent of the total, the figures are $7.44 per year for the Negro child against $35.34 for the white child, while the figures for Florida are respectively $11.41 and $75.07." These figures show why the "Jim Crow" schools of the South are generally rundown and badly equipped, why the teachers are usually poorly trained and atrociously paid, and why the school terms are anywhere from two to six months shorter than those for white children.

Racial prejudice in the United States extends to other minorities such as our indigenous Indian population, the French Canadians in New England, the Orientals in the West, the Mexicans in the Southwest, various immigrant groups from Europe, and especially the Jews. Unquestionably this country has of late seen an alarming growth in anti-Semitism, fanned by our continuing economic pressures and the heightened race consciousness caused by Fascist persecutions and the emigration of Jews from their homelands.

The Institute for Propaganda Analysis estimates that there are some 800 Fascist or semi-Fascist organizations in the U. S. carrying on anti-Semitic propaganda at the present time. Yet there has long been a strong anti-Jewish feeling in America which has expressed itself in various ways, from discriminating against Jews in business and the professions to excluding them from hotels and educational institutions. Again, Harvard taught me a good deal about the educational angle of the Jewish question when the reactionary Lowell regime tried to put through a percentage limitation on the number of Jewish students attending the College.

Let us make no mistake about the fact that the leaders and pacesetters of anti-Semitism in the United States have been the ruling capitalist class of native-born Anglo-Saxons, This class seldom considers even those Jews who are most useful to it, such as certain reactionary columnists, above the status of rather bright - lackeys. Though many American capitalists have been repelled by Hitler's excesses against the Jews and by his expropriation of their private property—a most dangerous precedent—it remains true that they themselves share a large measure of moral responsibility for American anti-Semitism.

Years before the hideous Nazi ideology arrived to plague the world these same capitalists were trying to lay the foibles and failures of the present system at the door of the Jews. And as part of its strategy of "Divide and rule," the capitalist class has ever tended to encourage anti-Semitic and other racial prejudices. In view of the position of racial minorities in this country, it always amazes me to hear upper-class Americans who talk about keeping Negroes and other "inferior" people "in their place" railing against the iniquities, of dictatorship in the Soviet Union, where the principle of racial equality is the lay of the land and the practice of the people. The same illogical stand is invincibly maintained by the small British aristocracy which throughout the Empire controls, on the basis of armed might and highly undemocratic government, colored subjects numbering more than 400,000.000. The fact is, of course, that the white ruling classes shudder at the very suggestion of extending the concept of democracy to include the black, brown and yellow peoples of the earth. Yet Christian ethics, which the capitalist classes profess to uphold, as well as any other genuine moral philosophy, cannot do otherwise than condemn racial prejudice as one of the most despicable things in our present-day world. For this insidious and illiberal attitude dooms, for the accidental quality of mere color or physiognomy, hundreds of millions of innocent persons generation after generation to an atmosphere of hate and humiliation and to a status of inferiority in the national and international community.

Coming to another important form of democracy, I think it is incontestable that no democratic system can be complete until women possess full and equal rights with men, both in law and established custom. In America the female sex did not win the suffrage until 1920. And though in general women have been relatively free in this country, there is still a long way to go. In the field of Education, for example, the opportunities for girls and young women are far less than for members of the male sex. Pitifully small sums are spent on women's institutions as compared with men's; and only a small proportion of the universities have opened their professional schools to the female sex. In most of the capitalist countries of Europe, and in all the countries of Asia, the significance of women achieving equality would be simply immense.

When we examine the question of cultural democracy, which I treat more fully in the next chapter, we see what very great inequalities of opportunity exist in America, In a recent book entitled *American Business Leaders* Professor F, W. Taussig and Dr. C. S. Joslyn, both of the Harvard faculty, analyse the 1927-28 edition of *Who's Who in America* and find that only 6.7 per cent of the persons listed have working-class fathers. And they add: "Most of the persons in 'Who's Who' (about nine-tenths) won their places by distinction in the professions, in the arts, or in letters——the very callings from which laborers' sons, by reason of the educational requirement, are virtually debarred." Thus Professor Taussig and his collaborator admit with entire frankness the lack of democracy in the realms of cultural and professional endeavor.

Yet for some strange reason, when through other studies They discover that the sons of working-class fathers constitute only slightly more than ten per cent of *business* leaders in the United States, they "strongly suggest" that this situation is due to lack of innate ability on the part of the proletariat. While I cannot undertake to endorse the statistics of Messrs. Taussig and Joslyn, their tabulation sounds reasonable. But what their elaborate figures strongly suggest to me is not that labor is wanting in native talent, but that the traditional claim that every American enjoys a fair and equal opportunity of working his way to the top is without foundation, which is what the radicals have been saying all along. How, indeed, can we possibly pretend that there is equal opportunity in any sense when, millions upon millions of able-bodied and able-minded Americans can find no jobs; when millions more are working only part-time, and when millions of others simply do not possess the financial means to obtain the good things of life?

Decades ago, with the disappearance of the frontier, it became impossible for individuals and families to solve their economic problems by moving to the rich open spaces of the West. Now a man has little choice but to stay where he is and fight it out in the economic wilderness of his own hometown. And with the omnipresent concentration of business enterprise it is not so easy, even if you do have a little capital to start with to set up on your own either in city or country. American class relations, which once were marked by considerable fluidity, have become, like those in Europe, more and more "frozen."

Clearly the old economic basis for American democracy, that of individuals owning their independent means of livelihood, has grown to be the exception rather than the rule. And no new form of economic democracy has become established in its place; nor can it become under the present system. True enough, the organization of all America workers into trade unions would constitute a most important step in the direction of real, economic democracy, But out of some 35,000,000 potential members only 8,000,000 are yet unionized: approximately 4,000,000 in the C.I.O; 3,500,000 in the A. F. of L.; and 500,000 in the Railroad Brotherhoods.

As regards political democracy, the underprivileged elements in this county are very far from having attained it in full measure. In the vital matter of elections, the substance, as distinct from the form, the power rests on the possession of sufficient economic resources to buy radio time and newspaper advertisements; to rent meeting halls and print pamphlets; to do the thousand and one things that vigorous and effective electoral campaigns demand. No one can suppose that the workers have anywhere near the funds which the capitalist class can make available for these purposes. Lack of financial strength is by no means the only thing which handicaps the political activities of the workers and of anti-capitalist minority groups. For the suppression of ordinary civil liberties has long been one of the outstanding features of the political scene in the capitalist democracies. And nowhere in allegedly democratic nations has this phenomenon been so marked as in our own United States, with its much-vaunted Constitution, including the famous Bill of Rights embodied in the ten original Amendments. Most crucial of all for civil liberties is the First Amendment, which reads as follows: "Congress shall make no law respecting an establishment of religion, or prohibiting the free exercise thereof; or abridging the freedom of speech or of the press; or the right of the people peaceably to assemble and to petition the Government for a redress of grievances." Other Amendments establish the right of trial by jury and give assurances against illegal search or seizure, excessive bail or fines, and cruel or unusual punishments.

The Bill of Rights was implemented by a section in the Fourteenth Amendment providing that, "No State shall make or enforce any law which shall abridge the privileges or immunities of citizens of the United States . . . nor deprive any person of life, liberty or property without due process of law." The Civil Rights Act of 1871 reinforced the constitutional provisions already cited. And in addition the various state constitutions also lay down guarantees for the maintenance of civil liberties, yet in spite of this galaxy of laws, American citizens have had to wage, from the earliest days of the Republic, a constant battle for the preservation of their constitutional freedoms.

One organization, the American Civil Liberties Union, was founded in 1920 for the sole purpose of aiding in this cause. As a member of its Board of Directors since 1932 I have had a particularly good opportunity over the past few years to keep abreast of the civil liberties situation in the United States. Let us now consider specifically this sector of affairs which is of such paramount importance So the future of democracy in this country.

2. The Violation of Civil Liberties

It is a sad and ironical fact that the majority of those

Americans who have recently been most vocal about "saving the Constitution" have never, in their lives raised a finger to protest against the continual violation of the civil liberties guaranteed in the Bill of Rights. Year after year, while workers have been shot down in cold blood, while Negroes have been lynched, while freedom of speech in every part of the country has been abrogated, these self-appointed defenders of the Constitution have kept silent as the grave. More than that, many of them, reactionary in their views and hard-boiled in their methods, have actually encouraged the use of violence against American citizens with whose opinions they happen to disagree. But let so much as a legislative whisper be heard implying some slight curtailment of property interests for the public good and these worthy gentlemen spring into swift and noisy action. They then suddenly discover the Constitution, and that it was drawn up for the sole and glorious purpose of protecting the rights of private property.

One of the reasons why these American capitalists care so little about civil liberties is that their civil liberties, are hardly ever infringed upon. Violation of the Bill of Rights revolves around labor, liberal and radical groups, because they are the ones who are urging reforms or fundamental changes in the social system which seem dangerous to the capitalist class. These and other such groups clearly add up to a majority of the population. It is on this account that Max Lerner, in his recent book on democracy, says quite correctly that the biggest problem is to preserve the civil liberties of the *majority* rather than of the minorities. For in the United States it is the ruling-class minority, attempting to impose its will on the rest of the people, which has been the chief offender against the Bill of Rights. Unquestionably the most serious and frequent violations of civil liberty in the United States have taken place over labor's right to organize, strike, picket, demonstrate, meet, and bargain collectively. The suppression of workers' rights is usually carried out in the name of "law and order," but in an overwhelming majority of cases this means in fact, anti-legal or extra-legal violence and intimidation on the part of employers, vigilantes, troops, special deputies, private thugs or police officers who neither know nor care about the Bill of Rights. Such attacks are far more serious than the restrictions imposed on civil liberties by ill-advised legislation, Now I do not for an instant claim that American workers are a lot of white-winged angels, always gentle and perfect in their behavior. Like American citizens in general they are proud, freedom-loving, quick to sense unfair tactics, and ready to fight back if pressed too far. Yet it is also accurate to say that 95 per cent of the violence that so often flares in labor disputes is started by the employers or their agents or by government authorities. In many situations the government authorities themselves are nothing more nor less than the "agents" of the employers, who are experts on ways and means of getting others to do their dirty work for them.

The revelations of the Senate Civil Liberties Committee, headed by Senator Robert M, LaFollette, Jr., regarding the methods used by big business and little business alike in fighting trade unionism and breaking strikes are as shocking as they are dramatic. The testimony of labor spies, of professional strikebreakers, commonly known as "finks," and of employers themselves has definitely established the fact that much of the violence attributed to strikers is purposely fomented, in order to discredit them, by agents provocateurs of various types.

Take, for example, the story sworn to on the witness stand by professional strikebreaker Edmund B. McDade, in the employ of the Wisconsin Light and Power Company: McDade described how a building was dynamited by strikebreakers and the blame placed on the strikers; and how the home of a company official was painted red by strikebreakers, and the strikers and their sympathizers then accused of the deed. To quote a representative passage from the report of the Senate Committee: "A Corporations Auxiliary spy sat in the meetings of the strike strategy committee of the Dodge Local of the United Automobile Workers in 1936 and urged the use of force and violence.

A Pinkerton spy in the International Association of Machinists in Atlanta sought to provoke a general strike A National Metal Trades spy in the Black and Decker strike at Kent,

Ohio, in 1936, urged his fellow unionists to dynamite the plant. The fact that strikes and violence increase the business of detective agencies is a contributing cause to this sort of conduct.

The LaFollette Committee found that labor spying is "a common, almost universal practice in American industry. . . . The known total of business firms receiving spy services is approximately 2,500. The list as a whole reads like a bluebook of American industry. Large corporations rely on spies. No firm is too small to employ them." The sums spent on spies are immense. For instance, the General Motors Corporation paid almost $1,000,000 to detective agencies for spy services from January of 1934 through. July of 1936. The Committee also revealed that many spies succeeded in worming their way into positions of high responsibility in the trade unions. Thus approximately 100, or one-third, of the spies employed by the Pinkerton agency were officials of unions, one being vice-president of an international union. Hand in hand with the spy racket has gone the expenditure of huge amounts by capitalist business on munitions, tear gas, and other forms of industrial armament. This is one of the main reasons why in labor troubles it is always the workers who are the chief sufferers. One never hears of an employer being injured or killed in a strike. During the steel strikes in the first half of 1937 many newspaper readers received the impression that the workers were resorting to widespread and illegal violence. The American Civil Liberties Union, however, made a careful survey of the entire situation on the basis of the available reports. It found that throughout America, from January 1st to the end of July, that twenty-four strikers and sympathizers were killed and 490 injured, chiefly on picket lines, and while not engaged in any act of violence. During the same period one police officer was killed and seventy injured. No non-striking workers were killed, and only thirty-one injured and 140 persons whose affiliation could not be determined were also injured. These proportions of the affiliations of those killed and injured are typical of the whole of American labor history. Almost half of the strikers' fatalities mentioned above occurred in the fearful "Memorial Day Massacre" at South

Chicago in which police brutally attacked a peaceful parade of workers on their way to demonstrate before a plant of Mr. Tom Girdler's Republic Steel Corporation. The police fired their revolvers point blank into a dense crowd of men, women and children, and then pursued and clubbed them unmercifully as they frantically tried to escape. Ten strikers were killed instantly or died later and ninety-seven other persons were badly injured. More than half of those killed or injured by bullet wounds were found to have been shot in the back.

While such incidents have happened again and again in this land of liberty, we are fortunate in this instance in possessing thorough and indisputable documentation in the form of a newsreel. Paramount News at first suppressed this film for fear that it would lead to riots, but later released it to the general public. The picture gives a gruesome and graphic presentation, accompanied by the roar of pistol shots, the thump of police clubs and the screams of the victims, of one of the most atrocious episodes in the long life of the American commonwealth. All of the policemen involved in this cruel and cowardly blood-fest were later completely whitewashed by a politically controlled Chicago grand jury.

What happened during the steel strike at Massillon, Ohio, in July of 1937 was, despite a much smaller death toll, in some ways even more revealing. For it showed undeniably the direct tie-up between capitalist business and illegal violence of the most brutal sort. As Chief Switter of the Massillon police force later testified before the Labor Relations Board on June 29t, Carl Meyers, district manager for Republic Steel in the Canton-Massillon district, sent for him. According to Chief Switter, "Meyers wanted to know what the hell was going on over there—letting those hoodlums run the town. He wanted to know why we hadn't done like the Chicago police had done. They knew how to handle a situation he said. He told me if the mills closed down, Massillon would be nothing but a junction point, with no need for a mayor or a chief of police or any other city officials."

Meanwhile a Law and Order League, composed of leading

businessmen, was urging Chief Switter to commission extra policemen who would be paid and equipped at the League's expense, Chief Switter declined the offer and emphasized that there had been neither loss of life nor serious disorder. But later, under added pressure from General Marlin, who had quartered two companies of the Ohio National Guard in the Republic plant, Switter gave way. On July 7 thirty to forty "loyal" Republic employees were sworn in as special policemen. On the evening of July 11 Chief Switter drove out of town on a picnic and Harry Curley, a retired army officer, took unofficial charge of the police department. Later that, night from fifteen to twenty of the new special policemen, armed with guns and tear gas, approached strike headquarters, where a considerable number of workers were standing around in front of their building. Without any more serious pretext than that they felt annoyed by the lights of a striker's automobile which happened to draw up, the police opened a murderous attack with gunfire and tear gas grenades, killing two workers and wounding fifteen. Also must be mentioned here, the loss of life at the labor strike massacre at Ludlow, Colorado.

The. scandalous outlawry of civil liberties in Jersey City by Mayor Frank Hague has centered, like so many other such situations, around labor's right to organize and the characteristic activities which that right involves. As far back as 1934 Boss Hague had conceived the bright idea of attracting new revenue-yielding business to the city by promising employers that he would prevent trade unions from bothering them. During the spring and summer of that year Hague's police made a regular practice of arresting peaceful pickets on trumped-up charges and throwing them into jail.

I myself at that time went over to Jersey City to make a test case on behalf of the Civil Liberties Union at a factory where members of the Furniture Workers Industrial Union were on strike. I was also interested in the matter as a trade unionist belonging to the New York Teachers Union. For the high crime and misdemeanor of walking quietly up and down in front of the plant in question and displaying an appropriate placard, I was arrested, arraigned, fingerprinted and put behind the bars in a cell of the main city jail for some five hours while waiting to get bailed out. Though the whole episode was over and done with in a few hours, I want to make clear that my day in Jersey City was distinctly not a lark, but rather constituted a grueling psychological experience. As a matter of fact, my case never came to trial, because the resultant publicity, first-class legal work, and other factors brought about the reversal of previous anti-picketing decisions, though not until they got beyond the lower courts. One of the most sinister things in the picture is that Hague's puppets sit on the bench and do his bidding. And in 1939 his son, Frank Hague, Jr., with little or no judicial experience, was appointed by a faithful Hague man, Governor Harry Moore, to the New Jersey Court of Errors and Appeals, the highest court in the state. So when Mayor Hague publicly stated, "I am the law," it was not mere bombast.

For a short time after the 1934 skirmishes Hague allowed picketing, but before long he was again violating the law, and his police were throwing strikers into jail and deporting sympathizers beyond the city lines. The situation reached a climax in the fall of 1937 when Hague decided to bar out completely the organizing efforts of the C.I.O. in Jersey City, He termed the C.I.O. organizing campaign and the attempts of the Civil Liberties Union to uphold the C.I.O.'s legal rights as a "Red invasion." In a public speech Boss Hague declared: "As long as I am Mayor of this city the great industries of the city are secure. We hear about constitutional rights, free speech and the free press. Every time I hear these words I say to myself, "that man is a Red, that man is a Communist." You never heard a real American talk in that manner," Later he advocated the exile of all whom he considered "Reds" to a concentration camp in Alaska. Hague's suppression of civil liberties and the counter-offensive of the C. I. O. and the Civil Liberties Union went on at full blast all through 1938. Interference with the Bill of Rights by the Jersey City administration extended to stopping and searching automobiles not having New Jersey licenses, prohibiting the distribution of leaflets on the streets, refusing permits for outdoor meetings or demonstrations by "undesirables," and intimidating local "hall owners so that they would not rent their premises for indoor meetings under the auspices of labor, liberal or radical groups. Meetings sponsored by the C. I. O, or the Civil Liberties Union were the first to come under the ban; later the same fate befell meetings organized by the Hudson County Committee for Labor and Civil Rights, the Socialist Party and the Catholic Worker, a religious periodical.

Highlights in the situation during 1938 were the successive "deportations" by Hague's police of Norman Thomas, head of the Socialist Party, and Representative Jerry O'Connell, Montana Democrat, both of whom journeyed to Jersey City to test the free-speech ban. The Federal courts, including (in June of 1939) the United States Supreme Court, finally declared unconstitutional Hague's ordinances and actions violating labor's rights and civil liberties in general, and granted a restraining injunction against the Jersey City administration. But the fact remains that for five years Mayor Hague was able successfully to defy, through the use of physical coercion, both the American Constitution and the Constitution of the State of New Jersey. And one cannot be too certain that even now Mr. Hague, with the full authority of the judiciary against him, will condescend to keep within the law.

In view of the fact that Boss Hague, is one of the most prominent Democrats in the country, controlling the state as well as the Jersey City Democratic machine and sitting on the Democratic National Committee as a Vice-Chairman, his behavior placed the Party of Franklin D. Roosevelt in a most awkward light. One of the salient features of Hague's onslaught on constitutional liberties is that he has enjoyed the enthusiastic support of local business, as represented by the Jersey City Chamber of Commerce. There can be no doubt, either, that reactionary capitalists in other parts of America looked with favor upon his tactics. Governor Aiken of Vermont underscored this point at the Lincoln .Day Dinner of the National Republican Club in 1938. "Would not Lincoln have been ashamed of us," he asked, "when Frank Hague, the Democratic boss of Jersey City, forbade free speech and free assemblage and no responsible voice in the Republican national leadership was raised in protest against his highhanded procedure? The reason was that free speech and free assemblage were being denied the C.I.O, and the Tom Girdlers of the Republican Party want the C.I.O. crushed even if a corrupt political boss of the opposing party has to tear up the Bill of Rights to crush them!"

It is noteworthy that throughout the United States the Bill of Rights fares worst where the underprivileged make some sort of conscious effort to limit the exploitation of the capitalists. Since the deepening tensions brought on by the Great Depression, reactionaries in widely separated parts of the country have resorted increasingly to the organization of vigilante groups and to the violent tactics formerly associated with the Ku Klux Klan. Thus in certain sectors, the embattled businessmen have outdone even Hague, setting up local reigns of terror with kidnapping, flogging and murder as the regular order of the day. This is or has been true in such places as Harlan County, Kentucky, and Gallup, New Mexico, where the coal miners have been attempting to organize; the Imperial Valley of Southern California, where the fruit and vegetable workers have been attempting to organize; and the cotton and farm area of eastern Arkansas, where share-croppers and tenants have been attempting to organize.

The Klan itself, originally founded in the South to maintain white domination over the Negroes, has extended its persecutions to all racial and religious minorities and to alleged Communists and radicals in general. Thus in 1933 Klan mobsters at Tampa, Florida, kidnapped from his home Frank Norman, an organizer for the International Labor Defense. His wife heard shots, and no trace has ever been found of him since. One night in 1935, Tampa Klansmen and city police officers kidnapped and "took for a ride" Joseph Shoemaker, an ex-manufacturer who was head of a progressive group known as the Modern Democrats, and two of his co-workers in the organization, Eugene F, Poulnot and Dr. Samuel J. Rogers. This mob in miniature stripped the three men, severely flogged them with chains and whips, and covered them with hot tar. Shoemaker was later found at the side of a road stripped of all clothing but a shirt, unconscious and half-frozen, his body bruised and burned. He died a few days later. Though the perpetrators of this crime were well known and were put on trial, they were all ·finally acquitted, due to their intimate connections with Klan-dominated government authorities in city and state. An organization closely akin to the Ku Klux Klan was exposed in 1936 in Michigan and neighboring slates; when it was discovered that the Black Legion, a secret terrorist society, had brought about the murder of Charles Poole, a white W.P.A. worker. On joining the Legion, members took an oath to protect Protestantism, Americanism and Womanhood and to wage war indiscriminately against Catholics, Jews, Negroes, Communists and aliens. Eight members of the Legion were indicted and sentenced to life imprisonment. On the stand they admitted that the Legion had kidnapped, beaten, or killed a number of others besides Poole. One Negro they shot to death "just for the hell of it." The Legion higher-ups, who were thought to include government officials, and the source of the organization's funds remained undisclosed.

Most of the vigilante bands operate on a local basis; but seemly it has become apparent that the vigilante spirit in America is countrywide. And in the programs and pronounciamentos of a number of organizations formed on a national scale, we find the outlines for what would be in essence an American Fascist revolution. And the high-sounding names taken by a few of the more prominent organizations of this type: the American Alliance; the American Coalition of Patriotic, Civic and Fraternal Societies; the American Defenders; the Associated Farmers; the Christian Front; the Crusaders; the German-American League (the Bund); the Knights of White Camellia; the National Civic Federation; the National Republic; the Patriot Guard of America; the Paul Reveres; the Sentinels of the Republic; the Silver Shirts; and the Vigilantes and Affiliated Organizations.

On June 6, 1937, the last-named organization issued a warning, quoted by Dorothy Thompson in her column in the New York Herald Tribune, which denounced President Roosevelt and John L. Lewis, head of the C.I.O., as Public Enemies Numbers One and Two. They threatened Mr. Lewis directly with "appropriate action that will let loose the dogs of civil war," and Mr. Roosevelt indirectly by stating that if certain legislation proposed in Washington passes, "an indignant army of citizens will be taking things into their own hands." The Key-Men of the Vigilantes and Affiliated Organizations [it is declared] have a large number of twenty-four-hour men who are ready to respond when called. These men have already received instructions and could converge on any designated point in overwhelming numbers, . . . When the time comes no quarter or consideration will be shown to the traitors to American democracy. Methods will be ruthless, swift, and sure, for when we start we must at any cost rid the nation of the subversive elements who today think they are riding the crest of the wave. When the zero-hour arrives, there will be no polite knocking upon doors.

Manifestos of this sort, strained and fantastic as they sound, can no longer be laughed off, as some worthy citizens seem to think. Against the general background of violations of civil liberties they have an ominous aspect. And taken in connection with public statements by persons in positions of power and influence, they make considerable sense. The anti-Semitic, Fascist outbursts of the Reverend Charles E. Coughlin have become a national scandal. In New York City we have George U. Harvey, leading Republican and Borough President of Queens, advocating in speech after speech that the police go out and beat up Communists with the well-known instruments of the rubber hose and the ax handle. At one American Legion Convention he ranted: "If the Communists push easygoing Americans too far, there won't be enough telegraph poles in the City of New York to take care of them."

Then there is ex-Ambassador James W. Gerard, a Democrat, who prophesies that Communists "will soon be hunted like mad dogs in our streets." The publisher, Bernarr McFadden, who in his social and economic views is a twin brother of William Randolph Hearst, openly suggests wholesale lynching of radicals and Communists: "Public enemies," he writes, referring to members of the Communist Party, "must be treated like man-eating tigers. The order given recently to policemen in many of our cities to shoot first and question afterward is a good policy in this dire emergency. 'Death to traitors' should be the slogan from now on." And Major General George Van Horn Mosley, retired, before a select audience of businessmen attending an annual meeting of the New York Board of Trade, publicly warned those whom he termed "domestic enemies" of a patriotic uprising against them which would "make those massacres now recorded in history look like peaceful church parades." Such statements on the part of reactionary organizations and individuals obviously amount to direct advocacy of violence, not at some vague, far-off, future time, but quite definitely, here and now. Yet no one ever hears of prosecutions on account of these incendiary exhortations. If labor leaders, Communists, or radicals in general ever talked this way, we can be certain that they would receive short shrift at the hands of the governmental authorities, who as it is are constantly prosecuting them for legitimate opinions and peaceful actions which in no sense constitute, in the late Justice Holmes' words, a "clear and present danger" to law and order. So we see that the capitalist classes are able both to advocate and to practice violence with little fear of prosecution; and at the same time, through the officials whom it controls, to terrorize labor and minority groups through illegal use of the law. Today it is possible to identify the capitalists and their agents as aggressors in the local or national community just as certainly as the Fascist governments in the international sphere.

In addition to the instances of violence and the development of fascist tendencies that I have been describing, there has gone on in the United States year after year the horrible lynching of Negroes, chiefly of course in the South. Since 1882, 5,120 of our fellow Americans have been lynched. The average annual number of lynchings over the past ten years, though showing a drop in comparison with the previous decade, stands at the shocking figure of sixteen. While some state administrations have recently been taking a determined stand against lynch mobs, government officials have as a rule, either openly sympathized with lynching

271

parties or made no attempt to bring the guilty, whose participation is almost always a matter of public knowledge, to book. Twentieth-century lynchers kill their prey as often by a volley of bullets or by burning alive as by actual hanging. Another modern feature is the usually sizable audience, frequently including women and small children. Entirely aside from the inhuman fate of the lynch victims there are the terrible psychological effects on the perpetrators and the spectators, whose most cruel and bestial impulses are given a powerful stimulus. The customary charge against Negroes who are lynched is that they have been guilty of criminal assault against a white woman. If prisoners arrested on this charge are not taken out of jail and slaughtered, it is only too likely that they will be railroaded to death through a trial that amounts to little more than a judicial farce. This is what was attempted in the celebrated case of the nine Scottsboro boys, who in 1931 were apprehended at Scottsboro, Alabama, and accused of criminal assault against two white girls of doubtful reputation who happened to be stealing a ride on the same freight train. They were quickly tried, in an atmosphere of passion and hysteria, and all but one, who was aged fourteen, sentenced to die.

Impartial investigation showed that beyond doubt the boys were innocent victims of a conscienceless frame-up. Seven years of legal struggles in the courts of Alabama and in the Supreme Court of the United States resulted in July, 1937, in the acquittal of four of the defendants. Since the original charges were made without discrimination against all of the nine boys, it is impossible to understand how some could be innocent and some guilty. The defense is still making strenuous efforts to obtain the release of the five remaining prisoners, all of whom are under what amount to life sentences. The Scottsboro case has at least had the good effect of causing an unprecedented publicizing of the wrongs perpetrated against the Negro people of the South and of making some dent in the southern custom of barring Negroes from juries.

One of the most vital spheres in the struggle for free speech is that of education. Unhappily, it would be possible to write a whole chapter or even a book on violations of academic freedom in this country. It was back in 1925 that there occurred the famous anti-evolution trial at Dayton, Tennessee, in which the biology instructor, John T. Scopes, was convicted and fined for disobeying the State law against the teaching of the theory of evolution in tax-supported schools. The State Supreme Court upheld the law, but purposely prevented a test in the United States Supreme Court by dismissing the charges on a technicality. The vast majority of academic freedom cases, however, arise over unorthodox views of teachers or students on social and economic affairs, or their participation in labor or radical activities. One would think that our educational institutions, with the labor movement and Socialist doctrines playing so important a part in modern life, would make special efforts to secure teachers who could discuss; such matters with knowledge and authority. On the contrary, our schools and colleges and universities make special efforts to keep out such teachers, but to get rid of those whom they already have. The prevailing attitude among those middle and upper-class groups who control America's educational system is, I fear that to which Mr. Silas Strawn, former President of the American Bar Association, gave expression in a commencement address at Middlebury College in 1935, "I am unable to sympathize,: he stated, "with the elastic conscience of those who inveigh against the capitalist system while on the pay-roll of a college whose budget or existence is due to the philanthropic generosity of those whose industry and frugality have enabled them to make an endowment...no one who is not a thorough believer in the soundness of the fundamental principles of our government should be permitted to teach either political economy, economics, social science or any other subject."

Out of scores of cases in which the spirit of Mr Strawns admonition has been applied, let me recount some typical examples: In 1931, Professor Herbert Adolphus Miller, prominent Sociologist of Ohio State University, was refused reappointment because of his support of the nationalist movement in India; his opposition to compulsory military training and his sponsorship of progressive causes. In 1934 Dr. Ralph E. Turner, Associate

Professor of History at Pittsburgh University, was dismissed because of his activities on behalf of labor legislation. This was the same institution which some years earlier had disbanded the Liberal Club and expelled two of its student officers for holding a meeting to urge the release of the California labor organizers, Mooney and Billings. The spirit of Pittsburgh was once well illustrated to me when, attending a social function there, I asked a prosperous-looking guest what all the trouble was about at the University. He replied, "Oh, don't Worry about that. We're just getting rid of the damned Reds."

In 1935, Granville Hicks, Assistant Professor of English at Rensselaer Polytechnic Institute at Troy, N. Y., was dropped for reasons of "retrenchment," but as indiscreet statements by the Institute authorities made clear, and as the American Association of University Professors later confirmed through special investigation, Mr. Hicks, acknowledged on all sides as a brilliant teacher, and writer, really lost his position because of his well-known Communist views. In 1936 Yale University refused to renew the appointment of Associate Professor Jerome Davis of the Divinity School, after twelve years on the faculty, because of his sympathy for Soviet Russia and Socialism.

And in 1937 Harvard faltered when it decided to drop two crack economics instructors, Drs, Alan R. Sweezy and J. Raymond Walsh, who had been active in the formation, of the Teachers Union and in labor causes. Of the older and more revered institutions of learning in America, Columbia University has undoubtedly made the most unsavory record in matters of academic freedom, particularly during the incumbency of President Nicholas Murray Butler, who has always posed as a great liberal. Dr. Butler had failed the crucial test of the war years by expelling Professor James McKeen Cattell and Professor Henry Wadsworth Longfellow Dana. The latter "cause celebre" induced the noted historian Charles A. Beard to resign from the faculty in protest. In a number of cases during the last decade Columbia has done much to re-establish its bad reputation. Especially scandalous in my opinion was the expulsion from the Columbia Medical School in

1935 of six students and three technicians for anti-war activities. In order to give some semblance of justification to their illiberal conduct, President Butler and his associates had pulled out of the hat a trick qualification of academic freedom to the effect that it does not allow the right to act contrary to "good manners." If a student or teacher says something or does something that the authorities do not like, it is always easy to rule him out on the ground that he has not lived up to Dr. Butler's definition of a gentleman.

When I was teaching philosophy and economics at Columbia, I well remember being warned by the higher-ups that to take publicly certain unorthodox and unpopular positions was equivalent to "bad manners," in fact, "like going to a dinner party in a golf suit." In 1932 "discourtesy" was one of the main charges that the administration brought against Reed Harris, militant editor-in-chief of the *Columbia Spectator,* which under his leadership had waged a constant battle for liberalism on the campus and had finally made a too, too telling attack on the management of certain dining halls. When I and fifteen other faculty members were about to make public a statement protesting Harris's summary expulsion, the College Dean's right-hand man, a full professor of long standing, summoned me and insisted that the protest should be quashed. When I absolutely refused to countenance any such move, he resorted to the bad manners argument and called me a "mucker." That was an unforgettable moment in my life. I walked out of the Professor's office tense and shaking, and personally issued, the statement to the press. My first experience in the ups and downs of free speech within academic walls had occurred years before when I was a Senior at Harvard College in 1924. At that time a movement was launched to invite some radicals to address the students at the Harvard Union, which provided its members with an annual program of lecturers. The Union's Undergraduate Committee, of which I happened to be Chairman, recommended that the organization ask as speakers Eugene V. Debs, the leader of the Socialist Party; W. Z. Foster, organizer of the great 1919 steel strike and later Secretary of the

Communist Party; and Scott Nearing, radical economics professor who had been dismissed from the University of Pennsylvania. The Governing Board of the Union, with six out of eight members officers in the University administration, opposed this move with all its power. And its course was strongly supported behind the scenes by President Lowell.

In view of the fact that the University authorities kept claiming that they were wholly in favor of free speech, I thought that their attitude was rather strange. A little later I felt somewhat enlightened when one of the college deans suggested to me that I was being decidedly untactful in stirring up such an issue when Harvard was just launching a campaign for $10,000,000. Needless to say, Debs, Foster, and Nearing were never invited to speak. When this episode took place back in 1924, I was very far from being a radical or a believer in Socialism. Along with many other students, however, I honestly wanted to hear the left-wing view of things. After the Harvard powers-that-be put up such a battle to prevent this, my suspicions became aroused and I started to study Socialism seriously for the first time. From then on I, became increasingly interested in and impressed by the radical analysis.

Over the last two decades or so only a handful of American colleges, such as Smith under President William Allan Neilson and Dartmouth under President Ernest M. Hopkins, have been really faithful to the principles of academic freedom. The sort of cases which I have cited are not only deplorable in themselves, but also result in the intimidation of thousands of teachers—not to mention students—who decide that silence is the better part of truth. During my association with Harvard, where I was a student for more than five years, and with Columbia, where I took a Ph.D. degree and taught for four years, I knew personally many teachers who, on all sorts of issues, felt it unwise to reveal openly what they actually thought. Most of the younger men, with impermanent appointments as instructors or lecturers, wanted to put off taking unpopular stands on controversial matters until they reached the rank of full professors. I have found, however, that one of the chief troubles with this strategy is that by the time such teachers achieve professorships, the habits of timidity and respectability are likely to have grown so ingrained as to be absolutely permanent.

There are a number of other important sectors where civil liberties are violated which I can do no more than mention. Such are the prosecutions under unconstitutional state syndicalism and sedition laws; the deportation of aliens for radical political beliefs and labor activities; the use of injunctions against the rights of labor; the forbidding or breaking up of meetings and demonstrations; the practice of police brutality and third-degree methods; the censorship of newspapers, magazines and books, of the theater, the motion picture and the radio; the arrests for disseminating birth-control information; the persecutions for religious scruples, such as refusal to salute the flag; the legal discriminations in many states against atheists and persons disbelieving in religion; and the unjust treatment of our Native American minority and our colonial populations.

It is not difficult to see that violations of the American Bill of Rights extend to practically all cultural, political and propagandist activities and to all sections of the nation and its territorial possessions. This means a constant abrogation of those principles and processes which are the very life blood of a healthily functioning democracy. And those Americans who make a habit of denouncing the lack of democracy in other parts of the earth would do well to examine more closely the glass house which they themselves inhabit. But there is, I feel, little ground for pessimism; for there are ways and means through which we can control this anomalous situation of undemocratic behavior within a democracy, though under Capitalism we can never put a complete end to it.

3. *The Preservation of Civil Liberties*

The free competition of ideas in the market place of public opinion is the best guarantee that truth and right will in the long run prevail. Any system of civil liberties worthy of the name, means therefore, that there must be civil liberties for everyone, without exception, whether we are considering persons as individuals or as members of specific groups. It also means the uncompromising maintenance of Voltaire's famous principle, which no one has ever formulated better: "I wholly disapprove of what you say and will defend to the death your right to say it."

The position of the American Civil Liberties Union since its founding over twenty years ago is, I believe, the only sound one to take. This organization supports freedom for all forms of agitation and propaganda not clearly associated with violence or other unlawful acts and which do not constitute direct incitement to violence or other unlawful acts, No practical joker, for instance, has the right to yell "Fire" in a theater, since that would be a direct incitement to riot. And no one has the freedom to indulge in libel or slander as defined by law. The Civil Liberties Union has defended on occasion individuals or groups varying as widely in their outlook as Communists, Republicans, Catholics, Ku Klux Klanners and Fascists. It has publicly come to the support of its bitterest enemies, even William Randolph Hearst and Representative Hamilton Fish, when it seemed that their constitutional prerogatives under the Bill of Rights were being violated, It protested to the National Labor Relations Board over a ruling against Henry Ford which appeared to go too far. And it has deplored lawlessness and violence on the part of organized labor on precisely the same basis as on the part of labor's opponents. Those who say that, yes, they are in favor of free speech, except for Communists or except for Fascists are playing with very dangerous doctrine. Whatever minority may be concerned, the violation of its civil rights and the use of illegal violence against it is not only an evil and a disgrace in itself, but necessarily builds up habits that threaten the liberty and welfare of everyone in the community. If Negroes are deprived of their privileges under the Bill of Rights, then sooner or later whites are too; and it is a significant fact that well over one-fourth of the total number of lynchings which I cited earlier were of white persons. If Communists are deprived of their constitutional guarantees, then sooner or later so are liberals, trade unionists, and, indeed, any persons who dare lift up their voices on behalf of social and economic justice. If Fascists are deprived of their freedom of expression, then sooner or later so are a host of other honest and well-meaning citizens who happen to hold conservative views. And if Jews are discriminated against under the law or outside of it, then in due course other religious groups such as the Catholics (take heed, Father Coughlin!) are likely to suffer the whips and scorns of insatiate fanaticism.

A good example of how legislative limitation of any group's freedom of speech is likely to react against groups very far afield has occurred in connection with an anti-Nazi law passed in New Jersey making illegal all statements which would tend to incite hatred or hostility against any religion. The first person arrested under this law was not a Nazi, but a member of the religious sect of Jehovah's Witnesses who had given utterance to anti-Catholic sentiments. And it is easy to see how ignorant or malicious officials could stretch such a law to gag legitimate and scholarly criticism of the Church and of religious theories by persons or groups even bitterly opposed to Nazism.

When it comes, however, to members of the Bund or any other political group participating in threatening acts such as parading and drilling in uniforms or with weapons, then it is high time to call a halt. I am in favor of enacting state or federal laws prohibiting private organizations from carrying on military drill or distributing uniforms that have a military significance.

In general I believe that our American democracy and its organs of government should take a vigorous and affirmative stand on behalf of civil liberties. I agree with Lewis Mumford's proposal in his militant *Men Must Act* that when, as in Jersey City, a local political organization year after year suspends the Bill of Rights and defies the courts, the Federal Government should intervene and restore, under martial law if necessary, the constitutional liberties of its citizens. If it is justifiable in some great emergency such for a flood or hurricane to invoke martial law to save life and property, it is surely justifiable to invoke it to save our democratic institutions!

During the period subsequent to 1932 when the Democratic

Party was strongly entrenched in nation and state, it can be said that governmental authorities, even to some extent in the lagging South, were on the whole more sympathetic to the cause of civil liberties than at any time for decades past. The enactment in 1935 by a Democratic congress of the National Labor Relations Act, guaranteeing the right of labor to organize and the setting up of the National Labor Relations Board to adjudicate disputes in the trade-union field, constituted a noteworthy step forward in that very sphere where civil liberties are subject to most frequent suppression. Indicative of a more alert attitude on the part of the Federal administration toward the Bill of Rights was the establishment in 1939, by Attorney General Frank Murphy, of a special Civil Liberties Unit in the United States Department of Justice. Similar Civil Liberties Units, it seems to me, ought to be a part of every State government.

Another most important contribution by public authorities toward sustaining the Bill of Rights was the work of the Senate Committee on Civil Liberties, with its sensational exposures of industrial espionage, violent and underhanded strikebreaking, and infringements of civil liberties in general. I hope very much that Congress will pass the legislation recommended by this Committee banning the possession or use of industrial munitions, restricting the zone of private guards to company property, and outlawing labor spies and strikebreaking activities.

I am also in favor of a national Anti-Lynching Bill designed to wipe out, with the aid and stimulus of Federal initiative, the utterly barbarous practice of lynching. If such a law would be an interference with states' rights, then so much the worse for states' rights! In non-governmental circles, one of the most significant moves of recent years was the establishment in 1938 by the American Bar Association of a Bill of Rights Committee, with Grenville Clark, conservative New York corporation lawyer, as Chairman. Of equal moment has been the progressive trend of late within the American Legion, long an organization deplorably zealous in urging repressive legislation and in extra-legal violence against labor and radical groups. The highest officers of the Legion have recently condemned participation by Legion members, officially or unofficially, in doings calculated to violate the Bill of Rights. In 1938 a Committee of the New York County American Legion issued a notable booklet on *Americanism* written by Mr. Cyrus Leroy Baldridge, Commander of the Willard Straight Post. Among other things this booklet stated that "Liberty demands Freedom of Speech because without Freedom of Speech there can. be no search for the Truth.

This search is vital to Americanism; for unless great numbers of people constantly seek and discover new Truths, we cannot know how to make our world a better place in which to live. Freedom of speech includes freedom of inquiry, freedom of discussion, and—most important—Freedom of Education. The freedom of teachers to teach facts without bias and of scholars to learn facts without bias must never cease. Never was it more necessary than now for all Americans to support their right to Freedom of Speech and Freedom to Listen and Learn. The re-actionaries in the American Legion raised a tremendous hue and cry over this booklet. But the civil liberties principles enunciated in it have won more and more backing in the Legion as a whole.

In spite of the many and ugly violations of the Bill of Rights, I think that since the Great War, its defenders have, by and large, more than held their own. While a number of deplorable episodes, such as the Chicago massacre and the Hague rebellion, have taken place, an equal or greater number of important victories have been registered, particularly in situations where there have been time and opportunity to join the issue. An outstanding case in point was the final pardoning, in 1939, of Tom Mooney by Floyd Olson, the Democratic Governor of California. Mooney had. been in prison for twenty-two years, as compared with the five-year incarceration of Captain Alfred Dreyfus, whose frame-up rocked France at the close of the last century.

It will be recalled that Mooney and another labor organizer by the name of Warren Billings were framed up and sentenced to life imprisonment for their alleged guilt in the fatal bombing of a

Preparedness Day parade in San Francisco in 1916. It was repeatedly proved that Mooney, around whom the basic issues in the case revolved, was convicted on perjured testimony and through the collusion of public officials and private businessmen who wanted to "get" him because he was an effective labor leader. Mooney and Billings, however, remained behind bars, partly because of legal technicalities and partly because of the reactionary attitude and proud stubbornness of California's capitalist class. It was much the same sort of situation that led to the judicial frame-up and execution of the anarchists, Sacco and Vanzetti, in Massachusetts back in 1927. Before Governor Olson can issue a pardon for Billings, certain legal proceedings must still be gone through.

American public opinion, then, especially since the minions of Fascism have begun to assert themselves so blatantly on the domestic scene, has been reacting more and more strongly against violations of civil liberties. While the anti-democratic drives of the Hearst press and of red-baiting agencies like the congressional committee of Representative Martin Dies have achieved minor gains here and there, they have succeeded mainly in arousing an alarmed citizenry to the menace confronting it, Americans have been in the habit of taking for granted that the U. S. A. is a really democratic country and that the Bill of Rights is the actual law of the land. When they suddenly wake up and find that this is by no means the case, they usually make their feelings of protest and disillusionment effective.

It seems to me that sincere conservatives as well as liberals and radicals ought to be able to unite on the wisdom and necessity of preserving intact the guarantees on civil liberties which our forefathers wrote into the Constitution. Freedom of speech and opinion is something that may well be called an eternal principle of mature civilization. It will be an evil day if the people of the United States are ever forced to surrender this principle. However drastically conservatives and radicals may disagree about current measures and ultimate ends, they surely can agree on the advisability of using the method of democracy. For this is the method of freedom and of reason. It is during times of social and economic stress that the upper class, feeling that its position is growing shaky, is most likely to succumb to the temptation of abandoning the democratic process. Accordingly, it is not surprising that recent violations of American civil liberties reached their high point during the economic low point of the Great Depression. Yet it is precisely during such periods that freedom of speech and opinion become more essential than ever for the working out of our basic problems.

Unlike other nations which have possessed practically no democratic institutions, we in America are fortunate in having behind us a long and powerful tradition of democracy and civil liberty. Unlike other nations which have abolished the democratic institutions which they had, our parliamentary form of government is still in a relative state of vitality. As long as civil liberties and the other procedures of democracy are strictly upheld, there can be no logical reason for a people resorting to violent revolution and running the gauntlet of adversities that inevitably come after. For with complete freedom of opinion the will of the majority is able to prevail, and extreme elements can let off steam in passionate oratory and tracts for the times. It is only when the free play of ideas is repressed that violence becomes a necessity for agitators, and revolution becomes the only way out for the underprivileged.

4. *The Transition to Socialism*

Now it is possible that in the future there will occur in the United States a tremendous swing to the Right, bringing with it a rigorous and Fascist-tending suppression of labor's rights, and of civil liberties. But as long as any chance remains of resolving our problems of the country through democratic and peaceful means. I am in favor of abiding by such means. Some radicals have taken the position that in every capitalist country Socialism can be achieved only by means of bloody revolution, since they claim that the capitalist class is sure to resist by force, the coming of a new social order. No class in history, the argument runs, has ever surrendered its power without a violent struggle. Hence, it is said, that the capitalist class today can be counted on to follow the example of its predecessors.

This thesis, in so far as it refers to organized, large-scale violence distinct from sporadic outbreaks, overlooks the fact that democratic processes and habits have never before been so highly developed as the capitalist democracies are at present. Karl-Marx himself declared in a speech at Amsterdam in 1872; "We know that special regard must be paid to the unions, customs, and traditions of various lands; and we do not deny that there are certain countries such the United States and England, in which the workers may hope to secure their ends by peaceful means." Many followers of Marx have tried to explain away this statement, but it is clear to me that in it the founder of modern Socialism was merely being realistic and recognizing the facts.

Since the aim of Socialism is the greater welfare of all mankind, the proponents of this new system naturally wish to bring it about with the least possible cost in suffering and not to repeat the awful violence which, for no less than five hundred years, accompanied the conquest of power by the capitalist class. It is an absurd and malicious caricature of Marxist policy to picture it in terms of armed workingmen dashing about and shooting down all well-dressed citizens. Even the most extreme Communists would prefer to win control of the state through the ballot; and no sensible radical, unless the necessity is absolute, wishes to initiate a violent revolution and to run the serious risk of giving up his life just as the vision he has worked for may be coming true.

A severe civil war, moreover does not only cause untold human misery and snuff out a vast number of human lives; it dislocates the whole economy of a country and sets back economic health and equilibrium for years or even decades. To attempt the establishment of Socialism upon the smoking ruins of a devastating civil conflict is a most unpropitious way of starting a new social order, and creates handicaps of the most serious nature. During the change to a Socialist society radicals will have enough problems on their hands without looking for trouble in the form of unnecessary quarrels.

My hope is that in Great Britain and its Dominions, in the United States and France, in Belgium and Holland and the Scandinavian commonwealths—all countries in which the democratic tradition is lengthy and strong—the transition to Socialism will take place through constitutional means. In spite of the enormous advantage which the capitalist class possesses in controlling most of the instruments of education and propaganda—that is, the bulk of the schools and colleges, the newspapers and magazines, the theaters and: movies, the radio and publishing business—and in spite of the constant suppression and distortion of facts unfavorable to Capitalism and favorable to Socialism, a good deal of information helpful to the Left does manage to seep through, often by way of extremely conservative mediums.

Then, too, the liberal and radical organs of opinion are quite numerous and exercise a wide and growing influence. In the United States even that bulwark of conservatism, the Supreme Court, under the invigorating influence of public opinion and the liberal justices appointed by President Roosevelt, has become increasingly sensitive to the needs of the time in its interpretation of the law. Such factors as these, together with the pressure of the economic situation and the ever more convincing example of Soviet Socialism, lead me to believe that if the present degree of freedom is maintained, the Socialist program will eventually win the right of way in the democracies, But many capitalists, as soon as they sense such a result in the offing, become bad sports about democracy. They refuse to keep on playing the game when they see that the score is going against them. As long as they can control in the main, public opinion, the elections, and governmental policy, they feel that political democracy is all right. The moment, however, that the people show signs of choosing for office enough radical and labor candidates to enact fundamental changes in property relations these reactionary capitalists become frightened and decide that perhaps the time has come to dispense with democracy.

An excellent example of this tendency, carried out under the cover of legal forms, was what happened to the five members of the Socialist Party who were elected 1919 to the New York State Assembly. As soon as the Assembly met in 1920 the two major parties, controlled by different groups of capitalists, got together and proceeded to expel the duly-elected Socialists from the legislature on the ground that because of their radical opinions, they were unfit to sit in that august body. This was, of course, at the height of the post-War reaction and the Bolshevik scare; but it showed how scandalously the Capitalist class, when it feels itself threatened, can treat the very essence of American political democracy. Since that time several states have barred the Socialist or Communist parties from the ballot or have put almost insuperable obstacles in the way of their getting on it. Such considerations demonstrate quite plainly how in these urgent times the continuation of democracy can easily become a class issue, with the capitalists trying to suppress democratic institutions and the rest of the people trying to conserve them.

It is not sufficient to say that the American capitalists have permitted all sorts of reform measures, such as the income tax and unemployment insurance, to go through without attempting to overturn democracy. Such elementary reforms have all taken place within the general and accepted framework of Capitalism. When, however, it becomes a question of doing away with the capitalist system itself, a very different situation arises. Then there is danger that the ruling class of today will follow the example of the southern slave-holding aristocracy which precipitated the Civil War when it felt that its power and its cherished institutions were threatened, Even the advance of trade unionism at present provokes a considerable amount of violence on the part of the capitalist class. These current episodes give a hint of more serious happenings when Socialism itself would draw near.

In other words, nothing can prevent some violence from taking place; in fact it has taken place and is taking place. But we can hope, by constant vigilance, to limit and localize that violence.

If and when a President, a Congress, and state legislatures are elected in the United States pledged to put Socialist economic planning into effect, I expect that capitalist groups here and there will attempt to thwart the will of the people by resorting to force. Our budding Socialist government must be on the watch for just such an eventuality and be fully prepared to crush the aggressor capitalists with swiftness and severity in order to keep scattered violence from developing into full-fledged and nation-wide revolt. If the die-hards start trouble, it will be their own fault if they get hurt. In any event, the first Socialist government in America cannot permit a repetition of the Spanish experience, in which a lax and unrealistic People's Front regime dozed in dreamy siesta while the Fascists and their generals went about blithely organizing a formidable and large-scale insurrection.

I doubt, however, if the American plutocracy will ever try anything on the scale of the Spanish Fascist rebellion. Spain, after all, was in 1936 just emerging from semi-feudal conditions and had about as little background in democratic institutions as the Russia of 1917. In fact, it can be definitely stated that in all those nations in which Fascist revolutions ether have been successful or have developed into a major threat, democratic traditions were relatively weak and of short duration.

But there is certainly a possibility that such movements will grow powerful in the democratic countries. Hence, while I am in favor of the working class and the radicals in nations like England and America relying on democratic methods, I also say that they must ever be on the lookout. In countries where Fascist or other types of autocratic dictatorship exist, the means of attaining socialism is a very different matter. Such a country was Tsarist Russia at the time of the overthrow of Nicholas II in 1917. There no other method was possible for the liberals and the radicals but revolution. There, no other form of government could have brought Socialism into being but a Left dictatorship. The other alternatives were the continuance of the iniquitous Tsarist autocracy, a military dictatorship of the Right; maintaining the same inhuman systems under slightly different forms; or complete and awful chaos.

With such alternatives on the agenda of history, what intelligent or humane person could fail to choose a radical dictatorship which would certainly be no more violent than other kinds, and which would lead Russia forward to a new and better social order? Some Americans claim that persons like myself are insincere because we have sympathized with the Communist revolution and dictatorship in Soviet Russia, and at the same time have been agitating for civil liberties and democracy in the United States. But our position is perfectly logical, it seems to me, when we take into consideration the vast differences in social structure between the Russia of 1917 and modern America. The same logic must lead progressive-minded people to recognize revolution as the necessary path to basic change in Fascist states, where democracy has been wiped out.

If, for instance, liberals, radicals and labor combining in a united front were able to oust by force the respective governments of Hitler and Mussolini, they would have to take the next step and set up temporary dictatorships, perhaps of very short duration, in order to stabilize their power and institute the proper measures for the creation of democratic Socialist republics, dedicated to the policy of domestic and international peace. In Germany and Italy the chief practical alternative at present to such regimes is the persistence of the brutal Nazi and Fascist imperialisms. Especially applicable to these lands is Strachey's trenchant generalization:

"The alternative to the violence entailed by the lifting of human life to a new level is the violence entailed by the decline of human society, the break-up of such world civilization as exists, the dawn of a new dark age of perpetual conflict." In the Fascist nations the only chance of a return to civilization, and democracy is an advance to Socialism. Again, what civilized man could fail to choose in favor of the Left?

However, let no one think for a moment that I like dictatorship of any variety as a form of government. In fact I sharply dissent from these radicals who sometimes portray a Left dictatorship as a lovely and beautiful thing in itself. But when it is obvious that dictatorship is essential for progress, I cannot do otherwise than to grit my teeth and support it, bearing as best I can the many cruel and violent things that it implies. I do not expect a dictatorship, even when managed by the most idealistic radicals, to avoid becoming involved in very un-idealistic actions. And that is why I have never been greatly surprised at the violence which has taken place in the Soviet Union, much of which I am convinced is an integral part of dictatorship as such, whether proletarian or otherwise.

As I have shown elsewhere in this book, the trend toward democracy has been very marked in Soviet Russia. There, in the world's one Socialist country, the people already enjoy economic, cultural, sex and racial democracy; they are well on their way toward full political democracy, and they stand unwaveringly for international democracy. This outcome of events in the U. S. S. R. is by no means the first example in history of democracy being advanced through revolution. It is, indeed, only the latest instance of this phenomenon. For it should not be forgotten that the democratic privileges and the-civil rights to which we have grown accustomed in the West were the result of centuries of bitter and violent struggle against monarchical and religious absolutisms upheld by intransigent ruling classes.

I was once cut off the radio when I came to a passage in an address in which I made a mild and qualified comparison between the Russian and the American Revolutions. But I think that I can safely state here that the American nation actually did win its characteristic institutions of democracy through a revolutionary war of five years duration. And for many years following the end of that war in 1781, the American Government did not treat at all gently the Tories who had sided with King George III or who still wished to see the newly founded Republic return to his rule. Americans, therefore, cannot with consistency deny the present right of oppressed peoples to throw off the yoke of twentieth-century autocracies, even if revolutions are essential to do the job; nor criticize too harshly drastic measures on the part of recently liberated nations to secure their gains against domestic and foreign enemies.

We should not forget, either, that the defenders of the

status quo always tend to minimize the amount of violence which is implicit in the functioning of the ordinary capitalist state. Without repeating my story of extra-legal violence on the part of government officials and of international war on the part of whole governments, I want to call attention to the fact that coercion or the threat of it, on behalf of certain socially recognized purposes, has been a necessary element in every state that has ever existed. The majesty of the law is only a shadow unless there stands behind it the physical power of enforcement. And the Marxist theory is that the coercive power of the state has on the whole been used, and often very harshly, on behalf of the ruling class in the community.

Since radicals are in general idealists and, in the ultimate sense, pacifists, they have often played into the hazels of the reactionaries, who are almost always hardheaded, realistic men who do not hesitate to use force whenever convenient. What Marx and Lenin and Stalin have taught the radical movement is that in order to succeed, or even survive, it must on occasion fight fire with fire and employ some of the traditional capitalist methods to defeat the capitalists. This does not imply the principle that the end justifies the means; what it implies is that *some* ends justify *some* means. Those liberals and radicals who have become disillusioned with the Communist dictatorship in the Soviet Union have in my opinion overlooked the fact that until we have a perfect society, we cannot expect to arrive at new social and economic forms through perfect methods; that until we have a perfect democracy, we cannot expect to bring about fundamental changes through perfectly democratic means. Communists and Socialists, who are in accord on most of the chief *ends* of Socialism, have disagreed primarily on the *methods* of attaining it. The traditional policy of the Socialist Party and its equivalents, such as the Labor Party in England and the Social Democratic Party in pre-Hitler Germany, has been to rely entirely on peaceful and parliamentary means for achieving a Socialist order. The Communist Party, on the other hand, has been more realistic by coming out forthrightly for revolution and proletarian dictatorship in those particular situations where no less drastic alternatives have seemed feasible.

The German Social Democratic Party threw away a magnificent chance, the Communists believe, when, having attained state power with the overthrew of the Kaiser in 1918, it permitted the capitalists, the landowners and the militarists to retain most of the key positions in the economic life of the country and many important posts in the governmental apparatus itself. Had the Social Democrats followed through with the revolution and seen the necessity of employing uncompromising measures against the capitalist class, there might well have been a highly developed Socialist economy in Germany today in place of Fascism. Instead, they dilly-dallied with technicalities and reform, and threw away their one great golden opportunity. Exactly the same holds true of the Social-Democratic Party in post-War Austria. And the Socialists in Italy likewise met disaster, at the hands of Mussolini, through their excessively pacifistic course.

As the sad case of Great Britain has demonstrated, however, it is not merely a naive and mystic faith in democratic and legal forms that has afflicted the Socialists. They have also on critical occasions exhibited an appalling lack of principle and courage. The most flagrant instance of this was, in my opinion, during the British financial crisis of 1931. In August of that year the late Ramsay MacDonald, leader of the Labor Party and Prime Minister, together with two other prominent members of the Labor Government, Philip Snowden and J. H. Thomas, deserted to the capitalists, joining with the Tories, of all people, to form a coalition National Government, MacDonald remained Premier in name for four years, but the power went to the Conservative Party and Mr. Stanley Baldwin. British labor stood betrayed by its own leaders, And Mr. MacDonald became even more than before a pathetic prisoner of the London "social lobby." Fortunately, the Socialists themselves have learned a good deal from the inglorious examples of the MacDonalds and their opportunistic, ever-compromising policies. Their education has been further stimulated by the rise and triumph of the German Nazis in 1933, by the slaughter and suppression of the Austrian Social Democrats in 1934, by the success of the Franco-Hitler-Mussolini revolt in Spain and by the alarming gains made by Fascism in the world at large.

At the present time the Socialists and Communists are much closer together than ever before in their general strategy of achieving power. In Spain they stood side by side on the firing line and in the Loyalist government. In all the Fascist nations they both work in underground movements which assume from the start that the only way to get rid of Fascism is through revolution. In the democratic commonwealths they both are in favor of proceeding through, constitutional means. The American Communist Party, for instance, long generally considered an advocate for revolutionary violence, unequivocally declared in its new 1938 constitution, allegiance to the United States Constitution and to the traditions of democracy.

But whatever method, whatever strategy, of transition Socialists, Communists or other varieties of radicals adopt in particular countries or in particular situations, they all agree that only through Socialism can the democratic promise be fulfilled, and that only a society which ultimately brings democracy in the broadest sense has the right to call itself Socialist.

5. *Socialist Democracy*

None but those who make their observations in the manner of the familiar ostrich can continue to think that Capitalism and democracy are synonymous. It is impossible to achieve democratic tranquility within nations, any more than peace between them, as long as Capitalism prevails. The riots and revolutions, the brutal violations of civil liberty and ordinary humanity, which keep taking place all over the capitalist world are, I am convinced, directly or indirectly due to the class struggle inherent in the capitalist system,—a struggle, in which the ruling class constantly tries to suppress the efforts of the proletariat and the other exploited sections of the people to obtain economic justice and a proper share in the abundancies of life. Radicals believe, in fact, that all through history the central role has been played by class struggles, revolving around conflicting economic interests and often expressing themselves in religious or nationalist manifestos and movements.

One does not have to be a follower of Karl Marx or a supporter of Socialism to believe in some such economic interpretation of history and politics. Before Marx was born, James Madison, fourth President of the United States and justly called "the father of the American Constitution," wrote:

> "The most common source of factions has been the various and unequal distribution of property. Those who hold and those who are without property have ever formed distinct interests in society. Those who are creditors and those who are debtors fall under a like discrimination. A landed interest, a manufacturing interest, a mercantile interest, a moneyed interest, with many lesser interests, grow up of necessity in civilized nations and divide them into different classes actuated by different sentiments and views. From the protection of different and unequal faculties of acquiring property, the possession of different degrees and kinds of property immediately results; and from the influences of these on the sentiments and views of the respective proprietors, ensues a division of society into different interests and parties."

Now it is the general status and relationship of the "different interests and parties" that determines the extent and form of democracy in any country. A completely democratic society requires appropriate economic foundations; democratic rights, whether in a political or some other sense, follow upon the possession of economic power.

The bourgeois class was able to overthrow the absolutisms of feudalism and to establish democracy, for itself, only when its economic power, as evidenced in the ownership of the means of production and distribution, had reached a high state of development. Similarly the working class in capitalist nations, though it has the strength to exert considerable pressure and win significant concessions, will not be able to attain full democracy until it achieves ultimate economic power through collective, ownership of the processes of production and distribution. And that means Socialism.

It also means the end of the class struggle, which has reached its final phase in the opposition between the capitalist class and the working class. For Socialism eradicates the class struggle by setting up a classless society in which the proletariat disappears as a separate class as well as the capitalists. Though the apparatus of government as an administrative agency continues, the state, as a super-policeman wielding a big stick for one class as against another class, "withers away." And there no longer remains any occasion for the curtailment of democracy or the violation of civil liberties.

As an instance of how the class struggle dissolves in the new order, consider what becomes of that apparently unceasing antagonism between workers and employers which manifests itself in strikes and results in the most frequent infringements on democratic rights. Strikes, which inevitably cause a temporary crippling of production, are not regarded by radicals as an eternal principle of things. Today strikes are a necessary part of labor's uphill fight, the most effective weapon in the trade-union arsenal. Tomorrow when the working class itself is running the economic machine, when there is no longer a capitalist class from which it has to wrest the very necessities of existence, when material security and growing prosperity are the sure possession of everyone, strikes will be few and far between. Accordingly in a Socialist America, though practically the entire working population will belong to trade unions and regular collective bargaining will go on with the managements of factories and other enterprises, there will be no great difficulty in arriving at satisfactory labor agreements. And most of the bitter bickering and long drawn-out disputes of the present will disappear.

Socialism's unlimited abundance in material goods lays the basis for a like abundance in democratic as well as cultural desiderata. A Socialist republic in the United States will not only preserve our democratic form of government, but will vastly enlarge our civil and political liberties by enforcing all constitutional guarantees in every corner of the land and by assuring equal political opportunity to individuals and groups through an equitable distribution of wealth. Religious and racial minorities will enjoy full political and social rights. Women will see the dawn of a new day for their sex. The extension and qualitative improvement of education will create such a high level of enlightenment that at last democracy will possess the proper intellectual bases. Socialization in the realm of culture does not mean that government authorities take over all cultural activities. Newspapers and magazines, for instance, while they will not be owned by individual proprietors, will be for the most part organs of trade unions, professional associations, co-operatives and other non-governmental bodies. And many such organizations will have their own educational institutions.

Under Socialism, as under any other, system, novel and unorthodox ideas will meet a certain amount of resistance and will be required to prove themselves. Undoubtedly, too, whenever the new society is forced to come into being through revolution and violence, there will be a transitional period during which rather strict controls will be maintained over opinion, But eventually and on the whole, the socialization of culture will usher in a milieu far more favorable to the reception of innovations in every field than has ever been known before. With the material security of men and of nations established on a firm footing, there will no longer exist the haunting fear that new theories will lead to catastrophe. Nor in the classless society will there be any privileged class interested in suppressing new truths.

The individual in a Socialist democracy, far from being regimented or permanently confined to some one particular job, has a much better chance of proving his worth than under any other system. Since economic advantage or disadvantage due to accidents of birth and environment is no longer a consideration, true equality of opportunity comes far nearer fulfillment. The old distinctions grounded in property and caste fade away; men are judged by what they are instead of by what they possess. And there results the closest possible approximation to a society in which there can emerge what the great American democrat, Thomas Jefferson, called "the natural aristocracy of talent and virtue." Of course, young men and women must prove their worth if they wish to rise, must take and pass examinations, and go through other tests of intelligence and ability. These are necessary and salutary processes in any kind of society.

There can be no doubt, then, that Socialism, reared on the firm foundation of economic democracy, will secure for us those other forms of democracy which are so essential to complete the picture. Here in the United States it will bring to final fruition that deep-lying democratic tradition, often thwarted but never downed, which has been so central in American life since the founding of our Republic. Furthermore, if we do not reconstruct our democracy on a Socialist basis by implementing it with an economic system that works and provides the material prerequisites for democratic privileges, there is grave danger of tensions becoming so aggravated that American constitutional government will be done to death in the resulting melee. Indeed, as long as Capitalism exists in any form, there always remains inherent in it be threat of anti-democratic Fascism. Thus the issue is likely more and more to become Socialist democracy or none at all.

Yet even under Socialism we must remain vigilant. Human liberty is not something that can ever become automatic. And no matter what social-economic system governs this country or the world, men will need to exert effort to maintain the freedoms already won and to win others we know not of.

Chapter VII
The Culture and Philosophy of Socialism

1. *Culture and Capitalism*

If we study the great periods of cultural upsurge in human history, we find that one and all of them sprang from a definite material base. They usually coincided with or followed a vigorous outpouring of economic energies, frequently resulting in relative prosperity, on the part of the people concerned. This was true, for example, in the case of ancient Egypt, of Greece in the fifth century B. C , of the high tide of medieval culture, of the Renaissance and Elizabethan England, and of Europe and New England during the nineteenth century. I do not mean that there has been anything equivalent to a scientific correspondence between material and artistic progress, No one could pretend, for example, that Western culture as a whole in the twentieth century, despite its extensive material foundations, has ever approached very closely the qualitative summits which Greek art, in a quite primitive economy, was able to attain. The point is that for art to flourish there must always be *some* material foundation, *some* accumulation of wealth beyond that providing for the bare necessities of life, to sustain the characteristic activities of culture, For the reason that surplus wealth in a community has ever been the monopoly of a small minority, full participation in and enjoyment of literature and the arts were, in the representative periods of civilization I have mentioned, confined to the ruling class and those upon whom it bestowed its favor and munificence. The upper class aristocrats have always claimed that the masses of the people are innately incapable of developing the mental capacity and aesthetic sense to appreciate art, and that education only does them harm by making them dissatisfied. But the truth of the matter is that never in all history have the masses had a fair and decent chance to enter into the broad and fascinating realm of culture. I do not hold in a literal sense that all men are born equal. What I do hold, though, is that all men, except those mentally sub-normal or belonging in asylums, are capable of relatively high educational and cultural development.

Just as the creation and enjoyment of art in a society as a whole requires certain material prerequisites, so does the work of the individual artist. He must either have money to start with or speedily acquire it from some source. Those geniuses who have arisen from the lower ranks have always been dependent on the financial patronage of wealthy individuals or of wealthy institutions like Church or State. For every artist who has succeeded in changing his lot from starving in a garret to dining at court and along the Park Avenues of this world, there have been twenty others, full of promise, whose careers poverty and lack of opportunity brought to a dismal end. The idea that under-nourishment and economic want are a great stimulus to artistic expression is on a par with the argument that insanity should be encouraged because some notable artists have been mentally abnormal.

Today under the capitalist system artists, writers and other professional workers are finding it increasingly difficult to make a living. Painters without patrons, actors without audiences, authors without publishers, teachers without schools, doctors without patients, lawyers without clients, engineers without employers— these have become common phenomena of our times. Usually in a business crisis we hear mostly about the declining stock market, about the huge drop in steel output, about the bankruptcies and the suicides, about the mounting millions of unemployed and the growing tension between classes and nations. But all the time there is a cultural crisis just as serious in its proportions and, in its own sphere, just as far-reaching in its effects, The books that are not written, the works of art that are not finished, the music that is not rendered—such things in any ultimate human sense are no less important than the sinking production schedules of factories and the falling off in domestic and foreign trade.

In the field of writing, the financial returns for the average author, never too lucrative under any circumstances, sharply diminish as publishing houses and bookstores, magazines and newspapers begin to feel the pinch, The business of writing must be carried on as a business, that is, as an enterprise that makes money, Few would claim that the profit criterion is an adequate one for evaluating literature; yet that must be the primary criterion of publishers under Capitalism, Authors themselves can hardly afford to overlook this little fact, In the sharing of profits, however, if there are any profits, the author, with his usual ten per cent royalties, lags pretty far behind. And I think it is possible to state definitely that relatively few writers are able to earn a minimum competence by their work. Reliable estimates indicate that the average writer of talent makes an annual profit of only about $300 for his first ten years of literary endeavor. It is no wonder that so many authors prostitute their gifts and, in a desperate effort to keep the wolf from the door, turn to writing cheap potboilers, lurid sex tales, and propaganda tracts for public utilities or other capitalist interests.

From the point of view of the reading public the situation is equally bad. In order to make his profit the publisher has to sell most books at so high a price that the masses of the people cannot ordinarily buy them. Selling 5,000 books at $3.00 is much more profitable than, selling 70,000 at $1.00. Though the potential book-purchasing public in the U.S.A. runs into the tens of millions, only 2,000,000 of America's population regularly buy books. Half the towns with populations of 5,000 to 100,000 are without bookshops of any sort. Our public libraries, excellent as has been their work, only partially redeem this situation. They are increasingly handi-capped by budget difficulties. And there remain 45,000,000 Americans completely without any library service at all.

What is true of publishing under Capitalism holds, with few qualifications, for every other aspect of culture. Painting sculpture, architecture, the theater, the opera, music, the radio, the motion picture and journalism are all in bondage to the profit system. While comparatively low prices have made mass distribution possible in radio, motion pictures and journalism, standards in these fields have been corrupted and vulgarized by the profit motive. Painting and sculpture, theater and opera, poetry and music of quality are still luxury products in the American scene.. They do not enter in a significant way into the life of the people as a whole.

In the sphere of education the situation is likewise far from ideal. To a large degree the extent and the quality of education depend upon the funds available for material equipment and the teaching staff; and upon the financial capacity of young people to take advantage of educational opportunities, To attend private institutions of course costs money; but to attend public ones also costs money. For the student cannot be at home helping his family or if he is old enough, working at a regular job and receiving wages. According to the United States Bureau of Education, approximately 45 percent of American youth do not attend high school, approximately 25 percent do not reach the eighth grade, approximately 14 percent do not reach the seventh grade, and approximately 10 per cent do not reach the sixth grade. Altogether more than 3,000,000 children between the ages of seven and seventeen are not going to school at present. Only slightly over 10 percent of American youth of college age go to college and fully 90 per cent of these come from middle income or upper income families.

The trials and tribulations which, since 1929, have descended in such abundance on our schools and colleges, our students and teachers show very clearly how educational conditions fluctuate in accordance with economic conditions. When there is a business crisis or depression, the capitalist-controlled city and state governments look around for reductions that can be made in the budget. And one of the first possibilities that comes to their attention is the appropriation for public education. For example, in 1939 the Republican majority in the New York legislature slashed more than $10,000,000 from the total allocated to education in Governor Lehman's budget. Ten other states have drastically cut their state aid to education during the past two or three years.

In private education during times of depression there is a tremendous falling off not only in donations to schools and colleges, but also in the interest on their endowments. Since 1929 there has been a shrinkage of approximately one-third in the return on such endowments. Even during good times private schools and colleges rarely have sufficient funds to carry out adequately their minimum functions and to give their staffs decent salaries. Furthermore, the distribution of financial resources is very uneven. In the field of higher education, for instance, a group of ten colleges and universities owns 43 percent of the recorded endowment funds, though it teaches only 17 per cent of the students; a middle group of ninety owns 38 percent of the total and teaches 42 per cent of the students; while the large number of 300 institutions owns only 19 percent of the endowment funds and teaches 41 per cent of the students. Quite evidently the modern concentration of capital extends into the cultural field.

The fact that private educational institutions are dependent on the gifts of the wealthy and well-to-do is a weighty reason for their well-known conservatism in social and economic affairs. The academic officials of great universities such as Harvard with an endowment of about $142,000,000, Yale, with an endowment of about $100,000,000, and Columbia with an endowment of about $70,000,000, feel that the welfare of these institutions is bound up with that of the capitalist system. In addition, since upper-class business and professional men are preponderant on most boards of trustees, whether of private or public educational institutions, it is inevitable that American education in general should pursue a course calculated to help preserve the *status quo.*

The permeation of American educational institution by the prevailing capitalist spirit and psychology leads them frequently to act toward their staffs and particularly toward their more humble employees in as thoroughly hard-boiled a manner as businesses with a backward labor policy. Thus, in 1929, Harvard University, of all places, peremptorily dismissed twenty scrubwomen in order to avoid paying them the 37 cents an hour minimum established by the Massachusetts Minimum Wage Commission, Harvard had been violating the Commission's decree by paying the women only 35 cents, an hour. The Treasurer of the University, backed by

President Lowell, actually had the gall to argue before a committee of the State legislature that there had been no underpayment because the wages of the women came to more than the required 37 cents if a twenty-minute rest period permitted during their working day was counted as time off without pay.

Few occurrences have ever so thoroughly aroused my indignation as this scrubwomen episode. I personally became the executive secretary of a group of distinguished Harvard alumni who made a public protest on the matter to the Harvard authorities and tried to persuade them to reverse their decision and pay the women the back wages due them. But Dr. Lowell and the Harvard Corporation stood pat. Eventually the alumni group raised from Harvard men. a special fund of $3,880 and itself paid back the scrubwomen. Today, I am glad to say, with Dr. James B. Conant as President, Harvard can boast of a labor policy that is liberal and enlightened.

Incidentally, the general public in America has an extremely exaggerated impression of the munificence of the capitalist class towards educational and charitable institutions. According to Phyllis A. and Omar P. Goslin in *Rich Man, Poor Man,* "the total gifts of all who filed income taxes has never amounted to as much as two per cent of their incomes," The great foundations which are constantly receiving such favorable publicity, and which have admittedly provided the economic wherewithal for a number of worth-while projects, possess an aggregate capital of less than $3,000,000,000, well under two-thirds of the approximate amount allocated by the U. S. Government to the army and navy in 1939. And the appropriations of two multi-millionaire capitalists, Andrew Carnegie and John D. Rockefeller, account for at least a third of this total.

From a careful study of the wills probated and estates appraised during four recent years in New York, the richest city in the nation, Professor Eduard C. Lindeman of the New School for Social Research finds that "only six percent of the wealthy distribute their estates among agencies and institutions. Moreover, the sum which they thus distribute amounts to only six per cent of the total wealth bequeathed. And, what is of greater significance, perhaps, is the fact that the bulk of wealth thus distributed flows into the treasuries of churches, hospitals and conventional charities." Of equal import was the statement made by the eminent sociologist, Abraham Epstein, in an article in 1931, that "the 360 American community chests, in spite of the energetic trumpeting, cajolery, and high-pressure salesmanship that go with them, do not raise more than $80,000,000 a year—less than half the sum now spent through workmen's compensation laws alone." Mr. Epstein went on to say: "That the slackers in the United States are not the poor people but the richest and most respectable as well known to persons engaged in the business of raising money for charitable purposes."

In so far as scientific research and progress are bound up with the great universities and technological institutes, they inevitably suffer when education in general suffers. In so far as they are directly bound up with business enterprise, they are retarded not only by lack of appropriations in times of economic stress, but also by the general effect of the profit motive. As I showed in a previous chapter, because of the fear of over-production, of technological unemployment, of costly machinery becoming obsolete and of new products taking away the markets for old, Capitalism, especially in its later monopoly stage, has seriously hindered the unfettered advance of applied science.

One of the most vital fields of science is that of medicine. And because of medicine's spectacular progress during the last century, health, like so many other things, has become largely a purchasable commodity. For it is the power of the purse that is able, to obtain not only proper medical supplies and services, but also the sort of working and living and recreational conditions in which the sound mind an the sound body naturally flourish. Public health work, held back everywhere by conservative physicians and laymen alike on the ground that it is Socialistic, has not filled more than an iota of the needs. At the same time, although there are not enough medical schools to take care of the young men and women who wish to enter the profession, there are not enough well-paid jobs to take care of the present graduates of medical schools.

The United States Public Health Service stated in 1938 that "one-third, perhaps one-half, of the population of the United States is too poor to afford the full cost of adequate medical care on any basis." The same report proved up to the hilt that health varies according to the economic status of the individual, disabling illness being the greatest, of course, among families on relief or having low incomes. "The non-relief group with an income under $1,000 showed a volume of disability of over twice that in the highest income group; families with incomes between $1,000 and $ 2,000 showed a 20 percent excess. Not only do relief and low income families experience more frequent illness than their neighbors, but their illnesses are of longer duration. An earlier report of the Health Service had estimated that the death rate, from the ten major diseases, among American families or single individual with incomes of less than $1,000 was double that of the rest of the population. Every year in America 144,000 babies, well over the entire death toll in the Great War are born dead or die within a few months of their birth. Proper medical care would save 45 per cent of them. Seventeen thousand American mothers die annually in pregnancy or childbirth. Proper medical care would save 66 percent of them.

Economically conditioned ill health and neuroticism are prime factors in establishing Capitalism as the greatest home wrecker that has ever been at large in the world. And there are other causes contributing to this result: the capitalist system drives millions of children to grueling labor at a tender age; it forces hundreds of thousands of young boys out of the home and onto the road, footloose and pathetic wanderers in a land of plenty; it leads scores of thousands of girls and women into houses of prostitution; it corrupts sexual love and the relationship between parent and child through considerations of money and property; it creates millions of widowed and fatherless homes through terrible civil and international conflicts; it makes satisfactory home life all but impossible for the masses of the people because of the execrable living conditions thrust upon them; it breaks up the families of the middle and upper classes as well as of the working class through the collapse of its moral codes and its failure to provide a worthwhile purpose and philosophy of living.

By no means unrelated to the state of the family is another field in which Capitalism has a very bad record, I refer to the matter of crime, which costs the United States the appalling sum of $15,000,000,000 every year. The Socialist view is that while subnormal mentality and sexual aberration, uncontrolled passion and the lure of excitement, all enter into the picture, crime is principally the result of an environment deficient in the social and economic prerequisites of wholesome living and often in the very necessities of existence. It was Marx who somewhere said, "Crime is the private war which the poor wage against the rich." But it was a leading capitalist, Daniel Willard, President of the Baltimore and Ohio Railroad, who, referring to unemployment in a public speech a few years ago, frankly remarked, " I would steal before I would starve." Many large-scale thieves and robbers, including our atrocious crop of kidnapers, having accepted the regular capitalist aim of getting rich quick, see in their profession an easy short cut to success. And not a few of them, as some of our recent business scandals have made plain, come from the highest ranks of capitalist enterprise.

Now if mere reform cannot, as we have seen, resolve the economic contradictions of Capitalism, then obviously it cannot cure the cultural deficiencies that stem from the present system. Under Capitalism there is precious little prospect of eliminating crime, of guaranteeing good health and physical well-being to the masses of the people, of making available to them the full fruits of art and education. If Capitalism is not able to distribute to its teeming millions even a sufficiency of material necessities like food and clothing and shelter, then what chance has it of enabling them to share in the enjoyment of good books, beautiful paintings and all the other products of culture? In any case I am most doubtful whether in a civilization that lays its primary stress on the making of money there can exist an atmosphere in which the things of the spirit will grow and flourish on the widest scale. It is surely no accident that the greatest and most highly developed capitalist nation, America, has given birth to so little in the realm of art that is unmistakably great. All in all, then I am constrained to say that though culture may yet experience occasional fits and starts which will temporarily look like progress, it can no longer fundamentally and in the large go forward under Capitalism. But in our present system it can retrogress far and quickly, as any study of what has happened in the book-burning, art-killing, genius-banishing Fascist states discloses. The one chance, as I see it, for culture to advance is in a planned Socialist society.

2. *Culture under Socialism*

Socialism drastically alters the whole cultural scene. It frees literature and art, education and science, from the economic ups and downs, the chills and fevers, the corrupting contagion and mortal illness of Capitalism. Under Socialism there are no depressions; no workers of hand or of brain unemployed or threatened with unemployment; no grounds for the curtailment of educational and cultural, programs. Consequently culture expands steadily along with the economic life of the country and with each annual increase in the national income. For income and basic wealth are always on the rise in a Socialist society. Such, a society will spend proportionately ten—no, a hundred times as much on culture as any upper class that has ever lived. It will invest in cultural activity, sums comparable, let us say, with what Capitalism puts into armaments and war.

Thus Socialism permanently releases both ordinary ability and genius from the cramping pressures of penury and the profit motive. Writers and poets are no longer compelled to choose between production for money and starving for their ideals; if their work has merit, they will easily earn the means of carrying it on. Publishers, too, will not have to subordinate literary standards to monetary profit. Science will make more rapid strides than ever before, both in the realm of pure research and of practical application, with labor-saving inventions becoming an immediate boon to mankind instead of a possible road to ruin. Scientific knowledge and the scientific spirit, with its cordial hospitality to new hypotheses, will everywhere replace the old religious, social and economic superstitions.

In a Socialist society education will finally come into its own; it will be planned on a country-wide basis; its proportion of the national budget will rise immensely. Its physical plant and equipment will expand accordingly and its teaching staff, no longer underpaid, will become ample in numbers, Schools and colleges will cease to be overcrowded; and classes will be reduced to that size which best combines the advantages of individual attention from the teacher with collective stimulus from the group. The Socialist curriculum will close the unfortunate cleavage between theory and practice that prevails today in capitalist countries, thoroughly integrating culture with economics, and what is learned inside school and college with the actualities of existence outside. The permanent purpose of Socialist education is to turn out individuals who are fully educated and who, to quote the French philosopher Henri Bergson, "will act as men of thought; and think as men of action."

It was America's Walt Whitman who said, " To have great poets there must be great audiences, too." Pushing this thought further, I think we can safely state that a Socialist commonwealth will provide writers and artists in general with an appreciative public practically as large as the whole literate population of a country, Under Socialism, with its economic security and progressively shorter hours of work, the leisure class is everyone. This new leisure class is not just a passive recipient and consumer of culture; it actively participates and creates, putting into effect the principle enunciated by the late American painter, Robert Hallowell, that "Each bears a gift for all," In the new society every individual becomes the practitioner of some cultural skill, at least as an amateur, and takes part in group cultural activities. Those of really professional ability enter the cultural field as a vocation and work upward toward the summits of achievement.

This spread of culture to the masses of the people does not

imply any letdown in standards; on the contrary, it results ultimately in just the opposite by raising to unprecedented, heights the general cultural level and by broadening to an unprecedented extent the ranks of first rate accomplishment and genius. At the same time the democratization of culture under Socialism brings art out from its cloistered retreats among the wealthy and the professional aesthetes, and transforms it from a thing apart, residing in private mansions and public museums, into a pervasive complement of man's work and play. The quality of beauty enters universally into the products of industry and the common objects of daily life. Science and art, no longer at cross-purposes, work harmoniously together to build a more beautiful world.

Literature and art in a Socialist society will without doubt express chiefly the fundamental principles and philosophy, problems and aspirations, of that society. In other words, writers and artists like other men will come to reflect their environment so completely and naturally that they will embody in their work, more or less unconsciously, the general features of the Socialist synthesis. Certain critics profess to find this prospect sinister. Throughout history, however, including the period of capitalist hegemony, writers and artists have always and everywhere given expression- to the particular economic, social and cultural characteristics of the civilization in which they have lived. As Marx puts it, "In every epoch the ruling ideas have been the ideas of the ruling class."

It can be said, I think, that the predominance of a generally accepted and pervasive set of cultural and philosophical principles is an aid and inspiration to literature and painting, sculpture and architecture. As John H. Randall, Jr., sums it up: "The supreme art has worked with the feelings and symbols of a great imaginative tradition. Periclean Athens, the Christian thirteenth century, Medicean Florence, the Elizabethan age, the last backward yearning of the Romanticists, not to go outside our own past— from these eras of a common faith and a common world of the spirit have come the great masterpieces of individualized genius." And there is every reason to expect that under Socialism, whether in the United States or elsewhere, a great art and literature will likewise in due course develop. But this outcome will take time, since the energies of the people must necessarily be preoccupied over a considerable period with laying deep and broad the foundations of the new order. It is well to remember that America's golden day of culture, the flowering of New England, did not reach its zenith until some six or seven decades after the Revolution.

That the Socialist economic system will significantly affect Socialist culture should not be considered as anything unusual. According to the doctrine of Historical Materialism as expounded by Marx and Engels, the underlying factor in the flow of human history at any particular time or in any particular place is the economic structure of society as embodied in the total relations of production. The existing mode of production expresses itself in certain property relations which are crystallized in definite class forms covering all the various aspects of social life. In Engels' words: "The political, legal, philosophical, religious, literary, artistic, etc., development rest upon the economic. But they all react upon one another and upon the economic base. Men make their own history, but in a given, conditioning milieu, upon the basis of actual relations already extant, among which the economic relations, no matter how much they are influenced by relations of a political and ideological order, are ultimately decisive, constituting a red thread which runs through all the other relations and enabling us to understand them,"

While, then, human minds and cultural activities possess plenty of efficacy in their own right, they are on the whole conditioned and channeled by the fundamental economic forces and relationships. For instance, the superb cultural phenomenon that we know as the modern symphony orchestra could never have occurred until certain economic and mechanical techniques had come into being with the Industrial Revolution and made possible certain complicated and delicately adjusted musical instruments. Nor could the airplane have become an actuality, no matter what brilliant and beautiful ideas men had about flying through the air, until firm foundations had been laid in the realm of economics and mechanics.

Marx's comment on Greek culture illuminates another aspect of the problem. "It is a well-known fact," he says, "that Greek mythology was not only the arsenal of Greek art, but also the very ground from which it had sprung. Is the view of nature and of social relations which shaped Greek imagination and Greek art possible in the age of automatic machinery, and railways, and locomotives, and electric telegraphs? Where does Vulcan come in as against Roberts & Co.; Jupiter, as against the lightning rod; and Hermes as against the Credit Mobilier? All mythology masters and dominates and shapes the forces of nature in and through the imagination; hence it disappears as soon as man gains mastery over the forces of nature."

As writers in a Socialist civilization will no doubt emphasize, one of the most profound qualitative advances under Socialism is that ordinary labor, always looked down upon with unconcealed contempt by the upper classes, possesses genuine social dignity. From this viewpoint, the carrying on of useful work is, to quote Marx again, not merely a means to live but is in itself the first necessity of living. Everyone will work under Socialism both because there is so much work to do and because having a job is recognized as a prerequisite for leading a full and satisfactory life. Capitalist America's wealthy idle would be far more normal and more happy human beings if they would take a hint from Socialist sagacity and substitute absorbing work for dull and trivial loafing.

Socialism envisages going much farther than establishing the dignity and universality of socially worth-while labor. Its goal is to overcome more and more the distinction between manual and intellectual work. As Engels phrased it: "Productive labor, instead of being a means to the subjection of men, will become a means to their emancipation by giving each individual the opportunity to develop and exercise all his faculties, physical and mental, in all directions; in which, therefore proactive labor will become a pleasure instead of a. burden. "The ideal, according to Marx, is "to replace the detail-worker of today crippled by lifelong repetition of one and the same operation and thus reduced to the mere fragment of a man, by the fully developed individual, fit for a variety of labors, ready to face any change of production, and to whom the different social functions he performs are but so many modes of giving free scope to his own natural and acquired powers."

Since Marx's day the tendency in a good many industries has been toward even greater specialization. The word "robot" is, after all, a twentieth-century invention. Yet we can still remain certain that under a fully developed Socialist system, where the employment of new inventions is geared to human well-being instead of to profit, a close approximation can be made to the picture Marx and Engels had in mind, in capitalist industry, as Mr. J. D. Bernal, eminent scientist of Cambridge University, informs us, "The machine is designed to employ the cheapest and, consequently, the most monotonous labor. This is completely contrary to the spirit of mechanical inventions. Those operations which are repetitive and monotonous are just those that could be done best by the machines themselves. What people speak of as the slavery of man to the machine is really the devotion of manufacturers to profits, If machines had been designed from the point of view of the worker rather than that of minimum cost of operation, they would be as interesting to work and far less laborious than farming or hunting."

Another goal of Socialism is to eliminate that sharp and unhappy distinction between town and country which capitalist industry and concentration has so accentuated. Only nation-wide economic planning can distribute industry and agriculture in such a way that productive efficiency and the living conditions of the population will both benefit to the utmost. No observer can deny that over-crowded cities with, their poisoned air and awful slums, are one of the chief banes of capitalist civilization, just as important as any material and geographic improvements required in the relationship between town and country is the drastic change which their cultural relationship demands. A primary plank in the Socialist platform is the elimination of the cultural lag of the rural areas. Proper educational planning will bring to these districts standards and services on a par with the wealthier urban sections.

The Socialist transformation of both town and country is of prime importance for the health program that the new order makes feasible, Socialism's provision of good housing and good air, as well as of good food and good clothing, is the natural foundation for good health. Adequate medical facilities will also become available to the masses of the people. And all sections of the population will have the time and financial means to enjoy America's superb recreational possibilities: cool beaches in the summer, the refreshing countryside, the myriad beauties of forest and mountain, the crisp and invigorating delights of winter ice and snow. Everyone will actively participate in the world of sports. But the usual capitalist commercialization of sport for the sake of private profit will be impossible; nor will there take place any prostitution of educational institutions to football in order to finance a general program, of athletics and attract donations from the more adolescent wealthy.

The new social and economic bases of life in a Socialist society exercise a profound effect on the family as on everything else. By guaranteeing economic-abundance and first-class living quarters to everyone, Socialism life domestic life to a new and higher plane. Parents, no longer fearing poverty or insecurity, feel free to go ahead and have as many children as they wish. Simultaneously, the general cultural advance greatly affects the home for the better, not only by giving the children vastly improved educational opportunities, but also by making sure that both mothers and fathers are educationally equipped to bring them up. No matter how excellent our schools and colleges become, the role of the parents in the education of the child, especially in the early formative years, will always remain most important. Another point is that in a Socialist society parents will possess far more leisure and vacation time to spend together with their children. Under Capitalism most of us, and especially husbands and fathers, are so busy trying to make the system work or trying to get rid of it entirely that we do not have one-tenth of the spare time that we would like to devote to home activities.

Not the least of Socialism's contributions to the institution of the family is its liberation of women. This means, among other things, that wives will no longer subordinate themselves morally and spiritually to their husband's careers, sacrificing their existence as independent human beings, giving up their freedom of opinion, and becoming mere reflections of masculine will and mind. Expectant parents will no longer, as so generally now, prefer a boy to a girl because of the discriminations and disadvantages that the latter will suffer throughout life, And whatever degree of sexual freedom the mores of the community sanction, there will be an end of the double-standard in which men have such freedom, but women do not.

While some radicals in the field of economics and politics have also been extremists in the theory or practice, or both, of sex relations, it is sheer nonsense to think that authentic Socialism ever envisaged "the abolition of the family" or a system of "free love." Friedric Engels himself wrote in his *Origin of the Family* that the monogamous family, "far from disappearing" with the advent of Socialism, "will then on the contrary be fully realized for the first time....Prostitution disappears; monogamy, instead of collapsing, at last becomes a reality—even for men." Lenin minced no words in denouncing sexual promiscuity and expressed particular repugnance for "the glass of water theory," which, held indiscriminate sexual intimacy to be a natural act no more to be criticized than drinking water when thirsty. "The revolution," he said, "demands concentration, increase of forces. From the masses, from individuals, it cannot tolerate orgiastic conditions, such as are normal for the decadent heroes and heroines of D'Annunzio. Dissoluteness in sexual life is bourgeois, is a phenomenon of decay. The proletariat is a rising class. It doesn't need intoxication as a narcotic or a stimulus——intoxication as little by sexual exaggeration as by alcohol."

Finally, Socialism, by improving so immeasurably the environmental aspects of human existence, does away with the poisonous atmosphere in which crime and vice are a natural growth, Simultaneously, because of its humane and intelligent attitude, it drastically reforms the whole theory and practice of penal administration. A Socialist regime treats persons who would ordinarily be classed as criminals as sick men, who have succumbed to a disease and must be put in quarantine until they recover. It runs its prisons on the basis of making its inmates feel like self-respecting citizens and of retraining them for normal life in the world outside. All prisoners will do or learn to do some form of useful labor in accordance with the principle that work is the most efficacious of curatives. And unlike the distressing situation under Capitalism, where released prisoners habitually wander from pillar to post hunting hopelessly for a position and often feel driven to take up crime again as a profession, prisoners unlike Socialism will always find a good job open to them when they have served their term.

There can no absolute proof, before the event, that a Socialist society in America and other capitalist nations will be capable of the cultural accomplishments which I have been reviewing. But there are many present-day indications that I have not been exaggerating. For instance, there is the general excellence, considering the many retarding economic factors, of those outstanding socialized institutions in America—our system of public education in school and college and our system of public libraries. Nor can we afford to overlook the striking achievements of the Federal Art Project, the Federal Music Project, the Federal Theater, including its special Radio Division, and the Federal Writers Project, all carried on under the aegis of the United States Government. When all is said and done, however, the most palpable proof of what Socialism can attain in the realm of culture lies in the astounding record, during the first two decades of its existence, of the Soviet Union, arising Phoenix-like out of the ashes of its semi-feudal and semi-barbarous past. That story I have told in an earlier chapter.

3. *The Transformation of Motives*

But how, asks the ordinary capitalist-minded individual,

can Socialism possibly bring about all the economic and cultural achievements I have discussed in this book, when there no longer exists the profit motive, supposedly the mainspring of human energy under Capitalism? This is a question which I must attempt to answer fully. And I shall begin my answer by denying that the profit motive is predominant with the majority of people working in the capitalist system. As I stated in Chapter II, profit is the money which a business makes above total costs in the selling of goods or services. It constitutes the basic regulator of capitalist enterprise and the basic motive of the capitalists owning and operating such enterprise. Workers and professionals under Capitalism are not spurred on by the profit motive; but it is the profit motive which leads businessmen to exploit them.

If a man, because of greater skill or ability, earns a higher wage or salary than his fellow, that does not in itself mean that he is working for the profit motive. Most Americans want substantial wages or salaries, not necessarily in order to indulge in great luxury or make some kind of social splurge, but in order to guarantee themselves and their families a decent standard of existence throughout the many economic vicissitudes which the present system makes inevitable. Accordingly, they need sufficient funds to build up reserves for whatever eventualities depression, ill health or old age may bring. Unfortunately, the indiscriminate identification of practically every form of making a living, or of manifesting self-interest, with the operation of the profit motive has brought endless confusion into the subject of incentives under Capitalism and Socialism.

The tens of thousands of devoted men and women in capitalist countries who have entered such vocations as teaching or medicine or scientific research can scarcely fail to recognize the absurdity of ascribing all professional endeavor either to the so-called profit motive or to economic considerations in general. For any physician worthy of the name, a motivation at least equal in importance with earning a living is that of preventing disease and preserving life; for any teacher worthy of his position, that of spreading knowledge and stimulating intelligence; for any scientist

315

worthy of his laboratory, that of searching for the truth and advancing the frontiers of authenticated fact. When Capitalism forces professionals to subordinate such motives to money-making, which it constantly does, it is corrupting; the very basis of profession ethics.

Even in the upper ranks of capitalist industry the profit motive is not nearly as controlling as the capitalists would have us think. As any number of reliable studies have pointed out, there is a growing separation in business between ownership and management. Most of the engineers, the superintendents, the administrative officers, and the more highly-paid white-collar workers are not profit-receivers in a direct sense however remunerative their salaries may be. Then, under Capitalism, there are the scores of thousands of employees in the local, state and national governments. These men and women can hardly be classified as working from the profit motive. And these public services would have completely broken down, with anarchy as the result, in the various capitalist governments, had the orthodox idea about the necessary profit motivation at the root of all useful endeavor been true.

We also have the lesson of the consumers' co-operative movement. The owners of the cooperatives are the owners. These organizations are run at cost and any surplus is paid back to the consumers in proportion to their purchases. The managers of the co-operatives receive a salary and do their work efficiently without benefit of the profit motive. The co-operative is now an important phenomenon in most non-Fascist industrialized countries. In Great Britain, for instance, the co-operatives carry on a retail business of more than a million dollars a year.

Whatever motives are operative in any society at any given time, every competent, modern psychologist or teacher knows that through the medium of economic processes and social pressures as well as through formal schooling, can achieve the most far-reaching changes in the basic attitudes of a people. This is true; whether a Socialist, Fascist, or democratic-capitalist system is determining the general outlines of what the people learn and of how they act. If your whole educational and economic system is geared to the idea that the profit motive is what makes the world go round, then the people may accept this myth as the gospel truth and become so conditioned to it that any other notion appears like an interference with the natural order of things. Theoretically, I suppose, they might become unable to perform their accustomed work on any other assumption; actually, however, we need have no such fear, since this myth of the all-ruling profit motive finds so little support in fact.

Clearly, fundamental alterations in motivation can be achieved regardless of the old adage, "You can't change human Mature." Or, rather, this hoary half-truth becomes irrelevant because its application all depends on which of a thousand and one definitions of human nature you use. As one eminent psychologist, the late Dr. Frankwood E. Williams, has put it, our conceptions of human nature are extremely unreliable, because under Capitalism we have been studying human nature "in captivity." In a sense, as Karl Marx himself once said, "the whole of history is nothing but the progressive transformation of human nature." In another sense, of course, there has been no real change in human nature, even under Soviet Socialism.

So we do not get very far by talking about human nature in the abstract, independent of time and circumstance. What we can definitely establish in the concrete, however, is that under certain economic and educational conditions human beings can perform wonders irrespective of the profit motive, or, indeed, of ordinary self-interest at all. When a nation becomes involved in war, for instance, the capitalists expect the workers promptly to forget about the money motive, to substitute for it sublime thoughts about patriotism, and to go out and die like heroes. And usually in the past they have succeeded through propaganda in persuading the masses to follow this very course.

Let us reflect for a moment, too, on the nature of the female sex. I do not suggest in the least that women are more noble than men; but it would be a rash observer indeed who could seriously maintain that women throughout the ages, in their characteristic functions as wives, mothers and managers of the household, have been mainly spurred on by the profit motive. Though a small percentage of women today do work for profit, 95 per cent of them throughout the world are still moved to all sorts of energetic and altruistic action for reasons entirely unconnected with profit-making.

The truth is that human nature, going through a process of change or not, is an exceedingly complex thing. It takes such a wide range of impulses and motives that psychologists find difficulty in even naming them. The classical economists of Capitalism constructed in their imaginations something called "the economic man," who is no less a monstrosity then "the warrior man" of those who wish to justify armed conflict and conquest, or the "sexual man," of those who stress the important of biological urges, expressed and suppressed. You cannot reduce man to a mere part of himself is such ways without grossly over-simplifying human nature. What Socialist psychology attempts to do is to view the *total* man in relation to his *total* environment. And in doing so gives due attention to all of the various factors—whether associated with economics, pugnacity, sex, intellect, play, or something else—which go to make up human nature. One of the most pressing tasks of this psychology today is to, incidentally, assimilate whatever is sound in the Freudian school with the existing body of the Marxist doctrine.

Though modern psychology has clearly shown, especially through the study of children, that human beings are innately *active*, the capitalists claim that the overwhelming majority of men need to be goaded into economic activity by the profit motive because they are naturally lazy and greedy. As Professor Harry F. Ward puts it: "This is the doctrine of total depravity in the economic field and that without remedy." It is one of the wonders of the modern world that men of scientific training, who indignantly reject "the Fall of Man" will yet locate him among the swine and insist that he can never get up from among them. Thus the argument for the profit motive comes full circle. It first asks us to accept a degrading view of life for the sake of economic efficiency and finally requires us to tolerate an inefficient economic process on the ground of a debasing concept of human nature."

What the usual argument for the profit motive essentially represents is an attempt to rationalize the stupidity of the capitalist system by grossly libeling mankind. It is on an exact par with the argument of those apologists for militarism who say that we can never get rid of war because human nature is afflicted with an instinct of pugnacity. Of course any number of businessmen recognize how intellectually disreputable is the latter proposition. But capitalists who talk about motivations seldom if ever seem to become aware of the mass of inconsistencies in which they are involved.

Thus they will argue hotly for the profit motive all week, but on Sunday they will piously plead, that belief in God and immortality constitute the central nerve of human initiative or that the Christian ethical ideals of love and brotherhood are the real inspiration of mankind. Few capitalists have the gall to stand up and say that their own main motivation in life is to pile up profits: they will always tell you that they are animated by the highest social and humanitarian considerations. And they sometimes actually have the moral complacency to state that it is chiefly the low-minded masses (only a tiny fraction of whom ever have the chance to make profits) who are swayed by the profit motive.

It likewise strikes my sense of the ludicrous to hear capitalists railing against the deplorable lack or incentive that Socialism would entail, when in the present capitalist order millions and millions of men, no matter what incentives they may have, *can't* work because there are no jobs. Again, some capitalists go so far as to assert that economic fear and insecurity are good things in that they keep the workers on their toes; but it is not noticeable that these same capitalists take pains to make their own children economically insecure. On the contrary, they usually endow them with a very considerable share of this world's goods. And it has never been clear to me why substantial subsidies from one's parents should necessarily result in hard work and nobility of character, whereas the guarantee of a mere living wage by the state, or even the granting of minimum unemployment relief, should corrupt men and ruin their initiative.

As a matter of fact, we all know well enough that the inheritance of great wealth, or its acquisition through other means, frequently turns men and women into idle, high-living, anti-social wastrels. Here again the general social milieu is the determining influence. In capitalist families where the tradition of work and achievement in the business or professional world remains strong the offspring usually do not degenerate into loafers and spend-thrifts; but there is always a fair chance that this tradition will grow weak in the second or third generation.

Several years ago the New York *World-Telegram* gave me a hearty laugh when it began a friendly editorial about me with the following: "He might spend his life cruising the seven seas in a yacht, his summers in Switzerland, his winters on the Riviera and all that sort of thing. Or if he didn't like that kind of navigation he could cruise the 36,000 speakeasies and night clubs that his home city affords. He could devote his days to polo if he chose. Or to golf or horse racing or roulette, or any of the other occupations that so many rich men's sons go in for." Now I am no Puritan and have visited in my time plenty of nightclubs, not to mention, speak-easies. But in the social atmosphere in which I happened to grow up there was not much danger that I or my brothers would go in for the playboy type of career so often satirized in the public prints, though the ruling class as a whole would no doubt much prefer the younger generation to become ne'er-do-well socialites than serious radicals.

All of which goes to prove that members of the capitalist class, including myself, do not inevitably have the will to work destroyed by the absence of economic fear and the possession of relative economic security. Thus again, the behavior of the capitalists themselves disproves their argument that under Socialism, where, every one has material security, individual initiative will, for that reason be undermined. The persistence of the notion that insecurity is required as a goad to productive work is largely due, I think, to the illegitimate hold-over of theories formulated in the long ages when an economy of scarcity made it inevitable that insecurity should in fact be the primary motivation for 99 per cent of those earning a living. The evolution of our present economy of abundance obviously makes such theories very much out of date.

Once in a while a capitalist, more intelligent and outspoken than the average, will admit much of what I have been saying about motivations. Thus one of our country's most important executives, Mr. Walter P. Gifford, President of the American Telephone and Telegraph Company, sees a growing change in business psychology.

> From the incentives of personal profit [he writes] the change to me is one of pride in the job and the satisfaction of rendering a public service. . . . More and more I encounter men of the highest ability who regard business not as a means to acquire personal wealth, but as a fascinating profession and as an opportunity for accomplishment. They do not seek more money from it than enough to give them comfortably only those things really worth having that money can buy—freedom from financial worry, security for their families, books, art and travel. But they do want outlet for their energies, exercise for their brains, and above, all, they genuinely want to be useful. Business is becoming a profession.

> New incentives to effort: are in force, I know it is popular to smile at the notion that the ideal of service, of a job well done, is an adequate substitute for mere acquisitiveness but it is becoming daily more evident that this is really so. Today, without the possession of great sums of money one may live well, and it is increasingly questioned whether great fortunes are a real help to happiness.

Now though Mr. Gilford gives expression to ideals which enter intermittently the minds of many capitalists, the trouble is that under the existing system businessmen in their characteristic business functions *must* make profit their major end or go to the wall. When, however, they are functioning as philanthropists, Sunday School superintendents, Commencement orators or heads of families, they may sincerely lend support to other motivations which for the most part they cannot possibly follow out in the day-to-day actualities of economic life.

Another illuminating slant on motives is to be found in a statement by the late Charles P. Steinmetz, next to Thomas Edison probably the most distinguished, inventor the electrical world has known. "Under Socialism, I would have even greater incentive that at present. If I invent anything now, the invention accrues immediately to the advantage of the General Electric and its full benefits reach society only after a long time, Under Socialism, anything invented could be used immediately by the entire industry and sold to the public at cost." The point made by Dr. Steinmetz brings out the fact that even if one has a job and a fairly-well paid job under Capitalism, one's sense of workmanship is likely to be frustrated. The scientist who sees the discoveries of years of experimentation resulting chiefly in higher profits for a little group of privileged capitalists; in suppression by some monopolistic corporation; in a disastrous increase in technological un-employment; or in the multiplied power of death-dealing military weapons, must feel as sick-at-heart as the artist who is driven to work that is lucrative in order to maintain his livelihood.

Steinmetz's belief that under Socialism, there would "be even greater incentive," has been thoroughly born out in the soviet Union. In view of the tremendous outpouring of energy in that country in the past twenty years, it is simply fantastic for comfortable Capitalists in other lands to claim that a Socialist system destroys initiative and to the human will to action. The impact of Socialism on psychology of motivation is such, to quote Dr. Ward again, as to bring about the most effective coordination of the egoistic and altruistic tendencies in human nature by developing a system of ownership which makes it true that when a man works for others he is also working for himself. Thus it has the chance to avoid the futility of Capitalism, which tried in vain to unite the same tendencies in the reverse order by saying that when a man worked for himself he also worked for others.

Most emphatically Socialism does not seek to abolish the basic motive of obtaining economic security and abundance, or to prove that all economic motivation is bad. On the contrary, its primary appeal to the masses of the people is precisely that only under Socialism can they win security and abundance. It has always been a part of Socialist theory that under Socialism the amount of compensation shall be according to the quality and quantity of work performed. I suspect that the idea, especially prevalent in the English-speaking world, that Socialism means absolute equality of wages is due in no small measure to Bernard Shaw's independent and non-Marxist views along these lines. The present inequality of wages in Soviet Russia does not in the slightest represent a return to the profit system, despite constant propaganda to this effect in the capitalist press. And there can be no doubt that Soviet Socialism has outlawed the profit motive proper almost 100 per cent.

The establishment or material security for everyone and the resulting disappearance of economic fear have been even more important than education and propaganda in changing the basis of motivation in the U.S.S.R. For genuine security makes it unnecessary for a man to carry on a bitter struggle with others to maintain himself and his family. It is difficult to feel full of brotherly love toward your neighbor when he is well-fed and you are half-starving, and when the competition for jobs and the brute necessities of life is so severe that another man's gain is likely to be your loss. Such is the kind of situation that the capitalist system is always making inevitable. Within a country its overwhelming urgencies are always turning well-meaning men into enemies; in the world at large the same pressures on a vast scale turn whole countries into enemies. Individual and national economic security make for *psychological* security and for tolerance and friendliness.

So only in the Soviet Union do the basic economic relationships harmonize with and support the highest ethical and social ideals instead of brutally contradicting and counteracting them, as elsewhere.

In the capitalist system the worker, thinking over the experience of the past, is quite prone to say to himself: "Why should I try to work harder and produce more when I know that the result may well be over-production and the consequent loss of my job?" Or he may object strongly to the installation of new machinery, which is also likely to make for unemployment. Trade unions have sometimes enacted such sentiments into a definite and considered policy. In the Soviet Union, however, the workers can be certain that increased production, far from leading to unemployment and economic misery, will raise the standard of living all around. They know, too, that no part of the fruits of their labor will be diverted, in the form of surplus value, into the pockets of a small group of private capitalists.

For these reasons the Soviet workers enter with eagerness into schemes for heightening productivity. Shock brigades, led by the Stakhanovites, set the pace in increasing the quantity and improving the quality of production. Individual factories, coal-mines, trade unions and other organizations enter into "Socialist competition" to do the same. "Socialism," writes Lenin, "does not do away with competition; on the contrary, it for the first time creates the possibility of applying it widely, on a really mass scale; of drawing the majority of toilers into the field of this work, where they can really show themselves, develop their abilities and disclose their talents, which have been an untapped source—trampled upon, crushed and strangled by Capitalism."

And Stalin adds: "Socialist competition and capitalist competition represent two entirely different principles. The principle of capitalist competition is: defeat and death for some and victory for others. The principle of Socialist competition is; comradely assistance to those lagging behind the more advanced, with the purpose of reaching general advancement." This very important fact of competition under Socialism has always made me think that it is highly confusing to call Capitalism, as a number of economists do, "the competitive system."

Socialist competition,, according to Stalin, has been a primary factor in the "radical revolution" in men's views of labor, "because it transforms labor from a disgraceful and painful burden, as it was reckoned before, into a matter of honor, a matter of glory, a matter of valor and heroism." The power of public opinion in the Soviet Union has been shifted from the money criterion of success to approval of socially useful labor in all fields, whether economic, cultural or governmental. At the same time the full weight of community *dis*approval is brought to bear on individuals who are acquisitive, inefficient or lazy. It is noteworthy that the new Soviet Constitution is the only national constitution in the world which writes into the basic law of the land the good old Biblical principle: "He who does not work, neither shall he eat.

In addition to these various sorts of incentive, there is in the Soviet Union the stimulus of the ordinary urge toward positions of greater responsibility and leadership; and also, of highest importance, the pervasive collective enthusiasm for carrying through the Five-Year Plans and constructing a Socialist society. The Soviet people fuel that they are writing into the realm of actuality an achievement of world historical significance and one that will exercise a more profound influence on humanity than either the American or French Revolutions. And they have, too, that same sense of daring and resolute pioneering in the race of enormous difficulties, of opening up a whole continent to a new civilization, that inspired our own American forefathers.

If and when other countries go Socialist, their peoples will discover much the same satisfaction and joy in their work that the Soviet people have today. In my opinion, what most men and women want the world over and have a right to obtain through their occupational activities, is a reasonable level of economic security and well-being, the money and leisure to enjoy the things of culture, the realization of their potentialities in useful and significant work, and social recognition of their abilities and achievements. Most persons are anxious to do a good job; they have a genuine sense of workmanship and a deep-seated desire to function effectively and well in the community. All the fundamental needs and wholesome wants, so terribly thwarted under Capitalism, will find fulfillment under a planned Socialist order.

Beyond all this is the spiritual imperative of the average person toward the pursuit of a worth-while purpose and toward the unification of his actions in the light of a general philosophy. Socialism not only provides the aim of building a more perfect society and the economic and political programs whereby this can be attained, but rounds out its synthesis by setting forth a carefully considered and consistent set of philosophical principles which are immensely superior to the confused medley of beliefs which Capitalism presents in this same realm. This philosophy of life is best described as *Socialist Humanism.*

4. *The Philosophy of Socialist Humanism*

The inclusive philosophy of Socialist Humanism has as its supreme ethical aim the welfare and progress on this earth of all mankind, irrespective of race or nationality, religion or occupation, age or sex. Its methods for achieving this goal—and here is where it differs most radically from other kinds of Humanism—are reliance on the principles of experimental science, of Socialist planning, and of democracy in the broadest sense. Extending the scientific outlook to the universe as a whole, Socialist Humanism maintains a world-view (in technical philosophical terms, a cosmology or metaphysics) which rules out all forms of the supernatural and looks upon humans as a fully natural part and product of the Nature that is their home. Since at the outset the principal field of my more serious studies and at my teaching was philosophy, it is not astonishing that I first became convinced that Socialism is right in its philosophical position and only somewhat later adopted its outlook in economics and politics.

The emphasis of Socialist Humanism is positive, not negative. It stands for the full-hearted enjoyment and affirmation of life, for a forward-looking and socially-minded attitude in relation to the problems of society, for the co-operative endeavor of liberated individuals toward making human, existence in this world attain those noble possibilities which have been the dream of every great prophet and statesman from Jesus and Plato to Lincoln and Lenin. To paraphrase Karl Marx, the philosophers of the past have only *interpreted* the world; but the point is to *change* it. Humanism carries out the most important function of traditional religion by giving to men and women a central and compelling purpose, around which to integrate their lives and through which to rise above their personal difficulties and dilemmas. And it offers, as a basis for happy and harmonious living, a philosophical and psychological outlook which is completely relevant to the conditions and spirit of modern civilization.

Socialist Humanism takes the position that Nature, as it discloses itself in .the facts of science and especially of biology and astronomy, does not show favoritism to humans or any other of its creatures. This little world of ours is only a tiny speck in an immense and unbounded universe, as vast in its spans of time as of space; and there is no reason to suppose that Nature cares more about our puny earth and what transpires upon it than about any other spot in the cosmos. What is primary, fundamental and prior in Nature is matter or energy. Mind appears on the scene only when, as on our planet and in the human species matter has become organized in a certain complicated manner after millions and millions of years or evolution. The truth of this world-view is not dependent on the definition of matter or energy in terms of a particular stuff, such as atoms, electricity or anything else. It is based simply on the proposition that there is objective reality existing independent of any sort of mind or minds.

In adopting this world-view, contemporary Humanism takes over and brings up to date the great tradition of Materialism and Naturalism in philosophy. This tradition started in the ancient world with Democritus, Aristotle and. Lucretius, came down in modern times to Hobbes and Spinoza, Feuerbach and Marx, and is supported in the twentieth century by noted American philosophers like George Santayana, Morris Cohen and John Dewey, as well as by all schools of Marxism. So Humanism throws into the discard every variety of, metaphysics that reads into the universe-at-large, human traits, whether they be mind or personality, love or purpose. And it definitely repudiates the religious bias running through most philosophies of the past. For "Divine philosophy," as Plato called it, has only too often been the philosophy of Divines.

Humanism puts the outcome of human's career in this world entirely up to humans and does not postulate any All-Guiding Providence or Cosmic Purpose that guarantees the ultimate triumph of humanity or its values. This philosophy, incorporating the indomitable spirit of Stoicism, encourages us to play the game boldly and well, come what may, it also contains an element of Puritanism in the sense that it recognizes the necessity, in times of great crisis, for humans to concentrate all their energies on the accomplishment of a certain task to the temporary exclusion of almost everything else. But Humanism does not coddle us like pampered children by saying that we are sure to enjoy victory in any particular mundane aim or as individuals in some otherworldly realm of immortality or as a society in some paradise on earth. This is why Humanism is pre-eminently a philosophy of sportsman-ship. It never loads the dice by assuming in advance the actualization of its ideals in the anthropomorphic operations of some omnipotent God.

Nevertheless Humanism is basically optimistic and is confident that humans have the courage and ability and intelligence to gain the day. In the tremendous achievements of the race so far, in the brilliant course of Socialism in Soviet Russia, it sees the promise of almost infinite progress. Looking very far into the future, it refuses to accept that doom for humans and this earth predicted by both Christian prophets and modern astronomers. It has faith that the advance of science and of social-economic planning on an international scale—bringing into being a sort of world mind which is the nearest thing to divine omniscience that Humanism can imagine as existing—will result in such further conquests of Nature that human life and culture will be indefinitely and perhaps "immortally" prolonged on this planet. Here again it is up to us humans. We may lose out. In any event the future is open and there is a good sporting chance of success. Thus Socialist Humanism presents an unending challenge to what is best and bravest in the human race.

Since humans are at least as much emotional as intellectual beings, one of the important functions of writers and artists in the new society will be to work out rites and ceremonies that give adequate and artistic embodiment to the central tenets of Socialist Humanism, and which appeal to the hearts as well as the minds of the people, capturing their imagination and giving their feeling for pageantry an outlet. Humanism definitely encourages intellectual and emotional activities which express our kinship with the Nature that produced and sustains us. It definitely discourages the attitude of shaking one's fist at the universe, as some disillusioned and despairing philosophers have done. Though Nature is neutral toward human aims, it can be well utilized on behalf of those aims, as the whole history of science demonstrates. Nor does Humanism belittle those natural reactions of awe and wonder which we all feel so keenly from time to time; Humanists, like others, look up at a beautiful night sky of stars and are overwhelmingly impressed with the sweep and majesty of the heavens. And they do not think that disbelief in the supernatural in any way detracts from the depth of such feelings.

In the Soviet Union we find the only nation in the world where Socialist Humanism, including the technical Marxist philosophy of Dialectical Materialism, is the prevailing doctrine and where the governmental authorities officially side with and support the campaign to substitute the procedures of modern science for those of old-time religion. It is essential to remember that the dominant Greek Orthodox Church of old Russia was in almost all respects, intellectually as well as morally, inferior to the Catholic and Protestant Churches of the West. As Professor Julius Hecker puts it, the ascetic outlook on life of the Orthodox Church "was directed not merely toward the mortification of the flesh, but equally toward the mortification of the mind." In Holy Russia before the Revolution, unlike as in Western Christianity, there never took place, any movements that were successful in substantially reforming or liberalizing the Church, all such attempts being promptly and harshly suppressed. Indeed; in 1917 the Russian Church had reached the very depths of decadence, with the corrupt, licentious and half-illiterate monk Rasputin controlling it through his personal sway over the Tsar and his court.

Most of the superstitions which the Soviet Union has been trying to eradicate are of a sort which the bulk of church members in America would consider relics of the Dark Acres. For example, part of the old agricultural protection ritual in Russia was to have a procession march through the fields led by a Greek Orthodox priest, who would sprinkle holy water over the earth to the accompaniment of a chant such as the following:

> Worms and grasshoppers!
> Mice and rats!
> Ants, moles, and reptiles!
> Flies and horseflies and hornets!
> And all flying things that wreak
> Destruction. . . .

> I forbid you in the name of the Savior come on earth to suffer for men. I forbid you in the name of the all-seeing cherubim and seraphim who fly around the heavenly throne. I forbid you In the name of the angels and the millions of heavenly spirits standing in the glory of God, I forbid you to touch any trees, fruitful or unfruitful, or leaf or plant or flower, I forbid you to bring any woe on the fields of these people.

No one can doubt that the Soviet farm program would have ended in failure had the peasants continued to rely on such primitive mumbo-jumbo.

The Russian Communists have naturally utilized every conceivable device that might help uproot the superstitions of the workers and peasants, including the very interesting and effective anti-religious museums, which are equally pro-science in many of the big cities. But most far-reaching of all in its consequences upon religion has been the great social and economic progress of the U.S.S.R. The Marxist theory is, in Lenin's words, that

> In modern capitalist countries the basis of religion is primarily *social*. The roots of modern religion are deeply embedded in the social oppression of the working masses and in their apparently complete helplessness before the blind forces of Capitalism. Fear of the blind force of capital—blind because its action cannot be foreseen by the masses—a force which at every step in life threatens the worker and the small businessman with a "sudden," "unexpected," "accidental" destruction and ruin, bringing in their train beggary, pauperism, prostitution, and deaths from starvation—this is THE tap-root of modern religion.

The truth is that the social-economic roots of religion are well on the way toward being totally abolished in Soviet Russia. With unemployment non-existent and economic security guaranteed, with health and education and old age all properly provided for, with art and culture constantly expanding and increasingly available, the masses of the people in the U.S.S.R. no longer have their old need for the consolations and escape-mechanisms of supernaturalism. And they no longer require the moral sanctions of traditional religion because the principles of Socialist Humanism are providing them with an inclusive code of life that unifies the country as a whole and also the individual personalities within it. In general it is possible to say that the situation in Soviet Russia indicates the prospect, for the first time in history, of a great and populous nation becoming totally free from supernatural distractions and able to concentrate wholly upon human welfare on this earth.

No one has described better than Sidney and Beatrice Webb the significance of the honest and thoroughgoing Humanism for which the Soviet Union stands. This philosophical position,

"has, it is claimed, the merit of a public and persistent repudiation of the equivocal hypocrisy in which the governments and churches of other countries, together with hosts of merely conventional Christians, are today implicated. That is, for the remaking of humankind, no small matter. It is not with impunity that .nations or individuals, outgrowing any genuine faith in a personal deity who hears their prayers and governs alike the ocean and the earthquake, the harvest and the hearts of people, can continue to practice rites and accept religious institutions as if they were still believers. No code of conduct professedly based on the supposed commands of an all-powerful, ruler will outlast the discovery that it has, in fact, no such foundation.

One result of this widely spread equivocation is seen in the practical abandonment at the present time by millions of young persons in Europe and America, not only of Christianity, but also, along with it; of nearly all the commandments by which their parents were guided, without acquiring any substitute. Another result is the actual retrogression, in principles and in acts, of this or that nominally Christian country, if not of many of them, to the characteristics not of civilization but of barbarism—the bloodlust and sadism accompanying the worship of a tribal god—out of which they seemed to have emerged centuries ago.[*]

In other words, lip service in the supposedly Christian nations of the West to an outworn faith and to an outworn code of morals derived from it, prevents the development, which has taken place in the Soviet Union, of a positive philosophy and ethics appropriate to a modern civilization based on science and the machine. It remains to be said that the progress of Socialist Humanism in the U.S.S.R, has not, as hostile reports would indicate, been tied up with the persecution of religion. In Tsarist Russia the official and government-supported Greek Orthodox Church was extremely active in persecuting all minority religious groups, whether Roman Catholic or Protestant, Hebrew, Buddhist, or Mohammedan, Today all religions in the Soviet Union are on an absolutely equal basis. And though localized excesses against the Church undoubtedly occurred in the first tumultuous years of the Revolution, the Government has from the start upheld the principles of freedom of conscience and religious worship, which are guaranteed in the Constitution. The bitterly hostile attitude of the Church toward the Socialist state since its inception shows clearly enough why priests and other religious persons have not infrequently been punished, and even shot, for counter-revolutionary activity against the Soviet Republic. In such cases they have simply been treated the same as others committing the same offence.

The Soviet Government, heeding the example of countries like the United States, early decreed the separation of Church and State, thus ending the special privileges, including public subsidies, of the Greek Orthodox religion. The government also took control of the schools away from religious organizations and ruled that the Church should confine itself to strictly religious activities, Parents can teach what they choose about religion to their children at home; and religious rites are freely permitted for

---

[*] Sidney and Beatrice Webb, *op. cit.,* p. 1134.

births, marriages and burials according to the desires of the family concerned. Of course, a great many churches have been closed and either demolished or converted into such secular institutions as schools, recreation centers or museums. No mere majority vote of the people in a community leads to the shutting down of a church; before this step is taken an overwhelming proportion of citizens must be in favor of it.

The number of churches, synagogues and mosques still open in the Soviet Union is as high as 60 per cent of the total prior to 1917, with more than 50,100 priests, rabbis, and other religious officials carrying on their accustomed duties. Those who travel through the U.S.S.R, can attend church services wherever they go and see for themselves, as I have done on numerous occasions, that religion is functioning freely and widely in Soviet Russia.

5. *Religion and Radicalism*

There can be no doubt that *organized* religion, whether in. its Christian or other forms, has on the whole strongly supported the capitalist system and its characteristic institutions. The Church everywhere has a heavy stake in the *status quo,* because of its interest-bearing investments in business enterprise, because of its huge land holdings and because it is the ruling classes which contribute the greatest share of the money to keep it going, In Tsarist Russia at the time of the Revolution, the Greek Orthodox Church had a bank account of 8,000,000,000 rubles (well over $4,000,000,000 in the US) and owned 20,000,000 acres of land. Marx; trenchantly summed up this matter of the relationship between the Church and private property when he said: "The Anglican Church will more readily pardon attacks upon thirty-eight of its thirty-nine articles, than upon one thirty-ninth of its income." During the twentieth century, as previously, the Christian hierarchy in general has maintained a conservative, if not reactionary, position in social and economic affairs and has tended to reflect the dominant capitalist attitudes of the day. In the imperialist war of 1914-18 the Christian Church throughout the world with almost one accord (there were exceptions among individual ministers) gave its enthusiastic backing to the various belligerent governments. The churches of all denominations suddenly transformed Jesus from the Prince of Peace into the Son of War, urged the soldiers of either side to go out and butcher one another "for Christ and country," and blessed them all in the name of the same God. Today certain elements in the Church, especially in the Catholic communion, tend to be apologists for Fascist dictatorship and aggression in Spain and elsewhere. In the United States probably the most dangerous influence of a Fascist variety is that of the broadcasting Catholic priest, Father Coughlin, who numbers among his followers many adherents of the Protestant faith.

At the same time, however, under the pressure of recent events, a notable awakening has taken place in many religious quarters. Scores of clergymen, particularly of the Protestant calling, have resurrected the radical tradition that always existed in the Church, discovering that Jesus was a leftist and that his Sermon on the Mount implies Socialism.

My own interpretation does not go so far. But while it is notorious that quotations can be found in the Bible to justify practically every social and economic view imaginable, it is not true that the general trend of the New Testament, ambiguous as it is in many places, is to support a co-operative society. This does not mean that Jesus foresaw the necessity of modem Socialism. It does mean, though, that his teachings about the "beauty of love, peace on earth; and the brotherhood of man," cannot today conceivably be fulfilled except in a Socialist order.

Likewise there runs through the New Testament a radically democratic spirit, a deep equalitarian feeling, which Capitalism betrays every day of its existence, I think that in my own case my thoroughgoing allegiance to democracy and to the ideal of the greatest happiness of the greatest number is due in a considerable degree to my early and intimate, acquaintance with the New Testament, in the superb King James version. As England's eminent Dean of Canterbury says Jesus "addressed his blessings to the common people, who welcomed him; people of the soil, peasants, fishermen and artisans like himself." He tells these common people that the new world is for *them,* not for the rich, the prosperous, the self-satisfied. It was the plight of these little people, borne down as our unemployed are borne down today, under social and economic burdens; the widow vainly seeking for justice; the penniless Lazarus begging bread at the door of the heartless rich man; the laborers standing all through the heat of the day in the village market place, ready to work but idle "because no man hath hired us, which called forth the anger of Jesus."

Thus Jesus was very much aware of the material needs of man. It is recounted that he himself fed the hungry and healed the sick. And in his Lord's Prayer recorded in the Book of Matthew he included as one of the major points: "Give us this day our daily bread." On other occasions Jesus said: "Ye shall know the truth, and the truth shall make you free" and " I am come that they might have life, and that they might have it more abundantly," statements singularly appropriate to the Socialist outlook.

As for the brutal selfishness and the profit motive which the capitalist system upholds as its activating principles, certainly they directly violate the ethics of Jesus. For it was Jesus, let us remember, who in indignation drove the money-changers out of the temple and who denounced the scribes and Pharisees, representing the ruling class of his time, with the withering words: "Ye serpents, ye generation of vipers, how can ye escape the damnation of hell?" And it was Jesus, too, who said: "The love of money is the root of all evil"; "It is easier for a camel to go through the eye of a needle, than for a rich man to enter into the kingdom of God." "No man can serve two masters."

Ye cannot serve God and Mammon"; and "What is a man profited if he shall gain the whole world and lose his own soul?" No wonder that Jesus was finally executed on the cross as a dangerous revolutionary.

Like the modern radical; Jesus, expected the last full measure of devotion to his cause. Thus he made it clear that he thought there were higher loyalties than to one's family, telling his disciples: "He that loveth father or mother more than me is not worthy of me, and he that loveth son or daughter more than me is not worthy of me. And he that taketh not his cross, and followeth after me, is not worthy of me. He that findeth his life shall lose it, and he that loseth his life for my sake shall find it. , . , Greater Love hath no man than this, that a man lay down his life for his friends." Nor, when the critical hour came, did Jesus hesitate to sacrifice his own life.

So even the rather drastic methods which radicals sometimes feel constrained to advocate in their endeavors for Socialism find significant support in the words and actions of Jesus. Pursuing this point further, I think it is essential to state that the Marxist stress on the class struggle and its concomitants is justifiable only in the light of existing conditions in a very imperfect society. It is a society in which hatred and ill-feeling already run rife. The Marxist radicals believe in harnessing these emotions to a good end and in trying to educate people to hate in the right direction. A civilized man, for example, *must* hate war; but he must go a step further and hate those who are responsible for war. Is it not true, therefore, that we ought to teach people to hate, with all their capacity, the Hitlers and Mussolinis and Francos of this world? And is it not true in general that a profound regard for the welfare of humankind necessitates an equally profound hatred for whatever and whom-ever bring misery to mankind? "

Let me quote a well-known American on the subject: "Love degenerates into a vague diffusion of kindly feeling unless it is balanced by the capacity for righteous indignation. Without abhorrence of evil, kindness becomes discriminating and flaccid; 'together they make the magnanimous man, who by as much as he loves his fellows, by so much hates the evils that destroy them," The author of these lines is no radical; he is the Reverend Harry Emerson Fosdick, pastor of the New York Riverside Church, writing in a forceful little book on Jesus called *The Manhood of the Master,* The "righteous indignation" which Dr. Fosdick discovers as one of Jesus' chief traits and which he recommends to all true Christians, partakes of, I believe, much the same emotional quality as the bitter and fervent class-consciousness of many radicals.

Such similarities as I have been discussing between Christianity and radicalism are not usually stressed by the orthodox Church and orthodox churchmen. In the light of contemporary affairs, however, they are bound to have a growing significance for religious people. Unquestionably an increasing number of Christians, including many individual Catholics; have come to realize more and more that only Socialism can bring their social ideals to pass, by setting up a society where the economic and political realities will entourage those ideals to flourish instead of stamping them under foot. They have come to see that the golden rule can be established only when the rule of gold—as typified in the heartless profit system—is forever broken.

Meanwhile during the past few years there has arisen a powerful anti-fascist sentiment among religious people in all countries. This is due not only to Fascism's assault on peace, democracy and culture in general, but also to its outright persecution of religious groups. The Fascist treatment of the Jews has become a world scandal; and its barbaric and anti-scientific racial theories have been excoriated by all the outstanding leaders of Christendom, including the late Catholic Pontiff Pius XL The Fascist attitude toward the Christian Church itself has also been most menacing, particularly in Nazi Germany. There Hitler, enraged by the outspoken opposition to him among the clergy, has thrown hundreds of pastors and priests into jail; while his followers write insulting pieces that denounce Christ as "that swine" and that Jewish tramp" and. refer to his Sermon on the Mount as "the first Bolshevist manifesto." For these various reasons, then, it is not surprising to find both clergymen and ordinary church members prominent in united front movements on behalf of liberal, labor and activist causes.

It is significant that in both Europe and America the Communist Party; reputedly the most hostile of all radical groups toward religion, has been making much of the policy of "the outstretched hand" toward Catholic workers and Catholic anti-Fascists. In Spain, of course, Catholics and all varieties of non-Catholic radicals fought together to save the country from reactionary Fascist dictatorship. In the United States Earl Browder, General Secretary of the Communist Party, explicitly stated, the attitude of his organization at its tenth national convention in 1938.

"Within the camp of democracy," he said, "are included the great majority of the members of the Catholic Church. We Communists extend the hand of brotherly co-operation to them, and express our pleasure to find ourselves fighting shoulder to shoulder with them for the same economic and social aims. The Catholic community, composing about one-sixth of the American population, shares fully all the hardships and aspirations for a better life of our whole people."

In 1939, in an address at the Community Church of Boston, Mr. Browder made it clear that the Communist Party "stands for unconditional freedom of religious beliefs and worship, as a matter of principle, for the complete separation of Church and State; for the removal of every element of coercion in matters of conscience, . . . Within our Party we place no tests of religion whatever upon our membership, which includes, as a matter of fact today, persons of all shades and tendencies of religious belief, as well as skeptics, agnostics and atheists." Mr. Browder also revealed the interesting point that there are more communicants of the Catholic Church who are members of the American Communist Party than of any other denomination.

Radicals, then, whether they be Communists or other kinds, while obliged to "oppose strenuously any specific anti-progressive manifestations masquerading in the mantle of the Church, are more than glad to co-operate with religious persons of any faith whatever in defense of democracy or in behalf of Socialism. On the other hand, it is perfectly possible for religious persons sincerely to believe in and work for the social and economic program of Socialism, without necessarily subscribing to the philosophy of Socialist Humanism. Brought up myself in a Presbyterian family and having many close personal ties with ministers, students of theology and other religious-minded individuals, I feel keenly that the place for all true Christians is in the struggle to create a Socialist society. Those of them who have already joined the ranks are the best of comrades; those who come later are assured of a warm welcome.

It remains legitimate to hope that many of those who enter the radical movement from one church or another will of their own volition ultimately adopt the philosophy of Socialist Humanism. For, to recapitulate, I submit that this philosophy constitutes a consistent and integrated interpretation of life worthy of the great traditions of the past and appropriate to the complex and dynamic conditions of the present. It is I believe, the best moral and intellectual guide that we moderns can possibly find. And I dare to hope that one day Socialist Humanism will command the allegiance of humans throughout the four corners of the earth, that it will become the first real world synthesis in philosophy.

Chapter VIII
The Prospects for Socialism

1. *General Considerations*

To try to estimate the prospects for Socialism in the world of today is very definitely to enter the dangerous field of political prophecy. Here more than anywhere else judgments have to be reached on the basis of probabilities. Yet there are a few indisputable facts with which we can begin this discussion. In the first place, there has of recent years been a growing unity among radical, labor and liberal groups in most countries, in spite of unfortunate splits here and there like that between America's C.I.O. and A.F.of L. Today's united front goes far beyond official Socialists and Communists to include all genuine radicals who envisage Socialism as their goal, and also all persons who, through the trade unions or otherwise, are seeking to advance the labor movement. On certain specific issues, such as the preservation of civil liberties or opposition to war and Fascism, the united front is bound to embrace many who call themselves liberals and even some who call themselves conservatives. In Germany it was the absence of such a united front of anti-Fascist forces and their splintering into hostile sects that finally made it possible for Hitler and his Nazis to win out.

The drift of radicalized proletarians and middle-class elements has everywhere in the last decade been toward Marxist tactics and the Marxist political organizations, that is, toward either the Communist Party or toward the Socialist Party and related groups such as the Social Democratic and Labor Parties of Europe. Spain and particularly its Province of Catalonia was the last stronghold of the Anarchists or Anarcho-Syndicalists; who aimed at the immediate abolition of the state, stressed economic rather than political action, and encouraged individual, terroristic deeds. These policies were always vigorously opposed by Karl Marx, who fought bitterly with the Anarchist leader Mikhail Bakunin, and by Marx's followers. Under the pressure of the Franco rebellion and the dire need for organization and discipline among the Loyalist workers, the Spanish Anarchists were steadily losing ground and compromising their philosophy. Now of course the victorious Fascists have wiped them out organizationally, except for what remnants may be functioning underground.

As between the Socialist and Communist Parties the most desirable step possible in every country would be the extension of their united front into actual organizational merger. In the trade-union field considerable progress has already been registered for such a policy. In France, for example, the Socialist and Communist unions have joined together in the great Confederation Generale de Travail. The Soviet trade unions, instead of continuing to promote the Red International of Labor Unions, known as the Profintern, have been working for affiliation with the International Federation of Trade Unions, which has its-headquarters at Amsterdam and has been composed of Socialist and non-Communist unions. Unhappily, the International Federation has not as yet been very responsive to the Soviet gestures of friendship. In the political sphere, the Communists have also been urging a merger .of the Socialist and Communist Internationals.

Since the time of Karl Marx, the labor movement has been formally organized on an international scale. The First International, initiated by Marx and Engels themselves, was established in London in 1864, and after, accomplishing much useful work, passed out of existence in 1876. The Second or Socialist International started in 1889, failed miserably in preventing a world war and-proletarian participation in that war, and continues to act at present as the representative of the various Socialist, Social Democratic, and Labor Parties. The Third or Communist International, usually called the Comintern, was founded in Moscow in 1919 by the Communist Parties and other groups which had broken away from Socialist leadership. The existence of a central international body for the guidance of the world radical movement obviously has great advantages. In its function as a center of information it can communicate its specialized and often "inside" knowledge to the labor and radical groups in every country. And in its function as a general staff it can attempt to co-ordinate the activities of these groups in view of the total international situation at any moment.

The Internationals, however, whether Socialist or Communist, run the danger of antagonizing nationalist elements, either by giving the capitalists a chance to claim that a secret foreign plot is being hatched or by making workers and radicals themselves feel that they are being dictated to from abroad. Thus there have sometimes been unfortunate reactions against the Comintern on the grounds that "we are not going to take orders from Moscow." Unquestionably a political movement in any country labors under a severe handicap if it is widely thought to be under the control of a powerful group in some foreign land. The leaders of the Comintern realize this fact well enough and have lately been taking pains to make clear that close collaboration between the different Communist Parties of the world, matching in its own way the close collaboration between capitalist groups throughout the world, need not and does not mean dictation from the Russian Kremlin or any where else.

For many years there have been rumors that the Communist International has given up its goal of bringing about Socialism over the entire earth and has become simply the creature of the Soviet Government, which allegedly, is interested only in building Socialism in the U.S.S.R. I do not think that there is much in this talk. The Comintern has certainly shifted its policy from time to time; but this means merely that it tries to keep abreast of changing conditions. And its support of the Peoples Front tactic at its Seventh World Congress in 1935 was a very sensible course. So far as the Soviet Union is concerned, Stalin's statement in 1938, reaffirming, "the ties between the U.S.S.R. and the workers of other countries," made perfectly clear the philosophy of internationalism inherent in Soviet Socialism.

A second fact from which we can reckon today is that the radicals have been more and more successful in welding together the theoretical and the practical; in giving theory its full and of course invaluable place, while bringing it down to earth and embodying it in action; in expounding the ends for which Socialism must stand, and also in working out the necessary means for their attainment. One of the chief banes of the radical movement has always been the presence of too many impractical idealists and intellectuals in its ranks, ultra-pure souls who prefer to keep their beautiful abstractions totally and eternally un-besmirched by reality, rather, than to make real progress toward Socialism by bowing in the direction of the hard facts. This type of theorist conceives of himself as an important thinker whose function it is to direct the battle, but to remain above it. He loves to argue over fine points of theory, to draw up blueprints for the Socialist Utopia, to puff his pipe and pucker his brow and think up splendid new ideas for the guidance of the working class.

But today in increasing measure the radical intellectuals have been coming down, from on-high and participating, in the necessary day-to-day organizational and trade-union, and political work of the radical movement. I believe, myself. that the greatest need of this movement still is for men and women of real business and administrative experience, people who know how to run an office; what it means to balance a budget; and how the ordinary political machine operates. For one major reason why the capitalists score so many victories is that they have most of the practical-minded persons, the common-sense business executives and politicians who understand when and how to compromise, when and how to retreat, and when and how to make the advance that checkmates.

Idealistic radicals sometimes become disillusioned over the fact that in the movement toward Socialism there are a lot of rather un-idealistic people to whom material well-being and personal advancement are more important than the progress of humanity. No great political movement, however, could ever hope to achieve success if it relied only on idealism. It is no secret that the advocates of Socialism, besides tapping so far as possible the sources of social altruism, count on winning-over the masses of the people through showing them that economically and culturally they will be far better off under a Socialist system rather than under a Capitalist system. When large numbers of people start to support the radical cause out of motives of self-interest and some even begin to view it as a good bandwagon to step aboard, then we may be certain that Socialism is well on the way to victory.

For that very reason, then, that a great mass movement attracts to itself an extremely varied assortment of individuals, the greater proportion of workers for Socialism can hardly be expected to be supermen either in an ethical or intellectual sense. They will be average persons who have seen the light of a new day in the distance and who are ready to work hard to make that light shine over the whole earth.

Naturally in this endeavor they will make many mistakes, both small and serious. One thing that rather disconcerts some people is that, in spite of the united-front spirit of today, there seems to be still much hot and useless vituperation on the Left, with the different radical groups frequently becoming more abusive of one another than of their common foe on the Right. Such bitter quarreling, however, among the advocates of social change has been a regular phenomenon all through history; and it would appear rather pointless to become agitated, about it at this late date. Politics is politics, whether on the Left or on the Right; and politics is not the vocation for those who expect to dwell in the calm and comforting atmosphere of sweet reasonableness. So I have come to the conclusion that radicals must steel themselves to be hard-boiled in the sense that they can "take it," if abuse becomes so savage that they can no longer laugh it off.

During my relatively short career as a radical I have myself been subject to a very generous share of insult and invective from practically all directions. Personally, a lot of the things I am called from time to time strike me as extremely funny. Whether it be that I delight in the stridency of battle or for some unknown reason, I have come rather to enjoy having good, full-blown epithets hurled at me. It is of course always flattering to be termed, as I am occasionally, "Public Enemy No.1." Then I cannot help chuckling over newspaper articles that refer to me as "an over-reformed blue blood," "a silk-shirt Communist" or "a young Park Avenue socialite whose palms have never known the corns and bunions of hard toil." I also am charmed with a tongue-twister like "pseudo-revolutionary with an acrobatic conscience." And I have even learned to smile when some indignant citizen tells me that I am "an associate of murderers," "knee-deep in blood" or "morally dead."

To return to our general summary, the third certainty on which we can base contemporary predictions is the power and influence of the Socialist Soviet Republic, standing ever more firmly, in a world of misery and violence, as the great beacon of hope for the masses of humankind, for beleaguered nations and oppressed races, for the unemployed, the downtrodden and the poverty-stricken of the earth. Despite all kinds of propaganda and censorship, the capitalist classes can no longer conceal from their peoples the exciting news about the economic and cultural advances of the U.S.S.R. In the end the truth knows no frontiers. And today the truth about Socialism in Soviet Russia cuts across and through all ordinary barriers of nation and of race, of religion and class and occupation. As this truth sinks-in, the people of other countries will ask more and more insistently, "Why do we not do the same and have Socialist planning here?"

The strategic geographical position which the Soviet Union has for influencing the rest of the world is rivaled only by that of the far-flung British Empire. The U.S.S.R. fronts on both Europe and Asia and is itself both a European and Asiatic country. Among the many different minorities which go to make up its population there are blood-brothers of almost every race and nationality which are to be found along its interminable frontiers—a favorable factor of weighty significance for the eventual spread of Soviet doctrines.

The influence of Soviet Socialism is becoming especially strong among the subject and colonial populations, who dwell upon the continent of Asia, whether in China or India, in Persia or Iraq or elsewhere. There hundreds of millions, hideously exploited in an economic sense and tragically humiliated in the moral sense by the Capitalist imperialisms cannot fail to be greatly stirred by realizing that the formerly oppressed peoples of the U.S.S.R. now live in freedom and security, with full legal and social equality their unquestioned right. The prestige of the Soviet Republic is already so great and its example so potent that any deep-going crisis, at least in the Capitalist lands of Europe and the East, can be counted upon to put Socialist regimes on the agenda of distinct possibilities. The profound apprehension of social revolution has been and still is one of the principal factors acting as a brake on those who juggle with the idea of risking a general war.

Unquestionably the Capitalists of the world, especially the European species, genuinely fear the radical movement. "A spectre haunts Europe—the spectre of Communism." These words of Marx and Engels are today, largely because of the Soviet Union, far more of an actuality than when they wrote them in the middle of the nineteenth century. For there is a contagious element about great social movements that all the doctors of reaction with all their counter-revolutionary anti-toxins have never been, able to cope with.

2. *The Effects of War and Fascism*

The last, but by no means the least important, fact that I wish to emphasize is that those husky twin brothers, War and Fascism, with all their sudden and unpredictable possibilities, continue to devastate large sections of the world. Large-scale military conflict has already engulfed, in the East, more than a fourth of the human race and promises at any moment to plunge the West likewise, into catastrophe. The immediate fortunes of Socialism are inseparably bound up not only with existing and possible war situations, but also with the course of events in the aggressor Fascist states. For Fascism is the most deadly enemy of Socialism and at the same time Capitalism's last defense against it. When the Fascist regimes crack up, it is more than probable that Socialism will take over.

Let us consider first what are likely to be the effects of war and Fascism In the Far East. In the Sino-Japanese struggle the indications are decidedly that China's 45O million will keep on resisting long enough to bring the Mikado's Fascist empire dangerously near to economic collapse. Generalissimo Chiang Kai-shek, with his headquarters in the vast, rich, quickly developing hinterland of western China, now possesses an army of several million men well-trained in guerilla strategy and well-equipped for this type of warfare. The Chinese tactics of constantly harassing the far-extended line of enemy communications in a large and hostile country are admirably suited to break down the military strength and morale of the Japanese. Success in this form of fighting is not dependent on heavy artillery, tanks, and the other highly mechanized weapons which are necessary for positional warfare and which China lacks; small arms and ammunition, which China can manufacture in considerable quantities, together with such airplanes and other supplies as she can obtain from abroad, ought to be sufficient to turn the trick.

Moreover, and one of our Far Eastern experts, Mr. F. V Field informs us, "China's very backwardness in economic development has the advantage of making her invulnerable to the destruction of highly organized economic nerve centers, which in her case do not exist. The backwardness, furthermore, provides China with a degree of local self-sufficiency which would not exist in a highly industrialized nation. Thus, no matter how many cities the Japanese capture along the coast and in the eastern part of China and no matter how many miles of railway their troops occupy, they find themselves unable to administer a decisive defeat in either a military or economic sense, but instead become bogged down deeper and deeper in the unending Chinese morass.

Then there is the growing pressure on Fascist Japan from abroad with a world-wide boycott movement against its goods. This greatly handicaps Japan, with its dwindling gold reserve, in the realm of foreign trade. Because it is a nation very poor in raw materials, and especially in those needed for heavy industry, it cannot possibly continue the war, or even maintain the home economy, without extensive imports from other lands. If the conflict goes into a third or fourth year, the cumulative strain will begin to shake Japan to its foundations. And even an eventual victory for the forces of Nippon is likely to be a Pyrrhic one and so exhaust the country so that Japanese Capitalism will never recover from its latest military exploits. It Looks to me as if its national symbol should be the suicidal act of hari-kari rather than the figure of the Rising Sun.

Revolution from the Left and toward Socialism is by no means excluded as a possibility in Fascist Japan. In several respects that country is today much like the old Russia of the Tsars. It is still semi-feudal in its aristocratic hierarchy, its political organization and cultural outlook; it is primarily a peasant country; and the great masses of the people live under conditions of economic misery and political terror. Socialist ideas, too, have been current in Japan for some time, having been imported from Germany many years ago along with German industrial technique and legal procedures.

In China one important result of the Japanese imperialists' aggression has been vastly to enhance the strength and influence of the native Communists. This is because of their own effective participation in the defense, because of the internal economic havoc which the war is causing, and because the Chinese people are now looking more and more toward Soviet Russia as their chief friend and potential ally in the world. Hence the Japanese assault is likely to make China psychologically ripe for a quick transition to a radical form of government. Furthermore, the pressure of hostilities has driven Chiang Kai-shek's administration to put certain Socialistic measures into effect, such as the nationalization of the munitions industry and strict governmental control over other economic enterprises essential to the conduct of the war. The Japanese propagandists have been quick to brand the Chinese Government as "Red" for taking those natural steps of self-defense forced upon it by the Japanese attack itself.

The Chinese Communists today, under the political leadership of Mao Tse-tung and the military direction of Chu Teh, actually rule a large area and population in the provinces of northwest China. Because the regions under their control have always been primarily agricultural, they have not been able to institute very far-reaching steps toward Socialism. Outside of their military feats, the "Reds" most effective and lasting work has thus far been educational. Now, since they are actively co-operating with Chiang Kai-shek's Government against the Japanese, they are subordinating their more radical aims to the present supreme task of driving out the invader. Once the war is over, the Communists will no doubt resume their campaign on behalf of a Chinese Socialist state.

Another significant element in the complex Chinese situation is the existence of the People's Republic of Outer Mongolia, a huge territory lying between northwest China and Soviet Siberia. It is almost a third as large as the United States, but has a semi-nomadic population of only 700,000. This republic is organized along Socialist lines, and maintains close economic and political co-operation with Soviet Russia. It has entered into a mutual assistance pact with that country for defensive purposes. This means that if the Japanese militarists attack Outer Mongolia, the Soviet Union will come to its aid. At the same time the U.S.S.R. recognizes official Chinese sovereignty over Outer Mongolia. Short of a sweeping victory of the Japanese imperialists over Soviet Russia itself, Outer Mongolia will in all probability remain a Socialist Republic and exercise a permanent radicalizing influence on its racial kinsmen in the adjoining Chinese Province of Inner Mongolia.

Should the various factors now operating in the Far East so eventuate as to bring into existence, within the next ten or twenty years, a Socialist government in industrially and culturally backward China, such a regime would face most of the difficulties with which the Soviet Union has had to cope and some fresh ones in addition. It will take decades to build a Socialist commonwealth in China, but it can be done. And there is the advantage of Soviet Russia being an adjoining country, with communication facilities that link it closely to the Chinese Republic being constantly improved. In any event, if a radical regime comes to power in either China or Japan, the repercussions will travel far and wide over the earth, especially throughout the East and including the huge Empire of India.

The extent to which the Japanese Government has become involved in China means that its usefulness as an active military ally for Germany and Italy is more than doubtful. This is one of the important reasons why, in case the Fascist powers force a general war on the world, I believe that France, Great Britain, Soviet Russia and their allies, even with the United States rendering the democratic bloc only economic aid, will be more than a match for their foes. Another important reason is that the populations of the democratic nations and their associates will be united in the spirit of self-defense. And in the Fascist states, however, despite all the militaristic propaganda, the people are getting bored with the idea of glory, and would much prefer three square meals a day and a little quiet to dying on the most glorious battlefield.

In Greater Germany only a few years ago almost a third of the people were voting Socialist or Communist; and the radical, tradition was so strong that the Nazis felt compelled to make a demagogic gesture in its direction by calling their party the National Socialist Workers' Party and by designating their goal as National Socialism.

We know for sure that numberless German workers and members of the middle class view a Nazi war of aggression with fear and loathing. And if Hitler plunges his country into the ordeal of battle, there will be, in addition to the sullen Czechoslovaks, millions of Germans; a large proportion of them in the army, eager to sabotage and defeat his plans. A protracted war, straining to the utmost the Reich's already dangerously debilitated economy, would undoubtedly transform the present underground movement in Germany into an immediate and substantial threat to the Nazi Government. As for Italy, although the holdover of the radical tradition is less potent there, it is well-known that Mussolini and other leading Fascists do not feel that the population would be over-reliable under the vicissitudes of a major conflict. Economically speaking, Italy is the weakest of the Great Powers and is even less able than Germany to stand the stresses of a big war.

If and when the Fascist regimes in Italy and Germany go

under, it is difficult to see what permanent alternative there would be to working-class governments with a Socialist program. Purely military dictatorships, might I suppose, temporarily replace Mussolini and Hitler. But they would be so much a replica of discredited Fascism and they would be so powerless to solve economic problems . that I cannot believe they would last very long. Nor is a return to a system of Capitalist democracy a major likelihood in Germany or Italy. Should these two nations go Left, it will mean that Socialism is well on its way toward winning the whole of Europe. Germany particularly, with its great productive efficiency and vigor, would give to Socialism elsewhere, a tremendous stimulus especially in the central eastern portions of the continent.

Even in the improbable event that the Fascist states win a World War, the results of international Capitalism will be disastrous. Can anyone imagine, for instance, a greater blow to the present order than the collapse and disintegration of the British Empire? If the first World War led to the establishment of Socialism to over one-sixth of the earth, the Second World War, no matter which group of powers are victorious, is likely to extend the sway of Socialism to over-one half of the earth. Fascist dictators who think that they can halt the radical movement by invading other countries stimulate in the long run the very thing that they fear. And they will in the end meet the same failure that came to Count Metternich and his allies in reaction when they tried, after the downfall of Napoleon in 1815, to suppress by force and armed intervention, the rising tide of liberalism and democracy throughout Europe.

Yet, the Fascist regimes, as I explained in Chapter II, are doomed if they remain at peace. This prediction applies to Spanish Fascism as well as to the other varieties. General Franco's government in Spain, ruling by means of terror, over an economically exhausted country and a deeply embittered population, is likely to prove extremely short-lived. This government, itself composed of diverse and dissident elements, has no program that can possibly cure the social-economic ills of the

Spanish people and still their revolutionary impulses. So, even without a fatal involvement on the Axis side in a general European war, the Franco regime will, in my opinion, fall within the next few years before a renewed upsurge of democratic and Socialist forces.

3. *The Non-Fascist Countries*

Capitalism in the countries of Eastern Europe—in Hungary and the Balkans, in Poland and the Baltic states—is so shaky already that the next definite move toward Socialism may come from one of them. In all of these lands the bulk of the population are desperately impoverished peasants seething under the oppression of great landlords and a semi-feudal economy. We can be certain that the spectacular rise of living standards on the collective farms of the Soviet Union is not being lost upon these peasants. Racial factors, are also important. For in Yugoslavia and Bulgaria, Poland, Lithuania, and Latvia, a very large proportion of the people are Slavs who feel a definite kinship with the Slavs of Soviet Russia.

Of course as long as the threat of Fascist aggression remains, it is most doubtful how far any European nation can go in the direction of Socialism without forceful intervention from beyond its borders. Even in so powerful a country as France the menace of war is the greatest obstacle holding back social progress. And it is tragic that some of the most important gains that the French people made during 1936 under the first Popular Front Government, headed by the veteran Socialist Leon Blum, were later nullified by the brink-of-war measures of Premier Daladier. It was, moreover, disagreement over the policy to be adopted toward the Fascist dictators that led to the split in the promising French Popular Front composed of the Communists, Socialists and Radical Socialists.

The virtue of the French Popular Front, which, actual war might well restore, was that it not only united all the workers, whether followers of the Socialist or Communist Party, in the anti-

Fascist struggle, but also drew in and educated numerous middle-class elements through the Radical Socialist Party, which, in spite of its name, is a good deal less radical than the Socialist Party. The weakness of all Popular Fronts is that if they initiate measures for establishing real Socialism, their right wings are certain to break away. For this reason the Popular Front strategy is principally worth-while in that it serves as a bulwark against Fascism and as a bridge to a more thoroughly leftist coalition which will undertake to abolish Capitalism.

The chances of such a coalition winning out in France, where radicalism is now stronger than in any other part of Western Europe, will be fairly good when the danger from foreign Fascism has finally abated. In Great Britain, though a Conservative Government has been in power since 1931, the forces of labor and Socialism remain quite powerful. With the Liberal Party gradually sinking into oblivion, Sir Oswald Mosley's Fascists negligible, and the relatively small Communist Party favoring co-operation and merger with the Labor Party, the Laborites constitute the substantial opposition in Parliament and in the general political life of the country. In the last general election in 1935, the Conservatives utilized the foreign crisis, precipitated by Mussolini's invasion of Ethiopia, to win a heavy majority. But the opposition, with Labor as its nucleus, made on the whole a promising show of strength by obtaining 184 seats out of 615 and by polling over 46 per cent of the popular vote. Meanwhile the Labor Party has been steadily gaining ground in the municipalities.

In-the fall of 1937 it won an absolute majority in fifty-seven out of 130 important Town Councils, and control of twenty-seven more in coalition with other groups. Very significant is the fact that since 1934 Labor has governed the city of London, where the able Socialist Herbert Morrison has been leader of the London County Council, a position, that corresponds roughly to that of Mayor LaGuardia in New York City.

Since the First World War socialization in Great Britain has gone ahead impressively, to a large extent, under the leadership of the Conservatives themselves. Municipal ownership and operation includes 80 per cent of the tramway services, 66 per cent of the electricity, and 40 per cent of the gas. The London Passenger Transport Board, for instance, the greatest public transport authority of any city in the world, owns and administers practically all transport Services over an area as large as the State of Delaware and for a population of more than nine million. This Board was established by Prime Minister Baldwin's Conservative Government. The same Government, in the national sphere, set up a Central Electricity Board to co-ordinate the generation and distribution of electric power throughout the country. The Minister of Transport appoints, on the basis of technical ability and not politics, the eight members of this Board. The British Broadcasting Corporation was also instituted during Mr. Baldwin's term. The Postmaster-General appoints the governors of this semi-public corporation, which on the whole has been successful in maintaining English radio standards on a decidedly high level.

Then in 1937 the Conservative Government of Prime Minister Neville Chamberlain, announced a bill for the nationalization of all coal mines in the United Kingdom. A special Coal Commission is putting this plan into effect over a period of five years and will determine the amounts to be paid as compensation by the state to the present four or five thousand mine owners. It is significant that the government has set the maximum total purchase price at less than half the sum demanded by the owners, the most substantial of whom are the Church of England and several members of the nobility. What is sometimes called "Tory Socialism" in England is indeed enough to make the hair of the average American capitalist stand permanently on end.

In other ways besides actual socialization Britain is much further advanced than the United States. Government unemployment insurance has been in effect since the Great War; minimum wages are the law in sweated industries; the Government spends, as a matter of permanent policy, huge sums on the improvement of housing in London and other urban communities; no court can set aside an act of Parliament as unconstitutional; there is no doctrine comparable to America's "States' Rights" theory to hold up social progress; and a relatively high proportion of the workers are organized into trade unions, which exist in unquestioned right in all forms of industrial life. In the light of this state of things in Great Britain, President Roosevelt's New Deal policies hardly look Communistic or even radical.

In certain of the British Dominions the process of socialization has gone beyond that in England. Public ownership in New Zealand and Australia covers almost all public utilities. The Australian Government, in addition, operates the radio, oil refineries, and the Commonwealth Bank; while individual Australian states have extended government ownership and operation to all sorts of enterprises, from coal mines and stockyards to canneries and butter factories. In Canada the public generation and transmission of electricity has made rapid strides since the turn of the century, particularly in the Province of Ontario. There the Hydro-Electric Commission, utilizing the immense power of Niagara Falls, has for many years been administering one of the most successful public projects in the world. And it has been able efficiently to provide electricity to all categories of consumers far more cheaply than private systems in the rest of Canada and in the United States.

In Australia the Labor Party has intermittently won control in several of the states and once, in 1929, captured the federal government itself; while in the Dominion of New Zealand the Labor Party has been in power for the past few years. Labor as a political entity has not made much headway in Canada and the Union of South Africa. Recently in Canada and particularly in the Province of Quebec, there have taken place dangerous curtailments of the rights of labor and radical organizations, with hints of Fascism in the air. In South Africa both labor and political issues are seriously complicated by the deep-seated antagonism between the ruling whites and the native Negroes, who make up four-fifths of the population. In India the advance of the labor and radical movement is bound up not only with racial factors, but also with the religious enmity between Hindu and Moslem and, above all, with the struggle for independence from Britain. Socialist and

Communist influence has been gaining, ground, however, among India's 350 millions, all of whom but a small minority, live at a bare subsistence level. And it is significant that the younger and more militant leaders, such as Nehru and Bose, view Socialism as the only eventual remedy for their nation's complex problems.

Though, again, a great deal depends on the fortunes of war and of Fascism, the movement toward Socialism in Britain and its Empire on the whole looks reasonably propitious, especially in England itself. During the next decade there is an excellent chance that British labor will win a clear and effective majority in Parliament. The main trouble with the 1924 and 1929 labor governments in England, besides the timidity and treachery of their leaders, was that they lacked a legislative majority and had to depend, therefore, on the uncertain support of the Liberals. Yet even a substantial majority in the House of Commons will not guarantee Labor's success. A real Socialist program is sure to meet resistance in the House of Lords. And if it is enacted with the gradualness which has so far ruled the tempo of British radicalism, the capitalists are only too likely to bring on an acute economic crisis either through conscious sabotage or through a panic caused by genuine fear of Socialist measures.

Another region of the world where the outlook for Socialism is favorable is in the Scandinavian countries of Norway, Sweden and Denmark, the last two or which I visited in 1938. In all three of these nations, Social Democratic or Labor governments control the state, and many of the municipalities; in all three, government ownership of public utilities and other services has gone far; in all three, the co-operative movement has made great headway. This is particularly true in Sweden, whose progress in co-operatives has been popularized by the American author, Marquis W. Childs, as "the Middle Way."

Though Nazi intrigue has not neglected the Scandinavian democracies, Fascism has gained even less of a foothold in them than in Holland and Belgium. I cannot conclude this survey of the prospects of Socialism in Europe without mentioning how certain developments in the United States have brought added difficulties to the ruling classes of the old world in holding down the boiling lid of unrest and revolution. Firstly, the restrictive immigration policy that Congress enacted after the Great War has reduced to a comparatively small stream the influx from abroad of poverty-stricken workers and politically oppressed dissents. The capitalist government, of Europe, repeatedly in the throes of internal crisis, can no longer count on the U. S. A. to perform this function of safety-valve for discontented Deputations.

Secondly, since the Great Depression, the beautiful dream which many workers in Europe cherished of America as a sanctuary of security and wealth has totally collapsed. The hope that similar promises could be created elsewhere under Capitalism has disappeared because the fancied American model, the fabulous "land of opportunity has itself plainly and indubitably disappeared.

Because of its spectacular failures and floundering since 1929, the Europeans know finally that the United States, whose weight and influence probably counts for between a third and a half of world Capitalism as a whole has no magic formula for making the capitalist system work. They know that Capitalism everywhere runs into the same general impasse. And this disillusionment is of inestimable significance.

4. *Mexico and South America*

From a radical point of view the most hopeful thing in the Western Hemisphere has been Mexico's noteworthy progress toward the Left during the past few years. On the surface it appears paradoxical that our southern neighbor, which is relatively so backward in the development of modern industry, should at present be advancing further along the path to Socialism than the United States. The While this seeming paradox resides in the fact that in the colonial and semi-colonial countries, contemporary movements for liberation from foreign imperialism and domestic feudalism tend, under twentieth century cannon, and influences, to go beyond these goals, telescoping two revolutions into one, and ending up with Socialism. This is precisely what happened in

Soviet Russia; what is happening now in China and Mexico and what may happen before long in India. And the. biggest reason why the capitalists of the imperialist states are desperately opposed to such countries trying to establish full national independence.

The Mexican people, in a revolutionary ferment since the overthrow of the Diaz dictatorship in 1910, have repeatedly found themselves betrayed by the weakness or corruption of the men they elevated to leadership, such as Presidents Madero, Carranzo, and Calles. In 1934 however, they elected as President Lazaro Cardenas, candidate of the National Revolutionary Party (the P.N.R,), a real friend of the common man and a radical who meant business. He soon broke with the rich and conservative ex-president, General Calles, ousted his sympathizers in the cabinet and in other important positions, and finally deported the General himself to the United States. The new President then proceeded to put teeth into the Six-Year Plan, which the P.N.R. had adopted in 1933, but which had largely consisted of eloquent generalities and verbiage.

Under the Cardenas administration the expropriation of land from large private estates for the benefit of landless peons and peasants has proceeded apace. In 1939 there was a total of more than 1,500,000 peasants living in communal farms on approximately 60,000,000 acres of tillable soil, so expropriated. The Government also financed much of the initial equipment and cultural services for these farms. Mexico, like Spain, and South America in general, is still primarily a peasant country with its agriculture organized on a semi-feudal basis. The Cardenas program represents both a return to the old Indian system of the communal farm, the "Ejido," which was destroyed by the Spanish conquest, and a step toward modern collective farming with its Scientific techniques and Socialist outlook. There is, however, a long way yet to go, since some 150,000,000 acres of land remain in the hands of the feudal landlords.

At the same time Cardenas and his associates moved steadily toward the restoration of the country's industry to the

Mexican people and toward actualizing the provisions of the 1917 Constitution, which vested in the nation ownership over all minerals and non-solid components of the subsoil such as petroleum and gas. Practically all Mexican industry—oil, mining, public utilities and textiles—was owned until recently by foreign corporations, mainly American and British. This has meant not only that the development of native business talent is held back, but also that the bulk of the profits flow abroad instead of staying to enrich Mexico itself.

The Mexican government has acted firmly though perhaps somewhat too hurriedly, in trying to remedy this situation. In 1937, it took over the National Railroads of Mexico, consisting of trackage throughout most of the country. Then in 1938, it made the far-reaching move of expropriating the foreign-owned oil properties representing an investment of $450,000,000 and turning them over for administration to the organized oil workers. The immediate cause of this measure was the refusal of the oil companies to abide by the decision of the Mexican Federal Labor Board, sustained by the country's Supreme Court, that wage scales in the oil industry should be substantially increased. The degree of expropriation promised indemnification of the foreign companies, but the exact amounts involved and the methods of payments to be used are still in controversy.

The present administration has, in addition to its expropriation, discouraged all varieties of foreign Capitalists, by supporting the workers and trade unions in their demands for higher wages and shorter hours, and better working conditions in general. The overwhelming majority of labor is organized in the Confederation of Mexican Workers, whose outstanding leader is Vicente Lombardo Toledano. Labor has all along supported Cardenas and has constantly used its influence to push him Leftward. Cardanas, on his part, has naturally been friendly and supportive of Labor. One of his latest and most significant measures was to set up a National Labor and Industrial Development Bank, to provide credit for co-operative factories run by the workers.

In the field of culture the achievements of the Cardenas Government have also been impressive. It has made substantial progress in cutting down illiteracy, has increased the number of rural schools by some 50 per cent, and has doubled the total federal appropriations for education. President Cardenas has continued the already established the policy of secularizing the schools and has supported the aim stated in the Six-Year Plan for Socialist education. The meaning of "Socialist" in Mexico is rather inexact and broad, though it implies at least a Marxian theoretical basis and opposition to religious supernaturalism. The educational policy of the administration is one of the fundamental reasons why the Catholic Church in Mexico is a bitter foe of Cardenas.

It is the opposition of the Church hierarchy, together with that of the big landlords, disgruntled officials, foreign capitalists and international Fascism itself, which has made a Fascist coup in Mexico enough of a danger for Cardenas and his supporters to be continually on guard. It was this vigilance that enabled the President to suppress swiftly the rebellion staged by ex-general Saturnino Cedillo, reactionary Governor of the State of San Luis Potosi, in the middle of 1938. The Mexican Government remains alert and has not failed to profit from the tragic example of Spain. Cardenas, himself a general and revolutionary fighter of long experience, has succeeded in transforming the Mexican army into a real people's army. By far the greater part of it, including the officers, can be counted upon to stand by him in a crisis and not go over to the Fascists as in Spain.

There is also now a uniformed and drilled workers' militia more than 100,000 strong, and outstripping the regular army in size by almost two to one. in addition a large number of loyal peasants have been armed. Without question the reforms of the last few years have won the vast preponderance of workers and peasants to militant support of the present regime. Filially, whatever Fascist elements there may be in Mexico, they can expect no support from the present Government of the United States. So it looks very much as if Fascism in Latin America will continue to find a formidable obstacle in progressive Mexico, standing as it does, for a liberal and leftward trend in economic affairs, serving as a ray of inspiration to the vacillating countries to the south, and providing a refuge for those exiled by dictatorship in various parts of the world.

Whatever the course of events in Mexico, the chances are not bright that Socialism will become established in the near future in any of the South American republics. On the other hand, it is easy to fall into the error of overrating the strength of recent Fascist tendencies in these countries. For democratic institutions in the south American nations have always been notoriously unstable and have frequently given way to old-fashioned military dictatorships, headed up by whatever president happens to be in office. The continuation of or reversion to such dictatorships at the present time does not, therefore mean Fascism. The nearest approach to genuine Fascist set-ups have been in Bolivia and Brazil. Since the latter country is the continent's largest, possessing an area bigger than that of the U.S. and vast natural resources, the course of events within it is of special importance. Getulio Vargas has been dictator of Brazil since he seized the government in 1930. In 1937 he foisted on his countrymen a "cooperative state" constitution, substantially a copy of Portugal's. But a little later he suppressed the Integralistas, the original Brazilian Fascists, entered into commercial and diplomatic feud with Nazi Germany, and drew closer to the United States. And it would not be accurate to say that Fascism has definitely been established in Brazil.

Most of the other nations of South America are under dictatorial rule, though they commonly retain a number of democratic forms. In the Republic of Colombia full political democracy still functions. In Chile, in the Fall of 1938, the Popular Front scored its greatest victory with the election of Pedro Aguirre Cerda to the presidency. Cerda's administration is proceeding with a vigorous program of economic reconstruction, including plans to weaken the hold of foreign imperialists in the country. The Popular Front movement in Latin America as a whole, including Cuba, received a strong impetus at the International Congress of

362

American Democracies held at Montevideo early in 1939. This Congress initiated an Inter-American organization to fight Fascism and issued a declaration of democratic faith and solidarity.

The whole Latin American situation is complicated by the crisscross of various foreign imperialisms throughout the continent and by the extent of their economic power in each country. The conflicting interests of American, British, German, Italian and Japanese Capitalisms meet at every turn and are everywhere entangled with national politics. One of the most significant of the last few years has been the energetic and successful Nazi trade drive. But whatever the maneuvering of foreign Capitalists against one another in Latin America, they agree in favoring rightist regimes and in opposing the advance of labor and the Left. American business of course pursues its old game of economic imperialism and chafes at the refusal of Washington to intervene more strenuously on its behalf in places like Mexico.

5. *The United States*

Though the highly developed United States, representing the quintessence of twentieth-century industrialism and machine technique, is uniquely in an objective economic sense for Socialism, up until recently the Americans, still feeling favored among the peoples of earth, have been quite unready in the psychological sense for anything approaching Socialism. Right up to the last few years of the nineteenth century, America had a frontier and rambunctious Indians, a yet unsettled region to absorb the pioneers still pushing westward and to relieve the economic pressures in the country's eastern sections. Then too, the democratic spirit of the new world and its lack of caste distinctions held back the development of Marxian Socialism, which lays such stress on class struggle and class consciousness. Likewise America's isolationist attitude, its underlying suspicion of foreign "isms," was unfavorable to the growth of Socialism in the European sense.

During the past twenty five years, however, a different

story has been unraveling. The American people, stimulated by the tremendous world events in which they have participated and disillusioned by repeated economic disasters on the domestic front, have seriously begun to question the system under which they live. They have begun to awake to the new relevance of radical doctrines and even of ones originating abroad. Few of them are now unaware that American Capitalism has been slipping badly. It would be absurd to call President Roosevelt's New Deal Socialist, but there can be no doubt that his administration has helped to loosen some of the accepted and traditional assumptions of the American people and has educated them to expect perhaps more drastic measures. And many Americans are, I believe, already sympathetic to Socialism without knowing it.

The groups working directly for Socialism on the American scene are still very weak in numbers, though their influence is surprisingly strong. The Communist Party, under the able leadership of Earl Browder, like Alfred M. Landon, a native Kansan, has a membership of over 75,000; active sympathizers, including youth groups, mounting up to more than ten times that figure; and numerous newspapers and magazines, together with extensive publishing facilities. The C.P., as it is familiarly known on the Left, not only has a far larger following than the sect-torn Socialist Party, led by Norman Thomas, a sincere and vigorous ex-minister, and is immeasurably superior in brains, energy and effectiveness. It is wholly evident, however, that at the present juncture of affairs, no American political party advocating the full agenda of a Socialist society has even a small chance of coming into power. Hence the Communists and other radicals in the United States have been putting more and more effort into the already substantial united-front movement, with its limited objectives.

In the economic sphere the united front expresses itself through the rapidly increasing unionization of American workers and in the effort to heal the unhappy breach between the C.I.O. and the A.F. of L. sections of labor. In the political sphere it supports labor and progressive candidates everywhere and advocates the idea of forming, at the proper time, an independent third party, probably to be called the Farmer-Labor Party. This party would have its base among wage-workers, both industrial and agricultural, numbering 30,250,000 in 1935 and constituting 59.3 per cent of the gainfully employed; the dissatisfied elements from the middle class, which is now more than 75 per cent composed of dependent salaried employees; and the small independent farmers. One of the main lessons of Germany's fate has been to teach the radicals in other Capitalist nations to take special pains to draw into the united front white-collar workers, professionals, small farmers, small businessmen, all of whom are promising material for the Fascists.

The Farmer-Labor Party would be able to go ahead on a broad and progressive social program un-handicapped by the reactionary ties which so hold back the Democratic Party. The Democrats still have as their chief stronghold the Solid South, the most reactionary section of America. In the North, in pivotal centers like New York City with its Tammany Hall; Jersey City with its Boss Hague; and Boston with its semi-Fascist Democratic-Catholic machine, they find themselves bound up with some of the most corrupt and politically backward elements in American life. In all probability Franklin D. Roosevelt and the progressive wing of the Democratic Party will meet increasing difficulty in shaking themselves loose from the right wing and at the same time preserving their own political power.

A Farmer-Labor Party would break across present political lines too unite all independent progressives with the progressives in both political parties. The conservative Democrats and the conservative Republicans would then presumably join together in one party. This would have a far-reaching and healthy political re-orientation on the basis of progressivism vs. conservatism. There have been numerous third-party movements in American history; the Republican Party itself, starting in 1854 and coming into power in 1860, was such a movement. Since that turbulent period in this country's evolution there has never been, until recently, any one big all-engrossing issue which goes to the very roots of the American system, nor the necessary alignment of political forces to take advantage of such an issue in a successful third-party movement. Today, however, with Capitalism so decidedly on the downgrade, this country is face to face with the most important issue that has ever arisen within it. At the same time, due to the increasing restiveness of the economically underprivileged elements in the population, the swiftly increasing organization of American workers into trade unions, and to the internal turmoil and disorganization within both old parties, the political prerequisites for a great and powerful third party on a national scale are clearly coming into being. The propitious moment for the launching of a Farmer-Labor Party depends largely on developments inside the Democratic Party. In the event that the progressive Democrats can win complete control of their party and drive out the reactionaries, a new political situation will have been created. In that case it may be possible for labor, progressive and radical groups to work as effectively through what would, in essence, be a new Democratic Party, as through a new party of their own creation.

The platform of the Farmer-Labor Party would at the start include planks for more adequate unemployment insurances more adequate unemployment relief and more adequate old age pensions; a system of public health providing proper medical care to low-income groups throughout the country, with special attention to the rural areas and to mothers and children; a far more extensive program of Public Works with a $5,000,000,000 appropriation for housing and a union scale of wages for those employed, on such projects, heavier income taxes, aid for poor farmers and agricultural workers, and the abolition of child labor; further protection of the workers' right to organize, the enforcement of civil liberties, and equal rights for Negroes; federal aid to education and the institution of a Federal Department of Education; the nationalization of coal; railroads and the munitions industry; and the adoption of a strong foreign policy, opposing war and favoring co-operation with other countries on behalf of world peace and collective security.

Finally, this party would stand for the passage of a

constitutional amendment granting Congress the power to make all laws which it considers necessary to the welfare of the American people. This last plank is, of course, aimed to make our governmental processes more democratic and more efficient by ending the veto power of the Supreme Court over congressional legislation. As time went on the adherents of Socialism within the Farmer-Labor Party would try to push it as far leftwards as the political situation at any time warranted. Thus the radicals would fairly soon press for the extension of public ownership and operation of all natural resources, all transportation and communications, and the banking system. In any case the Socialist and Communist Parties would maintain their organizational independence and continue to carry on vigorous education for the ultimate goals of Socialism.

Those impatient souls, the radicals-in-a-hurry, who are always becoming restive over what seems to them an infuriating slowness in the processes of history, need to be reminded that whether a Left party achieves office soon or late, it will have to enact a number of transitional measures before it proceeds to institute full-fledged Socialist planning. If some of these measures, such as the nationalization of certain industries, will be put into effect by prior administrations of a progressive character, then so much the better. For in that case, not only is the economic approach to Socialism facilitated, but also, the working out of the measures in question, has immense educational value in a Socialist sense, both for their administrators and the people in general.

One of the important points to which American radicals must give liberation in their political activities is the strategy of words and slogans. Stuart Chase's provocative book *The Tyranny of Words* throws considerable light on this matter, although Mr. Chase distinctly overdoes his theme. What I wish to emphasize here is merely that there are certain words and phrases which antagonize people and that there are also certain words and phrases which naturally arouse a favorable response. These "scare-words" and "charm-words" depend to a large extent on tradition, education, and the kind of propaganda that newspapers and other instrumentalities of opinion have been playing up. Words and phrases which evoke quick, deep and unthinking reactions, whether favorable or unfavorable, we call "stereotypes." The average person often reacts emotionally to the stereotype rather than rationally to the idea originally associated with it. An recent years we have become very familiar in the United States with such stereotypes as "un-American," "Communist," "Fascist" "Reds," "reactionaries," "economic royalist" and "the preservation of the Constitution."

Radicals and conservatives hurl terms like these at each other with equal vehemence and sometimes with good results. Stereotypes, however, can be overworked. During the presidential campaign of 1936, the Republicans tried in vain to pin the label of "Communist" on President Roosevelt. Only a year later,, in the New York City election of 1937, Jeremiah Mahoney, Democratic candidate for Mayor, absurdly attempted to make Mayor LaGuardia's alleged "Communism" the chief issue in the campaign. He charged that the American Labor Party, which was supporting LaGuardia, was "Red" and that LaGuardia himself had insidious tie-ups with Soviet Russia. In both cases the candidates who were accused so vociferously of being Communists won by unprecedented majorities. It is apparently becoming less easy to stampede the American people by means of artificial Red scares, and the right-wing forces will have to look hard for other electioneering methods.

Some expressions habitual to the proponents of Socialism are in their very nature conducive to misunderstanding. For instance, "the abolition of private property" is frequently interpreted as meaning to embrace *personal* property, so that many an American citizen is sincerely convinced that a Socialist system entails the nationalization of household furnishings and intimate belongings. "The elimination of the profit motive" is wrongly taken to imply absolute equality in wages, and the Marxist "withering away of the state" as equivalent to complete anarchy in the realm of government. I consider affirmative slogans such, as "production for use;" "Socialist economic planning;" and "an economy of abundance" much more effective than some of the older phrases. On the other hand, if we on the Left are to be clear in our own minds and make ourselves clear to others, there are some basic words, like some basic principles, that we cannot afford to desert.

Again, a number of peace-loving and democracy-defending radicals like to talk eloquently about "the Revolution" and evidently get quite a thrill from drinking loud toasts to it. What they mean by the term is the transference of political power from the capitalist to the working class and not necessarily any sort of bloodshed or violence. But the vast majority of Americans understand "revolution" as implying civil war, with force and violence sweeping the nation. I recommend this fact to the serious attention of our more exuberant Comrades. Because of my own faith in the American democratic process, and my desire to be strictly accurate, I have never come out for Revolution and have never called myself a "revolutionary." A radical, yes!

An important aspect of this general problem of language is the extant to which concrete terms can be used in place of large abstractions. Homely American political slogans like "a chicken in every pot ' and 'the full dinner pail" are effective because they are in the American idiom and clearly understandable to the average citizen living his everyday life. The Late Senator Huey Long's basic slogans, "Every man a king" and "Share the wealth" were successful for much the same reason. So were "The Square Deal" of president Theodore Roosevelt and "The New Deal" of President Franklin D. Roosevelt. It is interesting to note that in Russia, Lenin, who himself wrote an excellent piece "On Slogans," won the Revolution with the slogan and concrete battle cry, "Peace, bread, and the land." In the United States I do not think that any of the various labor and radical groups have yet hit upon the best possible slogans with which to put across their cause.

Lately the Communist Party especially has been paying more attention to the social realities of language in this country. This organization has even coined the slogan, "Communism Is Twentieth-Century Americanism. Its official newspaper in the

East, the *Daily Worker,* calls itself the "People's Champion of Liberty, Progress, Peace and Prosperity." Such attempts at Americanizing radical phraseology are to the good in my opinion. I am by no means certain that the best name for the third-party I have been discussing is "Farmer-Labor." It may scare off middle-class people who would otherwise be sympathetic. One third-party group has taken the name of 'The American Commonwealth Federation," which seems rather awkward and uninspiring to me. Perhaps the third-party would go farthest under the familiar but meaningful name of "Progressive."

Whether the third party I have in mind can become the instrument of eventually creating Socialism in America it is not possible definitely to say. It will certainly have to watch out against repeating the mistakes of the British Labor Party and the Social Democrats in general. Thus, in so far as it has a trade union base, it will have to guard against the creeping conservatism which sometimes affects labor officials when their organizations become powerful and well established. It will have to guard against faint-hearted and fickle leaders who go over to "the enemy" in moments of crisis, and against prima-donnas who have their heads turned by success or their egos disgruntled by criticism. And such a party will also have to guard against timid programs which do not differ fundamentally from those of the opposition and which are not able to arouse the enthusiasm of the electorate.

I believe that the great radical opportunity of this party, will come, not necessarily during the next big depression which American Capitalism is probably strong enough and rich enough to pull through, but in the depression following that. If our next and prolonged economic crisis takes place in the early forties, and another occurs ten years or so later in the early fifties, I suggest that during the latter period an alert and radicalized Farmer-Labor Party, a Progressive Party, a re-vamped Democratic Party, or whatever it may be called, will have the chance of laying the foundations in the United States of a planned Socialist order. And perhaps its winning slogan will be, "Make this the last depression!"

Socialism in America, like Socialism in all other countries, is bound to possess features which nobody can foresee. Those radicals who insist that a Socialist society is a failure unless it conforms to every last detail of some pre-ordained picture, unless every last hangover from the past is eliminated and every rough edge planed smooth, will continue to be deeply disillusioned. Socialism, we can be sure; is not going to usher in the final millennium and establish perfection in the affairs of humans. The choice between Socialism and Capitalism is not one between absolute good and absolute evil. And it is a mistake, I feel, to think of Socialism at all in terms of Utopias, especially those of the traditional sort, for those Utopias, like the after-life paradises of supernatural religion, have conceived of the ultimate society as a static place and as a sort of glorified rest-home where humans would be forever free from the arduous and soul-killing work with which they were afflicted in earthly life. When we adopt an evolutionary view and one which looks upon labor, under decent conditions, as a thing of dignity and value in itself, then any ideal society must always give to the people, big and creative and inspiring tasks to perform and must include also the hope of transcending itself. Thus Socialism will eventually give way to the ideal of a true Communal Society and eventually to an even higher form of social organization.

It is impossible to state with assurance how soon we may expect the definitive victory of Socialism in our present-day world. Certainly that victory is in no sense inevitable; and Capitalism has too many tricks in its bag for any radical to await complacently its demise. In some countries Socialism will come gradually, in others suddenly; in some peacefully, in others violently. In most it will be the story of the capitalists winning all the battles, but the radicals winning the war. And if we consult with reality, we must recognize that at least another hundred years will probably pass before the Socialist order is triumphant over the entire earth. Capitalism, let us remember, took something like five hundred years to achieve control of the world.

The pessimistic German philosopher, Oswald Spengler, has written two lengthy and erudite tomes about *The Decline of the*

West. But the only decline which we radicals recognize in either West or East is the Decline of Capitalism. Fortunately that need not be synonymous with the retrogression of society in general. No matter how bad things may seem at any specific time, a means does exist through which civilization can continue its advance. That is why, whether there is peace or war, economic crisis or another flashy period of recovery, the radical movement goes on, unshaken in its faith in the inexhaustible potentialities of humanity and firm in its conviction that a planned and democratic Socialist system can bring peace and security, happiness and freedom, to this modem epoch. Among all sorts and conditions of humans in all quarters of the globe, Socialism marches forward, as an economic program; as a political battle cry; as a cultural goal; as an inter-national commonwealth; as a compelling philosophy; as a total way of life that may well in this era become the way of life for an overwhelming majority of humankind.

~ ~ ~

This ends Corliss Lamont's originally intended final Chapter of his *You Might Like Socialism*, first. published 1939.

Here follows a tribute to Corliss Lamont written in 1995 for *The Humanist* magazine by Fred Edwords, then its Editor.

On Wednesday, April 26, 1995, the humanist movement lost its most prominent philosopher and social activist. Dr. Corliss Lamont, age 93, died peacefully at his home in Ossining, New York. A humanist funeral was held for close family and friends in New York City on April 29. Then on May 19, humanists celebrated his life at a special memorial service held during the fifty-fourth annual conference of the American Humanist Association. To Lamont's assembled friends and admirers, his wife Beth read a letter she had received a few days prior from Bill Clinton, who had met Corliss in 1992 and was familiar with his accomplishments. The letter read in part:

> Corliss gave a great deal to our country during his long, rich life. As a tireless advocate for America's civil liberties, he challenged our nation to honor its most basic covenant with its citizens. The many struggles he fought throughout his career have helped to preserve our precious freedoms for the generations to come.

Corliss Lamont was born March 28, 1902, in Englewood, New Jersey. The day happened to be Good Friday — a coincidence his mother hoped would prove an omen of future religious devotion. However, despite his regular attendance during his youth at the Presbyterian Church of Englewood, his study of the New Testament, and his tenure as a Boy Scout, Lamont gradually came to reject his family faith.

What he considered "the first big civics battle" of his life took place in 1919, when he was a student of 17 at Phillips Exeter Academy. He had learned that, on each night before a game, the coach of the academy's baseball team was cooking the balls that would be pitched by the opposing side. Because these oven-baked projectiles were harder, they flew further when struck by Exeter batters, accounting for his team's rising number of victories.

Lamont reported the unethical practice to the principal, resulting in the immediate dismissal of the coach and Lamont almost being thrown into the river by some of his disgruntled fellow students.

Corliss Lamont's father, Thomas, was a business partner of J. P. Morgan in what was then the leading banking firm in the United States. But, as Corliss declares in *Yes to Life*, his father's positions and actions on social issues "effectively contradicted the widely accepted stereotype of rich people and Republicans as conservative or reactionary plutocrats opposed to all forms of progress and liberalism." In November 1917, after the United States had entered World War I, Thomas Lamont became an unofficial adviser to President Woodrow Wilson, proposing that limited cooperation with the Soviets could help defeat Germany. Wilson, however, would hear none of it and, a few months later, sent troops into the new Soviet Union in an ill-fated attempt to topple Lenin's government. After the war, both of Lamont's parents were active in the peace process and the League of Nations.

It was therefore not surprising that, while Corliss was at Harvard during the early 1920s, he also supported the League of Nations, debating in print his classmate Henry Cabot Lodge, Jr., son of the U.S. senator most responsible for maintaining America's isolationist policies. But Corliss stirred additional controversy when, as student vice-chair of the Harvard Union, he proposed that Socialist Party President, Eugene V. Debs, communist labor organizer William Z. Foster, and radical economist Scott Nearing be invited to address the student body. His aim was simply to get an equal hearing for the viewpoints of the left. But when the governing board of Harvard Union bitterly fought his proposal, Lamont decided there might be some merit to socialism after all and launched into a serious study of the subject. Meanwhile, the speaker program at Harvard Union liberalized to a degree.

After graduating magna cum laude, Corliss Lamont studied for a year at New College in Oxford, England, living during that time in the home of Juliette and Julian Huxley. In the fall of 1925, Lamont began his doctoral studies at Columbia University and took a course under John Dewey. Then in 1928, Lamont became an instructor in philosophy at Columbia. One of the courses he taught used John H. Randall's *The Making of the Modern Mind* as a text. It was the reading of this book and the teaching of this course that turned Lamont from liberalism to democratic socialism. Later that same year, he married Margaret Hayes Irish, a writer and researcher who held convictions similar to his own.

In 1929, Lamont took up the cause of 20 scrubwomen who had been fired by Harvard when the Massachusetts authorities caught the university paying them only 35 cents an hour — two cents under the minimum wage. As secretary of the Harvard Alumni Association, Lamont raised $3,000 from his fellow alumni, which was paid to the women in lieu of back wages. A few years later, Harvard adopted a more enlightened labor policy.

Lamont completed his doctoral dissertation, *Issues of Immortality*, in 1932 and received his Ph.D. in philosophy from Columbia. This dissertation led to his 1935 book, *The Illusion of Immortality*, a work which, over time, became accepted as a prime reference on the nonexistence of a hereafter.

When *Humanist Manifesto I* was issued in 1933, Lamont felt that the document was too vague and incomplete to adequately express his own emerging humanist outlook, and he recoiled at its references to religious humanism. Nonetheless, he concluded that the manifesto's formulation was the best expression of his own beliefs he had seen so far. It enabled him to clarify his personal conclusions, which became thoroughly humanist and agnostic shortly thereafter. When many of the manifesto's signers founded the American Humanist Association in 1941, Lamont immediately joined.

After receiving his doctorate, Lamont was elected to the board of directors of the American Civil Liberties Union (a position he held for the next 20 years) and traveled with his wife on his first trip to the Soviet Union. Upon their return, he became chair of the Friends of the Soviet Union, an organization dedicated to Soviet-American cooperation.

From the start, his activism, writing, and teaching regarding the U.S.S.R. was misinterpreted. Red-baiting reporters and politicians accused him of being a "silk-shirt communist" — a falsehood he would find it necessary to deny repeatedly throughout the rest of his life. But many of his critics later admitted he was right when, in 1941, contrary to conventional wisdom, he correctly predicted that the Soviet Union would never fall to the Nazis but would, instead, thoroughly defeat them. In November 1942, Lamont and his father shared the podium with U.S. Vice-President Henry Wallace at a major Madison Square Garden rally in support of the U.S.S.R.'s war effort against Germany.

But Corliss Lamont erred in some of his sympathetic views of the Soviet system. During the late 1930s, for example, he defended the Moscow Trials, a judicial frame-up of certain Soviet leaders who Joseph Stalin wanted out of the way. Years later, Lamont corrected his mistakes.

His first civil-liberties case began upon his arrival home from his 1932 Soviet tour. Lamont had brought back what he described as "a number of lively posters, which illustrated public health work, reproduced works of art and ridiculed the capitalist system." U.S. Customs seized the posters as seditious material. After two months of legal protest, all but three were returned, these latter being retained because they included tiny photographs of U.S. currency.

Lamont's most significant civil-liberties battles, however, commenced after the end of World War II. Anti-communist hysteria was rife in the United States, and FBI Director J. Edgar Hoover ordered in January 1944 that Lamont be fully investigated. So in December 1945, the House Un-American Activities

Committee served Lamont, as chair of the National Council of American-Soviet Friendship, with a subpoena demanding that he hand over "all books, records, papers, and documents showing all receipts and disbursements of money" by the council and its affiliated organizations, as well as "all letters, memoranda or communications from, or with, any person or persons outside and within the United States of America." In response, Lamont called a meeting of the organization's board, which voted that the subpoena should be opposed as a violation of the First and Fourth Amendments and because the organization's members and contributors might be harassed.

On February 6, 1946, Lamont testified before the committee; a month later, Richard Morford, executive director of the council, also testified. Both refused to turn over any documents. Their cases went to the U.S. District Attorney in Washington, D.C., but only Morford (as custodian of the records) was indicted and subsequently found guilty. The U.S. Supreme Court refused to hear Morford's appeal, and he ended up serving a three-month jail term in the fall of 1950.

Nearly identical contempt cases during this time period put leaders of the joint Anti-Fascist Refugee Committee and the National Federation for Constitutional Liberties in jail. And the infamous "Hollywood Ten," citing the First Amendment in 1947, ended up serving one-year jail sentences. As Lamont later wrote in *Freedom Is As Freedom Does:*

[They] all deserve the gratitude of civil libertarians for their principled action in challenging the "Un-American Committee" on constitutional grounds. Although they did not achieve their ends, they set a splendid example and helped to educate the American public and the courts as to the true meaning of the Bill of Rights.

Though the government and press took notice at this time of Lamont's political views, his philosophical conclusions went largely ignored. From 1946 to 1959, he taught a lecture course at

Columbia called the Philosophy of Naturalistic Humanism. This developed in 1949 into his book, *Humanism As a Philosophy*, later re-titled *The Philosophy of Humanism*, which became and remains the definitive study of humanism.

With the deaths of his father in 1948 and his mother in 1952, Lamont came into control of a vast fortune. Over the years that followed, he contributed huge sums to Columbia and Harvard universities, as well as to the numerous causes he valued. Because of his commitment to civil-libertarian principles, and because the ACLU had too often given in to the government's efforts to hunt down leftists, Lamont left the ACLU board and, in 1951, founded the National Emergency Civil Liberties Committee, becoming its chair.

Corliss Lamont's next great civil-liberties battle began in 1953 when he was subpoenaed by Joseph McCarthy's Senate Subcommittee on Permanent Investigations. As Lamont later explained in *Freedom Is As Freedom Does:* [McCarthy] had uncovered the remarkable fact that the United States Army had included my book, *The Peoples of the Soviet Union*, in a bibliography. The listing had appeared, without my knowing about it, in an Army manual entitled *Psychological and Cultural Traits of Soviet Siberia*, published in 1953 by the Intelligence Section of the U.S. General Staff.

The subcommittee sought to prove that the U.S. Army had been infiltrated at its highest levels by communists and cited this reference to Lamont's work as evidence (this despite Lamont's publication earlier that year of a pamphlet, *Why I Am Not a Communist*). Understanding that taking the Fifth Amendment in similar hearings had not fared well in the courts, Lamont took a different tack: after affirming to tell the truth (but refusing to be sworn in and to state his reasons for such refusal), he began his testimony by making an objection to jurisdiction; this allowed him to read into the record a statement prepared by his attorney challenging the legal and constitutional power of the subcommittee to inquire into the political and religious beliefs and associational, personal, and private activities of private citizens. He also stated that he was "not now and never had been a member of the Communist Party." He then refused to answer most of the questions put to him, referring back each time to his prepared statement.

The hearing netted McCarthy no new information, so he demanded that Lamont be cited for contempt of Congress. The Senate voted in August 1954 and a federal grand jury handed down an indictment. Lamont was arrested, pleaded not guilty, and was released on $2,000 bail. In the two years that followed, *United States of America v. Corliss Lamont* went as far as the U.S. Second Circuit Court of Appeals before a unanimous decision came down in Lamont's favor. The precedent set by this case was successfully utilized by others.

In the summer of 1951, using his political views as justification, the U.S. State Department denied Lamont the renewal of his passport, thereby limiting his foreign travels to only Canada and Mexico. He battled the government on this issue, ultimately filing suit. Lamont's friend, artist Rockwell Kent, had previously sued on similar grounds; so when Kent won his case in the U.S. Supreme Court in 1958, Lamont automatically won his and was finally reissued his passport.

The 1960s saw Lamont's first marriage end in divorce. He then married author Helen Boyden Lamb. And there were new battles for civil liberties, as both husband and wife were put under surveillance and (years later) included on the Nixon administration's "enemies" list.

In 1963, Congress passed a law requiring the U.S. Postmaster General to screen all non-first class mail coming in from foreign countries and to issue postcards to the intended recipients of communist propaganda, asking if the literature was actually wanted. When Lamont received such a postcard regarding an unsolicited copy of the *Peking Review*, he filed another lawsuit.

He lost in federal court but appealed to the U.S. Supreme Court, which decided unanimously in his favor in 1965. *Lamont v. Postmaster General* was a landmark decision: it was the first time the Supreme Court had struck down a congressional law because it violated the First Amendment.

A decade later, Lamont learned that the FBI maintained a 2,788-page file on him and secured a copy under the Freedom of Information Act. He discovered that for 30 years agents had monitored his radio speeches, copied his articles and pamphlets, questioned his staff and friends — even his tennis partners — tapped his phones, inspected his tax returns, and reviewed his cancelled checks. These revelations resulted in yet another lawsuit, *Lamont v. Department of Justice*, which secured a federal ruling in 1979 that the government had failed to show how the FBI's surveillance was "related to the FBI's duties to enforce federal law." This case set a major precedent regarding adequate grounds for government surveillance of its citizens.

Next, Lamont sued the CIA in 1976 for damages in connection with its opening of 155 of his letters. The CIA admitted that its actions were illegal under the Fourth Amendment but contended that they were justified for "national security" reasons. In 1978, the federal district court in Brooklyn, New York, found in favor of Lamont and ordered the government to pay him $2,000 and send him a "suitable letter of regret." The court was particularly incensed over the opening of two love letters Lamont had written to his wife. It declared: "Illegal prying into the shared intimacies of husband and wife is despicable." (Helen had died in 1975 of liver cancer.)

Throughout its history, Lamont was active in the American Humanist Association and was named its president emeritus. His services were many, including representing the AHA in 1970 at the funeral of Bertrand Russell. In 1973, he was one of the original signers of *Humanist Manifesto II.* In recognition of his contributions to humanism and his commitment to civil liberties, the AHA bestowed upon him its highest honor in 1977: the Humanist of the Year Award.

In 1986, Lamont married Beth Keehner, a fellow humanist activist who shared and was devoted to advancing his ideas. And it was not long after this that Lamont's humanism and legal aggressiveness came together in one of the most important church-state battles of recent history. In February 1988, at the end of the Reagan administration, Lamont sued the government over its federal tax aid to sectarian schools overseas. *Lamont vs. Woods* was sponsored jointly by the ACLU and Americans for Religious Liberty and included such plaintiffs as AHA President Isaac Asimov, Reformed Rabbi Balfour Brickner, Unitarian-Universalist minister Bruce Southworth, and Florence Flast, president of the National Association for Public Education and Religious Liberty. Despite the Bush administration's argument that the $14 million in sectarian aid was part of foreign policy and, therefore, a political rather than religious issue, the U.S. Second Circuit Court of Appeals ruled in September 1991 that such aid was unconstitutional.

In June 1993, under the auspices of the Center for Cuban Studies, Corliss and Beth Lamont traveled to Cuba. Fidel Castro, who was well aware of Lamont's campaign of many years to lift the U.S. embargo of his country, gave him a lengthy audience, during which the two discussed the legal possibilities of Castro suing the U.S. government over the well-documented C.I.A. assassination attempts on his life.

Lamont's last two years were spent in active critique of U.S. government policies he opposed. In the closing paragraphs of his memoirs, *Yes to Life*, he summed up his never-ending commitment to such activism:

My final word is that in the battles that confront us today for America's freedom and welfare, our chief aim as public-

spirited citizens must be neither to avoid trouble, nor to stay out of jail, nor even to preserve our lives, but to *keep on fighting* for our fundamental principles and ideals.

With such an outlook, Corliss Lamont earned many famous friends and enemies. And because he truly lived his values, he was proud to have both.

~ ~ ~

The Humanist magazine continues to spotlight injustice and un-humanistic practices in the world, providing instances of ethical leadership toward a more humane and just democracy.

This brief description of the Philosophy of Humanism written by Corliss Lamont was published in *The Humanist* magazine.

What is Humanism?

Humanism is a philosophy of joyous service for the greater good of all humanity in this natural world and advocating the methods of reason, science and democracy. There are ten central propositions in the Humanist philosophy.

First, Humanism believes in a naturalistic metaphysics of attitude toward the universe that considers all forms of the supernatural as myth; and that regards Nature as the totality of being and as a constantly changing system of matter and energy which exists independently of any mind or consciousness.

Second, Humanism, drawing especially upon the laws and facts of science, believes that humans are an evolutionary product of the Nature of which we are a part; that our minds are indivisibly conjoined with the functioning of our brains; and that as an inseparable unity of body and personality we can have no conscious survival after death.

Third, Humanism, having its ultimate faith in human beings, believes that we possess the power or potentiality of solving our own problems, through reliance primarily upon reason and scientific method applied with courage and vision.

Fourth, Humanism, in opposition to all theories of universal determinism, fatalism, or predestination, believes that human beings, while conditioned by the past, possess genuine freedom of creative choice and action, and are, within certain objective limits, the masters of their own destiny.

Fifth, Humanism believes in an ethics or morality that grounds all human values in this-earthly experiences and relationships and that holds as its highest goal the this-worldly happiness, freedom, and progress—economic, cultural, and ethical—of all humankind, irrespective of nation, race, or religion.

Sixth, Humanism believes that the individual attains the good life by harmoniously combining personal satisfactions and continuous self-development with significant work and other activities that contribute to the welfare of the community.

Seventh, Humanism believes in the widest possible development of art and the awareness of beauty, including the appreciation of Nature's loveliness and splendor, so that the aesthetic experience may become a pervasive reality in the life of human beings.

Eighth, Humanism believes in a far-reaching social program that stands for the establishment throughout the world of democracy, peace, and a high standard of living on the foundations of a flourishing economic order, both national and international.

Ninth, Humanism believes in the complete social implementation of reason and scientific method; and thereby in democratic procedures, and parliamentary government, with full freedom of expression and civil liberties, throughout all areas of economic, political, and cultural life.

Tenth, Humanism, in accordance with scientific method, believes in the unending questioning of basic assumptions and convictions, including its own. Humanism is not a new dogma, but is a developing philosophy ever open to experimental testing, newly discovered facts, and more rigorous reasoning. Human beings, using their own intelligence and cooperating liberally with one another, can build an enduring citadel of peace and beauty upon this Earth.

By Corliss Lamont, 1990.

Here follows the Chapter III Section 3 entitled "Socialist Planning for America" of *You Might Like Socialism* **that the editor had extracted from the original Chapter sequence.**

It was removed from its proper sequence as being less relevant for specific planning today, 70 years later. Those who are inspired with the ideals of a more Socialistic Democracy will have hundreds, perhaps even thousands, of newer ideas about how to bring about the empowering changes in the public's perception that will be needed to promote this achievement.

You readers who are joining with other concerned citizens of the United States, acknowledging that this country is only one of many in the family of nations, may have a burning sense of urgency for change, and a fierce patriotism, feeling that the ideals to which we aspire have been totally betrayed. We fervently believe in this "experimental" democracy, a work evidently still-in-progress, that has a long way to go to actually achieve the freedoms and equalities, the right to life, liberty and the pursuit of happiness that tantalize us and our dreams. We know in our hearts that the United States has a deep obligation to perform in an ethical way upon the world stage, trying to make up for our fits of vengeful aggression. The Capitalist values that have been thrust upon us, that benefit only some and not all, promote greed, paranoia and chauvinism. Human Social values will provide prosperity for all and peace in this world. We will make the necessary changes.

This Section is here reproduced in its entirety, without further explanation. The detail that Corliss Lamont was describing as Socialist Planning for America in this Section was surely his courageous attempt to give some material substance to the Socialist ideals that he was envisioning. The specificity of these paragraphs seems less relevant in today's world. Remember, he was writing in 1939. Today, world-wide, we have at our fingertips new tools for communication and for organization undreamed of 70 years ago!

And now, back to the words of Corliss Lamont:

3. Socialist Planning for America

To make the picture of Socialist planning more concrete, let us visualize how it would work out in a definite country, And let us take as an example our own U.S.A. Suppose that in the elections of 1952, or sometime thereafter, the American people elect a President and a substantial majority in Congress pledged to establish Socialist planning throughout the country. Let us assume, furthermore, that the Supreme Court declares the legislative measures of the planning Party constitutional or that they are promptly made so through amendment of the Constitution at special state conventions. Leaving aside for the moment a discussion of the necessary transitional steps and without pretending to any finality, let us see what the pattern of American Socialist planning would in general be like. Apart from the political field, the key organization in the American planning system, as in any other, would be the National Planning Commission, with headquarters at Washington, D.C. The President, with the advice and consent of the Senate, chooses the eighteen members of the Executive Council of this Commission, including its Chairman, who sits as a member of the Government Cabinet, The appointments are non-politicial and are made from among experts especially qualified by wisdom and experience to deal with broad social and economic problems. The Commissioners are to regard themselves as trustees of the public interest. They will each receive salaries of $15,000 a year, except the Chairman, who will draw $20,000. Each of the Commissioners heads one of the eighteen different Divisions into which the Commission is organized. These Divisions, together with some of their more prominent Sections, are as follows:

Heavy Industry	Steel Machinery Housing Timber, Etc.

387

Light Industry	Clothing Footwear Furniture Motor Vehicles
Finance	Banking and Currency Capital Investment The Budget Taxation
Transportation	Railroads Motor Transport Air Transport Shipping (Domestic)
Communications	Telephone Telegraph Radio Post Office
Distribution	Retail Trade Storage Co-operatives Consumers' Needs
Social Welfare	Unemployment Insurance Pensions Public Health Recreation
Education	Primary Schools Secondary Schools Technical Institutes Colleges and Universities
Culture	The Arts Motion Pictures Science and Invention The Press

Fuel and Power	Coal Oil Electricity Gas
Agriculture	Cotton Wheat Dairy Livestock
Conservation & Reclamation	Forests Soil Flood Control Sub-soil Deposits
Foreign Trade	Exports Imports Merchant Marine Foreign Exchange
Defense	Army Navy Air Force Munitions
Labor	Wages and Hours Workers' Safety Employment Exchange Women Workers
Statistics and Research	Industrial Agricultural Population Social Trends
Organization	Education of Planning Experts Personnel
Co-ordination	Inter-Divisional Problems Public Relations

The functions of all but the last two of the Divisions are

clear enough from their names. The Organization Division has charge of managing and selecting the personnel of the Commission, which employs as trained statisticians or technical experts at least a thousand persons, as well as thousands of ordinary clerical workers, Appointment to a responsible position on the Planning Commission or the numerous subordinate commissions throughout the country is on a civil service basis, Only men and women who have fulfilled certain definite requirements are eligible for appointment. And one of the chief tasks of the Organization Division is to ensure the proper training of planning experts in a special Government institution or in already existing colleges and universities, which will establish special courses or graduate work for those who are aiming to enter the profession of planning. The Co-ordination Division, the head of which is always the Chairperson of the entire Commission, has the crucial task of constructing and synthesizing the final National Plan from the figures and projects submitted by the other Divisions and by the various sub-commissions throughout the country. It also oversees the relations between the National Commission and the Government, and through its Public Relations Section takes care of all publicity work for the Commission.

The Plans drawn up by the National Planning Commission and its subordinate commissions, while tremendously important and influential, are by no means final. Bills embodying the National Plans must be passed by Congress and signed by the President, They are subject to debate, criticism, and amendment like all other measures brought before the Senate and the House of Representatives. Since, moreover, the Commission is not an administrative body, its different Divisions, except those of Statistics & Research and Organization, must be matched in the national Government by corresponding administrative Departments, each of which has a planning board within it as one of its Bureaus. This naturally entails a considerable amount of reorganization in the structure of the Federal Government, The Departments of State and of Justice alone will retain their present set-up.

Each of the forty-eight states in the Union would have its

own Planning Commission, of which the ten members are appointed by the Governor. Each of the territories and dependencies, such as Alaska and Hawaii, the Pacific Islands and the Canal Zone, also has its separate Planning Commission; and in addition there is a special Regional Commission with responsibility for them all. There would also be nine regional Planning Commissions covering various states as groups according to the following arrangement:

New England Region	The six New England states	Headquarters at Boston
Middle Atlantic Region	New York down through West Virginia	Headquarters at New York City
South Atlantic Region	Maryland to Georgia, including Kentucky and Tennessee	Headquarters at Atlanta
Gulf Region	Florida west to Louisiana and Arkansas	Headquarters at New Orleans
Great Lakes Region	Ohio, Indiana, Illinois and Michigan	Headquarters at Chicago
Great Plains Region	Wisconsin in the east to the Dakotas in the west, and Missouri and Kansas in the south	Headquarters at Des Moines
Southwest Region	Texas to Arizona	Headquarters at Dallas
Rocky Mountain Region	Six mountain states with Montana in the north, Colorado in the south and Nevada in the west	Headquarters at Denver
Pacific Region	California, Oregon and Washington	Headquarters at San Francisco

Within the states each county and each city has its own Planning Commission. And in the more sparsely settled agricultural districts every unit of population amounting to 10,000 or more has a commission, There are also Planning Commissions for each industry as a whole and for each sub-division of each industry. For instance, the entire steel industry as a unit has its Planning

Commission; the-various regional steel trusts, of course publicly owned and operated, likewise have their separate commissions; as does each substantial producing unit within each trust. Finally there exist planning committees in each factory and even in each shop of each factory.

Thus, all of the workers in a steel factory combine to put through a plan for that unit; all the factories in a certain district combine to put through a central plan for the steel trust of which they are part; all the trusts combine to put through a plan for the steel industry as a whole; and then the steel industry itself, the co-ordinating centers of which are a Division of the Planning Commission and a Department of the Government, combines with every other industry and economic activity to put through a balanced Plan for the entire country. The geographical planning bodies operate on the same principle, that is, from the smaller up through the larger. The cities' plans fit into that of the county, the counties' into that of the state, the states' into that of the region, and the regions' into that of the entire country.

Planning under Socialism is, then, a complex process embodying three different but intimately related aspects. All of the plans are, in the first place, plans over a definite period of time. Taking the presidential term in America as an appropriate time-span, our Commission adopts for the nation a First Four-Year Plan, a Second Four-Year Plan, a Third Four-Year Plan and so on. Inside these Four-Year Plans there are one-year, quarterly and even one-month plans. In the second place, there is the geographic aspect of the plans. Besides the country as a whole, each region, state, county and city has its own four-year and one-year plan. In the third place, there is the functional aspect of the plans as applied to each industry and its sub-divisions.. These three fundamental aspects of planning—the temporal, the geographic and the functional—are thoroughly integrated by the National Planning Commission in each big Four-Year Plan. It is this Commission that welds together in one vast, integrated, long-range Plan all the minor plans and reports of all the various regions, states, counties, cities, industries, factories, distribution units, and cultural organizations throughout the entire United States. It is this Commission which takes the thousand and one estimates pouring in from all parts of the country and correlates them into the considered and rational whole which constitutes a National Plan. It is this Commission at Washington which from week to week, from month to month, from year to year, casts its all-seeing eye over the economic activities of the nation and shifts the schedules within the Plan to keep pace with new and unforeseen developments.

America's First Four-Year Plan would need careful and extensive preparation before it could be put into effect. If our planning Party is victorious in the national elections of November, 1952, it would have two months of leeway before the new President and Congress come into office in the first week of January, 1953. Accordingly, it can be expected to have ready for action by Congress, bills empowering the Government to take over at once a few key enterprises such as the railroads, communications, fuel and power, and, most important of all, the banks. Provision would be made for appropriate compensation of the owners over what must necessarily be a long period of years. The planning Party will also submit bills, establishing the general structure of the planning system and giving very general estimates of what is to be accomplished during the First Four-Year Plan. I expect that that the complete functional activization of existing capacity will be the main productive goal of this period. Eight months later, September 1, 1953, the National Planning Commission would be ready with a preliminary draft, giving detailed figures and measures for the First Four-Year Plan. During the next three months this draft will be published abroad throughout the land and given the widest kind of publicity in newspapers, magazines, radio programs, public meetings, educational institutions, scientific institutes and other organs of public opinion. At the same time the Planning Commission will send out to all subordinate planning organizations the provisional quotas to be fulfilled in the geographical or functional sectors for which they are responsible. Thus, the preliminary Plan will be discussed and criticized from one end of the country to another both by the public in general and by the specific planning, economic, and cultural agencies concerned in translating it into actuality.

"How can we improve the Plan?" will become a nation-wide slogan. By December 1 the various planning units, after careful consideration and in light of whatever suggestions have been made, will have returned revised drafts to the Planning Commission. During the next six weeks the Commission would proceed, after receiving all available information and criticism from its sub-commissions and other sources, to draw up a final Plan for presentation to Congress in the middle of January, 1954. Congress would then thoroughly discuss the Plan according to its regular procedures and will undoubtedly amend it to some degree. We can probably count on having the President's signature on the .final congressional planning bill by May 1, 1954, so that it can become definitely operative at the beginning of the fiscal year on July 1.

This means that the First Four-Year Plan (ending June 30, 1957) would be in operation as a completed and functional whole for only three years out of the full period. There is no way of avoiding this, however, for the first National Plan; but the second will overcome any time-lag and will go into effect July 1, 1957. All of the Plans will begin and end with the regular fiscal year. The Planning Commission will release its preliminary draft of the Second Year Plan (1957-1961) on July 1, 1956, to run the gamut of public opinion. Its final version it will have ready, promptly on January 1, 1957 for submission to Congress. The Commission will not wait for the formal completion of one Four-Year Plan before starting to draw up estimates for the next; and this preparatory work will ordinarily begin a full year before each Plan is due for presentation to Congress.

The standard-of-living goal for each family of four at the end of the First Four-Year Plan will be an annual minimum of $5,000 in consumers' values, including those made available by the extension of free government services. This goal will be achievable through the full utilization of our present labor supply, taking in the able-bodied unemployed but totally ruling out child labor, on the basis of a seven-hour day, a five-day week and a yearly holiday of three weeks. The minimum mentioned would be even higher if the new regime were able to eliminate America's soaring defense and armament expenditures. In any case, my $5,000 estimate by no means adequately represents the advantages which the American people will enjoy under Socialist planning. For it is impossible to evaluate in financial terms even the physical gains which will, for instance, accrue to the urban masses when they all live in houses or apartments which have plenty of room, good light and fresh air. And it is also out of the question to put a definite money value on the immense psychological boons which Socialism will bring, especially through insuring everyone a job and eliminating the chief economic worries of the present.

One of the most important problems that our planning experts will have to face is that of procuring trustworthy data on the capacities and needs of the various areas and of the country as a whole. It is not possible even to start planning without some such data yet it is not possible to obtain complete and reliable data until planning is well under way. For only an organization like the National Planning Commission, with its hundreds of subordinate agencies in different localities and economic enterprises through-out America, is equipped to gather in and organize all the necessary statistics. The Commission's own Division of Statistics & Research plays a central role here. Thus as planning makes head-way, we shall see a steady improvement and enlargement of the statistical base, making the intricate network of economic forces more and more measurable and bringing about what has aptly been called by economists complete economic visibility. In regard to this important matter of statistics, Socialist planning in America will not, as in Soviet Russia, have to start almost from scratch. For there already exist here a number of agencies, both public and private, which are constantly building up the kind of statistical knowledge that planning demands as a foundation. In the public field the most useful of these is the National Resources Planning Board, formerly called the National Resources Committee, which has published a number of volumes particularly pertinent to the subject of planning. Then we have the reports of the numerous local planning organizations, there being in the U.S.A. at present no less than 42 state planning boards, 400 county and over 1,100 municipal, all with very limited powers, of course.

In addition, each of the main Departments of the Federal Government carries on vital fact-finding activities, outstanding in this respect being the Bureau of the Census and the Bureau of Standards, both under the Department of Commerce; the Bureau of Internal Revenue and the U. S. Public Health Service, both under the Treasury Department; the Bureau of Labor Statistics, under the Department of Labor; the Bureau of Home Economics, under the Department of Agriculture; and the Geological Survey, under the Department of the Interior, There has also been established recently at Washington a Central Statistical Board to render information and advice in the working out of inter-departmental problems. Under private auspices we find the substantial studies-issued by the Brookings Institution and the Russell Sage Foundation, the reports of well-known research bodies such as the National Bureau of Economic Research and the National Industrial Conference Board, and the regular publications of organizations for the protection of the consumer such as the Consumers' Union. A huge aggregate of carefully organized and up-to-date statistics is as essential for the carrying out of a Four-Year Plan as for its preparation. For the National Planning Commission must keep informed on the progress or lack of progress that is being made throughout the country. For this reason the vast network of sub-commissions send into it frequent reports, at least once every two weeks. And the Commission has the duty, which is also an opportunity, of constantly revising the Four-Year Plans in the light of the specific situation at the beginning of each year, each quarter and each month. Whatever changes the Commission recommends to the Government Departments empowered to put them into effect, must of course fit in with the general perspectives laid down by the original Four-Year Plan, but need not conform exactly to the original figures. These periodic readjustments are essential because in large-scale and long-range planning there are sure to occur both under-fulfillments and over-fulfillments. Then, too, it is perfectly obvious that a Planning Commission, even if composed of the wisest persons in the world, is bound to make some miscalculations. Moreover, there exist certain factors which the most flawless technique of planning can hardly anticipate; weather conditions for example, affecting the fortunes of crops throughout the country; new inventions and new discoveries of mineral wealth, affecting the progress of industry and agriculture; the movement of world prices, affecting payments for needed imports; and the whole international situation, affecting the day-to-day psychology of the people and the proportion of the industrial plant which has to be geared to defense. All of these reasons combine to make intelligent flexibility a natural and fundamental principle of social-economic planning in the dynamic and ever-changing society of today; the notion that Socialist planning implies some sort of strait-jacket thrown over the life of the people is very wide of the mark. It is most important to note that the planning procedures which I have in mind make ample allowance for local initiative. The idea behind Socialism is not to set up a group of dictatorial supermen who sit in Washington and hand down orders to the rest of the country, but to provide for continuous and democratic interaction between the local planning units and the ones higher up, between the organizations on the circumference and those at the center. Within the framework of the National Plan it is possible and indeed highly desirable to give a good deal of leeway to the lower planning and administrative agencies in working out the details for their own particular sectors and in making final decisions on matters of primarily local significance.

The National Planning Commission or the Federal Government steps in only if decisions seem to violate or disturb in some way the objectives and schedules of the National Plan. Naturally enough, our Socialist planners are going to take full advantage of that bigness and concentration which is so marked a characteristic of American industry; and of the collectivism which objectively exists today in the form of mass concentration of workers in the factories, of extensive trade-union organization, and of the far-flung collective controls of corporate enterprise. A Socialist regime would find many problems solved in advance if it proceeded, for example, to take over the steel industry. For steel in the U. S. A., with a handful of monopolies ruling the roost, is already unified to such an extent that the step to total unification required by Socialist planning would be comparatively easy. And the same point holds true for a number of other basic industries. Indeed, if the present managements of these industries could be trusted to administer them faithfully on behalf of a Socialist commonwealth (and this is a very big if), they could be left substantially in charge. Undoubtedly, in some cases concentration has already gone too far for the highest efficiency. There is such a thing as administrative breakdown from sheer bulk. But the unification intended by Socialism does not rule out decentralization in production. The over-concentration of industries in urban areas, resulting in crowded living conditions, bad air and lack of decent recreational facilities, is one of the first things which Socialist planning aims to rectify. The principle to be followed throughout is that of the greatest possible degree of decentralization and autonomy consistent with nationwide coordination. The final guarantee that local initiative will flourish under Socialism is that in the last analysis the drawing up and execution of any social-economic plan depends on individuals.

The extent to which the beautiful blueprint of a Four-Year Plan is written into concrete material and cultural achievement rests upon the initiative and intelligence and energy of the workers and farmers, the technicians and professional people, throughout the length and breadth of America. Without their unceasing co-operation and support every Plan must fail. Hence the Public Relations Section of the National Commission has the vital task of educating every category of the population on the fundamentals of planning and of arousing their enthusiasm concerning the objectives and possibilities of the Four-Year Plans. It must bring to every individual an understanding of his part in the total planning set-up and the connection between his own function, and that of others. And this in itself constitutes one of the outstanding benefits of Socialist planning, since everyone in the community becomes able to see how and why his job fits into the larger scheme of things and to feel a significance and dignity in his work that was seldom present before. In this way central planning for the whole nation brings central planning into the activity of each person, pulling together the conflicting strands of his nature and making of them a potent unity.

Socialist planning, carried out in America in the American way, will present to the citizens of this country the greatest challenge they have ever had. Limited as war planning was in the U. S. and destructive as was its objective, it did show that the theory and practice of nation-wide planning is not something entirely alien to the American genius. It is my firm opinion that under Socialism all the idealism and practical engineering technique for which America is so noted, freed at last from the shackles of the profit system, will have unprecedented opportunity for fulfillment in projects of almost unlimited scope, and grandeur. There will be no lack of tasks to appeal to the imagination and ambition of new generations. And the American people in their boundless energy will sweep forward to conquer new heights of economic and cultural achievement.

~ ~ ~

Thus completes Corliss Lamont's *You Might Like Socialism*. With these closing words, we end this re-issue of his book, and Part One of *Lefties Are In Their Right Minds.*

Our most sincere wish is that this extensive research and advocacy by Corliss Lamont will be useful, first, to explain the original ideals of Socialism, and even more, to learn how many of its principles, adapted to present circumstances, might be just exactly what the people of the United States need to consider at this time for the purpose of modifying and controlling the abuses of unconscionable, unbridled Capitalism. We've lived long enough with the blatant lies and fear-mongering that Capitalism's vested interests have foisted upon the general public. Socialism's benefits and its concerns for the welfare of the people, equality, and of economic security, must no longer be associated in the minds of the people with totalitarianism. The truth is, totalitarianism is what you get when any power, no matter what it's called, is more con-cerned with sustaining and perpetuating itself, its own power, than exercising proper concern for the welfare of its own people. But we have People Power on our side; let's work together for change.

Special hello: Barack Obama Transition Team and Administration! PLEASE, DON'T ALLOW THE FEAR OF BEING LABELED SOCIALIST, PREVENT BOLD ACTIONS TO BENEFIT THE PEOPLE. PRESIDENT FRANKLIN ROOSEVELT WISELY LISTENED TO GOOD ADVICE; HE TOOK THE FIRST STEPS.

You're invited to read the next Book: Lefties, Part Two. Its chapters will present more of the works of Corliss Lamont, and copies of all the Pamphlets that Corliss Lamont created during his long activist lifetime. There will be additional material about him, and excerpts from relevant works, including addresses by other activists presented in his honor at a special Civil Liberties Forum marking the Centenary of Corliss Lamont in 2002 at Columbia University Law School. There'll be some updating commentaries from this Raging Granny, who loved and worked with him, and wishes for his works to inspire others to devote their lives helping to create a just and humane Democracy that respects and cares for the needs of its people.

~ ~ ~

INDEX

American Telephone and Telegraph Co., 70, 107, 321
American Soviet Friendship, National Council of, 376
Americanism, Cyrus Leroy Baldridge, 281
Americanism, 269, 281, 369
Anaconda Copper Mining Corporation, 70
Anarchists, 282, 341-342
anarchy, 26; 93, 96, 132, 245, 251, 316, 368, chaotic anarchy of
    unplanned Capitalism, 132
Anderson, Benjamin M., Jr. 128, 132-133
Annunzio, D', 313
anti-Communist hysteria, 26, 29, 32, 190, 191, 198, 376
Anti-Fascist Rescue Committee, 377; anti-fascist efforts, 59, 61,
    232, 338-339, 341, 354
Anti-Lynching Bill, 280
anti-Semitism, 164, 256-257, 262
anti-union provocateurs, 262
anti-war demonstrations, 32, 198, 275
Argentina, 244
Archangel, Siberia, 27
Aristotle, 154, 327
armaments, see manufacture of, 19, 89, 100, 102, 207-208, 214,
    228, 241, 248, 306; plan for taxation of, 36
Arnold, Thurman W., 127
Asimov, Isaac, president of AHA, 381
Assignment in Utopia, Eugene Lyons, 176
assassination, 25, 33, 59, 218, 381
Atheists, 26, 31, 277, 339
Attlee, Clement C.,69
Auden, W. H., 60
Australia, 133, 356
Austria, 89, 170, 209, 225, 231, 291
Austria-Hungary, 218-221, 225, 353
Azana, Manuel, 60

Bail Out Bill, (Act of Congress), 7
Bakunin, Mikhail, 341

bankruptcy, debt, borrowing, 6-9, 46, 88-89, 100, 114, 206, 208-209, 226, 293

Baldridge, Cyrus Leroy, 281

Baldwin, Oliver, 60

Baldwin, Roger N., 61

Baldwin, Stanley, Earl, 60, 291, 355

Balearic Islands, 234

Balkans, 220, 239, 353

Barlow, John Perry, *Declaration of Independence of Cyberspace,* 4

Baseball, Phillips Exeter Academy, protest re: sportsmanship, 373

Beard, Charles A., 274

Belgium, 285, 357

Bellamy, Edward, 61

Benton, Thomas, 61

Bergson, Henri, 307

Berle, Adolph A., Jr., 70, 93

Bernal, J. D., 311

Bessarabia, 141

betrayal, of the people, 4, 10-13, 22, 335, 385; by the FCC, 22; of Socialism, 92; of the Revolution, 54, 186, 291

Bible, 159, 335

Bill of Rights, 11, 19, 22, 24, 198-199, 260-262, 266, 268, 277-282, 377

Billinger, Karl, 59

Billings, Warren, 274, 281-282

binLaden, Osama, 17, 184

Bingham, Alfred, 61

Black Legion, 269-272

Bloor, Ella Reeve, 61

Blum, Leon, 59, 353

Bolivia, 362

Bolshevik Revolution, 23-26, 30, 189, 287; Bolshevik "scare," 286

Bolshevism, see Communism

Bose, Subhas Chandra, 61, 357

Boy Scout, 373

brain-washed, American public, 3; brain-washing, 9-11

Catholic Worker, The, 267, Catholic workers in Spain, 339
Cattell, James McKeen, 274
Cecil, Lord, 246
"celestial escape hatch," 13, 17, 18, 30
censorship, 277, 346
Census of Manufactures, 69
Center for Cuban Studies, 381
Cerda, Pedro Aguirre, 370
Chamberlain, Prime Minister, 241, 246, 362
Chart of Plenty, Harold Loeb and Associates, 78, 130
Chase National Bank, 71, 128, 147
Chase, Stuart, 367
Chavez, Hugo, President of Venezuela, 1
cheap labor, 19, see also labor
Cheney, Dick, 18
Chiang Kai-shek, 355-357
Chief Executive Officers, 15
Childhood of Humankind, 16
Childs, Marquis W., 365
Chile, 370
China, 59, 120, 172, 210, 217, 220, 233, 237, 244-248, 366
Chirac, Jacques, of France, suggested taxing armaments, 36
Christian, see Christianity
Christian appreciation for Socialist ideals, 346
Christianity, 52, 255, 258, 336, 339, 344
Chu Teh, 59, 357
Chunking, 243
church state battles in February 1988, 381
Civil Liberties, 19, 96, 167, 189, 204, 258, 260, 265-267, 270, 272,
      275, 282-283, 285-289, 293, 300, 348, 373, 382, 388, 390,
      393; preservation of, 283-289; Senate Committee, 268,
      286; violations of, 277, 300
Civil Rights Act of 1871, 265; state government units needed, 280
Clark, Grenville, 280
"class" prejudice, 250, 253-257
Clinton, Bill, 188, 373

Cliveden sets, 237
Cohen, Morris, 328
collective security, 169, 240-243, 246-247, 366
collectivization, 143-144, 147, 176
Colombia, 362
Columbia University, 8, 35, 56, 167, 186, 218, 274, 275, 280, 301, 375, 378, 400
Coming Struggle for Power, The, John Strachey, 74
Communism, 148, 177-178, 237-238, 354, 375, 377
Communist International, 239, 349, 350
Communist Manifesto, The, Marx and Engels, 57, 103
Communist Party, 32, 156, 164, 178, 193-194, 276, 281, 296, 298, 345-346, 348, 361, 371, 377, 388
Communist propaganda, 388
Communist, Why I Am Not A, (pamphlet by Corliss Lamont) 387
Communists, 103, 119, 124, 136, 202, 211, 217, 224, 262, 271, 280, 298; anti-communist hysteria, 25, 29, 376, 385
Conant, James B., 302
concentration, of corporations, 69; monopoly in banking field, 70; of revolutionary forces, 313; of workers, 397; of industries, 398
concentration camps, 99, 266
Confederation Generate de Travail, 342
Co-Intel Pro, 28
Congress, U. S., 6, 7, 10, 21, 29, 122, 155, 198, 260, 280, 286, 358, 367, 380, 387, 393; of Soviets, 155; of Communist Party, 175; Seventh World Congress, 343; contempt of, 379
Conservative Party, 291
consumers' boycott, 242
consumers' co-operatives and unions, 295, 316, 357, 396
consumers' goods, 81, 86; 87; with Socialist planning, 119, 130, 142, 145, 159, 151
Continental Planning Commissions, 133
Conversion to Peace Economy, Prof. Seymour Melman, 8, 36
cooperation with the Soviet Union, 374
Corliss, Mrs. Charles, 52

Denmark, 357
Department of Justice, 389
Dewey, District Attorney, 128
Dewey, John, Professor, 167,183, 186, 328, 375
Dialectic Materialism, 329
dictatorship, 3
Dies, Representative Martin, (Dies Committee), 282
domestic feudalism, 366
"domestic terrorism," 11; "domestic enemies," 271
Dreiser, Theodore, 61
Dreyfus, Alfred, Captain, frame-up, 281
Drobney, Sheldon, (*Report on Invasion of USSR*), 27
Dukakis, Michael, 29
Duranty, Walter, 140
Dutt, R. Palme, 217
Dzerzhinsky, Felix, 59

ecology, world, 20
economic warfare, 71, 73, 231, 252; "Priests of Economics," 2
economy, planned, 124
Edison, Thomas, 322
educational access, 3; public education, 261, 306-307, 320, 389
Edwords, Fred, 373
Egypt, 222, 297, 303
Electronic Freedom Foundation, 4
"enemies of the state," under totalitarianism 10, 11; list of enemies
        and dangerous persons compiled during McCarthy era, 90
"enemy combatants," re: torture as unlawful US Policy 19, 25
Engels, Friedrich, 55-57, 103, 309-311, 313, 342, 347
England, see Great Britain
Englewood, N.J., 373
Epstein, Abraham, 303
Equal Opportunity, ideal of, 48, 253; lack of, 258; equality for
        women, 390
Estonia, 141
Ethiopia, 100, 170, 209, 214, 230, 238, 234, 239, 241, 354

Greece, 56, 222, 224, 297, 303
Greek Orthodox Church, 139, 336, 340-341
Guantanamo, Cuba, 19; torture of alleged "enemy combatants", 25
Guaranty Trust Co., 70
Gulf of Tonkin, 18

HUAC; House Un-American Activities Committee, 376, 377
Hague, Mayor Frank, 265-268-273, 365
Hague, Frank, Jr., 266
Haiti, 229
Half-Moon Foundation, iii
Hallowell, Robert, 307
Hamilton, Alexander, 73
Hapgood, Powers, 61
hard-wired for wonderment and awe, 329
Harris, Lement, 61
Harris, Reed, 275
Harvard University, 25, 74, 259, 261, 263, 280-282, 307-308, 374, 378, Alumni Assn./scrubwomen, 375; Student Union, 374
Harvey, George U., 270
Hawaii, 400
Hayek, Professor, 89, 90
Haymarket, 28
health care, 3, 25, 32, 34, 190, 199, 310, 374; Public Health Services, 156-157, 303-304, 366, 377, 396
Hearst, William Randolph, 270, 278, 282
Hecker, Julius, 329
Hemingway, Ernest, 61
Hicks, Granville, 61, 274
historical relativism, 174
Hitler, Adolf, 161, 175, 187-188, 207, 214, 231-238, 250, 257, 288, 290-291. 337-338, 341, 351-352
Hobbes, 327
Holland, 127, 220, 223, 290, 365
Hollywood Ten, 377
Holmes, Justice, 271

412

Homer, 141, 210
Honduras, 229
Hoover, Herbert, President, 83, 93
Hoover, J. Edgar, 28, 376
Hopkins, Ernest M., 276
House Un-American Activities Committee, (HUAC), 376, 377
Huberman, Leo, 41, 81
Hudson, Manley O., 246
Humanism As A Philosophy, Corliss Lamont, 190, 378, 381
Humanism, Philosophy of, v, vi, 29, 31, 37, 199, 200, 326,
     principles of, 382, 388-391; at the UN, 31; Socialist
     Humanism, 326-340; Humanist Democracy, 199-200;
     ecumenical Humanism, 206
Human Rights, violations of, 12; Universal Declaration of, 1, 37
Humanist Magazine, 373, 382
Humanist Manifesto I & II, 37, 205, 375, 380
Humanist of the Year in 1977, 381
Hungary, 218-221, 225, 353
Huxley, Julian and Juliette, 375
hypocrisy, Capitalists embracing Fascism, 332; rabid Anti-Red
     violations of Free Speech in US, 28, 272. 275-278;
     Christian ethical ideals and the profit motive, 325

Iceland, 244
"illegals," 12
Illusion Of Immortality, The, 375; *Issues Of Immortality*, 375
imperialism, economic, 91, 358, 363; Capitalist, 215, 216, 219,
     227, 249, 346; Fascist, 98, 288; Tsarist, 170, 210
Imperialism, defined by V.I. Lenin, 215, 230
Immigration and Customs Enforcement, 12
immortality, focus on, "celestial escape-hatch" 12, 13, 197, 325,
     Issues of Immortality, 375, *Illusion of Immortality*,
     Corliss Lamont, 375
impeachment, 18, 32, 34
impunity, 15, 37, 202, 332
India, 61, 225, 230, 237, 256, 273, 346, 350, 364, 356, 357, 359,

Indian, Native Peoples, Indigenous, 1, 12, 225, 229, 256, 359, 363
industrial espionage, exposures of, 286
Industrial Revolution, 64, 71, 75, 153, 316
infiltrators, Co-Intel-Pro, 27
installment selling, 87
Institute for Propaganda Analysis, 261
International, First Communist, 348
International, Second Communist, 348
International, Third Communist, 169, 273
International Congress of American Democracies, 370
International Criminal Court, 15, 37, 187, 188, 197, 202, 332
International Labor Defense, 274; Standards, 20
International Planning Commission, 134, 398, 400, 404, 406
Internet, the, World Wide Web, sharing of information, 4, 123
"invisible hand," of the free-market, 6
Iran, 18
Iraq, 18
Irish, Margaret Hayes, Lamont, 384
It Is Later Than You Think, Max Lerner, 100, 261
Italy, 99, 100, 109, 133, 153, 168, 172, 176, 207, 214-216, 220,
        225, 229, 230, 232, 236, 238, 241, 244, 288, 291, 351, 352

Jackson, Gardner, 61
Japan, 59, 99, 109, 135, 138, 156, 170, 172, 177, 187, 120, 217-
        218, 220, 224, 229, 233-234, 237, 239, 240, 243, 245-249,
        254, 355, 370
Jaures, Jean, 59
Jefferson, President Thomas, vii, 296, 301
Jehovah's Witnesses, 284
Jersey City, 265-267, 279, 365
Jesus, 54, 335, "a socialist," 338; "dangerous revolutionary", 336
Jews, peace-marchers, 31; anti-Semitism, persecution of, 92, 137,
        163, 231, 254-257, 262, 279, 338; under Hitler, 257
Joslyn, C. S., 258

Keehner, Beth (Elberta) Lamont, 381

Materialism-Naturalism, 334; Historical, 315; Dialectical, 179, 336
Marx, Karl, 27, 51, 55-57, 95, 103, 140, 289, 290, 298-299, 311,
 314-317, 333-334, 341, 348
Marxian issues, 65, 81-83, 86, 161-162, 163, 176-178, 181, 195,
 296, 323, 325, 330, 336, 338, 344, 348, 368, 371, 376
Marxist theory, 27, 81, 163, 195, 296, 338
Mayor Hague, of Jersey City, 267
Means, Gardiner C., 69
meetings, banning of Socialist; refusing permits and rentals, 266
medical care, in U. S., disgrace of neglect, 156, 304, 366
Mein Kampf, Adolf Hitler, 236, 238
Melman, Professor Seymour, 8, 36
Memel, 170, 210
Men Must Act, Lewis Mumford, 285
Mesopotamia, 224
metaphysics, 333-334, 392
Metropolitan Life Insurance Co., 69
Metternich, Count, 359
Mexican War, 229
Mexico, 219, 236, 273, 366-369, 370, 388
Millennium Development Goals of United Nations, 37
Miller, Herbert Adolphus, 273
Mills, Ogden, 93
Minor, Robert, 59
Modern Age books, 26
Modern Corporation and Private Property, The, Adolph A. Berle,
 Jr., and Gardiner C. Means, 70
"money-changers," out of the temple, 10, 336, 343
Mongolia, Inner, 357; Outer, 357
Monopoly, 68, 70-71, 87; 108, 156, 220, 231, 303, 309;
  Committee, 70; growth of monopolistic tendencies, 71
Montezuma-Tripoli, 19
Mooney, Tom, 279; frame-up, 281, 287
Moore, Governor Harry, 271
"moral rearmament," 94; moral development, 14
Morford, Richard, 377

Morgan, J. P., 43, 70, 94, 222, 374
Morosov, Alexander, 57
Morris, William, 58
Morrison, Herbert, 362
Moscow Trials, "The Show Trials," 376"
Moseley, Major General George Van Horn, 361
Mosley, Sir Oswald, 361
Moulton, Harold G., 84
Mumford, Lewis, 285
Murphy, Attorney General Frank, 285
Mussolini, Benito, 99, 102, 164, 179, 210, 216, 234-236, 238, 241-
    243, 245, 288, 294, 297, 344, 351, 359, 361
Mussolini, Vittorio, 239; war as "sport," 288
NRA, 109, 110
Nation, The, 50
National Association Public Education & Religious Liberty, 381
National Bureau of Economic Research, 405
National City Bank, 70
National Council of American Soviet Friendship, 377
National Educational Association, 261
National Emergency Civil liberties Committee, 378
National Federation for Constitutional Liberties, 377
National Industrial Conference Board, 405
National Labor Relations Act, 93, 285
National Labor Relations Board, 184-185, 270, 285
National Planning Commission, 85, 94, 96, 130-131, 133, 397,
    399, 402, 404-405, 407, ; Divisions, 74-77; functions, 77
National Resources Committee, 75, 405
National Resources Planning Board, 405
National Revolutionary Party, 427
National Urban League, 260
nationalism, 174, 222, 230, 232, 242, 255
Native Americans, 1, 12, 225, 256, 277, 359, 363
Naturalistic Humanism, 327, 382
Nature, 5, 13, 57, 66, 75, 79, 97, 211, 212, 310; 326-329, 382-383;
    human nature, 159, 174, 205, 317-319

Nearing, Scott, 276, 374
Negrin, Juan, 60
Negroes, 250, 254, 254, 257, 261 271, 278, 284, 356, 366
Nehru, Pandit Jawaharlal, 64, 357
Neilson, William Allan, 276
Neutrality Act, U.S., 232, 246; neutrality, 245
New College, Oxford, 374
New Deal, 68, 76, 90, 93, 97. 108, 356, 364, 369
New School for Social Research, 52, 302
New Testament, 335, 373
New York Evening Post, 52
New York Herald Tribune, 174, 269
New York Legislature, 174, 269, 300
New York Times, The, 142
New York World-Telegram, 326
New York World's Fair, 154, 243
New Zealand, 363
News from Nowhere, William Morris, 58
Nicaragua, 229
Nicholas II, 140, 173, 293
Niebuhr, Reinhold, 59, 83, 203
Nixon Administration "Enemies List," 379
Norway, 364

Obama, Barak, US President, vii; advice to have courage, 400
O'Connell, Representative Jerry, 267, 272
Olson, Governor Floyd, 287
Olympic Games, 254
opium, international traffic in, 220
Origin of the Family, Friedrich Engels, 57, 313
Ossining, New York, 373
Our Siberian Adventure, by Gen. William Graves, 27
over-population, 216-217
over-production, 78, 153-154, 161, 309, 330
Owen, Robert, 60
Oxford Group, 54

PWA, 89
Page, Walter H., 223
Palmer Raids, 28
Panama Canal Zone, control of, Theodore Roosevelt, 226
Parker, Dorothy, 61
"Parlor Pinks," 53; "pinkos," 27
Parrish, Anne, 50
passport denial, US Supreme Court reversal 379
Patriot Act, 11, 34
peace bonds, 7
peacemaking mechanisms, 1
Pennsylvania Railroad, 69, 107
People's Front, 58, 235, 292, 350; in Chile, 370; in France, 349; in
        Spain, 58, 235, 292
People's History, A, by Howard Zinn, 29
people's movement, 2; mass movement, 352
Peoples Of The Soviet Union, by Corliss Lamont, 378
People's Right To Know, 22
Peking Review, magazine in Supreme Court censorship case, 379
Persia, 218, 346
personal property under Socialism, 131, 376
"personhood" immunity and unjustified power of corporations, the
        7, 20-21, 69, 72, 96, 127, 198, 201, 232
Peru, 216
Phillips Exeter Academy, 259, 373
philosophy, 3, 7, 22-23, 27, 49, 61, 80, 98, 157, 162, 179, 193,
        203-204, 243-244, 254-255, 259, 262, 280, 303, 311, 314,
        333-336, 340, 346-347, 349, 350, 379, 384, 387, 392
Philosophy Of Humanism, The, Corliss Lamont, 190, 378, 383
Philosophy of Naturalistic Humanism, 378
Pilsudski, Marshal, 140
"pinkos," 27
Pius XI, Pontiff, Catholic, 345
Plan, America's First Four-Year, 402; America's Second Four-
        Year, 403; flexibility of Four-Year, 406; Material, 113;

National, 112, 402, 407; Soviet Five-Year, 124, 144-154,
178, 332; Twenty-Year World, 134-135
planned economy, 8
planning, basic characteristic of, 125; collective economic, 120;
fundamental aspects of, 402; international, 134-136, 252;
most vital need of our times, 130; New Deal, 67, 75, 77,
90, 93, 108, 363, 371, 377; principles of, 107-121; public,
under Capitalism, 108; purpose of, in capitalist enterprise,
108; Socialist, for abundance, 105, 113, 130-131, 135, 150,
300, 306, 318, 329, 376; Socialist, purpose of, 48, 351
planned obsolescence, 131-132
Plato, 154, 200, 327-328
plutocrats, 43, 83, 85, 383
Poland, 138, 142-143, 190, 224, 360
police brutality, 277
political campaigns, financial inequality, 259
political conventions, 11
political power of Capital class, 264
Popular Front, see People's Front
Port of New York Authority, 127
Portugal, 220, 223, 370
Postmaster General (Lamont vs.), re: censorship, 379, 380
prejudice, 98, 166, 173, 179, 213, 260-263
Presbyterian Church, 373
Prestes, Luis Carlos, 61
"preventing the scourge of war," 36
Prodigal Parents, The, Sinclair Lewis, 55
profit motive, 3, 66, 74, 85, 95, 194, 206, 306, 309, 312; 321-326,
330, 343, 376; regulator of capitalist production, 79, 321;
result of, 66, 206, 307, 352
profit system, 32, 63-75, 79, 81, 91-94, 96, 122, 305, 330, 345, 407
Progressive Party, 370
propaganda, 2, 29, 33, 188, 196, 214, 228, 232, 261, 277, 283, 290,
305, 324, 330, 353, 358, 375, 387
Protestant Church, 336, 340, 342
provocateurs, "secret" US provocative Foreign Policy, 11, 198

Psychiatric & Cultural Traits of Soviet Siberia, Army manual, 378
public education, 261, 306-307, 320, 389
"public enemies," socialists accused and targeted as, 269-270
      list compiled in McCarthy era, 11, 270
Public Health, 156-7, 303-304, 366; 376, 396; needless deaths
      from lack of, 310, 404
publishing, for profit, 304-305; writers, 304-305; libraries, 304-305
"pump-priming" program, 89
Puritanism, 328

race prejudice, 260-262, inequalities in education 253-255
racial discrimination, 260, 263; discrimination against women, 78,
      263
Radical Socialist Party, 361
radicals, well-to-do, 44, 51-52, analysis of, 44, 51-52; arguments
      against, 45; problems of, 46; what they want, 53
Radio Corporation of America, 69
Raging Grannies, 18
Railroad Brotherhoods, 264
Randall, John H., Jr., 308, 375
Rasputin, 330
reason, appeal to, 46-47, 55, 61
Reed, John, 25, 61
Reconstruction Finance Corporation, 74
red-baiting, 288, 385; artificial Red scares, 375; "getting rid of
      Reds," 274; "exiling all Reds," 266; reporters, 376
regimentation, 124, 125, 301
Renaissance, 140, 157, 297, 303
Renn, Ludwig, 57
Rensselaer Polytechnic Institute, 274
Republic Steel Corporation, 269, 270
Republican Party, 90-91, 93, 273-274, 306, 373
Republicans as Conservatives, 374
Responsibility To Protect, United Nations Proclamation, 37
Rich Man, Poor Man, Ryllis A. and Omar P. Goslin, 302
"righteous indignation," Fosdick, 344

rights of majority, not minority, 266
Ripley, W. Z., 74
Robeson, Paul, 28
Rochester, Anna, 61
Rockefeller, John D., 302
Rolland, Romain, 60
Roosevelt, Eleanor, 37
Roosevelt, President Franklin D., 68, 76, 90-94, 108, 110, 242-246,
     267, 269-270, 285, 356, 364-365, 368-369, 400
Roosevelt, Theodore, 229, 369; re: Panama, 229
ruling class minority's violation of majority's rights, 262
Rumania, 220-221
Russell, Bertrand, 380
Russell Sage Foundation, 404
Russia, see Soviet Union
Russian Revolution, 23-24, 53, 137, 179, 185, 189, 340;
     revolutionaries, 23, 26-27, 141
Rust cotton-picking machine, 80

Saar basin, 221
Sacco, 282
sanctions, economic, 244-247; military, 172, 244-246; moral, 338
Santayana, George, 328
Sarajevo, 218
savings, capitalist, 70; 85, 87, 107, 114, 116, 118, 144; under
     Socialist planning, 114-148, 144
Scopes, John T., 273; "Scopes Trial," 273
Scott, Harold, 78
"Scottsboro Boys," 272
Scripps-Howard newspapers, 102
Second Five-Year Plan, 147-148, 150, 154-155
secret treaties, 220
Securities Exchange Act, 94
"seditious materials," violation of civil liberties, 384
Seldes, George, 61
Seligman, E. R. A., 218

Siberia, 27, 159, 240, 357

Soviet Union, 27, 45, 50, 124, 135-137, 139, 141-144, 146-148, 152-159, 160-167, 171-179, 181-186, 190, 192, 210, 235-237, 257, 289-290, 314, 322, 324-325, 330, 332-334, 343. 346-347. 350. 353. 374. 376. 378
Soviets, The, Albert Rhys Williams, 41, 153
Spain, 15, 54, 133, 142, 166, 172-174, 178, 219, 224, 266, 282, 289, 291
Spanish-American War, 229
Spartacus uprising, 57
Spencer, Herbert, 97
Spender, Stephen, 58
Spengler, Oswald, 371
Spinoza, 327
Spofford, William P., 61
stable economy, 7, 46
Stakanov movement, 199, 256
Stalin, Joseph, 94, 144, 150, 161-164, 167, 175, 179, 183, 186, 189, 192, 290, 324-325, 343, 376
Standard Oil Company, 70; of N. Y., 107
standardization, need for, 95
states' rights, problems with, Anti-Lynching Bill, 280, 286
Steffens, Lincoln, 61 127
Steinbeck, John, 61
Steinmetz, Charles P., 322
Stoicism, 328; Stoics, 251
Strabolgi, Lord, 60
Strachey, John, 41, 60, 74, 79, 227, 288, 294
"strangling the menacing infant of Socialism in its cradle," 27
Strawn, Silas, 273
Strikers, labor, 264; arrested, 265; labor spies and provocateurs, 263; Ohio Steel strike (Massillon) 264; Memorial Day Massacre, Chicago Republic Steel Corp., 263; Ludlow, 265
Strong, Anna Louise, 61
supernatural, vi, 16, 31, 160, 179, 333, 336, 338, 368, 378, 391
supervised regulation, 8
suppression of Civil Rights, 265

surplus labor-time, 82
surplus value, 82, 331
Sweden, 68, 365
Sweezy, Alan R., 274, 280
Switzerland, 210, 326

TVA, 108, 127
taming of corporate power, 20
Tammany Hall, 372
tariff, protective, obstacle to free trade, 71-73, 96, 232, 252; cause
    of wars, 132; Socialist abolition of, 252
Taussig, F. W., 258
taxation without representation, 24
Teachers Union, of New York, 265, 274
Technocrats, 78
Ten Days That Shook The world, by John Reed, 2, 25, 61
terrorists, 2, 11-12, 17, 193, 196
Third Five-Year Plan, 154, 156, 178, 181
Thomas, J. H., 291
Thomas, Norman, 61, 267, 364
Thompson, Dorothy, 269
Thompson, William Boyce, 23
Toledano, Vicente Lombardo, 360
Toller, Ernst, 59
Tolstoi, Count, 59
torture, violations by US, 19, 25; ethical principles regarding, 205
totalitarian, 3, 10, 14, 29, 99, 186, 198; systems becoming, 400
Townsendites, 92
trade unions, 69, 85, 92, 99, 119, 164, 176, 259, 263, 265, 294-295,
    324, 341-342, 356, 360, 366
Treaty of Brest-Litovsk, 139
Treaty of Versailles, 221, 247
Trotsky, Leon, 165, 167, 180, 183, 185, 186, 191
Trotskyites, 167, 178, 183, 190, 195
Turkey, 169, 225, 237
Turner, Ralph, E., 273

PHOTO GALLERY

A happy, confident Corliss Lamont in his student years

Corliss Lamont, the debonair man-about-town

Professor Corliss Lamont in his Study

Corliss Lamont's political campaign headquarters
on Upper Broadway in New York City

Beth and Corliss protesting the first Gulf War in Washington, D.C.
Photo thanks to friend, Ossining neighbor, and fellow Peacenik, Joan Indusi.

A smiling Corliss Lamont at a Bill of Rights Dinner
sponsored by the National Emergency Civil Liberties Committee

Corliss Lamont raising his glass of Champaign
at a Westchester People's Action Coalition Festival

Beth K. Lamont protesting U.S. Iraq policy of "Shock and Awe"
Courtesy of Norm Davis, Editor of *Haz Mat Review*
Photo by Marie Starr

Beth K. Lamont pointing out that patriots protect their homeland
Courtesy of Norm Davis, Editor of *Haz Mat Review*
Photo by Marie Starr

Beth and Corliss Lamont and Odie bidding you farewell at their backdoor

Printed in the United States
221096BV00005B/1/P

9 780578 007823